The Age of Deference

The Age of Deference

The Supreme Court, National Security, and the Constitutional Order

DAVID RUDENSTINE

OXFORD
UNIVERSITY PRESS

OXFORD

UNIVERSITY PRESS

Oxford University Press is a department of the University of Oxford. It furthers
the University's objective of excellence in research, scholarship, and education
by publishing worldwide. Oxford is a registered trade mark of Oxford University
Press in the UK and certain other countries.

Published in the United States of America by Oxford University Press
198 Madison Avenue, New York, NY 10016, United States of America.

Library of Congress Cataloging-in-Publication Data
Names: Rudenstine, David, author.
Title: The age of deference : the Supreme Court, national security, and the
constitutional order / David Rudenstine.
Description: New York, NY : Oxford University Press, 2016.
Identifiers: LCCN 2016009508 | ISBN 9780199381487 (hardback)
Subjects: LCSH: National security—Law and legislation—United States. |
Military law—United States. | War and emergency powers—United States. |
Political questions and judicial power—United States. | BISAC: LAW /
Constitutional. | POLITICAL SCIENCE / Political Freedom & Security /
Terrorism. | LAW / Legal History.
Classification: LCC KF7209 .R83 2016 | DDC 343.73/01—dc23
LC record available at http://lccn.loc.gov/2016009508

1 3 5 7 9 8 6 4 2
Printed by Sheridan Books, Inc., United States of America

For Zina

CONTENTS

PART THREE   JUDICIAL DEFERENCE

PART FOUR   BETWEEN ABDICATION AND USURPATION

ACKNOWLEDGMENTS

Completing a manuscript has many rewards, but one that is particularly gratifying is that it provides an opportunity to give thanks to those institutions and individuals who generously supported the endeavor.

The Jacob Burns Institute for Advanced Legal Studies at the Benjamin N. Cardozo School of Law of Yeshiva University provided irreplaceable financial support for the research and writing of this book. Melanie Leslie and Richard Bierschbach, Cardozo's current dean and vice dean, respectively, and Matthew Diller and Edward Stein, Cardozo's most recent former dean and vice dean, respectively, have been reliable and enthusiastic supporters of this book.

I owe a big debt of thanks to Jim Levine, my literary agent. From the beginning Jim was enthusiastic about this book, and once the idea of the book became a manuscript, Jim had very useful and important editorial suggestions. I also wish to thank Jim's literary assistants, Shelby Boyer and Matthew Huff, for keeping administrative matters going in the right direction.

David McBride, the editor-in-chief of social sciences at Oxford University Press, has been nothing short of an outstanding editor. In the beginning, he provided interest and enthusiasm for the subject, and then when the book was expanded in response to Edward Snowden's disclosures in 2013, he offered not mere patience in response to the fact that the book was going to take more time to complete, but outright cheerleading enthusiasm because he thought the expansion would make the book more important. Dave's editorial assistant, Kathleen Weaver, is competent, efficient, knowledgeable, and a storehouse of good judgment. Paul Tompsett, who oversaw the production of the book, has been prompt and effective in pushing the production process along at a rapid pace. Thank you to each of them.

The staff of the Cardozo Library has given me extraordinary support. Requests and inquiries—and there have been many—have been responded to with exceptional promptness and thoroughness. I wish to offer special thanks to former head librarian Lynn Wishart and to the current head librarian Carissa Vogel, as well as to librarian researchers Kimberly Ronning and Kathryn Mackey.

Many friends and colleagues have read either part or all of the manuscript. They are as follows: John Denatale, Max Frankel, Tom Gerety, Colin Greer, Arthur Jacobson, Alex Reinert, Gabor Rona, David Rosner, Steve Shapiro, and Stewart Sterk. To each of them I owe a profound debt of gratitude.

Over many years, many Cardozo students contributed to helping me throughout the preparation of this book: Bolutito Adewunmi, Michele Aronson, Brett Bacon, Justine Bernhardt, Amanda Coleman, Benjamin Cooper, Julia Forman, Adam Goebel, Brachah Goykadosh, Benjamin Gross, Todd Grabarsky, Laith Hamdan, A. Mark Irlando, Dening Kong, Elizabeth Langston, Rachel Wyzan Lasry, Elana Stiefel Lefkowitz, Arielle Matza, Victoria Edwiges Pinhas, J. David Pollock, and Adam Riff.

As is always the case, my friends and colleagues, as well as my research assistants, who have made the book better than it would have been, bear no responsibility for its lapses; they are all mine.

In writing this book, I have utilized some of my previous writings. Most specifically I wish to acknowledge two articles published in the *Cardozo Law Review* ("Roman Roots for an Imperial Presidency: Revisiting Clinton Rossiter's 1948 *Constitutional Dictatorship: Crisis Government in the Modern Democracies* (34 Cardozo L. Rev. 1063 (2013), and "The Irony of a Faustian Bargain: A Reconsideration of the Supreme Court's 1953 *United States v. Reynolds* Decision" (34 Cardozo L. Rev. 1283 (2013)); one article published in the *Texas Law Review* ("Self-Government and the Judicial Function" (92 Texas L. Rev. 161 (2013)); and one article published in the *University of Baltimore Law Review* ("The Courts and National Security: The Ordeal of the State Secrets Privilege" (44 U. of Baltimore L. Rev. 37 (2014)). I have also drawn on an essay entitled "Breaking the Tradition: The Case for the 640 Detainees in Guantanamo" published in *Guantanamo Bay and the Judicial-Moral Treatment of the Other* (Clark Butler ed.) (Purdue U. Press 2007).

To my Cardozo colleagues and students—past and present—I say thank you for fostering an environment for continued learning. You have elevated the value of learning to the highest of levels, and I have been one of the fortunate beneficiaries of your enduring commitments.

To my children, Aaron and Sasha, and their spouses, Olivia and William, and their children, Leila and Skye, I say thank you for being such reliable sources of optimism and energy as this book went from season to season.

And, lastly, to Zina, to whom I dedicate this book, I simply say that everything would have been so fundamentally different without you.

PROLOGUE

It was cold and wet when Franklin Delano Roosevelt stood before the Capitol building and took the oath of office for the presidency for a second time. By 1937, Hitler firmly controlled Germany, Mussolini dominated Italy, and the Spanish Civil War with substantial foreign involvement had been raging for six months. Yet on that momentous day, FDR spoke not a word on foreign affairs. Instead, he dedicated his remarks to the national condition that was still beset by the ravages of the 1930s economic depression and made clear what he saw: "I see one-third of a nation ill-housed, ill-clad, ill-nourished."[1]

Four years later—just eight days before the 1940 election—FDR told a Madison Square audience in New York City that by the Neutrality Act of 1935 "'we made it clear to every American, and to every foreign nation that we would avoid becoming entangled through some episode beyond our borders. Those were measures to keep us at peace . . . . Since 1935, there has been no entanglement and,' he categorically and chimerically promised, '*there will be no entanglement*.'"[2] A few days later in Boston, FDR told his audience: "'I have said this before, but I shall say it *again and again and again*: Your boys are not going to be sent into any foreign wars.'"[3]

FDR's views on America's role in world affairs were far more subtle and complicated than the isolationist stance he projected in these snapshots. Indeed, he was an internationalist and by the 1940 election "had more than doubled the size of the army and the national guard, and 800,000 young men would soon be trained for military service."[4] But isolationism, deeply rooted in American

---

[1] Susan Dunn, 1940: FDR, Willkie, Lindbergh, Hitler—the Election amid the Storm 23 (2013).

[2] *Id.* at 216.

[3] *Id.* at 229.

[4] *Id.* For example, FDR supported the idea of a United Nations. Rober Dallek, Franklin D. Roosevelt and American Foreign Policy, 1932–1945, 419–420, 422, 434–435 (1995).

policy and mind, was the popular siren call of the day, and in contrast to the Republican nominee, Wendell Willkie, who indulged in "predictions of war," Roosevelt offered the "opportunistic message of increased defense production, more military aid to Britain, and the promise of peace."[5] Historian Susan Dunn summed it up by quoting a reporter at the time who noted that "the president was playing his audience 'as a musician handles a fine violin.' "[6]

A year after FDR won a third term, Japan attacked Pearl Harbor, and within days the United States was at war with Japan and Germany. Three and one-half years later, Germany surrendered. Three months later, the United States dropped an atomic bomb on Hiroshima and then some days later on Nagasaki. Japan surrendered.[7]

With war's end came the emergence of the United States as the dominating world power with sole possession of an atomic bomb, as well as the collapse of isolationism as a dominating political force.[8] Perhaps no moment better captures that transformation than President Truman's speech to a joint session of Congress on March 12, 1947. Truman asked Congress to provide $400,000,000

---

[5] Susan Dunn, 1940: FDR, Willkie, Lindbergh, Hitler—the Election amid the Storm 230 (2013). The force of isolationism remained powerful even during the summer and fall of 1941. Thus, Ian Kershaw has concluded, even after the U.S. Congress passed the Lend-Lease Bill in March 1941, that President Roosevelt "still did not dare take any proposal to enter the war to Congress. The policy of isolationism had declined but still posed a significant influence." To Hell and Back: Europe 1914–1949, 351 ((2015).

[6] Susan Dunn, 1940: FDR, Willkie, Lindbergh, Hitler—the Election amid the Storm 230 (2013).

[7] The dropping of the atomic bombs on Hiroshima and Nagasaki in August of 1945 "remains among the most controversial actions in U.S. history." The Truman administration claimed that action was justified in order to "end the war quickly and spare the estimated half million to a million U.S. casualties that would be incurred in invading the Japanese home islands." Others questioned whether "the bomb was necessary to end the war" and accused Truman of dropping the bombs "mainly to bludgeon the Soviet Union into accepting America's postwar aims." According to historian George C. Herring, the controversy "has raged for more than a half century" and "goes to the very heart of what Americans believe about themselves and how other peoples view them." George C. Herring, From Colony to Superpower: U.S. Foreign Relations since 1776, 591 (2008).

[8] Isolationism as a political force did not immediately dissipate effective with the war's end. As historian Denise M. Bostdorff has noted, many Americans "were ready to return to isolationism after World War II." Denise M. Bostdorff, *Harry S. Truman, "Special Message to the Congress on Greece and Turkey: The Truman Doctrine"* (12 March 1947), Voices of Democracy: The U.S. Oratory Project (Jan. 18, 2008), http//archive.vod.umd.edu/internat/truman1947int.htm. Moreover, isolationism remained a pivotal tilt for the Republican Party, which had won "smashing victories" in the 1946 congressional elections, regaining control of both houses of Congress, and "vowing to implement massive budget cuts." Thus, when Truman decided to request assistance for Greece and Turkey, the Republican Senate Leader Arthur Vandenberg of Michigan told Truman that Republicans would in the end support the request but that Truman first needed to "scare the hell out of the country." George C. Herring, From Colony to Superpower: U.S. Foreign Relations since 1776, 615 (2008).

in assistance to Greece and Turkey, as part of his administration's effort to combat what it perceived to be serious Soviet Union threats to American security.

Truman's words to Congress constituted a revolution in American foreign policy. "One of the primary objectives of the foreign policy of the United States," he insisted, "is the creation of conditions in which we and other nations will be able to work out a way of life free from coercion." And to ensure "the peaceful development of nations, free from coercion," Truman added, "the United States has taken a leading part in establishing the United Nations," and furthermore, it must be "willing to help free peoples to maintain their free institutions and their national integrity against aggressive movements that seek to impose upon them totalitarian regimes." To assert these tenets, Truman went on, is to do "no more than [provide] a frank recognition that totalitarian regimes imposed on free peoples, by direct or indirect aggression, undermine the foundations of international peace and hence the security of the United States."

At that moment in world history, Truman maintained, "nearly every nation must choose between alternative ways of life . . . One way of life is based upon the will of the majority, and is distinguished by free institutions, representative government, free elections, guarantees of individual liberty, freedom of speech and religion, and freedom from political oppression. The second way of life is based upon the will of a minority forcibly imposed upon the majority" and relies upon "terror and oppression, a controlled press and radio. fixed elections, and the suppression of personal freedoms." Given that stark choice, Truman stated that he believed that "it must be the policy of the United States to support free peoples who are resisting attempted subjugation by armed minorities or by outside pressures" and to "assist free peoples to work out their own destinies in their own way."[9]

Given American attitudes and priorities in the 1930s, it is inconceivable that FDR could have given a speech during the Depression years comparable to Truman's. But by 1947, the world was different, and more importantly, so was the United States' place in that altered world. In response, Congress approved Truman's request.[10]

The fundamental change represented by Truman's speech to Congress—a change that became known as the Truman Doctrine—was driven home by Congress months later when it adopted the National Security Act. That statute created the Central Intelligence Agency, a National Security Council, a

[9] *Truman Doctrine*, The Avalon Project at Yale L. Sch., http://avalon.law.yale.edu/20th_century/trudoc.asp (last visited Sept. 20, 2015).

[10] Ian Kershaw's *To Hell and Back: Europe 1914–1949* (2015) provides a brief summary of the circumstances that gave rise to the Truman speech and its consequences. "The danger of the Greek Civil War providing the opening for Soviet expansion seemed real to the Americans, all the more so when the British Foreign Secretary, Ernest Bevin, told them in February that a financially enfeebled Britain could no longer provide military or economic aid to Greece and Turkey. From

cabinet-ranked Secretary of Defense, and the Joint Chiefs of Staff.[11] A few years later the National Security Agency was established.[12]

Within a short period of time—from FDR's speeches in the 1930s to Truman's address to Congress in 1947—the United States had gone from a nation with a sharply limited national security infrastructure that reflected isolationism to one with a highly robust national security infrastructure that included "a host of international commitments, launched scores of programs, and mounted a peacetime military buildup that would have been unthinkable just ten years earlier." The change, which "turned traditional U.S. foreign policy assumptions upside down,"[13] was designed to protect and advance global American national security interests—interests that required, among other things, as Truman stated, that the United States "support free peoples who are resisting attempted subjugation by armed minorities or by outside pressures."[14]

It was within these dynamic events that what I term the Age of Deference was born. The Supreme Court decisions that in retrospect gave rise to this era of judicial deference were certainly generated by their times, but they were not generated as part of a comprehensive jurisprudential plan. Rather, judicial

---

March 1947 onwards the United States provided the Greek Right with military aid and training that proved decisive in defeating the Left—though the huge losses (around 45,000 killed and immense material damage) and subsequent repression inflicted lasting harm on Greece's prospects for genuine national unity. For the USA, however, 'containment' had proved a success. The President, Harry S. Truman, had even declared it a 'doctrine'—support for 'free people' against 'totalitarianism' to hold back the spread of communism. It became the mantra of the Cold War" (pp. 511–512).

[11] George C. Herring, From Colony to Superpower: U.S. Foreign Relations since 1776, 614 (2008).

[12] *Id.* at 647. These developments combined to establish what has become known as the "National Security State," and as one student of the subject matter has observed: "No one doubts that the origins of the contemporary constitutional order in foreign affairs and defense policy, sometimes called the 'national security state,' lie in the cold war." Stephen M. Griffin, Long Wars and the Constitution, 5 (2013).

[13] George C. Herring, From Colony to Superpower: U.S. Foreign Relations since 1776, 595 (2008).

[14] President Harry S. Truman, Address Before a Joint Session of Congress, Recommending Assistance to Greece and Turkey (*Truman Doctrine*) (Mar. 12, 1947). http://avalon.law.yale.edu/20th_century/trudoc.asp. In his recent history of FDR's New Deal, which he defines as beginning in FDR's election and ending with the election of Dwight D. Eisenhower, Ira Katznelson, in referring to the confrontation between the United States and the Soviet Union in the years immediately following the end of World War II, wrote: "With the global face-off between the two great powers after the war, a confrontation exacerbated by the Soviet Union's acquisition of nuclear weapons and the standoff in the Korean War, it became impossible for the United States to return to isolation or to disarm, as it previously had done after prior large-scale military mobilizations. By the early 1950s, America's military was *ten times* the size it had been in 1939, creating a new political reality 'that could not be solved by a return to the happy days of 1939 or 1919 or 1914.'" Ira Katznelson, Fear Itself: The New Deal and the Origins of Our Time, 13 (2013).

voices—one by one—pointed the way, and in time profound judicial deference took root and sprouted across a very broad doctrinal landscape.

Nonetheless, there was one striking voice—that of Supreme Court Justice Robert Jackson—early on that may have done more than any other to kickstart the tilt toward deference and to shape its substance. His opinion in a case more or less otherwise lost in history is like the clarion call of a bugle when the wind is still and the sound rolls across the countryside.

Robert Houghwouth Jackson was born in a town in upstate New York. He made a name for himself in the rural part of the state as a brilliant lawyer, built a lucrative practice, became active in Democratic Party politics, and befriended Franklin D. Roosevelt. After FDR became president, Jackson moved his family to Washington and became active in the New Deal. Jackson had several appointments in the Roosevelt administration before President Roosevelt appointed him to be the Solicitor General and then the Attorney General, and in 1941 to be a Justice of the Supreme Court. Jackson was the last justice to be appointed to the Court who did not graduate from a law school, and he served on the Court until his death in 1954. In 1945, President Truman appointed Jackson to serve as the U.S. chief counsel for the prosecution of major Nazi war criminals.

Only months after Truman requested assistance for Greece and Turkey and Congress passed the National Security Act, Jackson wrote a court opinion[15] that included a passage that captured both the thinking and the feelings of judicial deference that permeated the decades ahead in cases implicating national security:

> The President, both as Commander-in-Chief and as the Nation's organ for foreign affairs, has available intelligence services whose reports neither are nor ought to be published to the world. It would be intolerable that courts, without the relevant information, should review and perhaps nullify actions of the Executive taken on information properly held secret. Nor can courts sit in camera in order to be taken in executive confidences. But even if courts could require full disclosure, the very nature of executive decisions as to foreign policy is political, not judicial. Such decisions are wholly confided by our Constitution to the political departments of the government, Executive and Legislative. They are delicate, complex, and involve large elements of prophecy.

[15] Chi. & S. Air Lines, Inc. v. Waterman S.S. Corp., 333 U.S. 103 (1948). Ian Kershaw's recent history of Europe from 1914 to 1949 reaffirms the general view that the Cold War, which provided an historical context for Jackson's opinion, dramatically crystalized during the 1947–1948 period. He wrote: "By 1947 ice was forming on the Cold War. The divisions—a largely monolithic Soviet bloc confronted by an increasingly anxious but resolute American-dominated western bloc—were already by that time becoming firmly entrenched. By the following year they were rigidely fixed." Ian Kershaw, *To Hell and Back: Europe 1914–1949*, 507 (2015).

They are and should be undertaken only by those directly responsible to the people whose welfare they advance or imperil. They are decisions of a kind for which the Judiciary has neither aptitude, facilities nor responsibility and have long been held to belong in the domain of political power not subject to judicial intrusion or inquiry.[16]

In sum, from Jackson's perspective it would be intolerable for courts to revise an executive decision to keep secret certain information. Judges are not competent to decide security questions implicated in cases because such issues are essentially political in nature.[17] Furthermore, national security decisions are so important to the welfare and future of the nation, they must be left to the politically accountable branches, the executive and the Congress. Although Justice Jackson seems to have changed his mind on these fundamental issues,[18] the 1948 opinion still echoes through Supreme Court opinions as a succinct and powerful statement of the deferential judicial mindset.

At the time, no one knew that a new and profoundly troubling era in American judicial history had commenced. But it had, and the era continues.

---

[16] Chi. & S. Air Lines, Inc. v. Waterman S.S. Corp., 333 U.S. 103, 111 (1948). For a recent reference to Justice Jackson's opinion in *Waterman*, see Justice Thomas's dissent in Hamdi v. Rumsfeld. Thus, Justice Thomas wrote:

> Several points, made forcefully by Justice Jackson, are worth emphasizing. First, with respect to certain decisions relating to national security and foreign affairs, the courts simply lack the relevant information and expertise to second-guess determinations made by the President based on information properly withheld. Second, even if the courts could compel the Executive to produce the necessary information, such decisions are simply not amendable to judicial determination because "[t]hey are delicate, complex, and involve large elements of prophecy." Third, the Court in *Chicago & Southern Air Lines* and elsewhere has correctly recognized the primacy of the political branches in the foreign-affairs and national-security contexts. (Hamdi v. Rumsfeld, 542 U.S. 507, 583 (2004) (Thomas, J., dissenting) (citation omitted))

[17] Justice Jackson made a comparable point a few years earlier in his dissent in Korematsu v. United States:

> In the very nature of things military decisions are not susceptible of intelligent judicial appraisal. They do not pretend to rest on evidence, but are made on information that often would not be admissible and on assumptions that could not be proved. Information in support of an order could not be disclosed to courts without danger that it would reach the enemy. Neither can courts act on communications made in confidence. Hence courts can never have any real alternative to accepting the mere declaration of the authority that issued the order that it was reasonably necessary from a military viewpoint. (Korematsu v. United States, 323 U.S. 214, 245 (1944))

[18] *See* United States v. Reynolds, 345 U.S. 1, 12 (1953) (Jackson, J., dissenting); Youngstown Sheet & Tube Co. v. Sawyer (Steel Seizure), 343 U.S. 579, 634–55 (1952) (Jackson, J., concurring).

PART ONE

FROM ISOLATIONISM TO GLOBALISM

1

The Republic Is Askew

The United States prizes individual liberty, the rule of law, a constitutional order premised on checks and balances, and democratic values. These are cornerstones to the nation's political order, and they are at risk for the most unexpected reason.

For the first time in American history, the very governing institution most responsible for protecting individual liberty, upholding the rule of law, and preserving the constitutional order—the Supreme Court—has generally betrayed for over seven decades its responsibilities to hold the executive meaningfully accountable in cases the executive claims implicates national security.[1] As extraordinary as this observation may seem, the Court has been excessively deferential to the executive branch of government in legal disputes that the executive claims implicate national security, and this dangerously deferential posture has seriously harmed American democracy, the rule of law, the governing order, and individual liberty.

Such judicial deference comes into play in a wide variety of cases, including such matters as challenges to surveillance activities, restrictions on expression, infringements on political associations, kidnapping and torture policies, preventative detention practices, policies that discriminate on the basis of religion or ethnicity that result in detention and harsh treatment, or secret Army experiments that cause irreparable harm to members of the armed services. This deference not only causes cases to be dismissed on technical legal grounds, but it has also prompted the Supreme Court to accommodate itself to a degree of secrecy in judicial proceedings that was previously unknown in the history of the American judiciary. Thus, the Supreme Court has accepted as part of

---

[1] I use this language—"that the executive claims implicate national security"—intentionally because past experience establishes that the executive will assert that a case implicates national security when it does not. In other words, the executive will assert a national security interest when in fact the interest is different.

the normal functioning of the federal judicial processes secret evidence, secret legal opinions, secret law, and secret courts.

Taken together in all of their manifestations, these dynamics have generated a judicial era that commenced after World War II when the United States ceased adhering to isolationism and became a global power with worldwide national security interests. As may be surmised, the ostensible main goal of this extraordinary judicial deference is the protection of the nation's security. But there is little to no evidence that such extreme judicial deference substantially protects this security. Moreover, the national security interests that prompted excessive judicial deference are unrelenting and unending, and as a result, there is no end in sight to the era of judicial abdication.

Following World War II, the Supreme Court created and implemented numerous legal doctrines that had the effect of insulating the executive from meaningful judicial review. These doctrines[2]—doctrines such as the state secrets privilege, the law of standing, the defense of quasi-immunity, and heightened pleading rules—work in tandem with one another to insulate the executive from meaningful judicial oversight, and when woven together they constitute an arsenal of legal weapons that the executive uses to protect itself from meaningful judicial review in national security cases, and that the judiciary invokes to shield arguably unlawful executive conduct from such review.[3] Because the doctrines complement one another in insulating the executive from meaningful judicial review, the reshaping of any one or two of these doctrines will not significantly increase judicial accountability of the executive because the other doctrines may expand to fill the void.[4]

---

[2] For example, courts have relied upon executive privilege, United States v. Nixon, 418 U.S. 683 (1974); the state secrets doctrine, United States v. Reynolds, 345 U.S. 1, 7–10 (1953); standing requirements, Clapper v. Amnesty Int'l USA, 133 S. Ct. 1138 (2013); new pleading rules, Ashcroft v. Iqbal, 556 U.S. 662 (2009); and the qualified immunity doctrine, Ashcroft v. al-Kidd, 563 U.S. 731 (2011).

[3] As any student of constitutional law developments knows, since President Nixon's four appointments to the Supreme Court in the early 1970s, the Court has developed legal doctrines that express judicial deference toward the Congress and the presidency across a range of substantive subject matters and that tend to close the courthouse door to individuals with claims against government officials at the federal, state, and local level. Thus, the post–World War II trend of judicial deference in cases implicating national security matters is in a sense an important aspect of this broader development. At the same time, as this book argues, the post–World War II era of judicial deference and secrecy in national security matters has such a profound significance for the rule of law and the constitutional order as to set the era quite apart from these other legal developments and to give it singular importance.

[4] I have previously used the image of a balloon to illustrate this dynamic. "Courts have used numerous legal doctrines to construct a 'balloon' that insulates the Executive from meaningful judicial review in cases the Executive asserts implicate the nation's security. When the scope of one doctrine that constitutes the balloon of insulation is diminished—or squeezed to follow through

In conjunction with the judicial fashioning of these insulating legal doctrines, the Supreme Court implemented a degree of secrecy in judicial proceedings that was unknown in the history of the American judiciary. Thus, during the last six decades, the Court has acquiesced to executive demands that it protect the confidentiality of secret evidence, secret law, and parts of judicial opinions, as well as certain judicial dockets. Furthermore, in 1978, the Court accommodated itself to the congressional establishment of a secret court, the Foreign Intelligence Surveillance Court, which was established to curtail improper executive electronic surveillance programs. This Court, which functions in secret and is not adversarial in character, is now criticized as a "kangaroo court with a rubber stamp"[5] for failing to exercise meaningful review over the executive's electronic surveillance activities.

Initially the Supreme Court's judicial deference in national security cases merely reflected the seminal worldwide changes that followed the last world war. But in time this deference did more than mirror it; it reinforced those changes and vested constitutional legitimacy in the Imperial Presidency and the rise of the National Security State. [6]

Moreover, the judicial deference to the executive that characterizes this accommodation has seriously injured the nation in many respects. It has denied judicial relief to individuals whose rights were arguably violated by the executive. It immunized unlawful executive conduct from meaningful judicial review so that courts not only permitted but perhaps enabled such conduct, and it weakened the constitutional governing scheme by diminishing checks and balances. It permitted a degree of secrecy in judicial processes that had not previously existed. It widened the gap between the nation's commitment to the rule of law and its reality. It distorted the constitutional order so as to threaten not only individual liberty but also the vitality of democratic processes.

with the imagery—in the expectation of increasing meaningful judicial review of the Executive, the effect is that the displaced air merely enlarges the balloon at some other place. This broadening of some other legal doctrine—such as standing or pleading rules—thus serves to preserve the insulation of the Executive. Built into the Age of Deference is a balloon effect the consequence of which is that the Executive's insulation is more or less constant no matter what modification may be made to any one doctrine that comprises the Age of Deference." David Rudenstine, *The Courts and National Security: The Ordeal of the State Secrets Privilege*, 44 U. Balt. L. Rev. 37, 45 (2014).

[5] See the comment by Russell Tice in Spencer Ackerman, *FISA Chief Judge Defends Integrity of Court over Verizon Records Collection*, The Guardian (June 6, 2013), http://www.theguardian.com/world/2013/jun/06/fisa-court-judge-verizon-records-surveillance.

[6] There are cases that constitute exceptions to the deferential stance that characterizes this era. Indeed, the history of the Supreme Court over more than two centuries is too complicated and subtle to permit a thematic synthesis without there being decisions that stand in contrast to the pattern. Thus, there are notable exceptions during the post–World War II decades. But as important as these cases were, they constitute an exception to the general rule of deference.

The judicial deference in national security cases so common in the post–World War II decades was not mandated by the Constitution, Congress, or prior cases. Instead, this deference resulted from the exercise of judicial discretion, a discretion so flexible that the high court could have decided the era's leading cases quite differently than it did. Thus, many of the touchstone cases were decided by the thinnest of margins, a five-to-four vote.[7] But that does not mean that the cases and doctrines central to this era of deference were in any way accidents of history. Rather, these doctrines were driven by highly questionable premises that a majority of the members of the Supreme Court—but not all—have adhered to since the commencement of the Cold War.[8]

This adherence was borne with the best of intentions and was aimed at advancing what is thought to be the nation's best interest. Indeed, the adherence rested on nothing less than the assumption that the premises mandate a degree of judicial deference toward the executive so as to protect the national security. But there is scant, if any, evidence that such judicial acquiescence to the executive in fact protected the nation's security. Indeed, there is evidence that the decades of deference may well have harmed the nation's security, an ironic outcome of inestimable proportions.[9] As a result, a well-meaning Court has caused the nation serious harm that only it can diminish or eliminate by exercising the very same judicial discretion it employed in creating and expanding the doctrines of deference.

[7] See, for example, Clapper v. Amnesty Int'l USA, 133 S. Ct. 1138 (2013); Ashcroft v. Iqbal, 556 U.S. 662 (2009); Mitchell v. Forsyth, 472 U.S. 511 (1985); Harlow v. Fitzgerald, 457 U.S. 800 (1982); and Laird v. Tatum, 408 U.S. 1 (1972).

[8] Concededly, claiming that constitutional interpretations exist within an historical context and can only be understood as an expression of that context is at odds with those who claim that the Court either does or should interpret the Constitution quite devoid of historical trends, changing mores, traditions, and values. For example, in the late nineteenth century, many conceived of law as a "brooding omnipresence" waiting to be discovered, a concept that Justice Holmes famously attacked as failing to understand that the law was dynamic and was the expression of history and morals. Oliver Wendell Holmes, The Common Law 5 (Mark DeWolfe Howe ed., 1963). In the late twentieth century, and partially in reaction to the force of the "realism" jurisprudential school and the perceived "liberalism" and "activism" of the Warren Court, political and judicial conservatives adopted "originalism" as an interpretive methodology intended to assure the public that there was only one correct answer to the meaning of the Constitution and that meaning was the meaning of the Constitution to the public when the Constitution became effective. The effect of originalism is to make judges appear modest in that they do no more than study historical sources and render decisions that are devoid of personal inclination and outlook. This is a fundamentally flawed interpretative methodology. See generally Jack M. Balkin, Living Originalism (2011); David A. Strauss, The Living Constitution (2010); David Rudenstine, Self-Government and the Judicial Function Cosmic Constitutional Theory: Why Americans are Losing Their Inalienable Right to Self-Governance. By J. Harvie Wilkinson III., 92 Tex. L. Rev. 161 (2013) (book review).

[9] For a discussion of the harms generated by judicial abdication, see Chapter 14.

As noted, the Supreme Court's adherence to exceptional deference in cases implicating national security has had many serious consequences. Thus, courts deny individuals the possibility of a judicial remedy without assessing the merits of their claims. So instead of fulfilling one of the highest aims of civil society—providing a remedy for unlawful government conduct—the Supreme Court betrays that lofty aspiration and clothes the denial of a remedy in a technical legal doctrine permitting the executive officials who may have committed an unlawful act to escape judicial accountability.[10]

Moreover, because judicial deference supports an executive official's expectation that unlawful conduct will not have judicial consequences, such deference not only permits but possibly encourages these officials to ignore legal norms in the future. In other words, the doctrines of deference have unleashed a dynamic that certainly insulates and perhaps promotes unlawful conduct by executive officials. The irony of this development is profound given that it is the Supreme Court, more than any other governing body, that has primary responsibility to uphold and to strengthen the rule of law and to assure that checks and balances within the constitutional structure—designed to assure that power is not overly concentrated and abused—remain meaningful.

But the Supreme Court has done more than deny relief to an individual and to shield the executive; it has effectively elevated the executive in national security cases above the law,[11] and thus it has contributed not only to the emergence but also the continued strengthening of the presidency and the departments and agencies that comprise the National Security State.[12] In other words, the judicial arc of deference that began after World War II as a response to the demands of the National Security State has over time yielded decisions that have not just permitted but enabled the rise of the Imperial Presidency and the emergence of the National Security State by granting them constitutional legitimacy.

Furthermore, the rise of the National Security State has created a context that has permitted a departure from the traditional judicial model that emphasizes the

---

[10] For cases in which the Supreme Court lets stand circuit court opinions denying relief on technical legal grounds, *see generally* Mohamed v. Jeppesen Dataplan, Inc., 614 F.3d 1070 (9th Cir. 2010) (en banc), *cert. denied*, 131 S. Ct. 2442 (2011); Arar v. Ashcroft, 585 F.3d 559 (2d Cir. 2009), *cert. denied*, 130 S. Ct. 3409 (2010); El-Masri v. United States, 479 F.3d 296 (4th Cir. 2007), *cert. denied*, 552 U.S. 947 (2007); ACLU v. NSA, 493 F.3d 644 (6th Cir. 2007); Halkin v. Helms (*Halkin I*), 598 F.2d 1 (D.C. Cir. 1978).

[11] Two law professors have argued that the executive is constrained by important dynamics that keep the president within lawful bounds. For a reference to their book and to several highly critical reviews, see note 31.

[12] *See generally* Bruce Ackerman, The Decline and Fall of the American Republic (2010); Peter M. Shane, Madison's Nightmare: How Executive Power Threatens American Democracy (2009); Garry Wills, Bomb Power: The Modern Presidency and the National Security State (2010).

public nature of judicial proceedings so as to guard against the abuse of authority by judges or lawyers. Thus, one legal doctrine, the so-called state secrets privilege,[13] results in presumptively public courts using secret evidence—evidence available only to the executive and not even necessarily a judge and certainly not to the opposing side—to dispose of a case, and in the rendering of judicial opinions that are themselves secret because they describe secret evidence. The Foreign Intelligence Surveillance Court, which was established as a reform measure in the mid-1970s to impose meaningful judicial oversight on executive surveillance conduct, is today widely criticized as having failed to meet expectations.[14] In addition to the acceptance of secret evidence, secret opinions, and secret courts, the post–World War II decades also witnessed the development of secret law.[15] And as odd as it may seem that law should be secret, it is and there is no reason to expect that the idea of secret law is in danger of becoming extinct.

Although these consequences are sufficient to raise profound concerns about the wisdom and efficacy of the doctrines of deference, there are even more fundamental consequences flowing from this development. Judicial acquiescence in national security cases undermines the structural checks and balances scheme central to the constitutional distribution of power. The nation's fundamental ideal of preserving and strengthening the national commitment to the rule of law is betrayed by the very governing institution—the courts—primarily charged with preserving and strengthening the ideal, which in turn runs the risk of the courts undermining their own legitimacy. More generally, because the constitutional order is premised not just on a doctrine of separation of powers among the three coequal branches of government,[16] but on a complicated system of checks and balances,[17] which assumes that the executive will not be above the law,[18] excessive judicial deference threatens the constitutional order.

The post–World War II era of deference has no antecedents in American history. Although the Supreme Court had been profoundly deferential to the

---

[13] See Chapters 5 and 6 for a discussion of the state secrets privilege.

[14] See Chapters 8 and 9 for a discussion of the Foreign Intelligence Surveillance Court.

[15] See Chapter 7 for a discussion of secret law.

[16] For cases in which the Supreme Court asserted its role as an independent and coequal branch of government, see Hamdi v. Rumsfeld, 542 U.S. 507 (2004), New York Times Co. v. United States, 403 U.S. 713 (1971), and Youngstown Sheet & Tube Co. v. Sawyer (Steel Seizure), 343 U.S. 579 (1952).

[17] *See generally* Clinton v. City of New York, 524 U.S. 417 (1998); INS v. Chadha, 462 U.S. 919 (1983).

[18] *See generally* Clinton v. Jones, 520 U.S. 681 (1997); *see also* United States v. Nixon, 418 U.S. 683 (1974).

executive in certain cases that arose during wartime,[19] those periods were circumscribed, and for the most part the Court in those cases decided the merits of the dispute and did so in public, as opposed to dismissing the action on technical legal grounds or hiding the result in secrecy.[20]

In contrast, post–World War II judicial deference developed as a response to America's dominant power in the world with exclusive possession of atomic weapons, the expansion of its national security interests to encompass the globe, the demands of the National Security State, and the emergence of the Imperial Presidency during the Cold War. These developments influenced judicial attitudes toward the role of the judiciary in cases the executive claimed implicated national security, and in the end these developments created a context for the shaping of a juristic mind of deference that prompted the Supreme Court to shape and employ technical legal doctrines to dispose of cases. Moreover, in the cases the Court did decide prior to World War II that implicated national security, the Court for the most part decided the merits of the case, as opposed to disposing of the case on technical legal grounds, an approach that generally has failed to engage the public's attention. In short, the role of courts in national security cases during the last seven decades breaks ranks with the period prior to World War II, just as America's engagement in the world following the end of World War II breaks ranks with America's historic isolationism.

The juristic mind that is so central to these postwar decades congealed only in the post–World War II years. Several interrelated considerations combined to shape this judicial disposition. Judges are understandably concerned about their competence to make decisions affecting national security.[21] This is so because judges may lack education and experience in the area and may be worried that judicial processes—the rules of evidence and procedure—may not permit them to have access to all of the relevant and important information. Judges are also concerned that because they are not politically accountable, they should refrain from reviewing executive decisions on matters as important as national security.[22] Judges may seek to avoid, as the Supreme Court termed it in one case, a "showdown"[23] with the

---

[19] For a discussion of these wartime cases, see Chapter 2.

[20] After the Civil War, the Supreme Court did decide a few very important cases on technical grounds, resulting in their dismissal without a decision on the merits. For a discussion of these cases, see Chapter 3.

[21] Justice Robert Jackson's opinion in Chi. & S. Air Lines, Inc. v. Waterman S.S. Corp., 333 U.S. 103 (1948), is one of the cornerstones of this line of reasoning.

[22] For a discussion of this consideration, see Chapter 15.

[23] Chief Justice Vinson used the term "showdown" to describe a conflict between the Supreme Court and the executive branch of government in his state secrets opinion in United States v. Reynolds, 345 U.S. 1, 11 (1953).

executive in national security cases out of concern that the executive may embarrass the courts by not complying with a judicial order, or that the Congress will utilize its authority to regulate the courts by imposing restrictions on the courts' jurisdiction or remedial power. At some point during the last seventy years, the very fact that courts had deferred to the executive in so many cases implicating national security itself created a body of precedent which, quite apart from all other factors, added to the current sweeping judges along in a tide of deference.

Judges may be insulated from public accountability, but they are not immune from public opinion. Thus, when fear and insecurity penetrated the American psyche in the years immediately following the end of World War II,[24] the members of the Supreme Court were not oblivious to the public demands for executive leadership and national security. Indeed, they responded[25] by quickly taking the first judicial steps in shaping the law of deference.[26] And although the considerations that frame the juristic mind and the doctrines it has spawned have their place in a legal regime, the perceived demands of the National Security State and the Imperial Presidency prompted such an expansion of the legal doctrines of deference that the reasons that gave rise to the doctrines in the first place have now been so unreasonably stretched, pulled, and expanded that they cannot legitimate the vast doctrinal structure that depends upon them.

These are strong claims, but they should not be misunderstood. There is no claim that the Supreme Court has never deviated from a disposition of deference that insulates the executive. For example, in 1952, the Supreme Court ruled President Truman's seizure of the nation's steel mills unconstitutional;

---

[24] In the few years following the end of World War II, the Soviets developed an atomic weapon, China fell to the Communists, the Korean War erupted, and McCarthyism ignited both charges of communist spying (for a fascinating review of the litigation involving Julius and Ethel Rosenberg, see Brad Snyder, *Taking Great Cases: Lessons from the Rosenberg Case*, 63 Vand. L. Rev. 885 (2010)), and infiltration of the federal government (for example, see generally, Alistair Cooke, A Generation on Trial: U.S.A. v. Alger Hiss (1968), and Richard H. Rovere, Senator Joe McCarthy (1973)).

[25] For an example of a case which demonstrates the impact that events had on judicial thinking, consider Dennis v. United States, 341 U.S. 494 (1951). In that matter, leaders of the American Communist Party were convicted under federal law of a conspiracy to engage in speech that constituted advocacy to teach the duty or necessity of overthrowing the government of the United States by force or violence. In other words, the defendants were not convicted of a conspiracy to overthrow the United States government nor were they convicted of actually giving a speech in which they urged that outcome. Instead, they were convicted of a conspiracy in which they planned to produce publications or to give speeches which contained such advocacy.

[26] Justice Jackson's opinion in Chi. & S. Air Lines, Inc. v. Waterman S.S. Corp., 333 U.S. 103 (1948), which was written during these tense years, contains a classic statement of the reasons prompting deference. By 1953, Jackson seems to have changed his mind on the relevant issues when he dissented in a state secrets case, *United States v. Reynolds*, 345 U.S. 1 (1953).

in 1971, the Court denied President Nixon's administration an injunction barring the *New York Times* and the *Washington Post* from publishing excerpts from a highly classified Pentagon history of United States involvement in Vietnam from 1945 to 1968;[27] in 2004, the Court required the executive to grant a U.S. citizen detained in the United States and accused of taking up arms with al-Qaeda against United States forces an administrative hearing to determine whether the individual was in fact properly identified as an enemy combatant;[28] and in 2008, the Court concluded that detainees had the right to file a petition for a writ of habeas corpus in a United States District Court in which the legality of their detention was challenged.[29] These are important cases, but they do not undermine the claim that for seven decades, the general disposition of the Supreme Court in cases implicating national security has been and is to defer to the executive.[30]

Nor is there any claim presented herein that the Supreme Court's rulings have taken the United States to the precipice of tyranny. Thus, although two prominent law professors have criticized scholars and commentators for claiming that the United States is about to slip or has slipped into tyranny, there is nothing in this book that would constitute what these law professors term "tyrannophobia."[31] Democratic processes live along a continuum of vitality, and in the United States this continuum is highly complicated and nuanced because of the diversity and size of the American population, the numerous and distinctive geographical regions, and the complicated nature of American

---

[27] Perhaps the two most prominent exceptions are the Steel Seizure case, *Youngstown Sheet & Tube Co. v. Sawyer* (Steel Seizure), 343 U.S. 579 (1952), decided against President Truman's 1952 seizure of the nation's steel mills during the Korean War, and the Pentagon Papers case, *New York Times Co. v. United States* (Pentagon Papers), 403 U.S. 713 (1971), decided against President Nixon's effort to stop publication by newspapers of excerpts from a top-secret history of U.S. involvement in Vietnam in 1971 during the Vietnam War. *See also* Boumediene v. Bush, 553 U.S. 723 (2008); Rasul v. Bush, 542 U.S. 466 (2004); Hamdi v. Rumsfeld, 542 U.S. 507 (2004); David Rudenstine, *Breaking the Tradition: The Case of the 640 Detainees in Guantanamo, in* Guantanamo Bay and the Judicial-Moral Treatment of the Other 15 (Clark Butler ed., 2007).

[28] *Hamdi*, 542 U.S. 507.

[29] *Boumediene*, 553 U.S. 723.

[30] Chapter 13 discusses judicial deference in the context of the Guantanamo detainees.

[31] The two professors are Eric A. Posner of the University of Chicago Law School and Adrian Vermeule of Harvard Law School, who wrote *The Executive Unbound: After the Madisonian Republic*. In their book, they criticize a "tradition" they term "legal legalism," which they state may in simplified terms be defined as holding that "representative legislatures govern and should govern, subject to constitutional constraints, while executive and judicial officials carry out the law. The basic answer that liberal legalism supplies, then, is that law does and should constrain the executive." Eric A. Posner and Adrian Vermeule, The Executive Unbound: After the Madisonian Republic 3 (2010). Posner and Vermeule assert that proponents of liberal legalism—and they identify James Madison, Bruce Ackerman, Richard Epstein, Albert Venn Dicey,

federalism. One of the central elements of the continuum is the role of the Supreme Court as a third and coequal branch of government that functions as a meaningful check on the powers of the presidency and the Congress, and as the most important governing body that upholds individual liberty and the national commitment to the rule of law. Thus, the argument presented herein is not that the Court's disposition of deference has resulted in a tyranny that expunges the democratic impulse, but that the Court's deferential stance has substantially harmed the nation—and done so needlessly—by compromising individual liberty, the rule of law, and the democratic process. This is a serious claim, but it is a far cry from the idea that the Supreme Court has contributed to a context in which the United States is about to slip, is slipping, or has already slipped into a tyrannical state. That is an important difference that should not be overlooked at a time when prominent academics use exaggerated terms that are more useful for attracting attention to an argument than explicating it.

Arguing for a different perspective on the question of deference is not premised on an idealization of the judiciary. Instead of idealizing the judiciary, the evidence and the analysis set forth herein portray the judiciary in a very sobering and disturbing light.[32] Nonetheless, the Supreme Court should reshape the doctrines of deference to assure more meaningful judicial review, and this can be accomplished without replacing judicial abdication with judicial usurpation. No one should want government by the

---

and David Dyzenhaus as examples of proponents of liberal legalism—are so "intensely anxious about executive power" because of the stark limitations of law to constrain executive power that they can be characterized as having "tyrannophobia," an "unjustified fear of dictatorship." *Id.* at 5. Drawing "upon the thought of the Weimar legal theorist Carl Schmitt," *id.* at 4, Posner and Vermeule contend that the "central fallacy of liberal legalism . . . is the equation of a constrained executive with an executive constrained by law," and that liberal legalists overlook the de facto political constraints that have grown up and, to some degree, substituted for legal constraints on the executive. As the bonds of law have loosened, the bonds of politics have tightened their grip. The executive, "unbound" from the standpoint of liberal legalism, is in some ways more constrained than ever before. *Id.* at 5. Posner and Vermeule's book has been subject to trenchant criticism. *See, e.g.,* Aziz Z. Huq, *Binding the Executive (By Law or By Politics),* 79 U. Chi. L. Rev. 777 (2012) (book review); Benjamin Kleinerman, *The Executive Unbound: After the Madisonian Republic,* 90 Tex. L. Rev. 943 (2012) (book review); Julian David Mortenson, *Law Matters, Even to the Executive,* 112 Mich. L. Rev. 1015 (2014) (book review); Richard H. Pildes, *The Executive Unbound: After the Madisonian Republic,* 125 Harv. L. Rev. 1381 (2012) (book review); Harvey Mansfield, Book Review, *Is the Imperial Presidency Inevitable?* N.Y. Times, Mar. 11, 2011, at BR12.

[32] See, for example, the assessment of the judges in cases involving the state secrets privilege in Chapters 5 and 6, the authority of the Court to provide a damage remedy for the violation of constitutional rights in Chapter 11, the construction of doctrinal hurdles preventing individuals from securing relief for the violations of federal rights by senior executive officials in Chapter 12, and the failure of the Supreme Court to uphold the rule of law with regard to Guantanamo prisoners in Chapter 13.

judiciary.[33] At the same time, no one should want government without meaningful judicial review.[34] Fortunately, these are not the only alternatives. There is a substantial spectrum separating abdication and usurpation that permits the Court to exercise a form of review that is both meaningful and respectful. The details of such a perspective vary from one doctrine of deference to another, but there can be no doubt that the Supreme Court could redefine the doctrines of deference so that they provide a more demanding form of review while still being respectful of the executive in national security cases.[35]

The claim against the exaggerated sense of deference is not premised on a cynical disposition toward the executive. Recognizing that the executive is an exceedingly complicated branch of government with thousands of agents responsible for its daily administration that may err in discharging its authority or that may abuse its authority is to do nothing more than what Chief Justice Fred Vinson acknowledged in a seminal state secrets case, when he asserted that it was important for the Court to shape a legal doctrine to guard against executive "caprice."[36] Indeed, almost ninety years ago, Supreme Court Justice

---

[33] Critics of the role of the Supreme Court in American life frequently claim that the Court has exceeded its constitutional authority and damaged government by the people by instituting government by the judiciary. And that charge is leveled by individuals criticizing the Court from a politically liberal position, as was the case with Louis Boudin, in his 1932 book entitled *Government by the Judiciary*, as well as individuals criticizing the Court form a politically conservative position, as was the case with Raoul Berger, in his 1977 book entitled *Government by the Judiciary: The Transformation of the Fourteenth Amendment. Compare* Louis B. Boudin, Government by Judiciary (1932), *with* Raoul Berger, Government by the Judiciary: The Transformation of the Fourteenth Amendment (1977). Too frequently critics of the Court assume that there are only two avenues the Court can go down in making important constitutional decisions. One avenue is headlined "judicial deference," and the other avenue is headlined "judicial usurpation." One of the themes of this book is to emphasize that there is a broad spectrum separating deference or abdication, on the one hand, and usurpation, on the other, and that it is far too simplistic to simply charge the Court with government by the judiciary, as is often done.

[34] David Rudenstine, *Self-Government and the Judicial Function Cosmic Constitutional Theory: Why Americans are Losing Their Inalienable Right to Self-Governance. By J. Harvie Wilkinson III.*, 92 Tex. L. Rev. 161 (2013) (book review).

[35] There is no question that the Supreme Court exercises an extraordinary power over American life. The highly respected historian Gordon S. Wood succinctly stated the matter: "Certainly the federal judges, and especially the justices of the Supreme Court, precisely because they do not periodically have to face an electorate, have exercised an extraordinary degree of authority over American's society and culture. The Supreme Court not only sets aside laws passed by popularly elected legislatures but also interprets and construes the law with a freedom that sometimes is virtually legislative in scope. Nowhere else in the modern world do courts wield as much power in shaping the contours of life as the Supreme Court does in the United States." Gordon S. Wood, Empire of Liberty: A History of the Early Republic, 1789–1815, 442 (2009).

[36] United States v. Reynolds, 345 U.S. 1, 10 (1953). For example, consider the Iran-Contra scandal in which President Ronald Reagan's secret diplomatic initiative—"trading arms for hostages

Louis D. Brandeis observed that the "greatest dangers to liberty lurk in insidious encroachments by men of zeal, well-meaning, but without understanding."[37] By redefining legal doctrines so it moves from a disposition of undue
deference to meaningful judicial review, the Court will still exhibit respect for
the executive, but it will temper that respect with a realism shaped by experience about the exercise of executive power.[38]

The war on terror has been understandably dominant in the American mind
since 9/11, and, as a result, many may conclude that contemporary judicial deference toward the executive in national security cases commenced with the
war on terror and will fade away when that war becomes an historical event.
As understandable as the assumption may be, it is an error. The doctrines of
deference long preceded 9/11, and they are tied intimately to global national
security interests of the United States—interests that are broader than those
related to the war on terror and that will long outlast those interests. Thus,
the Supreme Court's undue deference toward the executive in national security matters will long survive past the war on terror and will end only when

---

in Iran and aiding contra rebels in Nicaragua—was a foreign policy disaster from almost any political perspective." Stephen R. Weissman, *A Culture of Deference: Congress's Failure of Leadership
in Foreign Policy*, 4 (1995). Stephen R. Weissman concluded that the United States "armed Iran
but failed to reduce the number of American hostages or to moderate the revolutionary regime,"
opened itself up to blackmail by those who might reveal the secret deal, undermined U.S. credibility in foreign affairs by radically departing in secret from public pronouncements, lost $10 mil-
lion to the contras, and enriched intermediaries with arm sales profits. Stephen R. Weissman, A
Culture of Deference: Congress's Failure of Leadership in Foreign Policy, 4 (1995). Or consider
Constance C. Menges, who wrote in a book on foreign policy during the Reagan presidency that
she "encountered a small but influential group of foreign policy officials who believed they knew
better than the president what was best for the country and who could and would manipulate
events to attain their preferred course of action." Menges, Inside the National Security Council:
The True Story of the Making and Unmaking of Reagan's Foreign Policy, 11 (1988).

[37] Olmstead v. United States, 277 U.S. 438, 479 (1928) (Brandeis, J., dissenting).

[38] In 1970, three years before what became publicly known as the Nixon Watergate scandals,
the then Assistant Attorney General William H. Rehnquist testified before a congressional subcommittee chaired by Senator Sam J, Ervin, Jr. regarding government investigations and the
threat they presented or did not present to individual privacy. During his testimony Rehnquist
claimed that the American public had nothing to fear from the executive branch because " 'self-
discipline on the part of the executive branch will provide an answer to virtually all of the legitimate complaints against excesses of information-gathering.'" Senator Sam J. Ervin, Jr., Privacy
and Government Investigations, 1971 Law Forum 137, 147 (1971). Or to use Chief Justice
Vinson's words, Rehnquist asserted that executive self-discipline protected the American public
from executive 'caprice.'" United States v. Reynolds, 345 U.S. 1, 10 (1953). In response, Senator
Ervin characterized Rehnquist's statement as an "amazing theory" (p. 147), and then argued that
"recent events have shown that there is indeed a need for strict legislation in this area of the" and
that self-discipline "is not enough" (p. 148). To illustrate his point, Ervin made reference to many
privacy intrusions such as those by the Army, the Census Bureau, and the Secret Service (p. 148).

the Supreme Court itself comes to accept that its responsibilities require it to change its disposition.

Since the early 1970s, the Supreme Court has effectively closed the courthouse door on many civil rights and civil liberties claims to which many justices are unsympathetic.[39] Because of that, the Supreme Court's deference in national security cases is part and parcel of a broader legal development. At the same time, deference in security cases is sufficiently different from this broader dynamic that it stands quite apart from it. The doctrines of deference are primarily a response to national security considerations, and their supporters and opponents do not fit neatly into a simple categorization as conservative or liberal. Moreover, deference in these cases has not just denied individuals a judicial remedy, but it, as noted, has bolstered the Imperial Presidency and the National Security State, diminished the potential transparency of the executive, permitted if not encouraged unlawful conduct by executive officials, and undermined the rule of law and the constitutional order.[40] And because the doctrines of deference are inextricably intertwined with the rise of the United States as a world power with global national security interests, they will continue until the members of the Supreme Court conclude that the

---

[39] The Supreme Court has effectively made it increasingly difficult for individuals to sue public officials to vindicate federal rights by redefining a variety of legal doctrines that essentially close the courthouse door, such as the law of standing and ripeness, the law pertaining to the right of an individual to secure damages against pubic officials, the quasi-immunity defense, and the requirements for setting forth sufficient detail in the plaintiff's complaint. For a general introduction to this, see Erwin Chemerinsky, The Conservative Assault on the Constitution (2010), and Susan N. Herman, Taking Liberties: The War on Terror and the Erosion of American Democracy (2011).

[40] The literature on transparency and secrecy in government is enormous, and no effort is made here to review that important and broad subject. What is worth noting is that President Obama "has boasted of running 'the most transparent administration in history,'" and yet his administration has mounted a fierce resistance to making public secret legal memoranda President Obama himself has stated demonstrates why it is lawful for the United States to kill a United States citizen outside of a combat zone. See Chapter 7. Moreover, during the Obama presidency certain federal agencies such as the Drug Enforcement Agency, the Peace Corps, and the F.B.I. are refusing to comply with requests submitted by the inspector-general system that was created "in 1978 in the wake of Watergate as an independent check on government abuse." That development has prompted Paul Light, a New York University professor, to observe that the Obama administration's response to the investigations constitutes "the most aggressive assault on the inspector general concept since the beginning" and in total is a "complete evisceration of the concept. You might as well fold them down. They've become defanged." Eric Lichtblau, *Tighter Lid on Records Threaten to Weaken Government Watchdogs*, N.Y. Times, Nov. 27, 2015. The dynamics in government that yield a penchant for secrecy are powerful and, in the end, seem overwhelming, perhaps in part because those who assume office as reformers themselves become in time vulnerable to the power of the dynamics that produce secrecy; they often conclude that untutored instincts embraced before assuming office must give way to a new "realism" engendered by the burdens of being a responsible office holder.

harms inflicted by undue deference in national security cases exceed whatever national interests the deference may be thought to be advancing.

The overall significance of this post–World War II development is often unnoticed, and that is true even though the development occurred in full public view. That is so for several reasons. The idea of seven decades of profound judicial deference runs against the dominant narrative defining the role of courts in national security cases in American history.[41] That narrative maintains that courts unduly defer to the executive's judgment on security matters during wartime such as the Civil War, World War I, and World War II, when the nation's fears intensify and it loses its perspective.[42] The consequences of this are that political dissent is suppressed, as during World War I, and citizens are detained in camps, as the Japanese American citizens were during World War II. These periods of national peril caused the judiciary to lose its perspective and to overreact to situations, thus causing serious harm. According to the dominant narrative, once the crisis has passed or the war has ended, courts regain their perspective, change the tenor and substance of their decisions, and perhaps even express regret for past judgments. Baked into this ingrained narrative is the premise that the national perspective is lost for only comparatively short periods of time—a handful of years—and not seven decades. Thus, the idea of a seven-decade era of deference is inconsistent with the premises of this ingrained narrative.

Many liberal court watchers are certainly aware of the doctrines of deference and criticize their robustness. But their analysis tends to frame the discussion as one that pits liberty and security as clashing fundamental values in a zero-sum confrontation, and their focus is on moving the boundary to protect liberty. As a result, they may place less emphasis on the doctrines of deference that cause cases to be dismissed without a decision on the merits, and their analysis tends to downplay the significance of the consequences of deference for checks and balances, separation of powers, and the rule of law.

On the other side of the political fence, many conservative observers of the high court applaud judicial (as well as congressional) acquiescence to the executive in matters the executive claims implicate national security. Although they may believe that such a disposition is warranted because judges lack competence to decide such matters, it is also the case that they favor security over liberty, scorn the idea of checks and balances that interfere with presidential authority, emphasize the importance of near-term security considerations over long-term security concerns, and define security exclusively in concrete military and intelligence terms as opposed to preserving and enhancing "soft

---

[41] For a discussion of dominant narrative, see Chapter 2.
[42] For a discussion of these themes, see Chapter 2.

power" and the United States' security interests in its free institutions and in the liberty of the individual. Such advocates are sometime termed "presidentialist," meaning that they have a radical conception of an all-powerful president—a Prometheus unbound—who is able to utilize enormous power to advance the nation's security.[43] One scholar summarized "presidentialist" as follows:

> For the last quarter century, the checks and balances of American government have been increasingly battered by the merger of two powerful currents. One is the gathering concentration of power in the hands of the federal executive, a trend nurtured since the New Deal by Presidents both Democratic and Republican, although at different rates of acceleration. The second current has been the relentless campaign of the right wing of the Republican Party since 1981 to steer the capacities of our national government toward the fulfillment of a conservative social, economic, and foreign policy agenda. Together, the growing concentration of executive power and the campaign for partisan predominance have produced an era of aggressive presidentialism, a theory of government and a pattern of government practice that treat our Constitution as vesting in the President a fixed and expansive category of executive authority largely immune to legislative control or judicial review.[44]

For the presidentialist, the very idea that judges have significant responsibility under the current constitutional scheme to adjudicate cases that the executive argues implicate national security is anathema.

The importance and scope of the judicial deference pattern have also failed to galvanize public attention because cases are generally dismissed on technical legal grounds doctrines as opposed to judicial decisions that decide the merits of the dispute.[45] Such grounds—the state secrets privilege, the failure of the law to provide a remedy, a quasi-immunity defense, the law of standing, and heightened pleading rules—are difficult for the public to dissect and

---

[43] For an historical and endorsing account of what is often referred to as the "unitary executive," see Steven G. Calabresi and Christopher S. Yoo, The Unitary Executive: Presidential Power from Washington to Bush (2008). For a critical account of the exercise of presidential power during the administration of George W. Bush, see Charlie Savage, Takeover: The Return of the Imperial Presidency and the Subdivision of American Democracy (2007).

[44] Peter M. Shane, Madison's Nightmare: How Executive Power Threatens American Democracy, 3 (2009).

[45] One example of a major exception to the general statement that Supreme Court decisions resting on technical grounds fail to attract public attention is a set of decisions resting on the state secrets privilege involving claims of kidnapping and torture. See David Rudenstine, The Courts and National Security: The Ordeal of the State Secrets Privilege, 44 U. Balt. L. Rev. 37, 40 n.24 (2014).

do not stir public debate the way legal decisions do that concern abortion, the boundary between church and state, or same-sex marriage. As a result, although such decisions are not completely lost in the daily news cycle, they rarely receive enough attention to trigger a strong public reaction.

The Supreme Court's role in the rise of the National Security State and the Imperial Presidency generally is overshadowed by Congress's role in these developments. That is so because the Constitution has delegated to Congress substantial power such as the power to declare war, to raise and support armies, and to provide for a navy, and it has delegated to the Senate the power to approve treaties and the appointment of ambassadors. Moreover, the Congress controls income and expenditures, which means that it must approve expenditures for military and nonmilitary matters.

In addition, not only is there more of a focus on Congress than on the courts because Congress has substantially more power than the courts to balance off the executive, but also because it is generally thought that Congress has over time abdicated its power. Arthur M. Schlesinger, Jr. stated the commonly held view as follows: presidential assumption of the war-making power was "gradual and usually under the demand or pretext of emergency. It was as much a matter of congressional abdication as of presidential usurpation."[46] Referencing developments in the 1970s, 1980s, and early 1990s, Stephen R. Weissman reached a similar conclusion that "Congress—Democrats and Republicans alike—has largely lost its will to co-determine American foreign policy with the president . . . It is not too much to say that Congress has substantially ceded its fundamental constitutionally role in foreign policy . . . [and that the] executive branch has been the main beneficiary of Congress's default, but narrow special interests have also gained."[47] More recently, and focusing on the transformation engineered by George W. Bush, Charlie Savage wrote: "The expansive presidential powers claimed and exercised by the Bush-Cheney White House are now an immutable part of American history . . . [and the] importance of such precedents is difficult to overstate."[48] Lastly, Garry Wills, looking back on the post–World War II decades, offered this thumbnail sketch of the ineffectiveness of the Congress to rein in a powerful presidency:

> All the forces traced in this book have moved toward a concentration of power in the presidency, far from the design of the framers of the Constitution, who were determined not to have a monarch

[46] Arthur M. Schlesinger, Jr., The Imperial Presidency, ix (1973).

[47] Stephen R. Weissman, A Culture of Deference: Congress's Failure of Leadership in Foreign Policy, 2–3 (1995).

[48] Charlie Savage, Takeover: The Return of the Imperial Presidency and the Subversion of American Democracy 330 (2007).

like the king they had just rebelled against. From World War II, the secrecy and unchecked power of Leslie Groves set a pattern repeated in the CIA, the NSA, and the President's private monopoly over nuclear weaponry. The undeclared wars against Korea and Vietnam endorsed presidential control of military power and created a cult of the President as Commander in Chief. The attempt to push back with the War Powers Resolution, CIA oversight, and the FISA court did little or nothing to check Presidents defying the WPR in Lebanon, Grenada, Panama, Libya, Haiti, Kosovo, Bosnia, and elsewhere. But these foreign adventures cannot compare with the full-court press of warmaking powers asserted by the administration of George W. Bush.[49]

But as potentially powerful as Congress is, and as much constitutional room as may exist for Congress to change its ways and to assert control over executive conduct, Congress alone cannot solve the distortions in the governing scheme that have developed in the postwar decades. Whatever Congress may do to exercise more thoughtful oversight of the executive in national security matters, the Congress cannot take the place of the courts. For example, although the Congress may theoretically provide a remedy to an individual who has been seriously and wrongfully harmed, such a remedy is rare and exceedingly difficult for an individual to secure. Nor can the Congress replace the capacity of the courts to hold the executive accountable for its action that holds out the possibility of deterring the executive from future unlawful conduct. Nor can the Congress meaningfully replace the Supreme Court's unique role in the scheme of government in upholding the rule of law. In short, if the governing scheme is to be righted so that the executive is not above the law, so that an unlawful executive is not exempted from judicial accountability, so that allegedly wronged individuals have legal remedies and are not sacrificed because of a judicial utilitarian calibration in the name of national security, so that the rule of law is not only an ideal but a reality, then the courts will need to abandon a posture of acquiescence in favor of shaping legal doctrines that make the executive toe the legal line and respect the rule of law.

In response to these and other security threats, the idea that the Supreme Court should modify its unduly deferential stance in cases implicating national security may strike some as unsound on the grounds that it may enhance the risks to national security. This is a totally understandable response. National

---

[49] Garry Wills, Bomb Power: The Modern Presidency and the National Security State 222 (2010).

security considerations remain of paramount importance.[50] Thus, a decade and a half after 9/11, terrorist security threats remain high in the United States and in Europe. ISIS is expanding "beyond its base in Syria and Iraq to establish militant affiliates in Afghanistan, Algeria, Egypt and Libya . . . raising the prospect of a new global war on terror,"[51] and individuals, either on their own as a "lone wolf"[52] or in conjunction with recognized terrorist organizations in the Middle East,[53] attack or kill or both those whose actions are deemed offensive. Moreover, and going well beyond the war on terror and the conflicts that now occupy so much of the Middle East, one recognized military authority has "branded Russia the No. 1 'existential threat'" followed by North Korea, China, and the Islamic State.[54] The former chairman of the Joint Chiefs of Staff, General Martin Dempsey, said in a 2015 report that the current "global security environment is the most unpredictable I have seen in 40 years of service."[55] Thus, not only are national security threats substantial and continuing, but a proposal that courts be less deferential in national security cases than they have been does constitute a departure from previous norms, and that departure understandably may give rise to doubts that challenge the merits of the proposal.

But the claim that a less deferential judiciary would injure the national security is purely speculative. There is no evidence that some alteration of the judicial stance in cases implicating national security will increase the risk of national danger. Indeed, in cases in which federal judges have exercised meaningful judicial review, they have, in terms of national security, impressively acquitted themselves. Furthermore, there is reason to believe that a judiciary that

[50] For example, by Friday, December 4, 2015, the F.B.I. was treating the attack in San Bernardino, California, a few days before, which left fourteen individuals dead, as "an act of terrorism." Michael S. Schmidt and Richard Perez-Pena, *F.B.I. Treating San Bernardino Attack as Terrorism Case*, N.Y. Times, Dec. 5, 2015. On Friday, November 14, 2015, several terrorist attacks in Paris caused the death of over 120 individuals, with ISIS claiming responsibility and terming the deaths "miracles." For coverage of the attacks, see generally N.Y. Times, Saturday, November 14, 2015. The ISIS claim and the term "miracles" is in a report by Rukmini Callimachi, *ISIS Claims Responsibility for Paris Attack, Calling Them "Miracles,"* N.Y. Times, Nov. 14, 2015.

[51] Eric Schmitt and David D. Kirkpatrick, *Islamic State Sprouting Limbs Beyond Its Base*, N.Y. Times, Feb. 14, 2015, at A1.

[52] Liam Stack, *Texas Police Kill Gunmen at Exhibit Featuring Cartoons of Muhammad*, N.Y. Times, May 4, 2015, at A14.

[53] Dan Bilefsky and Maia de la Baume, *Terrorists Strike Charlie Hebdo Newspaper in Paris, Leaving 12 Dead*, N.Y. Times, Jan. 8, 2015, at A1.

[54] General Joseph Dunford Jr. made this claim at his confirmation hearings as the nominated chairman of the Joint Chiefs of Staff. Editorial, *Who Threatens America Most?* N.Y. Times, Aug. 12, 2015, at A18.

[55] *Id.*

holds the executive more accountable than it has in the past will enhance the nation's security because the possibility of such judicial review might cause the executive to proceed with greater deliberateness than it might otherwise do and that such deliberateness may in turn result in wiser decisions.

In addition, the executive demand for judicial deference relies in part on the assumption that security rests solely on a strong military defense, but that assumption is incorrect. As one district judge, Murray Gurfein, eloquently stated when he denied the Nixon administration a preliminary injunction in the Pentagon Papers case: "The security of the Nation is not at the ramparts alone. Security also lies in the value of our free institutions."[56] In other words, the concept of national security is complex and encompasses many factors that give the nation its character and enhance its standing in the world, such as the strength of American private and public institutions, the scope of individual liberties, and the commitment to the rule of law.[57] Therefore, even assuming that the Supreme Court's seventy-year hands-off approach in national security cases may have advanced some short-term security interests, it has put at risk other national security concerns, especially longer-term considerations. What Gurfein and so many others understood, and what the insistence on narrowly defined, short-term security claims minimizes or ignores, is that while there is no law without security, there is no security without law.

Altering a seven-decade pattern of judicial deference may seem a radical idea to some, but the really radical idea is that national security requires that the courts continue along a path that denies injured individuals a judicial remedy, erodes the nation's commitment to the rule of law, and undermines checks and balances so central to the governing scheme.[58] In short, remaining

---

[56] United States v. New York Times Co., 328 F. Supp. 324, 331 (S.D.N.Y. 1971).

[57] Joseph S. Nye, Jr. developed the idea of what he termed "soft power" in his book *Soft Power: The Means to Success in World Politics* (2004). Nye stated that soft power "arises from the attractiveness of a country's culture, political ideals, and policies" (p. x). He offered as examples the impact of President Franklin D. Roosevelt's Four Freedoms in Europe after World War II, Radio Free Europe on Eastern European youths before the Soviet Union collapsed, and the Statue of Liberty on Chinese students protesting in Tiananmen Square; and Afghans asking for copies of the Bill of Rights after the Taliban were ousted in 2001 (p. x). Nye argued that the United States knew how to use soft power effectively during the Cold War and hopes that "we can do it again" (p. 147).

[58] As long ago as 1807, when the republic was still properly understood to be a vulnerable experiment in self-government, federal judge William Cranch, the Chief Judge of the Circuit Court of the District of Columbia, understood the important duties of the judiciary during times of peril that are frequently put aside today in favor of judicial deference and the felt needs of security. In a case involving treason claims against Aaron Burr, Chief Judge Cranch wrote:

> In times like these, when the public mind is agitated, when wars, and rumors of wars, plots, conspiracies and treasons excite alarm, it is the duty of a court to be peculiarly watchful lest the public feeling should reach the seat of justice, and thereby precedents be established

on this course presents a fundamental challenge to the constitutional order and the failure to change course is not just a radical position but also a dangerous one.[59]

By addressing a central dynamic in the American governing scheme that is now woven into national security structures, this book addresses critical paradoxes that the United States now confronts. To what extent should the United States adopt policies, practices, and tactics to defend itself when these very same policies, practices, and tactics may themselves threaten the very institutions and values they are designed to protect? How far should the United States go—indeed, how far may it go—in defending its governing structures, its democratic values, its individual liberties, and more generally its Western values against foreign and domestic enemies without abandoning them along the way? Although such issues present timeless political theoretical problems that reflect back on each other in a way that brings to mind T. S. Eliot's elegant phrase of "wilderness of mirrors,"[60] they are, in the current context, pragmatic questions demanding a practical response from the courts that the courts have both the responsibility and authority to grant.

There is no perfect or eternal solution to the conundrums generated by the factors that have generated judicial abdication in national security cases. But it

---

which may become the ready tools of faction in times more disastrous. The worst of precedents may be established from the best of motives. We ought to be upon our guard lest our zeal for the public interest lead us to overstep the bounds of the law and the constitution; for although we may thereby bring one criminal to punishment, we may furnish the means by which an hundred innocent persons may suffer. The constitution was made for times of commotion. In the calm of peace and prosperity there is seldom great injustice. Dangerous precedents occur in dangerous times. It then becomes the duty of the judiciary calmly to poise the scales of justice, unmoved by the arm of power, undisturbed by the clamor of the multitude. Whenever an application is made to us in our judicial character, we are bound, not only by the nature of our office, but by our solemn oaths, to administer justice, according to the laws and constitution of the United States. No political motives, no reasons of state, can justify a disregard of that solemn injunction. In cases of emergency it is for the executive department of the government to act upon its own responsibility, and to rely upon the necessity of the case for its justification; but this court is bound by the law and the constitution in all events. When, therefore, the constitution declares that "the right of the people to be secure in their persons" "against unreasonable seizures," "shall not be violated," and that "no warrants shall issue but upon probable cause, supported by oath or affirmation," this court is as much bound as any individual magistrate to obey its command. (United States v. Bollman, 24. F. Cas. 1189, 1192 (C.C.D.C. 1807))

[59] Aharon Barak, former president of the Supreme Court of Israel, has written a remarkably perceptive, thoughtful, and inspiring book that discusses with unusual wisdom the problem of courts, democracy, and terrorism. Aharon Barak, The Judge in a Democracy, 283–305 (2006).

[60] T. S. Eliot, Gerontion, T. S. Eliot: The Complete Poems and Plays: 1909–1950, 21 (1958).

is certain that the judiciary's current posture of being exceedingly deferential to the executive in national security cases has more or less turned the judiciary into an extension of the executive, a dynamic that makes Alexander Bickel's observation of about a half century ago with regard to the Vinson Court appropriate for the entire seventy-year epoch: "Far from entering new claims to judicial supremacy, it seemed at times to forget even its independence."[61]

What is now required is for judges to accept, as one federal judge put it sixty years ago, that federal judges are "public officers whose responsibility under the Constitution is just as great as that of the heads of the executive departments,"[62] and to recognize what another federal judge more recently offered as a fundamental tenet of the American political system, namely, that in the "United States, for better or worse, courts are, almost universally, involved"[63] in granting redress to citizens arguably wronged by the executive.

Seven decades of deference have resulted in a serious and very harmful distortion in the governing scheme, and the Supreme Court and the judges who preside over the lower federal courts need to strike a new balance in cases implicating national security so the executive is accountable, individuals secure relief, and the rule of law is upheld. To that end, there is no doubt that the Court can be properly respectful of the executive and the Congress in national security matters while still exercising meaningful judicial review because an important and broad spectrum of doctrinal choices exists between judicial abdication and usurpation.

No thoughtful observer of the justices now on the Supreme Court would expect a majority of those justices to accede to this perspective. These justices have espoused their views too often over too long a period of time to leave open the possibility that their minds are anything but closed on the question of the Court's role in cases involving national security. But the Court's membership will change in time, and the purpose of this book is to influence the shape of things to come.

---

[61] Alexander M. Bickel, The Supreme Court and the Idea of Progress 5 (1970).

[62] Reynolds v. United States, 192 F.2d 987, 997 (3d Cir. 1951), *rev'd*, 345 U.S. 1 (1953).

[63] Arar v. Ashcroft, 585 F.3d 559, 638 (2d Cir. 2009) (Calabresi, J., dissenting).

2

The Ingrained Narrative

The idea of an era of judicial deference, which emerged from the ashes of World War II as the United States became the dominant world power, is out of step with the generally accepted narrative regarding the role of courts in cases implicating national security during times of war and peril. Moreover, the ingrained narrative described is not only out of step with the post–World War II era, it is a misleading description of American judicial history from 1789 to 1945. Nevertheless, whether by comparison to the classical narrative or by comparison to a revised narrative set forth in the next chapter, the post–World War II decades are a distinct and important period in American judicial history.

The ingrained narrative emphasizes that the nation predictably overreacts during wartime to real or imagined security threats by curtailing liberties: that courts, insulated from political pressure so that they can protect fundamental constitutional commitments from the public's emotional impulse, become themselves swept up in the intensity of the times and surrender their independence and their judgment to the executive branch out of concern for protecting the nation's security.[1] That narrative goes on to posit that once the war ends the nation recovers its perspective and judgment, as reflected in judicial outcomes, and in time comes to accept that it has needlessly oppressed liberties.

Supreme Court Justice William J. Brennan gave a speech in Jerusalem in 1987 in which he set forth the ingrained narrative. Justice Brennan stated that "as adamant as my country has been about civil liberties during peacetime, it has a long history of failing to preserve civil liberties when it perceived its national security threatened." Brennan explained that a "sudden national fervor causes people to exaggerate the security risks posed by allowing individuals to exercise

---

[1] Judge Learned Hand wrote understandably of this dynamic: "It may be that the peril of war, which goes to the very existence of the state, justifies any measure of compulsion which Congress deems necessary to its safety, the liberties of each being in subjection to the liberties of all." Masses Publ'g Co. v. Patten, 244 F. 535, 538 (1917).

their civil liberties and to become willing 'temporarily' to sacrifice liberties as part of the war effort." For Brennan these failures were "particularly frustrating" in that they resulted "not from informed and rational decisions that protecting civil liberties would expose the United States to unacceptable security risks, but rather from the episodic nature of our security crises." Brennan observed that this cycle of repression meant that the "peacetime jurisprudence of civil liberties leaves the nation without a tradition of, or detailed theoretical basis for, sustaining civil liberties against particularized security concerns." Brennan went on to note that even though the nation realized once the perceived threat had subsided that "the abrogation of civil liberties was unnecessary," it was "unable to prevent itself from repeating the error when the next crisis came along."[2]

A recent White House report—*The NSA Report: Liberty and Security in a Changing World,* prepared by The President's Review Group on Intelligence and Communications Technologies—echoed Brennan's analysis.[3] After noting that "it is always challenging to strike the right balance between the often competing values of national security and individual liberty," and it is *"particularly* difficult to reconcile these values in times of real or perceived national crisis," the Report observed that too often the United States has "overreacted in periods of national crisis" and "taken steps unnecessarily and sometimes dangerously jeopardized individual freedom" and then later, with "the benefit of hindsight," recognized its failures, reevaluated its judgments, and "attempted to correct our policies going forward."[4]

---

[2] William J. Brennan, Associate Justice, Supreme Court of the United States, Remarks at the Law School of Hebrew University, *The Quest to Develop a Jurisprudence of Civil Liberties in Times of Security Crises,* 1–2 (Dec. 22, 1987). Chief Justice Earl Warren embraced a similar view in a 1962 speech he gave at New York University Law School: "I do not propose to discuss in detail other cases that have been decided in a wartime context, for the risk is too great that they lie outside the mainstream of American judicial thought. War is, of course, a pathological condition for the Nation. Military judgments sometimes breed action that, in more stable times, would be regarded as abhorrent. Judges cannot detach themselves from such judgments, although by hindsight, from the vantage point of more tranquil times, they might conclude that some actions advanced in the name of national survival had in fact overridden the structures of due process." 37 N.Y.U. L. Rev. 181, 191–192 (1962).

[3] Richard Clarke et al., The NSA Report: Liberty and Security in a Changing World (2014).

[4] *Id.* at 10–11. William M. Wiecek's volume on The Birth of the Modern Constitution: The United States Supreme Court, 1941–1953, 285 (Stanley N. Katz ed., Volume XII 2006) begins with a chapter entitled *Total War and the Constitution,* which marches to the beat of the same narrative drummer:

> *Silent enim leges inter arma,* declared Cicero two millennia ago. (Wiecek relied on N.H. Watts' translation of Cicero's Latin phrase: "For the laws fall laws silent amid the clash of war." William M. Wiecek, The Birth of the Modern Constitution: The United States Supreme Court, 1941–1953, 285 (Stanley N. Katz ed., Volume XII 2006).) Edmund Burke concurred: "Laws are commanded to hold their tongues

Legal opinions written by Supreme Court justices have had a shaping hand in fashioning this narrative. A few examples illustrate the point. Only months after the fighting ended in the Civil War,[5] Justice David Davis observed that the war had distorted judicial temperaments and perhaps the substance of judicial constructions of the Constitution. "During the late wicked Rebellion," Justice Davis wrote, "the temper of the times did not allow that calmness in deliberation and discussion so necessary to a correct conclusion of a purely judicial question." But now, he observed, that "the public safety is assured, this question, as well as all others, can be discussed and decided without passion or the admixture of any element not required to form a legal judgment."[6]

amongst arms; and tribunals fall to the ground with the peace they are no longer able to uphold." American historical experience suggests that there is some truth in their observation. Law as a constraint on authority in the United States has never severely impeded military operations. In the principal wars the United States fought between 1789 and 1940, the relative position of the Supreme Court vis-à-vis the other branches receded during hostilities, while the powers of the president increased dramatically, though temporarily. *Id.*

In a similar vein, one of the members of the Review Group, Geoffrey Stone, in a highly praised study, has summarized this perspective: "[T]he United States has a long and unfortunate history of overreacting to the perceived dangers of wartime. Time and again, Americans have allowed fear and fury to get the better of them. Time and again, Americans have suppressed dissent, imprisoned and deported dissenters, and then—later—regretted their actions." Geoffrey Stone, Perilous Times; Free Speech in Wartime 5 (2004).

[5] The fact that a perceived crisis prompts the government to seriously diminish substantive rights is about as old as the republic. Thus, as may well be familiar, within a decade of the effective date of the current constitution, John Adams and Federalist Party supporters claimed that a threat of insurrection warranted a radical curtailment of speech critical of the government. The result was the Sedition Act of 1798, which made it a crime punishable by a $5,000 fine and five years in prison for any person to "write, print, utter or publish . . . any false, scandalous and malicious writing or writings against the government of the United States, or either house of the Congress . . . or the President . . . , with intent to defame . . . or to bring them, or either of them, into contempt or disrepute; or to excite against them, or either or any of them, the hatred of the good people of the United States." Sedition Act, ch. 74, 1 Stat. 596 (1798). The Act allowed a defendant only the defense of truth, which had the effect of criminalizing erroneous statements. This meant that the press had no "breathing room" to make errors, and breathing room is essential to a free press, for as Madison observed "[s]ome degree of abuse is inseparable from the proper use of every thing; and in no instance is this more true than in that of the press." New York Times Co. v. Sullivan, 376 U.S. 254, 271 (1964). That horrific statute, which expired by its own terms in 1800, prompted President Thomas Jefferson to pardon those who had been convicted and sentenced under the Act and to remit their fines, and it caused the Congress four decades later to repay the fines on the ground that the act was unconstitutional. Although the constitutionality of the act was never "tested" before the Supreme Court, Justice Brennan concluded in a 1964 opinion involving the *New York Times* that "the attack" upon the Act's "validity has carried the day in the court of history." *Sullivan,* 376 U.S. at 276.

[6] Ex parte Milligan, 71. U.S. 2, 109 (1866).

A half-century later during World War I, Justice Oliver Wendell Holmes, Jr. concluded that the war prompted the Court to interpret the Constitution differently than it would have during peacetime. "When a nation is at war," Holmes wrote, "many things that might be said in time of peace are such a hindrance to its effort that their utterance will not be endured so long as men fight and that no Court could regard them as protected by any constitutional right."[7]

Three decades later, in the aftermath of World War II, Justice Robert Jackson gave his twist to the same theme. "The Government asserts," Jackson wrote, "no constitutional basis for this legislation other than this vague, undefined and indefinable 'war power.'" Jackson insisted that no one doubted that this power is "the most dangerous one to free government in the whole catalogue of powers." That was mainly so because it "is invoked in haste and excitement when calm legislative consideration of constitutional limitation is difficult" and because it is "executed in a time of patriotic fervor that makes moderation unpopular." But Jackson went on to maintain: "And, worst of all, it is interpreted by Judges under the influence of the same passions and pressures." Furthermore, Jackson continued to push his point: "the Government urges hasty decision to forestall some emergency or serve some purpose and pleads that paralysis will result if its claims to power are denied or their confirmation delayed."[8]

This conventional narrative of the role of courts during wartime is supported not only by judicial observations but also by a pattern of judicial outcomes. A brief review of a few cases arising during the Civil War, World War I, and World War II that are generally relied upon to support the efficacy of the ingrained narrative illustrates the pattern.

In May of 1863, Clement Vallandigham, an Ohio politician and forceful advocate for the Copperheads, a vocal northern group who opposed the Civil War and favored peace with the South, was arrested by Union soldiers for violating a military order by publicly criticizing the war and President Lincoln. Vallandigham argued that a military commission lacked authority over him because he had a constitutional right as a civilian to criticize government leaders and policies. The military commission rejected the argument, found Vallandigham guilty of violating a military order, and recommended that he be imprisoned for the duration of the war.

Vallandigham's arrest and detention became the subject of a petition for a writ of habeas corpus. Ohio federal Judge Humphrey H. Leavitt initially denied Vallandigham's petition, even though the military order that arguably provided legal grounds for Vallandigham's detention was not authorized by an act of

---

[7] Schenck v. United States, 249 U.S. 47, 52 (1919).
[8] Woods v. Cloyd W. Miller Co., 333 U.S. 138, 146–147 (1948) (Jackson, J., concurring).

Congress, a specific executive order signed by President Lincoln, or even a directive from a cabinet member such as the secretary of war. In reaching this result, Judge Leavitt offered the following assessment of the judiciary's inability to enforce an order in the face of executive noncompliance: "[I]f [the writ were] granted, there is no probability that it would be available in relieving Mr. Vallandigham from his present position. It is, at least, morally certain it would not be obeyed. And I confess I am somewhat reluctant to authorize a process, knowing it would not be respected, and that the court is powerless to enforce obedience."[9] When Judge Leavitt wrote these lines he almost certainly had in mind the fact that in 1861 President Lincoln ignored Chief Justice Taney's order in the *Merryman* case,[10] an order that directed a military general who had taken John Merryman of Maryland prisoner to explain to the civilian court why Merryman's imprisonment was lawful.[11]

In 1864, the Supreme Court decided in the *Vallandigham* case[12] that it lacked power to issue a writ to a military commission since the pertinent

---

[9] Ex parte Vallandigham, 28 F. Cas. 874, 924 (1863).

[10] Ex parte Merryman, 17 F. Cas. 144 (C.C.D. Md. 1861). More generally with regard to Lincoln and the Constitution, Supreme Court Justice Robert Jackson wrote that President Lincoln "at the outset of his administration, suspended the writ of habeas corpus and resorted to wholesale arrest without warrant, detention without trial, and imprisonment without judicial conviction. Private mail was opened, and Cabinet officers simply sent telegrams ordering persons to be arrested and held without communication or counsel. The power was given to generals of various of the northern states to suppress newspapers and suspend the writ." Robert H. Jackson, The Supreme Court in the American System of Government 75 (1955). To put Lincoln's conduct in a comparative context, there is evidence that President Franklin D. Roosevelt was, similar to Lincoln, prepared to ignore a Supreme Court ruling. In a draft speech, "prepared in the event that the Court were to decide it was unconstitutional for the Government to abrogate 'gold clauses' in federal obligations (which in the end it did not)," Roosevelt was going to announce in 1935 that he would not "stand idly by and permit the decision of the Supreme Court to be carried through to its logical, inescapable conclusion" because it "would imperil the economic and political security" of the nation and, as a result, the elected leaders of the country "must look beyond the narrow letter of contractual obligations, so that they may sustain the substance of the promise originally made in accord with the actual intention of the parties." Kathleen Sullivan and Noah Feldman, Constitutional Law 246 (18th ed. 2013). In 1942, seven months after the Japanese attack on Pearl Harbor, FDR told his attorney general, Francis Biddle, that no matter what the Supreme Court might rule he would turn the Nazi saboteurs over to civilian authorities. Francis Biddle, In Brief Authority 331 (1962). For Biddle's reference to the Nazi saboteurs, see Ex parte Quirin, 317 U.S. 63 (1942).

[11] The *Merryman* case is discussed in Chapter 3.

[12] Vallandigham made many arguments, including the following three. A federal statute limited the authority of a court-martial or military commission to persons who are "in the military service of the United States, and subject to the articles of war," and since Vallandigham was not in the military and not subject to the articles of war, he argued that he should be released immediately. Ex parte Vallandigham, 68 U.S. 243, 248 (1864). Article III, § 2 (3) of the Constitution guaranteed a jury trial in the trial of all crimes, and that this important procedural guarantee was violated by the military commission procedures. The military commission lacked jurisdiction over him because he had not committed "an offense known to the law of the land, and that

statute—a provision of the 1789 Judiciary Act—limited its appellate juris-diction to appeals arising from the "circuit courts and courts of the several states."[13] Justice Wayne did not mention District Judge Leavitt's observation that General Burnside would almost certainly ignore his order. But it would be naive to think that this consideration was not present in the mind of the jus-tices, as it had been only two years since Lincoln ignored Chief Justice Taney's decision in the *Merryman* case. Of course, one might well conclude that the high court had more than sufficient reason to avoid yet another embarrassing confrontation with the executive branch that would undermine the Court's legitimacy and public standing. At the same time, it is profoundly disquieting that the Court used its discretionary authority to shape legal doctrine so that it could sidestep the merits of a case it was eager to avoid.[14]

A second Civil War case also illustrates the conventional narrative. Lamdin P. Milligan, a United States citizen and a resident of Indiana, was alleged to be part of a secret society known as the Order of American Knights or Sons of Liberty, which aimed at overthrowing the government of the United States.[15] Milligan was arrested at his home on October 5, 1864, pursuant to a military order.[16] He was charged with being part of a "[c]onspiracy against the Government of the United States," "[a]ffording aid and comfort to rebels against the authority of the United States," and "inciting insurrection, [d]isloyal practices, and [v]iolations of the laws of war."[17] Milligan was brought before a military commission, found guilty, and sentenced to be hanged.[18]

On May 10, 1865, one month after Robert E. Lee surrendered to Ulysses S. Grant at the Appomattox Court House and nine days before Milligan was

General Burnside had no authority to enlarge the jurisdiction of a military commission by the General Order No. 38, or otherwise." *Vallandigham*, 68 U.S. at 248.

[13] Justice James Moore Wayne wrote on behalf of the court, saying: the Court has "no power to review by certiorari the proceedings of a military commission ordered by a general officer of the United States Army, commanding a military department." *Id.*

[14] To gain a perspective on the claim that the Court has discretionary authority to decide the *Vallandigham* case differently, compare the outcome in the Vallandigham case with Ex parte Milligan, 71 U.S. 107 (1866), also discussed in this chapter. Clinton Rossiter's comment on the Supreme Court's ruling in the *Vallandigham* case is worth recalling. "It is one thing for a Court to lecture a President when the emergency has passed, quite another to stand up in the middle of the battle and inform him that he is behaving unconstitutionally. There is no intention here to deride the Court for executing its retreat of 1864. At the time discretion was indeed the better part of valor, and the Court practically confessed the futility of judicial restraint on a President actively exercising his war powers in defense of an embattled nation." Clinton Rossiter, The Supreme Court and the Commander in Chief 38 (1976).

[15] Ex parte Milligan, 71 U.S. 107, 118 (1866).

[16] *Id.* at 107.

[17] *Id.*

[18] *Id.*

scheduled to be hanged, Milligan filed a petition for a writ of habeas corpus, a matter that was decided by the Supreme Court in its December 1866 term.[19] The issue presented focused on the legality of the military commission's jurisdiction over Milligan. In framing the issue, the majority emphasized that Milligan, arrested while at home, was not a "resident of one of the rebellious states, or a prisoner of war, but a citizen of Indiana for twenty years past, and never in the military or naval service."[20] Supreme Court Justice Davis wrote that "no graver question was ever considered" before the high court,[21] and then in equally strong terms he summarized the argument in favor of the military commission's jurisdiction over Milligan:

> The proposition is this: that in a time of war the commander of an armed force . . . has the power, within the lines of his military district, to suspend all civil rights and their remedies, and subject citizens as well as soldiers to the rule of *his will*; and in the exercise of his lawful authority cannot be restrained, except by his superior officer or the President of the United States.[22]

Davis rejected the claim that "for, if true, republican government is a failure, and there is an end of liberty regulated by law" since the consequence of martial law is to destroy "every guarantee of the Constitution, and effectually renders the 'military independent of and superior to the civil power . . . ' "[23] Davis asserted that neither the president nor the Congress could constitutionally establish military comissions except in war zones where the civil courts were closed. Davis contended that the Constitution was the supreme law when the nation was at peace or at war and that its guarantees of liberty and its limitations on governing power could not be set aside in the name of the "theory of necessity":[24]

> The Constitution of the United States is a law for rulers and people, equally in war and in peace, and covers with the shield of its protection all classes of men, at all times, and under all circumstances. No doctrine, involving more pernicious consequences, was ever invented by the wit of man than that any of its provisions can be suspended during any of the great exigencies of government. Such a doctrine

[19] *Id.*
[20] *Id.* at 118.
[21] *Id.* at 75.
[22] *Id.* at 124.
[23] *Id.* at 78.
[24] *Id.* at 121.

leads directly to anarchy or despotism, but the theory of necessity on which it is based is false; for the government, within the Constitution, has all the powers granted to it, which are necessary to preserve its existence; as has been happily proved by the result of the great effort to throw off its just authority. [25]

The *Milligan* opinion did two quite contradictory things. First, it illustrated the conventional narrative that courts are more willing to stand in opposition to Congress or the executive when there is peace as compared to when the nation is at war. Second, it rejected the premise of the conventional view and insisted that the "constitution . . . is a law for rulers and people, equally in war and in peace, and covers with the shield of its protection all classes of men, at all times, and under all circumstances."[26] Strong words, brave words, but words written only after the war had ended and in that only lent further evidence to support the merits of the ingrained perspective.[27]

The World War I cases involving political opposition during World War I provide another snapshot of the Supreme Court's interaction with cases implicating national security during war. In total, there were four cases decided within eight months of one another. The first three were decided on

[25] *Id.* at 120–121. Four justices concurred in the result vacating the military commission's conviction and sentence. But they parted company with the majority over its reasoning. The majority claimed that the military commission held in Milligan's case was unconstitutional and nothing could be done by Congress to change that conclusion. The concurring judges asserted that Congress had the constitutional authority to authorize a military commission in Indiana at the time the commission tried Milligan, but that it had not done so and because of the lack of congressional authorization the military commission lacked jurisdiction over Milligan. The concurrence based its conclusion on the idea that Congress had the authority to authorize military tribunals when the "nation is involved in war, and some portions of the country are invaded, and all are exposed to invasion," in those areas vulnerable to "imminent public danger," which was the situation in Indiana in 1864. *Id.* at 140 (concurring opinion). There is no reason to doubt that the concurrence was as loyal and supportive of republican government and individual liberty as was the majority, but that it concluded that the preservation of republicanism and liberty required risking the vesting in the governing authorities the authority to authorize martial law and the use of military commissions in areas imminently threatened by armed conflict but not yet engaged in such conflict.

[26] *Id.* at 120–121.

[27] Clinton Rossiter, The Supreme Court and the Commander in Chief 127–128 (1976). "Third, whatever limits the Court has set upon the employment of the war powers have been largely theoretical and rarely practical. Even admitting that *Ex parte Milligan, United States v. Cohen Grocery Co.,* and *Duncan Kahanamoku* have their uses as warnings to the political branches to fight our wars constitutionally, the warning is merely moral. Future Presidents are likely to pay about as much attention to these decisions as did Lincoln, Wilson, and Roosevelt; the first and third were long dead, Wilson but three days from the end of his term, when the great limiting decision of each one's particular war was announced by a stern-visaged Court." *Id.*

March 3 and 10 of 1919, and the fourth was decided on November 10.[28]
Holmes wrote the majority opinion in the first three and then wrote an historic dissent in the last case.[29] A review of all four of these cases is beyond
what is required to illustrate the dominant narrative of the court's role in
national security cases. Instead, a review of the lead case, *Schenck v. United
States,* is sufficient.

In that case, the defendants were convicted of conspiring to violate the 1917
Espionage Act of June 15, 1917, in that they conspired to obstruct or attempted
to obstruct the "recruiting and enlistment service of the United States, when
the United States was at war with the German Empire, to-wit, that the defendant willfully conspired to have printed and circulated to men who had been
called and accepted for military service under the Act of May 18, 1917. . .."[30]
The Supreme Court affirmed the conviction. To appreciate the degree to
which the Supreme Court was deferential in this case, a review of the evidence,
as summarized by Holmes, is required.

The evidence that provided the basis for the finding that the defendants intended to "influence" those subject to the draft in order "to obstruct the carrying of it out" consisted of a two-sided printed leaflet mailed to "men who
had passed exemption boards."[31] On one side the leaflet quoted part of the
Thirteenth Amendment of the United States Constitution and "said that the
idea embodied in" that amendment "was violated by the Conscription Act and
that a conscript is little better than a convict."[32] Holmes stated that the leaflet
used "impassioned language" to intimate that "conscription was despotism in
its worst form and a monstrous wrong against humanity in the interest of Wall
Street's chosen few."[33] Although the leaflet asserted that individuals should not
"submit to intimidation," the leaflet, as Holmes stated, "in form at least confined itself to peaceful measures such as a petition for the repeal of the act."[34]
In other words, this side of the leaflet characterized the draft as a tool of Wall
Street financiers who stood to profit from the war, claimed that it constituted
a violation of the Constitution, and urged its readers to exercise rights guaranteed by the First Amendment "to petition the Government for a redress of
grievances," which in this situation meant, as Holmes conceded, the "repeal

---

[28] Schenck v. United States, 249 U.S. 47 (1919); Frohwerk v. United States, 249 U.S. 204
(1919); Debs v. United States, 249 U.S. 211 (1919); and Abrams v. United States, 250 U.S. 616
(1919).

[29] Abrams v. United States, 250 U.S. 616 (1919).

[30] Schenck v. United States, 249 U.S. 47, 49 (1919).

[31] *Id.* at 49–51.

[32] *Id.* at 50–51.

[33] *Id.* at 51.

[34] *Id.*

of the act."[35] The leaflet's second side was headed by the phrase "Assert Your Rights," and, as Holmes wrote, it set forth reasons "for alleging that any one violated the Constitution when he refused to recognize 'your right to assert your opposition to the draft,'" or in other words, a person had a right to oppose, not obstruct, the draft, and that anyone who did not recognize a right to oppose the draft was ignoring rights protected by the Constitution.[36] Holmes went on to quote the leaflet: "If you do not assert and support your rights, you are helping to deny or disparage rights which it is the solemn duty of all citizens and residents of the United States to retain."[37] Here again, the leaflet is not urging a violation of the draft law; it is urging readers to "assert and support" their "rights" to protest.[38] Holmes stooped so low in his opinion that he stated that the leaflet described the arguments favoring the war and the draft as coming from "cunning politicians and a mercenary capitalist press,"[39] as if characterizing those favoring the war and draft as "cunning" and "mercenary" made a difference as to whether the defendants violated the Espionage Act. Holmes brought to a close his summary of the leaflet by stating that the leaflet "denied the power to send our citizens away to foreign shores to shoot up the people of other lands," and urged young men to do their "share to maintain, support and uphold the rights of the people of this country." [40]

After summarizing the facts that he thought supported the charges, Holmes set forth the relevant law. The essence of Holmes's view for the court was premised on there being a meaningful, significant, and discernible distinction between what can be said during times of peace and times of war. Here is how he phrased his thoughts:

> We admit that in many places and in ordinary times the defendants in saying all that was said in the circular would have been within their constitutional rights. But the character of every act depends upon the circumstances in which it is done. [citation omitted] The most stringent protection of free speech would not protect a man in falsely shouting fire in a theatre and causing a panic. It does not even protect a man from an injunction against uttering words that may have all the effect of force. [citation omitted] The question in every case is whether the words used are used in such circumstances and are of such a nature

[35] *Id.*
[36] *Id.*
[37] *Id.*
[38] *Id.*
[39] *Id.*
[40] *Id.*

as to create a clear and present danger that they will bring about the substantive evils that Congress has a right to prevent. It is a question of proximity and degree. When a nation is at war many things that might be said in time of peace are such a hindrance to its effort that their utterance will not be endured so long as men fight and that no Court could regard them as protected by any constitutional right.[41]

Congress may criminalize words that create a clear and present danger, and although what constitutes a clear and present danger is a matter of "proximity and degree" and depends on the "circumstances in which it is done," and although the national interest in curtailing speech in war is greater than in "ordinary times," Holmes did not state what he meant by "proximity," "degree," or "circumstances." But the fact that Holmes found that the evidence in the case was legally sufficient to affirm the conviction meant that the clear and present danger standard meant nothing more than that Congress had the authority to criminalize speech that had a "tendency" to cause a danger no matter how speculative that danger might be, no matter how improbable it may be, and no matter how remote in time it may be. Thus, in *Schenck*, on behalf of a unanimous court, Holmes gave the government all the authority it could have desired to regulate speech it considered threatening. Indeed, putting Holmes's four highly quotable words—"clear and present danger"—aside, and focusing just on the evidence and the outcome, it is hard to imagine how the government could have hoped for a better outcome.

Schenck has never been overruled, and Holmes not only never criticized his opinion in *Schenck*, but he almost seemed to go out of his way in his famous *Abrams* dissent to state that *Schenck* was in his mind still "good law." What he said was: "I never have seen any reason to doubt that the questions of law that alone were before this Court in the cases of *Schenck*, *Frohwerk*, and *Debs*, were rightly decided."[42]

A third prominent example of America losing its senses during wartime, which is often understood to be the prime example of the Supreme Court recklessly crushing individual liberties in the name of national security, was the decision to confine 120,000 Japanese Americans during World War II in what one Supreme Court justice termed "concentration camps."[43] In early 1941, just weeks after the Japanese attack on the United States Naval Base in Pearl

---

[41] *Id.* at 52.

[42] Abrams v. United States, 250 U.S. 616, 627 (1919) (Holmes, J., dissenting).

[43] Korematsu v. United States, 323 U.S. 214, 226 (1944) (Roberts, J., dissenting). Another infamous World War II case that exhibited deplorable judicial acquiescence to the executive is *Ex parte Quirin*, 317 U.S. 1 (1942).

Harbor, Lieutenant General John L. DeWitt, commanding general of the Western Defense Command, issued an order that "prohibited the presence of persons of Japanese ancestry" in much of the West Coast after a specific date. Fred Toyosaburo Korematsu was convicted, as the executive's brief stated, "solely of remaining where he had no right to be."[44]

The executive's brief stated that Korematsu was a "native-born citizen of the United States, born in Oakland, Alameda County, California, on June 30, 1919, to Japanese nationals resident there."[45] It asserted that Korematsu had "never renounced his American citizenship; that he has never departed from the continental limits of the United States; that his birth has not, with either his consent or knowledge, been registered with any consul of the Empire of Japan; and that he does not possess any form of dual allegiance and does not owe allegiance to any country other than the United States."[46] It also contended that Korematsu "registered for the draft and testified that he is willing to bear arms for this country and to render any service requested of him in the war against Japan."[47] The brief conceded that Korematsu had no sympathy for Japan, that he was assimilated "in the American community," and that he continued to "work and live in Alameda County" after the effective date of the exclusion order "because of friendly relations with its residents, and particularly with a girl who was not of Japanese ancestry, and because he considered himself an American and did not want to be evacuated."[48]

The executive argued that Lieutenant General DeWitt's orders were warranted because "there was ample ground to believe that imminent danger then existed of an attack by Japan upon the West Coast,"[49] that the West Coast contained "a large concentration of war production and war facilities,"[50] that approximately 88 percent of all persons of Japanese descent in the United States lived in the restricted areas, that some persons of Japanese ancestry had "formed an attachment to, and sympathy and enthusiasm for, Japan," that it would be "impossible quickly and accurately to distinguish these persons from other citizens of Japanese ancestry,"[51] and that presence of individuals in the restricted areas who "might aid Japan was peculiarly and particularly dangerous."[52]

---

[44] Brief for Respondent at 17, Korematsu v. United States, 323 U.S. 214 (1944) (No. 22).
[45] *Id.* at 4.
[46] *Id.*
[47] *Id.* at 4–5.
[48] *Id.* at 5.
[49] *Id.* at 11.
[50] *Id.*
[51] *Id.* at 12.
[52] *Id.*

A divided Supreme Court upheld the controversial exclusion orders. In doing so, the Court, in an opinion by Justice Black, plainly stated that "all legal restrictions which curtail the civil rights of a single racial group are immediately suspect" and are subject to the "most rigid scrutiny." That said, the Court went on to make it clear that not all such classifications are unconstitutional and that "[p]ressing public necessity may sometimes justify the existence of such restrictions; racial antagonism never can."[53]

With those few but important considerations that suggested that the Court would impose the "most rigid scrutiny" in examining the evacuation program, the majority embarked on an analysis that was quite deferential to the challenged national security judgments. The majority stated that it "was unable to conclude that it was beyond the war power of Congress and the executive to exclude those of Japanese ancestry from the West Coast war area at the time they did."[54] The Court stated that "[n]othing short of apprehension by the proper military authorities of the gravest imminent danger to the public safety can constitutionally justify" the evacuation, but that the military authorities had concluded that such evacuation was central to preventing "espionage and sabotage."[55] To the contention that it was unlawful to confine all 120,000 persons of Japanese ancestry when there was not even evidence to suspect a cadre of 5,000[56] individuals of being so loyal to Japan that they might engage in sabotage or espionage, the Court said the following:

> It was because we could not reject the finding of the military authorities that it was impossible to bring about an immediate segregation of the disloyal from the loyal that we sustained the validity of the curfew order as applying to the whole group. In the instant case, temporary exclusion of the entire group was rested by the military on the same ground.[57]

And because the Court deferred to the judgments of the military authorities that it could not distinguish between those for whom suspicion existed from the others, the Court said that the evacuation was a "military imperative" and that the existence of such an imperative was a complete response to the charge that "the exclusion was in the nature of group punishment based on antagonism to those of Japanese origin."[58]

---

[53] Korematsu v. United States, 323 U.S. 214, 216 (1944).
[54] Id. at 217–218.
[55] Id. at 218.
[56] Id. at 219.
[57] Id.
[58] Id.

In upholding the exclusion order, the majority emphasized that it was "not unmindful of the hardships imposed by it upon a large group of American citizens."[59] "But," the court insisted,

> [H]ardships are part of war, and war is an aggregation of hardships. All citizens alike, both in and out of uniform, feel the impact of war in greater or lesser measure. Citizenship has its responsibilities as well as its privileges, and in time of war the burden is always heavier. Compulsory exclusion of large groups of citizens from their homes, except under circumstances of direst emergency and peril, is inconsistent with our basic governmental institutions. But when under conditions of modern warfare our shores are threatened by hostile forces, the power to protect must be commensurate with the threatened danger.[60]

The Court's perspective was warped. The majority identified the "hardship" as the compulsory exclusion of citizens from their homes. If that were the case, that would have been a terrible "hardship" that would likely result in irreparable harm. But that was not the "hardship" persons of Japanese ancestry experienced. The result of a combination of the various military orders issued between March and May of 1942 was not just the exclusion of persons of Japanese ancestry from their homes, but their detention in what the majority termed "relocation centers" and what Justice Roberts in dissent termed "concentration camps."[61] The majority insisted that it was only addressing the legality of the exclusion order,[62] but to decide the *Korematsu* case pretending that the only issue before the Court was the exclusion order and not the detention consequences was, as Justice Roberts stated in dissent, "to shut our eyes to reality."[63]

But the majority's willingness to dilute what it termed the "most rigid scrutiny" into meaningless judicial review is evidenced in other parts of the opinion it submitted. The majority made no inquiry into the evidence that supported the claim that threats of sabotage and espionage actually existed. It sought no evidence to review any threats the military claimed emerged solely from persons of Japanese ancestry. It accepted without question the military judgment that it was not possible to distinguish between those who were suspected of possible espionage and sabotage from the others. It did not ask the military

---

[59] *Id.* at 219.
[60] *Id.* at 219–220.
[61] *Id.* at 226 (Roberts, J., dissenting).
[62] *Id.* at 223 (majority opinion).
[63] *Id.* at 232 (Roberts, J., dissenting).

whether other means were available that would protect the nation from espionage or sabotage aimed at facilitating an invasion.

The deferential posture that Justice Black assumed in his majority opinion resulted in an outcome that two prominent constitutional law scholars have stated has "come to live in infamy."[64] Eventually in 1984, a United States District Court in California "issued a writ of *coram nobis* vacating Korematsu's conviction . . . on the grounds of governmental misconduct in the submission of false information to the Supreme Court in the 1940s."[65] Four years later, Congress enacted a law "apologizing for the World War II internment program and providing for reparations of $20,000 each to surviving victims."[66]

Implicit in this conventional perspective is the idea that major wars, such as the Civil War and the two world wars, create special circumstances in which courts should—or must—defer to the executive. Furthermore, so goes this line of thinking, as dreadful and horrific as they may be, some legal outcomes that arise during these perilous times are driven by the exigencies of war, and although these decisions may cast a shadow over the future scope of liberty and the strength of democratic values, the nation's security requires the sacrifice of these fundamental values.

James Madison seems to have appreciated that dynamic when he observed in the midst of the national fears over war with France: "Perhaps it is a universal truth that the loss of liberty at home is to be charged against provision against danger, real or pretended, from abroad."[67] Lincoln certainly embraced this perspective when he asked rhetorically—and perhaps with acute frustration when criticized for suspending the writ of habeas corpus during the opening months of the Civil War: "Are all the laws, but one, to go unexecuted, and the government itself to go to pieces, lest that one be violated?"[68] And Franklin

---

[64] Kathleen Sullivan and Noah Feldman, Constitutional Law 639 (18th ed. 2013). For a different analysis of the *Korematsu* decision, see Mark Tushnet, *Defending* Korematsu?: *Reflections on Civil Liberties in Wartime*, Wisconsin L. Rev. 273 (2003).

[65] Korematsu v. United States, 584 F. Supp. 1406, 1409 (N.D. Cal. 1984). Not quite three decades after the district court's ruling in the *Korematsu* case, Acting Solicitor General Neal Katyal conceded that the Solicitor General in the *Korematsu* case made errors. See *Confession of Error: The Solicitor General's Mistakes During the Japanese-American Internment Cases*, Neal Katyal, Acting Solicitor General of the United States, U.S. Dep't of Justice (May 20, 2011), http:blogs.justice.gov/main/archives/1346?print=1.

[66] Kathleen Sullivan and Noah Feldman, Constitutional Law, 639 (18th ed. 2013).

[67] Madison Writings, Letter from James Madison to Thomas Jefferson, May 13, 1798, 588 (Jack N. Rakove, ed., Library of America (1999)).

[68] President Abraham Lincoln, Message to Congress in a Special Session (July 4, 1861). The Library of America, Abraham Lincoln, Speeches and Writings 1859–1865, Speeches, Letters, Miscellaneous Writings, Presidential Messages and Proclamations 253 (Don E. Fehrenbacher ed., 1989).

Roosevelt's attorney general, Francis Biddle, understood the president's attitude toward the internment of Japanese Americans during World War II to rest on the assumption that war is different and may permit what would otherwise be unthinkable. As Biddle wrote: "Nor do I think that constitutional difficulty plagued him. The Constitution has not greatly bothered any wartime President. That was a question of law, which ultimately the Supreme Court must decide. And meanwhile—probably a long meanwhile—we must get on with the war."[69] National aspirations and the rule of law are important, but for a president responsible for security, they may be at the margin when a nation is at war.

From this perspective—and neither Lincoln nor Roosevelt would apologize for this perspective—the nation overreacts to perceived national security threats and all too quickly compromises its liberties and its commitment to a government structured by checks and balances so that security is strengthened by granting the president substantial power unfettered by bothersome judicial accountability and individual liberties. But with comparable certainty, this view insists that the nation regains its senses, restores its liberties, reasserts its checks and balances in the governing scheme, regrets its conduct during war, learns from its past errors, and reaffirms its fundamental commitment to the rule of law.

Oddly enough, this narrative that draws a sharp distinction between war and peace and seems so condemning of America's failure to uphold the nation's liberties and governmental structures is at the same time remarkably cleansing of the nation's betrayal of its aspirations. The narrative assesses the Civil War, World War I, and the infamous internment of Japanese American citizens during World War II as historical moments when, as a result of perceived peril, a collective America lost its mind. By so doing, this narrative emphasizes the continuing American commitment to liberal democracy—a political theory that places importance on the fracturing of power and places individual liberty at its core. From this perspective of American liberalism, the failure of courts

[69] Francis Biddle, In Brief Authority 219 (1962). The summer of 2015 marked the seventieth anniversary of the dropping of the atomic bombs on Hiroshima and Nagasaki, which brought to the fore many recollections and much commentary on the decision to drop the bombs. One comment by Leona Marshall Libby, "probably the most well-known female scientist in the Manhattan Project," made during this period may have captured in straightforward words what Biddle described in more cloaked terms when he referred to FDR. In reflecting on her role in building the bombs, Dr. Libby stated: "I have no regrets. I think we did right, and we couldn't have done differently. In wartime, it was a desperate time. . . . When you are in a war to the death, I don't think you stand around and ask, 'Is it right?'" Susan Southard, *A Debate over Hiroshima and Nagasaki, 70 Years Later: Nagasaki, the Forgotten City*, N.Y. Times (Aug. 11, 2015), http://www.nytimes.com/ 2015/08/11/opinion/a-debate-over-hiroshima-and-nagasaki-70-years-later.html?_r=0.

to uphold the rule of law and fundamental liberties during times of crisis are characterized as exceptions to the grandeur of the noble tradition that characterizes courts as the guardians of the rule of law and the constitutional order, and the periods of repression are exceptions to the long and continuing march toward the highest aspirations of political liberalism.

In a contemporary context, this narrative places great emphasis on the attacks of 9/11 and suggests that it is the post–9/11 era, as opposed to the post–World War II era, that constitutes the modern deferential age. Also implicit in this view is the assumption that the Court's highly deferential stance will dissipate once the war on terror is quelled. By uncoupling the judicial abdication in national security cases from the rise of the National Security State and the Imperial Presidency, this dominant narrative has many shortcomings. It fails to identify the driving force behind the Age. It fails to explain how the Age not only mirrors these fundamental changes in American society, but how it has over time both strengthened and legitimated these developments. It fails to appreciate that the Age will outlast the threats presented by terrorism unless the Supreme Court changes its posture in national security cases.

3

A Second Look

The conventional narrative is unimpeachable insofar as it maintains that courts are generally highly deferential to the executive during wartime in cases implicating national security. But when the narrative is considered in light of the Court's entire history, it seeks to explain too much on the basis of too little. A broader historical focus suggests that the high court is exceedingly deferential to claims involving not only the nation's security from external threats during war but also to claims involving internal order and stability when the nation is not at war. Furthermore, on occasion the Court will rule against the executive in a case implicating national security even during wartime. To modify the conventional perspective and make it more nuanced and complicated is important, for it sheds light on the Court's historic role in American life. But even against this modified perspective, the post–World War II era of deference breaks ranks with the past. Before those issues are addressed, it is important to first take a second look at the ingrained narrative.

One group of cases that undermines the conventional narrative was decided during the years immediately following the Civil War. In those postwar cases, the Court was nonetheless exceedingly cautious about asserting judicial authority.

There is no doubt that these cases arose at a time when the Court was under siege. During those volatile years, not only did the Supreme Court have to accept that the executive might refuse to comply with an order directed against it or fail to enforce an order directed against others, but the Court also had to accept the fact that Congress was deeply distrustful of the Court and president. Indeed, the Court could fairly assume that Congress would use its authority to retaliate against it if it believed that the Court threatened its reconstruction initiatives. And the Court knew that the Congress was so distrustful of President Johnson that it had taken the extraordinary step of reducing the number of Supreme Court justices from ten to seven as members died in office or retired, so that Johnson could not make appointments that might be hostile to the congressional reconstruction initiatives.[1] The ingrained narrative, which places great emphasis on the distinction between war and peace, cannot account for these cases.

Three cases illustrate the issues. Over President Andrew Johnson's veto, Congress passed the Reconstruction Statutes of March 2 and 23 of 1867,[2] which imposed military rule on the former Confederate states, except for Tennessee, which had already ratified the Fourteenth Amendment to the Constitution, ratification being a condition for readmittance to the Union.[3] In response, the state of Mississippi sued President Johnson and the local military commander, seeking an injunction barring them from "carrying into effect an act of Congress alleged to be unconstitutional."[4] Chief Justice Salmon P. Chase's short opinion denied the "motion for leave to file the bill," stating that the Court had no jurisdiction over a bill "to enjoin the President in the performance of his official duties."[5]

From one angle, the opinion is a victory for the presidency in that the Court concluded that it had no authority to enjoin the president from enforcing a congressional enactment on the ground that it was unconstitutional. But from another perspective, the outcome constituted a victory for the Congress in that the effect of the ruling was to leave the constitutionality of the Reconstruction Acts unaddressed and to leave in place the military occupation of the states that rebelled against the Union.

What is remarkable about the opinion is Chase's candor in explaining the outcome. If the Court had declared the Reconstruction statutes unconstitutional and granted the requested injunction, President Johnson might well have refused to obey it, as Lincoln had done in the *Merryman* case, leaving the Court powerless to respond to executive disobedience.[6] In contrast, if President Johnson complied with the order, his actions might cause the "House of Representatives [to] impeach the President . . ."[7] To avoid either outcome, the Court did not decide the merits of the matter, but rather concluded it lacked authority to grant the requested relief.[8]

A second case involved William H. McCardle, a newspaper editor in Vicksburg, Mississippi, who was arrested after writing editorials critical of the

---

[1] Charles Fairman, The Oliver Wendell Holmes Devise, History of the Supreme Court of the United States 169 (Paul A. Freund ed., Volume VI, Part One 1971).

[2] *Id.* at 317–333, 591–598.

[3] Eric Foner, Reconstruction: America's Unfinished Revolution 1863–1877, 261 (1988).

[4] State of Mississippi v. Johnson, 71 U.S. 475, 498 (1866).

[5] *Id.* at 501.

[6] *Id.*

[7] *Id.* at 500–501. The House did impeach Johnson in 1868 and Chase presided at the Senate trial, which ended in an acquittal.

[8] State of Mississippi v. Johnson, 71 U.S. 475 (1866).

military occupation, Reconstruction Acts, and local military commander, and then charged with "disturbance of the public peace," "inciting to insurrection, disorder, and violence," "libel," and "impeding reconstruction."[9] McCardle challenged the legality of his detention and his case ended up before the Supreme Court at its December 1867 term. After the case was argued on the merits and submitted to the Court for a decision, Congress, fearful that the Supreme Court might declare the Reconstruction Acts unconstitutional, passed over President Johnson's veto of the so-called Repealer Act, which repealed the statute that McCardle relied upon as a statutory basis authorizing his appeal to the Supreme Court.[10]

McCardle's case involved the Court in the "fierce conflict then ensuing between President Johnson and the Congress over Reconstruction policies."[11] Congressional Republicans insisted upon military control of the former Confederate states "until the States should be reorganized and admitted back into the Union upon acceptance of such conditions as Congress should choose

---

[9] Ex parte McCardle, 73 U.S. 318 (1867).

[10] Supreme Court Justice Robert Jackson termed President Johnson's veto message an example of noteworthy "political courage," since Johnson's impeachment trial in the Senate was going on at the time. Robert H. Jackson, Wartime Security and Liberty Under Law, 2 Buffalo L. Rev. 102, 122, n.23 (1951). At the time of the veto message Johnson was under enormous congressional attack in part because Congress feared that he, and some members of the Supreme Court, were strongly opposed to the congressional effort to adopt statutes that became central to the Reconstruction. Nonetheless, in vetoing the Repealer Act, Johnson submitted the following as part of his veto message to Congress.

> The legislation proposed in the second section, it seems to me, is not in harmony with the spirit and intention of the Constitution. It cannot fail to affect most injuriously the just equipoise of our system of government; for it establishes a precedent which, if followed, may eventually sweep away every check on arbitrary and unconstitutional legislation. Thus far during the existence of the Government the Supreme Court of the United States has been viewed by the people as the true expounder of their Constitution, and in the most violent party conflicts its judgments and decrees have always been sought and deferred to with confidence and respect. In public estimation it combines judicial wisdom and impartiality in a greater degree than any other authority known to the Constitution; and any act which may be construed into or mistaken for an attempt to prevent or evade its decisions, on a question which affects the liberty of the citizens and agitates the country, cannot fail to be attended with unpropitious consequences. It will be justly held by a large portion of the people as an admission of the unconstitutionality of the act on which its judgment may be forbidden or forestalled, and may interfere with that willing acquiescences in its provisions which is necessary for the harmonious and efficient execution of any law.

President Johnson's veto message may be found at Cong. Globe, 2165 (1868).

[11] Charles Warren, Vol. III The Supreme Court in United States History 418 (1926).

to impose."[12] President Johnson and his supporters "openly stated" that such legislation was subject to judicial challenge, which meant that the Supreme Court "might become the final arbiter of the situation,"[13] and on that score, the congressional Republicans were "apprehensive as to the attitude of the Court."[14]

The Supreme Court had several options. It could have ruled that Congress did not intend the Repealer Act to apply to a case already pending before the high court. It also could have decided that if Congress intended the act to apply to a pending case, the application of the statute was unconstitutional because it would constitute an improper intrusion by the Congress in the internal affairs of the judiciary. Or it could have upheld the application of the Repealer Act not only in general, but in particular to the *McCardle* case and dismiss the proceedings for want of jurisdiction.[15] If the Court had concluded that it had jurisdiction, it could have decided that the Reconstruction statutes were unconstitutional—which would have put the Court in direct conflict with the Congress—or it could have decided that they were constitutional—which would have given constitutional legitimacy to the continued military occupation of the Confederate states, even though the rebellion had ended. In the end, the Court avoided both of these outcomes by using its discretion to argue that it lacked jurisdiction to decide the matter because of the Repealer Act. The Court's very short opinion suggested that the Court thought that the less said in explanation of the outcome the better.[16]

Mississippi yielded one more dramatic case that thrust the high court into the national struggle of Reconstruction. Edward M. Yerger, another newspaper editor, was accused of stabbing the acting mayor of Jackson to death, arrested by military authorities, and placed on trial before a military commission. During the trial, Yerger filed a petition for a writ of habeas corpus in the circuit court in Mississippi, challenging the authority of the military jurisdiction to try him. Once the court denied the writ, Yerger appealed to the Supreme Court under the provisions of the 1789 Judiciary Act (as opposed to the Judiciary Act of 1867 that Congress had repealed). One week after the argument,[17] the Court, in an opinion written by Chief Justice Chase, upheld the Court's jurisdiction under the 1789 Act.[18]

The central question the Court had to decide was whether the so-called Repealer Act of 1868, which was determinative in the *McCardle* case, withdrew

---

[12] *Id.* at 418–419.

[13] *Id.* at 419.

[14] *Id.*

[15] Ex parte McCardle, 74 U.S. 506.

[16] *Id.*

[17] Charles Warren, II The Supreme Court in United States History 491 (1926).

[18] Ex parte Yerger, 75 U.S. 85 (1868).

the Court's jurisdiction over the appeal otherwise authorized by the 1789 Judiciary Act. The Repealer Act did not by its terms repeal any jurisdictional statute other than the 1867 statute, but that left open the question whether the Repealer Statute repealed the 1789 statue "by implication."[19]

The Court reasoned that if the Repealer Statute repealed the 1789 statute by implication, it must also have repealed by implication other statutes conferring jurisdiction on the Court. Because the Court found a repeal by implication unacceptable, Chase wrote for the Court: "Our conclusion is, that none of the acts prior to 1867, authorizing this court to exercise appellate jurisdiction by means of the writ of *habeas corpus*, were repealed by the act of that year, and that the repealing section of the act of 1868 is limited in terms, and must be limited in effect to the appellate jurisdiction authorized by the act of 1867."[20]

After the court's opinions in *Mississippi v. Johnson* and *McCardle*, these words in the *Yerger* opinion might have suggested that the Court was infused with renewed independence and conviction about its important role in the governing scheme. But that impression would have been misleading. After asserting that repeal by implication was "not favored," Chase went on to recite the facts in *McCardle* that caused the court in *McCardle* to dismiss the appeal.[21] There was no need for Chase to recite the *McCardle* facts to decide the *Yerger* case unless Chase was signaling to Congress that Congress could make this case vanish from the Court's docket, and thus avoid a possible confrontation between the branches, by repealing the jurisdictional basis for the suit as it had done in *McCardle*. In the end, the Supreme Court did not have to decide the matter because the parties settled the case.[22]

Taken as whole, these post–Civil War cases express remarkable timidity. The Court expressly conceded that it would not decide the merits because it had no confidence that its order would be obeyed, it granted Congress the authority to withdraw its jurisdiction over a case that had been argued on the merits and submitted to the court for decision in order to avoid a confrontation, and it asserted that it had jurisdiction over a dispute but invited Congress to withdraw its jurisdiction to eliminate the possibility of yet another showdown. And all of this was done after the Civil War had ended.

A second cluster of cases resulting from the Civil War provides another example that undermines the conventional narrative. This group concerns the rights of the newly freed slaves during the last decades of the nineteenth century. Three cases—the *Slaughter-House Cases* decided in 1873, *The Civil Rights*

---

[19] *Id.* at 105.
[20] *Id.* at 106.
[21] *Id.* at 105.
[22] Charles Warren, II The Supreme Court in United States History 496–497 (1926).

Cases decided in 1883, and *Plessy v. Ferguson* decided in 1896—involved construction of the Thirteenth and the Fourteenth Amendments.[23] These were complicated cases separated by almost a quarter of a century and thus at first blush may seem as if they push against a straightforward characterization. But as different as the three cases were, and as complex as the legal issues were, the cases involved the rights of the newly freed slaves and thus presented a challenge spanning a quarter of a century to civil peace.

The Fourteenth Amendment to the Constitution was adopted in 1868 and included three important clauses designed to advance, among other interests, the rights of the newly freed slaves as they daily confronted prejudice and discrimination. Combined, the three clauses prohibited states from making or enforcing any law that abridged the "privileges or immunities of citizens of the United States," or deprived "any person of life, liberty, or property, without due process," or denied "any person within its jurisdiction the equal protection of the laws." Those constitutional provisions, in conjunction with legislation that granted lower federal courts jurisdiction over suits raising federal questions,[24] as well as legislation that authorized the federal courts to grant relief against state officials, not only constituted a revolution in the relationship between the federal and state governments,[25] but also sought to assure that the newly freed slaves would be able to secure judicial relief that gave important meaning to these newly adopted constitutional provisions.

As unlikely as it may seem, the first major case decided by the Supreme Court construing the Fourteenth Amendment was brought by white butchers in Louisiana who challenged a statute that granted a butchering monopoly to a corporation. The opinion construed the so-called Privileges or Immunities Clause of the Amendment so that it did not guarantee any new rights—as opposed to those rights provided for in the Constitution that existed before the adoption of the amendment—a person could assert against a state. As a result, instead of this potentially dynamic clause being a basis for protecting individuals from unfair or oppressive state regulation, the high court's construction of the clause rendered it essentially a nullity.[26] A decade later, the Supreme Court

---

[23] Plessy v. Ferguson, 163 U.S. 537 (1896); The Civil Rights Cases, 109 U.S. 3 (1883); Slaughter-House Cases, 83 U.S. 36 (1872).

[24] Richard H. Fallon Jr., John F. Manning, Daniel J. Meltzer, and David L. Shapiro, Hart and Wechsler's The Federal Courts and The Federal System 779–784 (7th ed. 2015).

[25] The key provision today is codified as 42 U.S.C. §1983, which was adopted in 1871. *See generally id.*

[26] In keeping with his broad effort to minimize the scope of judicial discretion in interpreting the Constitution, Justice Felix Frankfurter commented favorably on the majority opinion's construction of the Slaughter-House Cases by stating that its narrow construction of the clause avoided "the mischievous uses to which that clause would lend itself if its scope were not confined to that given it" by the majority opinion. Adamson v. California, 332 U.S. 46, 61 (1947)

limited the authority of Congress to enforce the Fourteenth Amendment by giving a narrow construction to the meaning of the word "state" as that word is used in the Fourteenth Amendment that prohibits the "state," as opposed to private parties, from infringing upon various rights.[27] And a dozen years later, the Supreme Court decided the infamous *Plessy v. Ferguson* case, in which it concluded that a state did not violate the Equal Protection Clause of the Fourteenth Amendment by mandating race segregation on railway cars.[28]

Taken together, these dismal decisions decimated the capacity of the Fourteenth Amendment to be used as a sword by African Americans in their effort to become full and equal citizens, and although there are multiple layers of reasons that prompted the precise legal opinions in these cases, it is difficult to accept that they were not partially driven by a fear that a different result in each case would ignite social unrest, as judicial decisions challenged social structures and political practices, especially in the former Confederate states. Thus, in his magisterial and award-winning history of Reconstruction, Eric Foner noted that in some areas of the South during the years following the end of the Civil War, "violence against blacks reached staggering proportions."[29] In his judgment, the "pervasiveness of violence reflected whites' determination to define in their own way the meaning of freedom and their determined resistance to blacks' efforts to establish their autonomy, whether in matters of family, church, labor, or personal demeanor."[30] Foner observed that the violence against the newly freed slaves illustrated:

[H]ow day-to-day encounters between the races became infused with the tension inevitable when a social order, with its established power relations and commonly understood rules of conduct, has been swept away and a new one has not yet come into being. Only over time would the South's new system of social relations be worked out. As David L. Swain, former governor of North Carolina, remarked in 1865, "With reference to emancipation, we are at the beginning of the war."[31]

Ultimately, according to Foner, the violence against blacks during these years was of historic proportions: "In its pervasive impact and multiplicity of

(Frankfurter, J., concurring). Nonetheless, in recent years, a majority of justices on the Supreme Court did rely upon the clause as basis for a person's right to travel. Saenz v. Roe, 526 U.S. 489 (1999).

[27] The Civil Rights Cases, 109 U.S. 3 (1883).
[28] *Plessy*, 163 U.S. 537.
[29] Eric Foner, Reconstruction: America's Unfinished Revolution 1863–1877, 119 (1988).
[30] *Id.* at 120.
[31] *Id.* at 123.

purposes, however, the wave of counterrevolutionary terror that swept over large parts of the South between 1868 and 1871 lacks a counterpart either in the American experience or in that of the other Western Hemisphere societies that abolished slavery in the nineteenth century."[32]

There are not many indications in the judicial opinions signaling that the potential of social unrest and horrific violence prompted judicial outcomes that reinforced the status quo preferred by whites. But Justice Brown's opinion in *Plessy v. Ferguson,* which gave constitutional legitimacy to "Jim Crow" laws by upholding a Louisiana law requiring separate cars on public transportation for African Americans and Caucasians, provides some evidence that this concern was at least in his mind as he penned the majority opinion. Drawing a distinction between political and social rights, Justice Brown argued that the legal challenge to the Louisiana law:

> [A]ssumes that social prejudices may be overcome by legislation, and that equal rights cannot be secured to the negro except by an enforced commingling of the two races. We cannot accept this proposition. If the two races are to meet upon terms of social equality, it must be the result of natural affinities, a mutual appreciation of each other's merits, and voluntary consent of individuals . . . Legislation is powerless to eradicate racial instincts, or to abolish distinctions based upon physical differences, and the attempt to do so can only result in accentuating the difficulties of the present situation.[33]

In Brown's mind, coerced commingling—and whether it resulted from legislature or judicial order was not a significant distinction—would not eradicate racial prejudice or lead to social equality, but it would "result in accentuating the difficulties of the present situation," which was surely a reference to racial tensions in America at the time.[34]

A third group of cases out of harmony with the ingrained narrative was decided during the 1920s. According to the war-and-peace paradigm, once

---

[32] *Id.* at 425.

[33] *Plessy,* 163 U.S. 551.

[34] A dramatic example of the Supreme Court using its authority to further domestic security challenged by the late nineteenth-century labor movement is *In re Debs,* 158 U.S. 564 (1895). The United States sought an injunction against Eugene Debs and other officers of the American Railway Union on the ground that the Union's strike interfered with the capacity of the government to deliver the mails. In granting the equitable relief, as opposed to requiring the government to pursue relief via the criminal sanction or damages, Justice Brewer stated that "under this government of and by the people the means of redress of all wrongs are through the courts and at the ballot box, and that no wrong, real or fancied, carries with it legal warrant to invite as a means of redress the co-operation of a mob, with its accompanying acts of violence." *In re* Debs at 599. William

World War I ended, the Supreme Court should have offered more protection to political dissenters than it did during the war. That is, after all, what Holmes implied on behalf of the Court in the *Schenck* case when he wrote: "When a nation is at war many things that might be said in time of peace are such a hindrance to its effort that their utterance will not be endured so long as men fight and that no Court could regard them as protected by an constitutional right."[35] But that is not what the Court, in fact, did.[36] For example, in *Gitlow v. New York* and *Whitney v. California*,[37] both decided in the 1920s, a majority of the Court was very deferential to the states in the name of perceived threats to stability and order. In the *Gitlow* case, the Supreme Court sustained the conviction of political dissenters pursuant to a New York statute that made their speech a crime even in the absence of an imminent threat, and even though the dissenters did not advocate unlawful conduct. In the *Whitney* case, the Court upheld the conviction of the defendant because the defendant was an active member of a socialist organization that was considered a threat to the political order.

Apart from these cases, which are at odds with the dominant narrative because they were decided during times of peace, there were a handful of cases decided during wartime in which the judges were in fact not deferential. For example, consider a case that arose during the first months of the Civil War in which the chief justice of the Supreme Court and the president collided. Shortly after Abraham Lincoln became president, he authorized military commanders along the eastern seaboard to suspend the writ of habeas corpus so as to assure the safe passage of troops from the north to Washington, D.C., which was threatened by Confederate soldiers. At that point, Union troops arrested and imprisoned John Merryman because he was suspected of being a southern sympathizer and participating in the destruction of railroad bridges that linked Maryland with the nation's capital.

Merryman's lawyer prepared a petition for a writ of habeas corpus challenging the legality of Merryman's detention by the military and presented it to Chief Justice Roger B. Taney in his capacity as circuit judge.[38] The writ was

---

M. Wiecek's history of the Stone and Vinson Courts offered this comment on the *Debs* case: on behalf of a unanimous court, Brewer "upheld the labor injunction, the most potent weapon in the judicial arsenal of labor-suppressive techniques. Brewer extolled federal executive, judicial, and military power as the ultimate force for preservation of order in a society that he and his colleagues feared was veering out of control." William M. Wiecek, The Birth of the Modern Constitution: The United States Supreme Court, 1941–1953, 25 (Stanley N. Katz ed., Volume XII 2006).

[35] Schenck v. United States, 249 U.S. 47, 52 (1919).

[36] Harry Kalven Jr., A Worthy Tradition, Freedom of Speech in America 147 (Jamie Kalven ed., 1988).

[37] Gitlow v. People of State of New York, 268 U.S. 652 (1925); Whitney v. California, 274 U.S. 357 (1927).

[38] Ex parte Merryman, 17 F.Cas 144 (1861).

issued the same day and addressed to General George Cadwalader. The next day, one of the general's aides appeared in court without Merryman.[39] Taney then directed that an attachment be issued against the general that the marshal could not effectuate because he was prevented from entering the fort. In response, Taney ruled that only Congress had the authority to suspend the privilege of the writ of habeas corpus, and thus Lincoln's suspension was unconstitutional and the military imprisonment of Merryman was unlawful. Lincoln ignored Taney's ruling and only alluded to it when he prepared his famous July 4, 1861 message to Congress explaining his actions, in which he argued that the suspension of the writ was justified because it was necessary to preserve the Union.[40] He famously put the matter this way: "[A]re all the laws, *but one*, to go unexecuted, and the government itself go to pieces, lest that one be violated?"[41]

Taney's *Merryman* opinion is discounted on the ground that he was a southern sympathizer whose sympathy for the South made him hostile toward Lincoln and his polices and thus willing, if not eager, to rule against Lincoln. Be that as it may, Taney's personal disposition, at least in this case, does not mean that his constitutional interpretation in *Merryman* was unsound. Rather, it would seem that Taney had the better of Lincoln on this constitutional question—only Congress had the constitutional authority to suspend the writ.[42]

As is evident, *Merryman* is out of line with the idea that judges bend over backwards during wartime to defer to the executive. At the same time, its net effect was likely to reinforce the Supreme Court's deference to the executive, at least during wartime, for fear that the executive would fail to comply with a judicial order in a showdown.

The post–World War II cases illustrate the questionable narrowness of the dominant narrative. During the Korean War in 1952, when a union strike threatened to shut down the nation's steel industry, President Truman directed his secretary of commerce to seize the steel mills in order to keep them open and running. The president argued that a strike would imperil the war effort since the armaments industry required a dependable supply of steel.

---

[39] See William H. Rehnquist, All the Laws But One, Civil Liberties in Wartime 26–35 (1998) for historical background.

[40] The Library of America, Abraham Lincoln, Speeches and Writings 1859–1865, Speeches, Letters, Miscellaneous Writings, Presidential Messages and Proclamations 346 (Don E. Fehrenbacher ed., 1989).

[41] *Id.* at 253.

[42] But as sound as Taney's legal analysis was, he lost out in the court of history. Lincoln's suspension of the great writ is respected as driven by necessity, and the fact that he made his decision public at the time and sought to explain and justify it to the Congress—which retained the authority to impeach the new president—added strength to the nobility of Lincoln's cause.

The legal arguments were complicated, but in the end the court voted six to three that the executive seizure was unconstitutional absent congressional authorization. This case certainly put the president and the Court on a collision course and this time, unlike the Court in the post–Civil War cases, the Court did not blink. Moreover, the president complied with the ruling, which was followed by a strike that did not lead to a shortage of steel.[43]

In June of 1971, while the United States continued to fight a land war in Vietnam, the *New York Times* began a ten-part series based on a top-secret Pentagon history of the United States involvement in Vietnam from 1945 to 1968. The Nixon administration initiated a lawsuit seeking a prior restraint to bar the newspaper from publishing its complete series. The administration argued that the study contained information that would seriously harm the national security if disclosed. It was precisely the kind of dispute where one might expect the high court to defer to the president's claims, even if it meant censoring the press. But in the end the Court ruled six to three against the Nixon administration, claiming that the administration did not present evidence that satisfied its heavy burden, given that it sought to enjoin the press from publishing information the press possessed.[44]

And then, after 9/11 and after no weapons of mass destruction were found in Iraq, the Supreme Court, first in 2004 and then in 2006 and 2008, issued a total of three rulings that constituted serious judicial defeats for the Bush administration. In one case of limited application, the Court concluded that an American citizen identified as an enemy combatant and detained in the United States had a right to an administrative hearing to contest his identification as an enemy combatant.[45] In the other two cases, the high court insisted that federal courts had jurisdiction over writs of habeas corpus submitted by detainees held in Guantanamo.[46]

These cases are out of alignment with the pattern put forth by the conventional narrative. They indicate that on occasion the Supreme Court folds its tent and retreats from a collision with the executive during peacetime, and that, conversely, it will not, on occasion, shy away from a showdown with the executive during wartime.

In describing the role of courts in cases implicating national security, the dominant narrative draws a sharp distinction between times of war and peace. But

---

[43] This case was Youngstown Sheet & Tube Co. v. Sawyer, 343 U.S. 579 (1952). See Chapter 15 for discussion of this case.

[44] This case is New York Times Co. v. United States, 403 U.S. 713 (1971). See Chapter 15 for a discussion of this case.

[45] Hamdi v. Rumsfeld, 542 U.S. 507 (2004).

[46] Boumediene v. Bush, 553 U.S. 723 (2007); Hamdan v. Rumsfeld, 547 U.S. 1016 (2006).

placing so much emphasis on that distinction constitutes an oversimplifica-
tion that is both over- and underinclusive. The conventional narrative is underinclusive in that the Court has been highly deferential to the executive in cases
implicating national security during times of peace, and it has been overinclu-
sive in that the Court has ruled against the executive during times of war.

Nonetheless, even a more nuanced understanding of the Supreme Court's
role in cases affecting security in the nation's history leaves intact the claim
that the post–World War II decades constitute a distinct era in Supreme Court
history. That is so because the Supreme Court's approach in cases implicating national security during the post–World War II era is tied to changed historical circumstances—the emergence of the United States as a global power
with global national security interests—a development with an antecedent in
American history.

4

Breaking Ranks

Whether by comparison to the conventional narrative of the role of the Supreme Court in matters concerning security or by comparison to the more complicated perspective, the fact is that Supreme Court decisions in cases implicating national security since World War II break ranks with the Court's prior history.

What sets the post–World War II era apart from earlier periods in American history is the collapse of isolationism as a dominant force in shaping the American mind and policy. Isolationism runs deep into American history. Indeed, one prominent historian has speculated that American isolationism found expression as early as the seventeenth century, when the first European settlers arrived in New England and John Winthrop declared that "Americans dwelt in a 'city upon a hill,'" which suggested that Americans were "not simply distant from the Old World but different from it as well,"[1] and should, as a result, remain separate and apart. Be that as it may, there is little doubt that keeping Europe at a full arm's length was partially the result of an "accident of geography" in that America had "grown to national maturity on a remote continent in the absence of threats from abroad."[2] And, as is well known, the first leaders of the current republic were strong advocates of shunning European entanglements. For example, recall George Washington's Farewell Address when he warned "[a]gainst the insidious wiles of foreign influence" and advised that the nation "steer clear of permanent alliances with any portion of the foreign world,"[3] and Thomas Jefferson's Inaugural Address when he set forth what he termed one of the "essential principles" of his administration: "peace, commerce, and honest friendship with all nations, entangling alliances with none."[4]

[1] David M. Kennedy, Freedom From Fear: The American People in Depression and War, 1929–1945, 86–87 (1999).

[2] *Id.* at 386.

[3] President George Washington, The Address of General Washington To the People of the United States on his Declining of the Presidency of the United States (Washington's Farewell Address) (Sept. 19, 1796). http://avalon.law.yale.edu/18th_century/washing.asp.

[4] President Thomas Jefferson, First Inaugural Address (Mar. 4, 1801). http://avalon.law.yale.edu/19th_century/jefinau1.asp.

The Spanish-American War with annexation of "territories" around the globe, and then a decade and a half later the involvement of the United States in World War I, might well have signaled an end to the isolationist mindset. But that was not the case. In fact, America's controversial entrance into the Great War in the hope of ending all wars had just the opposite effect. As the respected historian David M. Kennedy has written:

> No people came to believe more emphatically than the Americans that the Great War was an unalloyed tragedy, an unpardonably costly mistake never to be repeated. More than fifty thousand American doughboys had perished fighting on the western front, and to what avail? So far from being redeemed by American intervention, Europe swiftly slid back into its historic vices of authoritarianism and armed rivalry, while America slid back into its historic attitude of isolationism.[5]

In the years immediately following the war's end, "Americans said no to Woodrow Wilson's League of Nations, no to the French security treaty, no to freer trade policies, no to pleas from France and Britain to forgive their wartime loans from the U.S. Treasury, and no to further unlimited immigration from Europe."[6]

The ramifications of this isolationism, which molded American politics in the 1920s and 1930s,[7] were significant. After World War I, the size of the army was drastically reduced, a cap was placed on naval capacities, and there was no commitment to exploiting and pressing the opportunities presented by air power. There was also retrenchment in intelligence activities as immortalized by Henry Stimson, who learned shortly after his appointment as secretary of state in 1929 that the United States had "maintained a highly successful code-breaking unit, known as the Black Chamber, ever since the end of World War I," when he said, "Gentlemen do not read each other's mail."[8]

During the 1930s, American isolationism remained dominant even as the lamps of Europe were going out yet again and another war seemed certain.[9]

---

[5] David M. Kennedy, Freedom From Fear: The American People in Depression and War, 1929–1945, 386 (1999).

[6] Id.

[7] Id. at 381–464.

[8] John Ranelagh, The Agency: The Rise and Decline of the CIA 27 (1986). Ranelagh states in a footnote that there is "some question whether Stimson ever actually said this. But the sentence and its authorship were ascribed to him during his lifetime, and he never denied them." Id.

[9] The phrase "lamps of Europe" is drawn from the eloquent foreboding of Sir Edward Grey, British foreign secretary, on the eve of World War I: "The lamps are going out all over Europe. We

Thus, the United States resisted the development of a powerful military service, an effective intelligence service, and a coordinated and directed diplomatic service aimed at protecting the national security. Indeed, President Roosevelt even "moved swiftly after his inauguration in 1933 to shrink the already skeletal 140,000-man army,"[10] and during the decade, his "White House had no national security adviser or formal foreign policy decision-making apparatus,"[11] even as he tried to move the Congress and the nation away from the isolationist frame of mind.

The Japanese attack on Pearl Harbor on December 7, 1941, and Germany's declaration of war on the United States a few days later abruptly challenged America's historic isolationist stance. And by the time the United States dropped two atomic bombs on Japanese cities and World War II hostilities ended with the United States as the dominant power in the world, it would have seemed as though the isolationist impulse was permanently buried. But, as peculiar as it may seem, that judgment was premature. Isolationism was an irrepressible frame of mind, and as soon as the war ended, the inclination toward isolation once again reasserted itself. In keeping with that frame of mind, President Truman, for example, disbanded the Office of Strategic Services (the immediate forerunner of the CIA) in September of 1945, as he tried to figure out how the nation could have a "sound, well-organized intelligence system,"[12] without having a "Gestapo under any guise or for any reason."[13]

But what had been irrepressible was indeed finally repressed. Following the Soviet Union's annexation of Lithuania, Latvia, and Estonia, and the

---

shall not see them lit again in our lifetime." Ian Kershaw, To Hell and Back: Europe 1914–1949, 9 (2015).

[10] David M. Kennedy, Freedom From Fear: The American People in Depression and War, 1929–1945, 388 (1999).

[11] *Id.* at 389.

[12] 1 Memoirs by Harry S. Truman: Year of Decisions 98 (1955).

[13] *Id.* at 99. Tony Judt's Postwar: A History of Europe Since 1945 offers a brief summary of relevant considerations:

> The United States in 1945 and for some time to come seriously expected to extricate itself from Europe as soon as possible, and was thus understandably keen to put in place a workable settlement that would not require American presence or supervision. . . . The abrupt ending of Lend-Lease was part of a general cutting back of economic and military commitments to Europe. The American defense budget was reduced by five-sixths between 1945 and 1947. At the end of the war in Europe the US had 97 combat-ready ground divisions in place; by mid-1947 there were just twelve divisions, most of them under strength and engaged in administrative tasks. The rest had gone home and been demobilized. (Tony Judt, Postwar: A History of Europe Since 1945, 109 (2005))

establishment of subordinate regimes in Eastern Europe, Winston Churchill, who had been the British Prime minister from 1940 to 1945, gave a speech in Fulton, Missouri, in which he observed that the Soviet Union had pulled down an "iron curtain" separating Eastern and Western Europe.[14] Soon thereafter, in 1947, George Kennan published his highly influential "X" article in *Foreign Affairs* that argued in favor of "a policy of firm containment, designed to confront the Russians with unalterable counter-force at every point where they show signs of encroaching upon the interest of a peaceful and stable world."[15] And then in the early months of 1947, after American officials concluded that the withdrawal of British forces from the eastern Mediterranean would permit Stalin to dominate Greece and Turkey and through them other neighboring countries, Truman addressed a joint session of Congress and announced what later became known as the Truman Doctrine. "I believe," he declared, "that it must be the policy of the United States to support free peoples who are resisting attempted subjugation by armed minorities or by outside pressures. I believe that we must assist free peoples to work out their own destinies in their own way."[16]

It was in that year that the United States fully embraced what one authority, Herring, termed "the Magna Charta of the national security state,"[17] and fundamentally changed its relationship with other nations and its role in world events. This "Magna Charta" consisted of the National Security Act of July 1947 that created an independent Central Intelligence Agency; established a National Security Council in the White House to coordinate policymaking, and a cabinet-level, civilian secretary of defense responsible for the previously separate army, navy, and air force departments; and established the permanent Joint Chiefs of Staff.[18] This Magna Charta was supplemented a few years later by a seven-page presidential memorandum signed by President Harry S. Truman on October 24, 1952. This memorandum, which was classified top secret and stamped with a code word that was itself classified,[19] established

---

[14] II Memoirs by Harry S. Truman: Years of Trial and Hope 95 (1956).

[15] George F. Kennan, *The Sources of Soviet Conduct*, Foreign Aff., July 1947, 566.

[16] II Memoirs by Harry S. Truman: Years of Trial and Hope 106 (1956). George Kennan thought Truman's position was "too strong," whereas Clark Clifford "thought it too weak." Dean Acheson, Present at the Creation: My Years in the State Department 221 (1969); *see also* Clark Clifford and Richard Holbrooke, Counsel to the President: A Memoir 130–140 (1991); John Lewis Gaddis, George F. Kennan: An American Life 254–58 (2011).

[17] George C. Herring, From Colony to Superpower: U.S. Foreign Relations since 1776, 614 (2008); *see also* George F. Kennan, *The Sources of Soviet Conduct*, Foreign Aff., July 1947, 566.

[18] *See* George C. Herring, From Colony to Superpower: U.S. Foreign Relations since 1776, 614 (2008).

[19] James Bamford, The Puzzle Palace: Inside the National Security Agency, America's Most Secret Intelligence Organization 15 (1983).

the National Security Agency (NSA, or "No Such Agency," according to "wags"). The initial purpose of the NSA was to "listen in on enemy communications and crack codes."[20] Together, these developments put in place a set of national security agencies that have been the foundation of the national security structure ever since.[21]

These initiatives responded "to the turmoil that was the new world 'order' and to a perceived global threat from the Soviet Union," and in combination with one another and over a few short years, roughly 1945 to 1953, they "turned traditional U.S. foreign policy assumptions upside down." The United States, which had been a country "accustomed to free security," now "succumbed to a rampant insecurity through which nations across the world suddenly took on huge significance." Moreover, "[u]nilateralism gave way to multilateralism [] [t]hrough the policy of containment," as the Truman administration undertook "a host of international commitments, launched scores of programs, and mounted a peacetime military buildup that would have been unthinkable just ten years earlier." As Professor Herring concludes: "The age of American globalism was under way."[22]

One simple but dramatic example of the globalization of American national security interests was the substantial increase of overseas United States military bases since the end of World War II. Although the United States "had

---

[20] George C. Herring, From Colony to Superpower: U.S. Foreign Relations since 1776, 647 (2008).

[21] There were other expressions of America's new and dominating role in world affairs. For example, in 1949, the United States signed the North Atlantic Treaty, which in Article 5, provided that an armed attack on any of the signatories "shall be considered an attack against them all," and in the event of such an attack each party shall "assist the Party or Parties so attacked by taking forthwith, individually and in concert with the other Parties, such action as it deems necessary, including the use of armed force, to restore and maintain the security of the North Atlantic area." NATO, The North Atlantic Treaty (Apr. 4, 1949), http://www.nato.int/cps/en/natolive/official_texts_17120 htm.

[22] George C. Herring, From Colony to Superpower: U.S. Foreign Relations since 1776, 595 (2008); *see also* Michael J. Glennon, National Security and Double Government (2015); Frederick A.O. Schwarz Jr. and Aziz Z. Huq, Unchecked and Unbalanced: Presidential Power in a Time of Terror 4–5 (2007):

> The cold war and the 1947 National Security Act brought a new institutionalization of intelligence powers. Until the 1940s, the United States, unlike the former Soviet Union and Great Britain, had no organized secret intelligence services. What previously was ad hoc and informal became bureaucratic, regularized, and effective—a powerful tool concentrated almost exclusively in presidents' hands. The FBI's domestic security activities burgeoned. The CIA and the National Security Agency (or NSA) were born and rapidly expanded to enormous proportions. In 2005, the federal government spent $44 billion on the intelligence community's sixteen agencies and 100,000 staff.

some bases in foreign lands,"[23] before the last world war, it has only been since the end of that war that "the idea" that the United States "should have a large collection of bases and hundreds of thousands of troops permanently stationed overseas" has become "a quasireligious dictum of U.S. foreign and national security policy."[24] Pursuant to that policy, the United States, as of 2015, controls approximately 800 bases outside the fifty states and Washington, D.C.[25] One scholar of the subject matter, David Vine, has written that, according to the Pentagon, there are today "174 U.S. bases in Germany, 113 in Japan, and 83 in South Korea. There are hundreds more dotting the planet in Aruba and Australia, Bahrain and Bulgaria, Colombia, Kenya, and Qatar, to name just a few. Worldwide, we have bases in more than seventy countries."[26] Vine concludes that the United States "probably" has more bases "in other people's lands than any other people, nation, or empire in world history."[27]

This seismic shift changed America.[28] Two vignettes illustrate the change. The first is a scholarly study published in 1948 by Clinton L. Rossiter,

---

[23] David Vine, Base Nation: How U.S. Military Bases Abroad Harm America and the World 3 (2015).

[24] *Id.* at 5.

[25] *Id.* at 6.

[26] *Id.* at 3.

[27] *Id.* at 3. As yet another development in the expansion of military bases around the world, on December 10, 2015, the *New York Times* reported that the Pentagon has "proposed a new plan to the White House to build up a string of military bases in Africa, Southwest Asia and the Middle East" as at least one initiative to "grapple with the expansion of the Islamic State beyond its headquarters in Syria." Mark Mazzetti and Eric Schmitt, *Pentagon Seeks to Knit Foreign Bases Into ISIS-Foiling Network*, N.Y. Times, Dec. 10, 2010.

[28] In July of 1946, John Dewey wrote an Afterword to a book written twenty years earlier. The first paragraph reflected Dewey's sense that the American experience in World War II buried isolationism, and his single fact symbolizing the shift was America's refusal to join the League of Nations after World War I and its membership in the United Nations after World War II.

> This book was written some twenty years ago. It is my belief that intervening events confirm the position about the public and its connection with the state as the political organization of human relationships that was then presented. The most obvious consideration is the effect of the Second World War in weakening the conditions to which we give the name "Isolationism." The First World War had enough of that effect to call the League of Nations into being. But the United States refused to participate. And, while out-and-out nationalism was a prime factor in the refusal, it was reinforced by the strong belief that, after all, the main purpose of the League was to preserve the fruits of victory for the European nations that were on the winning side. There is no need to revive old controversies by discussing how far that belief was justifiable. The important fact for the issue here discussed is that the *belief* that such was the case was a strongly actuating consideration in the refusal of the United States to join the League. After the Second World War, this attitude was so changed that the country

who at the time was just commencing his academic career and who later became a nationally prominent political scientist at Cornell University. Rossiter discussed the overwhelming significance of the changes sweeping across America at the time, and of the struggle between the United States and the Soviet Union, in a study with the ominous title of *Constitutional Dictatorship: Crisis Government in the Modern Democracies*. In the second sentence of his study, Rossiter asked the fundamental and paradoxical question that Abraham Lincoln once posed and that he sought to answer in his study, which he considered of paramount importance because of the challenges confronting the United States at the time: "Must a government of necessity be too *strong* for the liberties of its people, or too *weak* to maintain its own existence?"[29] Rossiter posited that complex democracies are designed to function during times of peace, and that during times of crisis, democratic governments must have the power to "*overcome the peril and restore normal conditions,*" which will mean that the "*government will have more power and the people fewer rights.*"[30]

Rossiter was hopeful, but his hopefulness required a fundamental enhancement in governmental power. From Rossiter's perspective, the development of the atomic bomb,[31] the subsequent threat of nuclear proliferation, and the emergence of the Soviet Union as a potent adversary meant that the allocation of power within the national government must change and that the power of government over its people must be enhanced.[32] "From this day forward," he

joined the United Nations. (John Dewey, *The Public and Its Problems* 221 (Swallow Press Books 1954))

[29] Clinton L. Rossiter, Constitutional Dictatorship—Crisis Government in the Modern Democracies 3 (1948).

[30] *Id.* at 5 (emphasis in original).

[31] In his 2010 book, Bomb Power: The Modern Presidency and the National Security State (2010), Garry Wills argued that the development of the atomic bomb "altered our subsequent history down to its deepest constitutional roots. It redefined the presidency, as in all respects America's 'Commander in Chief' (a term that took on a new and unconstitutional meaning in this period). It fostered an anxiety of continuing crisis, so that society was pervasively militarized. It redefined the government as a National Security State, with apparatus of secrecy and executive control. It redefined Congress, as an executor of the executive. And it redefined the Supreme Court, as a follower of the follower of the executive. Only one part of the government had the supreme power, the Bomb, and all else must defer to it, for the good of the nation, for the good of the world, for the custody of the future, in a world of perpetual emergency superseding ordinary constitutional restrictions" (p. 1). A few pages later Wills ends his first chapter with this line: "Executive power has basically been, since World War II, Bomb Power" (p. 4).

[32] Clinton L. Rossiter, Constitutional Dictatorship—Crisis Government in the Modern Democracies 314 (1948).

insisted, "we must cease wasting our energies in discussing whether the government of the United States is to be powerful or not. It is going to be powerful or we are going to be obliterated." The challenge, Rossiter argued, was to "make that power effective and responsible" and to "make any future dictatorship a constitutional one." Thus, he wrote that "power can be responsible, that strong government can be democratic government, that dictatorship can be constitutional."[33]

Rossiter used the term "constitutional dictatorship" more for shock value than to convey any substantive set of reforms for changing the governmental structures. But Rossiter was deadly serious that the atomic bomb had changed the alignment of power under the constitution, and as a result, "[n]o sacrifice is too great for our democracy, least of all the temporary sacrifice of democracy itself." Rossiter was not urging the abandonment of the 1789 Constitution, but that the nation could not restore power structures that existed before World War II: the nation "can't go home again; the positive state is here to stay, and from now on the accent will be on power, not limitations."[34]

President Eisenhower's 1961 farewell address to the nation is a second vignette illustrating the swift and dramatic change sweeping over the United States immediately following World War II.[35] Eisenhower made it clear that a "vital element in keeping the peace is our military establishment," and he insisted that our "arms must be mighty, ready for instant action, so that no potential aggressor may be tempted to risk his own destruction." But Eisenhower was deeply troubled by the seismic shifts then underway in the United States. Today, he remarked, our military organization "bears little relation to that known by any of my predecessors in peacetime, or indeed by the fighting men of World War II or Korea." He recalled that:

> Until the latest of our world conflicts, the United States had no armaments industry. American makers of plowshares could, with time and as required, make swords as well. But now we can no longer risk emergency improvisation of national defense; we have been compelled to create a permanent armaments industry of vast proportions. Added to this, three and a half million men and women are directly engaged in the defense establishment. We annually spend

---

[33] *Id.* at 314.

[34] *Id.*

[35] President Dwight D. Eisenhower, Military-Industrial Complex Speech (Eisenhower's Farewell Address) (Jan. 17, 1961). http://avalon.law.yale.edu/20th_century/eisenhower001.asp.

on military security more than the net income of all United States corporations.[36]

Eisenhower argued that this "conjunction of an immense military establishment and a large arms industry is new in the American experience," and that its total influence "is felt in every city, every State house, every office of the Federal government." Eisenhower accepted the imperative nature of this development, but he cautioned that "we must not fail to comprehend its grave implications," and "we must guard against the acquisition of unwarranted influence, whether sought or unsought, by the military-industrial complex." Eisenhower concluded that the American people

> [M]ust never let the weight of this combination endanger our liberties or democratic processes. We should take nothing for granted. Only an alert and knowledgeable citizenry can compel the proper meshing of the huge industrial and military machinery of defense with our peaceful methods and goals, so that security and liberty may prosper together.[37]

Eisenhower cannot be accused of failing to value the importance of a strong military, an aggressive CIA,[38] a resourceful NSA, and a dominant role of the United States in world affairs. And yet he was alert to the profound risks inherent

---

[36] *Id.*

[37] *Id.* As one student of Eisenhower and his legacy, James Ledbetter, has emphasized, Eisenhower was "no pacifist, but he was a lifelong opponent of what he called a 'garrison state,' in which policy and rights are defined by the shadowy needs of an all-powerful military elite." James Ledbetter, Opinion, *What Ike Got Right*, N.Y. Times, Dec. 14, 2010, at A35. Ledbetter conceded that the United States "isn't [] a garrison state today," but he claimed that Eisenhower "would likely have been deeply troubled . . . by the torture at Abu Ghraib, the use of martial authority to wiretap Americans without warrants and the multiyear detention of suspects at Guantánamo Bay without due process." And to further support the rise of the National Security State, Ledbetter pointed out that during the last half century there have been "very few years in which the United States has spent less on the military than it did the year before," and that that was true whether the United States was "actively fighting a war, whether it has an obvious and well-armed enemy or whether Democrats or Republicans run the White House and Congress." *Id.* Two years after Eisenhower delivered his farewell address, Earl Warren warned of the dangers of "the military in a democratic society.'" A military was a "necessary organ of government," but its "reach must be carefully limited" to preserve the proper balance between "freedom and order." Warren made clear that as he cautioned Americans he had in mind the dominance of the military in totalitarian governments behind the "iron curtain," as well as "many countries that have all of the formal trappings of constitutional democracy." Earl Warren, *The Bill of Rights and the Military*, 37 N.Y.U. Law Rev. 181, 182 (1962).

[38] For a recent history of the CIA during the Eisenhower years, see generally Stephen Kinzer, *The Brothers: John Foster Dulles, Allen Dulles, and Their Secret World War* (2013).

in the fundamental changes that had swept through the nation during and immediately after World War II. He was worried that the rise of the National Security State was at odds with "our liberties or democratic processes," and that it would in fact constrict liberty and undermine democracy. Eisenhower did not necessarily trust national political leaders or the courts to keep the tiller straight as the ship of state navigated its own dangers between its own Scylla and Charybdis. Instead, he placed his reliance on an "alert and knowledgeable citizenry," for he thought that in the end only it can "compel the proper meshing of the huge industrial and military machinery of defense with our peaceful methods and goals, so that security and liberty may prosper together."[39]

Rossiter and Eisenhower—one a youthful scholar and one a celebrated military commander elected president—perceived the shape of things to come. And come they did. By the mid-1950s, the structure of the modern-day National Security State was basically established and the hallmark of the Imperial Presidency acting in secret through the CIA, the NSA, and the FBI was operational. Although Congress certainly has important powers and the courts on occasion intercede to curb executive power, the president is without doubt at the head of the table and he is without a close second. And although that has always been the hallmark of the presidency, it has become much truer since the end of World War II than before. As two political scientists recently observed: "Sometime in the second half of the twentieth century, the president moved into the driver's seat of our political system."[40] But it was left to Arthur M. Schlesinger, Jr. to coin the term "The Imperial Presidency" as the title of his enormously influential book, in which he sought to identify the presidency of Richard M. Nixon as the time when the presidency became an "imperial" one, and thus threatened the constitutional order.[41]

Schlesinger observed that the constitutional system of checks and balances "would not work at all unless one of the three branches took the initiative and that it worked best in response to vigorous presidential leadership" because such leadership "was necessary to overcome the tendency toward inertia" and "enabled the American republic to meet the great crises of its history." Nonetheless, Schlesinger observed that presidential "energy," as Hamilton termed it, "produced" by the early 1970s "a conception of presidential power so spacious and peremptory as to imply a radical transformation of the traditional

---

[39] President Dwight D. Eisenhower, Military-Industrial Complex Speech (Eisenhower's Farewell Address) (Jan. 17, 1961). http://avalon.law.yale.edu/20th_century/eisenhower001.asp.

[40] Matthew Crenson and Benjamin Ginsberg, Presidential Power: Unchecked & Unbalanced 11 (2007).

[41] Arthur M. Schlesinger, Jr., The Imperial Presidency (1973).

polity." Indeed, in Schlesinger's view, the contemporary ramifications of the historical trend were extreme and profoundly threatening: "In the last years presidential primacy, so indispensable to the political order, has turned into presidential supremacy. The constitutional Presidency—as events so apparently disparate as the Indochina War and the Watergate affair showed—has become the Imperial Presidency and threatens to be the revolutionary Presidency."[42]

Schlesinger's theme has been restated and updated in recent decades. For example, *New York Times* correspondent Charlie Savage paid tribute to Schlesinger and his influence by even paraphrasing Schlesinger's title: *Takeover: The Return of the Imperial Presidency and the Subversion of American Democracy.* In *Takeover*, Savage makes the compelling point that the "accretion of presidential power ... often acts like a one-way ratchet: It can be increased far more easily than it can be reduced." As a result, Savage concludes that the "expansive presidential powers claimed and exercised by the Bush-Cheney White House are now an immutable part of American history .... [and are] difficult to overstate."[43] Or consider the conclusions of a legal scholar, who, after conceding that controversies "over the use of executive power have existed throughout American history," went on to state:

> But they took on a completely new dimension following the enormous expansion in the capacities of government necessary to prevail in World War II and the Cold War. Seen in this light, the deeply problematic aspects of the Bush administration's "war on terror" belong to

[42] *Id.* at viii. Thirty years after Schlesinger's book was published, David J. Barron and Martin S. Lederman wrote an unusually impressive law review article that seeks to revise the view that portrays the Congress as having over two centuries surrendered its substantial powers to the president. They wrote: "Specifically, the history shows that the legislative abdication paradigm is not only ill-suited to the present moment but severely overdrawn insofar as it purports to describe longstanding practice. As much as Congress may have ceded ground over the last two centuries when it comes to the President's unilateral power to use military force and deploy troops, Congress has been an active participant in setting the terms of battle (and the conduct and organization of the armed forces and militia more generally), to the extent that war powers scholarship has not fully acknowledged." David J. Barron and Martin S. Lederman, The Commander in Chief at the Lowest Ebb—A Constitutional History, 121 Harv. L. Rev. 941, 947 (2008).

[43] Charlie Savage, Takeover: The Return of the Imperial Presidency and the Subversion of American Democracy 329 (2007). Two constitutional law scholars who carefully studied constitutional war powers and the potential conflict between the presidency and the Congress over the making and conduct of war reached the same conclusion as Savage. The constitutional law supporting the enhancement of presidential power "is often made through accretion," and "once claimed by the Executive" such powers "are not easily relinquished." David J. Barron and Martin S. Lederman, The Commander in Chief at the Lowest Ebb—A Constitutional History, 121 Harv. L. Rev. 941, 1111 (2008).

a family of constitutional crises that include Watergate in the Nixon administration and the Iran-contra affair in the Reagan administration. These crises are part of a pattern of recurrent policy disasters and constitutional problems linked to the war power that run back to the Truman administration and include both covert and overt military operations such as the Bay of Pigs and the Vietnam War.[44]

The operational apparatus of the Imperial Presidency has grown so much since its first days that the scope and size of the agencies that comprise the nation's security front line dwarf what went before. Thus, a half-century after Eisenhower gave his Farewell Address, the *Washington Post* published a lengthy three-part series entitled *Top Secret America: A Washington Post Investigation*, which provides a contemporary snapshot of the National Security State that Eisenhower worried about. The report concluded that about "1,271 government organizations and 1,931 private companies work on programs related to counterterrorism, homeland security and intelligence in about 10,000 locations across the United States;" approximately 854,000 individuals "hold top-secret security clearances"; since 9/11, 33 building complexes for "top-secret intelligence work" have been built or are being built, and together they are in size "the equivalent of almost three Pentagons or 22 U.S. Capitol buildings."[45]

The post–World War II emergence of the United States as a dominant world power with global national security concerns constituted a departure of singular importance from its prior history when isolationism was central to the American outlook. And that definitive departure has had significance of extraordinary importance for the constitutional order.

Above all else the departure has resulted in the emergence of a National Security State that, because of what seems to be persistent and never-ending

---

[44] Stephen M. Griffin, Long Wars and the Constitution 1–2 (2013).

[45] Dana Priest and William M. Arkin, *Top Secret America: A Washington Post Investigation*, Wash. Post (July 19, 2010), http://projects.washingtonpost.com/top-secret-america/articles/a-hidden-world-growing-beyond-control/1. One way to appreciate the scope of the change that occurred as a result of World War II is through its military bases. As David Vine has written in Island of Shame, from the Roman Empire to the British and French empires, "bases have long been essential tools for securing empires and political, economic, and military control over vast lands." David Vine, Island of Shame: The Secret History of the U.S. Military Base on Diego Garcia 42 (2009). Before World War II, "the United States had few bases outside its territory," but by the end of the war, it had "more than 30,000 installations at more than 2,000 base sites globally." And that expansive system of bases and installations increased substantially since that time so that today, Vine writes, the United States "has what is likely the largest collection of military bases in world history, totaling more than 5,300 globally and an estimated 1,000 bases outside its own territory of the 50 states and Washington, DC." *Id.*

challenges or threats to United States security, is itself more or less continually in a state of emergency, or as Garry Wills as termed it a "permanent war in peace."[46] That dynamic has created a national climate that distorted the constitutional order by facilitating the powerful dominance of the presidency over the other two coequal branches of the federal government and the incapacity or unwillingness of the Congress to regularly insist upon asserting its formidable powers in foreign and military affairs affecting the national security. The departure has also had profound consequences for the federal judiciary in cases implicating the national security that have resulted in the needless loss of liberty, undermined democratic values, eroded the rule of law, and distorted the constitutional order.

Thus, the National Security State created a context for the increased use of secret evidence and secret legal opinions in courts that are normally committed to public processes. It has enhanced the range and scope of secret law, a dynamic that permits the executive to argue to the public that certain conduct is lawful while not disclosing the legal precedents and reasoning it claims eliminates any doubt of the conduct's legality. In the name of curtailing executive power, the departure made it possible to think of the creation of a secret court as an important step toward disciplining and controlling executive surveillance activities while simultaneously not diminishing public confidence in the courts.

But the rise of the National Security State did far more than introduce an unprecedented degree of secrecy in American judicial proceedings. Because of the expansion in the scope of matters that were deemed to threaten national security interests and because the geographical range of these interests became global, the number of individual cases implicating national security increased exponentially during the post–World War II decades by comparison to earlier periods. Moreover, the Supreme Court often responded by developing technical legal doctrines of deference that resulted in the dismissal of these cases without the Court deciding the merits. Such dismissals rarely ignited public debate and scrutiny, which undercut the possibilities of a national discussion of the policy at stake if the Court had decided the merits of the case. Because of that, the judicial stance of deference has contributed to the lack of transparency of national security matters while enhancing the cloak of secrecy that shrouds the functioning of the security agencies. Furthermore, because the Supreme Court has been so deferential to the executive in security cases, it has for the first time in the nation's history created a powerful and expansive judicial dynamic that ends up shielding unlawful executive conduct from judicial accountability.

---

[46] Garry Wills, Bomb Power: The Modern Presidency and the National Security State 57 (2010).

The national security state that engenders judicial secrecy and deference is not transient. It has been central to the United States for seven decades, and there is no reason to doubt that its centrality will continue into the indefinite future.[47] That means that the Supreme Court's acceptance of secrecy and deference will also continue indefinitely unless the court itself alters its disposition. That too sets the post–World War II era apart from earlier periods of judicial deference that were responsive to particular circumstances which created a sense of national peril or insecurity but that did not seem as though they would last indefinitely.

[47] The basic nature of the presidency and the National Security State is not likely to change with presidential administrations, even when that change involves a change in political party for the incoming incumbent. For example, President Barack Obama, a Democrat, was elected at least in large part because of many promises that he would take a different approach by comparison to President George W. Bush, a Republican, with regard to such policies as the deployment of American military in foreign armed conflicts, the use of torture, the detention of detainees in Guantanamo, and surveillance initiatives by the National Security Agency. Thus, as Professor Owen Fiss concluded after studying the policies of Bush and Obama, "the essential truth is one of continuity." Obama "sought to block judicial inquiries into extraordinary rendition"; "continued the policy of imprisonment without trial"; "sought to deny the writ of habeas corpus to the prisoners now being held in Bagram"; "continued to use military commissions to try terrorist suspects"; and "continued the policy of warrantless wiretaps." Owen Fiss, A War Like No Other: The Constitution in a Time of Terror 123 (2015). Charlie Savage reached a similar conclusion in Power Wars: Inside Obama's Post-9/11 Presidency 35 (2015). When the Christmas Day bomber of 2009 failed in his attempt to blow up a plane, Savage wrote, "the entire episode became the functional equivalent of the 9/11 terrorist attacks, which transformed the Bush-Cheney administration. The result of the stomach-churning near miss of a mass murder over American soil and its political fallout would have profound implications for Obama's legal policy, hardening his administration's approach to counterterrorism. The ambiguous, ambivalent balance of the first year tilted; Obama's policy choices that departed from Bush-era programs dwindled, and those that continued—or even expanded—Bush-era programs rose, from a fierce campaign of drone strikes whose targets would include an American citizen to the perpetuation of a sprawling and voracious surveillance apparatus."

PART TWO

JUDICIAL SECRECY

5

Looking through a Keyhole

It is unusual for one case to represent a complicated era. It is even rarer that that representative case begins about when the era commences and comes to a final end nearly six decades later, thus continuing in one form or another for almost the entire era. But that is true with *United States v. Reynolds*, which arose out of a 1948 plane crash in the skies over Waycross, Georgia, and ended with Supreme Court inaction in 2006.[1] Because the *Reynolds* case is such a poignant symbol, it offers a compelling window on a complicated era.

At 1:28 p.m. on October 6, 1948, a fifty-ton United States Air Force B-29, popularly known as a "Superfortress," with a 141-foot wingspan roared down the Robbins Field runway in Waycross, Georgia, carrying eight crew members, five civilian electronic experts, and secret military electronic equipment. As Bomber #866 lifted off the runway, it was out of compliance with Air Force regulations requiring heat shields designed to minimize engine fires, a constant threat to the B-29. Forty minutes into its scheduled five-hour mission, the Superfortress's engine number one caught fire, the plane went into a tailspin, and then it exploded midair, killing five servicemen and four civilians.[2]

Three hours later, a neighbor knocked on the apartment door of twenty-year-old Patricia Reynolds, whose twenty-four-year-old husband, Bob, was one of the civilian engineers on the flight: "[T]here's been an accident down at Waycross," he said. "We don't know who survived."[3]

During the next three hours, state police and military officials "ignored" Patricia Reynolds—they "wouldn't even look at her"—as she waited in the state police headquarters for word as to whether her husband was alive or

---

[1] United States v. Reynolds, 345 U.S. 1 (1953).

[2] For an exhaustive account of the accident and the subsequent lawsuit, see David Rudenstine, *The Irony of a Faustian Bargain: A Reconsideration of the Supreme Court's 1953* United States v. Reynolds *Decision*, 34 Cardozo L. Rev. 1283 (2013).

[3] Barry Siegel, Claim of Privilege: A Mysterious Plane Crash, a Landmark Supreme Court Case and the Rise of State Secrets 49 (2008).

dead.[4] Finally, a representative of Radio Corporation of America, Bob's employer, told Patricia what many others had known for hours: Bob was dead.[5]

One year after the crash, Patricia Reynolds joined Phyllis Brauner and Elizabeth Palya in suing the United States of America for damages pursuant to the Federal Tort Claims Act, alleging that the accident that killed their husbands was caused by government negligence. Shortly after the commencement of the lawsuit, Francis Biddle, a Philadelphia lawyer, submitted thirty-one written questions to the Air Force and requested that the Air Force turn over a copy of its official investigatory report that assessed the causes of the crash and the written statements of the three surviving servicemen. The Air Force submitted false written responses to the plaintiffs' questions and refused to turn over the investigatory report.[6] The report that the Air Force refused to allow the plaintiffs to read stated that Bomber #866 lacked the required heat shields designed to minimize the risks of engine fires and that the plane was plagued by so many problems that it was "not fit for flight."[7]

The Air Force sought to hide these findings. It did so because in 1947, the Air Force had become an independent service separate and apart from the Army, and, as a result, there was fierce competition among the Army, Navy, and Air Force for congressional support for enlarged budgets to finance personnel and weapon development.[8] The Air Force feared that disclosure of the accident report would be deeply embarrassing and sorely injure its reputation in the Congress, on Main Street as well as Wall Street.[9] Thus, the Air Force's deceit and refusal served ends far more compelling than merely trying to escape liability to three widows of the civilian engineers.[10]

At that point the plaintiffs asked the trial judge, William H. Kirkpatrick, to compel the Air Force to turn over the disputed documents. Judge Kirkpatrick was experienced, having joined the Army Judge Advocate's Corps during World War I, served one term in the House of Representatives from 1921 to 1923, and been a district judge since 1927.[11] In response to the plaintiffs' motion to compel, the Air Force gave Kirkpatrick the impression that the report contained information injurious to national security.[12] To assure himself that the

---

[4] *Id.*

[5] *Id.*

[6] *See* David Rudenstine, *The Irony of a Faustian Bargain: A Reconsideration of the Supreme Court's 1953* United States v. Reynolds *Decision*, 34 Cardozo L. Rev. 1283, 1312–1317 (2013).

[7] *Id.* at 1292.

[8] *Id.* at 1320.

[9] *Id.* at 1318–1320.

[10] *Id.*

[11] *Id.* at 1321 n.233.

[12] I use the word "impression" as a shorthand for a complicated analysis, *id.* at 1339–1346.

report contained such sensitive information, Kirkpatrick directed the Air Force to submit the disputed documents to him so he alone—without permitting the plaintiffs, their lawyers, or anyone else—could review the documents. The Air Force refused. It would not permit even Judge Kirkpatrick to review the investigatory report alone in his private chambers.[13]

In response, the judge made findings of facts against the government on the critical question of negligence and barred the government from submitting evidence contesting those facts. The consequence of that ruling was a factual finding that the accident resulted from government negligence and, as a result, the government was liable to the plaintiffs for damages. At that point, the trial judge conducted an evidentiary hearing on the remaining question of damages and awarded the plaintiffs damages in the amount of $225,000.[14]

The Third Circuit ruled against the Air Force. It denied the Air Force's claim that a federal judge lacks the authority to compel the disclosure of the investigatory report that allegedly contained information injurious to the national security if improperly disclosed. In doing so, the three-judge panel stated that federal judges are "public officers whose responsibility under the Constitution is just as great as that of the heads of the executive departments" and these judges may be "depended upon to protect with the greatest care the public interest in preventing the disclosure of matters which may be fairly characterized as privileged."[15]

The Air Force took the case to the Supreme Court, and on April 13, 1953, that Court, by a vote of six to three, reversed the judgment favoring the widows and announced for the first time in the nation's history a set of rules that continue to this day to guide courts in the application of the highly controversial state secrets privilege. Although those rules appear to constitute a Solomonic compromise—blending competing claims involving national security, individual justice, and a system of constitutional checks and balances—the rules amounted to a ringing victory for the executive because they in effect granted the executive a de facto absolute right to control the disclosure of information in most, if not all, legal cases when it asserted a state secrets privilege.[16] Indeed, over the last decades, courts have vastly expanded the reach of these rules so that cases may be dismissed at a very early stage, and they have resisted altering these rules even in the face of serious criticism.

[13] *See* David Rudenstine, *The Irony of a Faustian Bargain: A Reconsideration of the Supreme Court's 1953* United States v. Reynolds *Decision*, 34 Cardozo L. Rev. 1283, 1345–1350 (2013).

[14] *Id.* at 1346.

[15] *Id.* at 1351–1352.

[16] *See* David Rudenstine, *The Irony of a Faustian Bargain: A Reconsideration of the Supreme Court's 1953* United States v. Reynolds *Decision*, 34 Cardozo L. Rev. 1283, 1371–1372 (2013).

Equally important, *Reynolds* became the first and central pillar of the judicial deference that characterized the post–World War II decades in national security cases. During this era the Supreme Court spawned several distinct, judicially created and shaped legal doctrines. [17] Although each is important and although each serves different purposes and promotes different values, their ultimate significance can only be understood when they are understood as interlacing with one another in a way that permits the judiciary to knit together a comprehensive protective shield that generally insulates the executive from meaningful judicial review, thus undermining the rule of law and constitutional plan.

Reynolds is a worthy window on the post–World War II decades for reasons that are important well beyond the importance of the state secrets privilege, or even beyond the numerous doctrines of deference the high court utilizes in national security cases. The story behind the *Reynolds* case, a story that begins some years before the 1948 plane crash, discloses the unexpected factors that came together in unpredictable ways to shape the case, and it discloses dispiriting Supreme Court conduct that falls far short of national aspirations for the fair-minded application of the law.

The initial impetus behind the executive branch's effort that resulted in the modern state secrets doctrine had little to nothing to do with national security.[18] Rather, the executive branch's litigation strategy that resulted in the *Reynolds* decision had its origins in its efforts during the 1940s to limit the reach of pretrial discovery procedures authorized by the Federal Rules of Civil Procedure in 1938. In its most ambitious expression, that complex effort sought an extremely broad and essentially absolute privilege that would have

---

[17] The *Reynolds* decision announced the rules for the contemporary state secrets privilege that federal courts upheld in appropriate cases. During the last thirty-five years, that privilege has gone from a rarely invoked privilege to a frequently invoked, highly controversial, and enormously important one. *See, e.g.,* David Cole and Jules Lobel, Less Safe, Less Free: Why America Is Losing the War on Terror 42 (2007) ("Perhaps the most troubling invocation of secrecy has been the administration's invocation of the state secrets privilege to block judicial oversight of some of its most dubious practices."); Susan N. Herman, Taking Liberties: The War on Terror and the Erosion of American Democracy 198 (2011) ("Take the state secrets privilege. The Bush and then Obama lawyers have invoked this privilege . . . to keep cases out of court altogether, sometimes without even allowing the court to review whether an asserted national security concern is credible."); Robert M. Pallito and William G. Weaver, Presidential Secrecy and the Law 86 (2007) ("The state secrets privilege is the most powerful weapon in the presidential arsenal of secrecy . . . ."); Charlie Savage, Takeover: The Return of the Imperial Presidency and the Subversion of American Democracy 169–170 (2008) ("[U]se of the State Secrets Privilege essentially established the president and his department heads as the sole arbiters of which matters could receive judicial review.").

[18] *See* David Rudenstine, *The Irony of a Faustian Bargain: A Reconsideration of the Supreme Court's 1953* United States v. Reynolds *Decision,* 34 Cardozo L. Rev. 1283, Part III.A–B (2013).

provided the executive branch with a breathtakingly broad shield against discovery efforts to secure information from the government.[19] Although the executive's sweeping claim for a privilege was not initially termed "executive privilege," that was the term the executive eventually used in its legal briefs filed with the Supreme Court by 1950.[20] Thus, although *Reynolds* announced significant rules guiding courts in cases that, the executive claimed, implicated national security—the initial impetus for the executive's strategy in that case had no connection to the nation's security.

The fact that the executive branch ended up using a case that arose out of a 1948 B-29 plane crash that killed four civilian engineers and five servicemen and that had little to nothing to do with national security as a Trojan Horse for pressing its request for a sweeping executive privilege was a complete happenstance. For its part, the Air Force needed to keep certain highly embarrassing documents that were in dispute confidential in the *Reynolds* case,[21] and as for the Department of Justice, it was urgently in need of a case to use to press its executive privilege claim, a claim it had previously unsuccessfully pressed in the courts.[22] As a result, the interests of the Air Force and the Department of Justice unexpectedly came together in the *Reynolds* case, and the accidental nature of this intersection goes a long way toward explaining the mysteries surrounding *Reynolds*. Mysteries such as why a routine tort case became a seminal national security landmark; why the executive branch delayed so long before asserting the executive privilege in the *Reynolds* litigation, and then engaged in the manipulation and misrepresentation of the evidence once it did assert the privilege; why, as is now known, there was in fact no information in the disputed documents that were at the heart of the *Reynolds* litigation that would injure national security if disclosed; and why the Supreme Court's opinion in

[19] *See* Brief for Petitioner, United States of America v. Cotton Valley Operators Comm., 339 U.S. 972 (1950) (No. 490), 1950 WL 78566. Harvard Law Professor Paul A. Freund wrote the foreword for the *Harvard Law Review*'s review of the 1973 Supreme Court term, in which he stated that the earliest usage of the phrase "executive privilege" that he could discover was in the executive's brief in the *Reynolds* case. Paul A. Freund, *Foreword: On Presidential Privilege*, 88 Harv. L. Rev. 13, 18 n.29 (1973). The executive's brief in *Cotton Valley*, however, makes use of the phrase three years earlier. Brief for Petitioner, United States of America v. Cotton Valley Operators Comm., 339 U.S. 972 (1950) (No. 490), 1950 WL 78566, at *19–20; *see also* David Rudenstine, *The Irony of a Faustian Bargain: A Reconsideration of the Supreme Court's 1953 United States v. Reynolds Decision*, 34 Cardozo L. Rev. 1283, 1336–1338, nn.306–317. And, as will be discussed in this chapter, the executive's brief in *Reynolds*, including the use of the term "executive privilege," drew extensively from the executive's brief in *Cotton Valley*.

[20] *See* Brief for Petitioner, United States of America v. Cotton Valley Operators Committee, 339 U.S. 972 (1950) (No. 490), 1950 WL 78566, at *18–19.

[21] *See* David Rudenstine, *The Irony of a Faustian Bargain: A Reconsideration of the Supreme Court's 1953 United States v. Reynolds Decision*, 34 Cardozo L. Rev. 1283, Part I.E. (2013).

[22] *Id.* at Part III.C.

Reynolds was riddled with deceit and pretense. It also turns out that the *Reynolds* case sheds light on a complicated and entangled set of events involving the Air Force, Department of Justice lawyers, and the Supreme Court, aimed at, among other things, shielding the Air Force from substantial public embarrassment.[23]

The Air Force's effort to protect itself began immediately after the plane crash that gave rise to the *Reynolds* case, when the Air Force conducted a limited investigation into the causes of the crash.[24] The Air Force's effort to protect itself from public humiliation and criticism continued when the Air Force kept a second report confidential reviewing the causes of the crash, submitted false responses to a routine set of interrogatories submitted to the Air Force by the plaintiffs' lawyer, and deceived a senior Radio Corporation of America (RCA) executive about the causes of the plane crash.[25] Thereafter in the litigation, senior Air Force officials submitted two affidavits to the federal court that contained misleading and deceptive statements[26] in the hope of securing a ruling that protected the confidentiality of the investigation-related documents.

The Air Force's effort to protect itself from public embarrassment soon swept Department of Justice lawyers within its orbit. From the available evidence, it seems that the Department of Justice lawyers shielded themselves from discovering information that would have prevented them from asserting claims that the Air Force was determined to present to the courts in the hope of protecting its reputation and public standing. This complicity first occurred in the district court[27] and then repeated itself throughout the appeal process.[28]

But this effort to conceal the truth about the plane crash involved more than the executive branch. Eventually, the opinion in the *Reynolds* case, written by Chief Justice Fred M. Vinson, was yet one more major step taken to protect the Air Force from public criticism. Thus, although the Supreme Court in *Reynolds* set out rules that appear to constitute a blending of competing claims involving national security, individual justice, and the maintenance of a governmental system of checks and balances, the opinion invited executive branch caprice by granting the executive a de facto absolute right to control the disclosure of information. Moreover, the justices on the Court who reversed the judgment of the lower courts in favor of the widows had reason to doubt, at the very time they decided the case, that the disputed Air Force documents contained any information harmful to national security.[29] Furthermore, although

---

[23] *Id.* at Part III–VI.
[24] *Id.* at Part I.C–F.
[25] *Id.* at Part I.D–F.
[26] *Id.* at Part III.C.
[27] *Id.* at Part II.B.2.
[28] *Id.* at Part V.A.3.
[29] *Id.* at Part VI.A.2.a.

the opinion suggested that it would be possible for the widows to establish the cause of the crash without relying upon the evidence that the Air Force insisted should be privileged, there was no reasonable basis for such a representation.[30] In the end, although the outcome in *Reynolds* was probably in accord with Chief Justice Vinson's willingness to curtail, if not eliminate, meaningful judicial review in cases implicating national security, it seems implausible that Vinson would have written the particular opinion he did in *Reynolds* unless he had received information about the case from President Truman. And although the evidence relevant to whether Truman disclosed information about the case to Vinson is only circumstantial, it is highly suggestive.

The Supreme Court decision in *Reynolds* constituted a serious error. That decision provided a doctrinal basis for legal developments that have emboldened the executive at the expense of the courts and denied judicial remedies to individuals, thus undermining the rule of law. In *Reynolds*, the high court pretended that it was not making any of these problematic changes, which in turn only undermines the public trust in the Court, which is the essence of its legitimacy.

In early 2000, Judith Palya Loether, a daughter of Albert H. Palya, one of the civilian engineers who died in the 1948 crash, "came across an internet website offering access to recently-declassified military aircraft accidents reports."[31] Subsequently, she obtained the Air Force Investigation Report and the three witness statements that senior Air Force officials had represented, a half century earlier, contained military secrets that would injure the national security if disclosed.[32] To her surprise, the confidential documents contained "nothing approaching a 'military secret.' There is not one mention of the secret mission or the secret equipment that had occupied these men on the day" they died in the crash of the B-29 bomber.[33] Eventually she and others,[34] including Patricia J. Reynolds (now Patricia J. Herring, the spouse of Robert Reynolds)

---

[30] *Id.* at Part VI.A.3.

[31] Independent Action for Relief from Judgment to Remedy Fraud on the Court at 2, Herring v. United States, No. 03-CV-5500-LDD (E.D. Pa. Sept. 10, 2004), 2005 U.S. S. Ct. Briefs LEXIS 2430, at *104, *105–107 [hereinafter Independent Action for Relief from Judgment to Remedy Fraud on the Court]. This complaint was filed in the United States District Court for the Eastern District of Pennsylvania by Wilson M. Brown III and Jeff A. Almeida of Drinker Biddle & Reath LLP, a Philadelphia law firm that represented the three widows in the original damage action authorized by the Federal Tort Claims Act against the United States. *Id.* at 15–16, 2005 U.S. S. Ct. Briefs LEXIS 2430, at *104, *125–127.

[32] *Id.* at 11–12, 2005 U.S. S. Ct. Briefs LEXIS 2430, at *104, *119–122.

[33] *Id.* at 2–3, 2005 U.S. S. Ct. Briefs LEXIS 2430, at *104, *105–109.

[34] The other parties to the suit included Susan Brauner, Catherine Brauner, William Palya, and Robert Palya, as living heirs of the deceased William H. Brauner and Phyllis Brauner, and Albert H. Palya and Elizabeth Palya. *Id.* at 1, 2005 U.S. S. Ct. Briefs LEXIS, at *104, *104–105.

secured legal representation from the same law firm that brought the original case—the Philadelphia law firm of Drinker Biddle & Reath LLP—and initiated suit to reopen the case and "to set aside the settlement agreement reached fifty years earlier on the grounds that the settlement was procured by the Air Force's claim of privilege, through which it committed a fraud on the Court actionable under Rule 60(b)'s savings clause."[35]

They claimed that the Air Force's accident report and the three witness statements contained no military secrets.[36] Instead, they maintained, these recently declassified documents established that the B-29 that crashed in 1948 was not fit for flying,[37] that the crew had not previously flown together,[38] and that the civilian engineers who died in the crash had not been instructed about emergency exit procedures.[39] Thus, the descendants claimed that high government Air Force officials had deliberately and intentionally submitted false information to the court, that the submitted information was central to the court's reasoning and judgment in the case, and that this fraud on the court warranted the exceptional relief of vacating the earlier final judgment.[40] After two efforts before the Supreme Court, one before a United States District Court and another before a Court of Appeals, these family members lost in their effort to gain a hearing to reopen the judgment in the case.

[35] Herring v. United States, No. Civ.A.03-CV-5500-LDD, 2004 WL 2040272, at *2 (E.D. Pa. Sept. 10, 2004), aff'd, 424 F.3d 384 (3d Cir. Sept. 22, 2005).

[36] Independent Action for Relief from Judgment to Remedy Fraud on the Court, 11, 2005 U.S. S. Ct. Briefs LEXIS 2430, at *104, *119–121.

[37] Id.

[38] Independent Action for Relief from Judgment to Remedy Fraud on the Court, 1, 12, 2005 U.S. S. Ct. Briefs LEXIS 2430, at *104, *121 (Complaint); id. Exhibit J, at 103, 110, 2005 U.S. S. Ct. Briefs LEXIS 2430, at *198, *205 (Persons Report).

[39] Id. Exhibit J, at 103, 113, 2005 U.S. S. Ct. Briefs LEXIS 2430, at *198, *210. As the report stated in its official language: "The aircraft is not considered to have been safe for flight because of non-compliance with Technical Orders 01-20EJ-177 and 01-20EJ-178," "Fire developed in the No. 1 engine as a result of the failure of the right exhaust collector ring," and "AF Regulation 60-5 was violated in that the passengers and crew were not properly briefed." Id. Exhibit J, at 103, 116, 2005 U.S. S. Ct. Briefs LEXIS 2430, at *198, *213–214. Taken together, the findings had the following implications: the plane was unfit for flying because it lacked heat shields designed to prevent engine fires as required by Air Force technical orders; the lack of heat shields contributed to causing the fire that the extinguishers failed to extinguish; the crew had not previously flown together in violation of Air Force rules and the lack of flying experience as a team contributed to misjudgments that, in turn, contributed to the crash; and the crew had not trained the civilians in escape procedures, which contributed to the outcome that the civilian engineers did not parachute safely from the plane.

[40] Independent Action for Relief from Judgment to Remedy Fraud on the Court, 2005 U.S. S. Ct. Briefs LEXIS 2430, at *104.

Initially the families sought relief before the Supreme Court because it was the Supreme Court that had issued the highly important 1953 decision.[41] But on June 23, 2003, the Court refused to consider the matter.[42] At that point, the families applied to the United States District Court for the Eastern District of Pennsylvania for relief, the very court in which the original damage action was first filed. They claimed that the settlement agreement reached fifty years earlier was the result of the Air Force successfully asserting a fraudulent claim of privilege.[43]

United States District Judge Legrome D. Davis denied relief. He stated that although the disputed documents provide "no thorough exploration of the secret mission"[44] and do not "refer to any newly developed electronic devices or secret electronic equipment,"[45] the report did "describe the mission in question as an 'electronics project' and an 'authorized research and development mission.'"[46]

The family members appealed Judge Davis's judgment to the Court of Appeals for the Third Circuit.[47] That court, sitting in a panel of three judges— Judges Samuel A. Alito, Franklin Van Antwerpen, and Ruggero Aldisert—affirmed the district court's judgment in an opinion written by Judge Aldisert. Judge Aldisert wrote that the affidavits submitted by senior Air Force officials did not constitute fraud on the court during the original litigation because they had claimed that the disputed documents contained information that was in fact in the disputed documents, indicating that the B-29 that crashed was engaged in a secret mission testing secret military equipment.[48] More precisely, the opinion stated that the affidavits submitted by Secretary of the Air Force Thomas K. Finletter and Judge Advocate General Reginald C. Harmon "can be reasonably read to assert privilege over technical information about the B-29," such as the plane's "mission," its "operation," or its "performance," as opposed to just the "confidential equipment" it had on board for testing.[49]

The families had one last hope: an appeal to the Supreme Court. They filed their papers; the government responded with its papers. A decision to review

---

[41] The descendants sought leave from the Supreme Court to file a petition for a writ of error coram nobis, which the court denied. *In re* Herring, 539 U.S. 940 (2003).

[42] *Id.*

[43] Herring v. United States, No. Civ.A.03-CV-5500-LDD, 2004 WL 2040272, at *2 (E.D. Pa. Sept. 10, 2004), *aff'd*, 424 F.3d 384 (3d Cir. Sept. 22, 2005).

[44] *Id.* at *6.

[45] *Id.* at *8.

[46] *Id.* at *6.

[47] *See* Herring v. United States, 424 F.3d 384 (3d Cir. 2005).

[48] *Id.* at 392.

[49] *Id.*

the case required four of the nine Justices to vote in favor of granting certiorari and reviewing the case. The ultimate vote is not known, but the disposition is. At least six members of the Court did not favor review. The families' petition was denied.[50] That ended the appeal, and the litigation begun a half-century earlier came to an end for a second time.

In the effort to reopen this tragic case, the descendants hit a judicially constructed brick wall. That was not altogether a surprise. The policies against reopening a judgment are strong and the legal requirements for vacating a judgment on grounds of fraud are demanding.[51] But it is likely that the judicial resistance to reopening the judgment in *Herring* was reinforced by another factor.

By the time the families had moved to reopen the case, the federal courts, pursuant to the Supreme Court's direction, had for over a half-century displayed the "utmost deference" toward the executive branch in cases implicating national security.[52] Although the family members of the civilian engineers who died in B-29 #866 in 1948 over Waycross, Georgia, initially lost before the Supreme Court in 1953 because of the state secrets privilege, they lost before the federal courts for a second time in 2005 because of a broad rule of deference the *Reynolds* case helped generate. Thus, the *Reynolds* decision forms two bookends demarking the Age of Deference—the 1953 Supreme Court decision that helped launch the era and the 2006 Supreme Court refusal to review the case, a decision emblematic of the era's maturity.

Thirteen federal judges—one district court judge, three circuit judges, and nine Supreme Court justices—participated in the review of the *Reynolds* case in light of the previously confidential Air Force documents. That process produced two opinions, one at the district court and one at the circuit court; no one on the Supreme Court wrote an opinion in this case. Neither of the two published opinions contains the faintest criticism of the conduct of the executive branch or of the government lawyers in the original litigation. This was the case even though it seems totally implausible that judges who reviewed the case did not conclude that Air Force officials and Department of Justice lawyers had manipulated, misled, and deceived the courts in the initial case. Indeed, the reasoning of both published opinions makes it seem as if reasonable judges were willing to go to unreasonable lengths to construct—indeed,

---

[50] Herring v. United States, 547 U.S. 1123 (2006).

[51] In *Herring v. United States*, the Third Circuit stated the challenge facing any party wishing to reopen a case on grounds of fraud as follows: "The presumption against the reopening of a case that has gone through the appellate process all the way to the United States Supreme Court and reached final judgment must be not just a high hurdle to climb but a steep cliff-face to scale." Herring v. United States, 424 F.3d 384, 386 (3d Cir. 2005).

[52] United States v. Nixon, 418 U.S. 683, 710 (1974).

invent—an explanation as to why Air Force officials sixty years earlier had acted in good faith and with sufficient cause.[53]

By so doing, these thirteen members of the federal judiciary seem to fulfill Associate Justice Robert Jackson's pessimism that in times of national crisis, the nation's judges cannot be relied upon to uphold restraints upon the exercise of raw power. In an opinion rendered in the year of the *Reynolds* plane

[53] For example, consider the opinion of the Third Circuit written by Judge Aldisert. That opinion claims that the privilege was properly sustained if Finletter's affidavit can be "reasonably read to include . . . the workings of the B-29." *Herring*, 424 F.3d at 391. Judge Aldisert asserts that if the privilege asserted by Finletter can be understood to include the "workings of the B-29" as opposed to the secret electronic equipment, "the Appellants' assertion that the Air Force claim of military secrets privilege misrepresented the nature of the information contained in the accident report over which the privilege was asserted falls apart." *Id.* At that point, Aldisert claims that Finletter and Harmon objected to disclosure of the plane's mission, as well as "information concerning its operation or performance," and that such an objection was properly protected by the privilege at the time. *Id.* at 392 (quoting Claim of Privilege). Judge Aldisert's claims about what information was properly privileged in 1950, when Finletter and Harmon signed their affidavits, have no support in the historical record. As already noted, the news reports of the crash of Bomber #866 revealed that the plane was on a special mission to test secret electronic equipment. *See* David Rudenstine, *The Irony of a Faustian Bargain: A Reconsideration of the Supreme Court's 1953* United States v. Reynolds *Decision*, 34 Cardozo L. Rev. 1283, 1294 n.40 (2013). Furthermore, the *New York Times* had already published many reports on the operation and performance of the B-29. *See* Anthony Leviero, *Robot-Piloted Plane Makes Safe Crossing of Atlantic*, N.Y. Times, Sept. 23, 1947, at 2. Also, the Soviet Union had three American-made B-29 planes in its possession which it used to manufacture its own version of a B-29. But Judge Aldisert argued the following in footnote three of the opinion: "Even if we concluded that the Air Force's claim of privilege could not be read to include concern about revealing the workings of the B-29, we would be obligated to consider whether certain information contained in the accident report actually revealed sensitive information about the mission and the electronic equipment involved." *Herring*, 424 F.3d at 391 n.3. At that point, Aldisert made reference to three concerns: "that the project was being carried out by 'the 3150th Electronics Squadron,' that the mission required an 'aircraft capable of dropping bombs' and that the mission required an airplane capable of 'operating at altitudes of 20,000 feet and above.'" *Id.* (quoting Report of Special investigation). Although there may not have been public reports identifying the 3150th Electronics Squadron as the unit involved in the tests, the other factors were established as part of the public record. *See* David Rudenstine, *The Irony of a Faustian Bargain: A Reconsideration of the Supreme Court's 1953* United States v. Reynolds *Decision*, 34 Cardozo L. Rev. 1283, 1302, nn.112–113 (2013) and accompanying text. United States District Judge Davis's opinion relied upon reasoning and factual allegations similarly unsupported by the historical record. The relevant portion of Judge Davis's discussion of the matter follows:

> In 1948, amid Communist paranoia, it is hardly shocking to contemplate an Air Force eager to protect from public view the accident investigation report that mentions modifications needed for the B-29, and by extension the Tu-4. [The Tu-4 was a Soviet version of the B-29 that was made possible when three B-29s were forced to land in Vladivostok, Russia, in 1944. The Soviets released the crew but kept the planes and used reverse engineering to build a copy of the B-29—the Tu-4. Herring v. United States, 2004 WL 2040272, at *8.] By no means, will this Court draw firm conclusions as to military

crash, Jackson upheld rent control legislation under the banner of the "unde-fined and undefinable 'war power' ":[54]

> No one will question that this power is the most dangerous one to free government in the whole catalogue of powers. It usually is in-voked in haste and excitement when calm legislative consideration of constitutional limitation is difficult. It is executed in a time of pa-triotic fervor that makes moderation unpopular. And, worst of all, it is interpreted by judges under the influence of the same passions and pressures.[55]

> intelligence concerns in existence some fifty years ago. Rather, we will examine the events contemporaneous to the accident only in order to shed light on factors surround-ing the Air Force's assertion of military privilege. It is at least conceivable that were the accident investigation report released, it might have alerted the otherwise unaware Soviets to a technical problem in the Tu-4 that the May 1, 1947 technical order sought to remedy in the B-29. Though the Plaintiffs argue that the Air Force deliberately hid its obvious negligence behind fraudulent affidavits, disclosure of this now seemingly innocuous report would reveal far more than the negligence Plaintiffs read; it may have been of great moment to sophisticated intelligence analysts and Soviet engineers alike. Viewed against this political and technical backdrop, it seems that the accident inves-tigation report may have reasonably contained sufficient intelligence, if not about the secret equipment or mission, then about ongoing developments in Air Force technical engineering, to warrant an assertion of the military secrets privilege. (Herring, 2004 WL 2040272, at *9 (footnotes omitted))

Judge Davis's reasoning is unsupported by history. The Soviets did not need the Persons in-vestigation report to alert them to the B-29 engine fire problem. The Soviets were alerted to the B-29 engine fires because the B-29s that made emergency landings in Russia were "on fire," *How Soviets Copied America's Best Bomber During WWII*, CNN.com, Jan. 25, 2001 (on file with author), and because news reports made it clear that the B-29s frequently experienced devastat-ing engine fires; *see* David Rudenstine, *The Irony of a Faustian Bargain: A Reconsideration of the Supreme Court's 1953* United States v. Reynolds *Decision*, 34 Cardozo L. Rev. 1283, 1298–1299 nn.78–79 (2013) and accompanying text. Moreover, the Soviets did not need the disclosure of the *Persons Report* to inform them that the Air Force was trying to remedy the B-29 engine prob-lem because the *New York Times* reported that fact a full six weeks before the *Persons Report* was even completed, and a full ten months before Secretary Finletter and Judge Advocate General Harmon submitted statements to District Judge Kirkpatrick claiming that the report was privi-leged. The newspaper reported that fact when General Hoyt S. Vandenberg, Air Force chief of staff, ordered grounded all B-29s "that have not been modernized mechanically," to limit, what General Curtis LeMay, head of the Strategic Air Command, stated was "too many engine fires." *U.S. Grounds B-29s as Another Crash Kills 5 in Florida*, N.Y. Times, Nov. 19, 1949, at 1. Judge Davis's claim that the *Persons Report* contained information about the design of the so-called heat shields intended to minimize or eliminate engine fires was false. The report contained no such information.

[54] Woods v. Cloyd W. Miller Co., 333 U.S. 138, 146 (1948) (Jackson, J., concurring).
[55] *Id.*

In reaching their results, these judges surely acted in good faith, but their conceptions of their responsibilities as Article III judges seem disturbingly deferential. Rather than understanding federal judges to be "public officers whose responsibility under the Constitution is just as great as that of the heads of the executive departments," as one judge wrote,[56] these judges seem to understand their role in cases implicating national security as little more than being an extension of the executive branch.[57]

By any fair measure, the judges in the *Herring* case owed more by way of basic fairness and decency to the descendants whose family members had died in the service of the nation than they delivered,[58] and they owed more to the nation by way of a forthright statement of reasons in support of the judgment than they offered in their opinions. Indeed, their judicial

[56] Reynolds v. United States, 192 F.2d 987, 997 (3d Cir. 1951), *rev'd*, 345 U.S. 1 (1953).

[57] In considering the relationship between the judiciary and the executive, it is worth noting former Supreme Court Justice John Paul Stevens's observation:

> Burger's opinion for the Court in *United States v. Nixon* (1974) required President Nixon to produce the tape recordings that eventually led to his resignation. The decision not only had a historic effect on American politics and society but also powerfully illustrated the integrity and independence of the Court. It may well have done more to inspire the confidence in the work of judges that is the true backbone of the rule of law than any other decision in the history of the Court.

John Paul Stevens, Five Chiefs: A Supreme Court Memoir 114 (2011). It was in the *Nixon* case that Chief Justice Burger also stated that the Court should show the "utmost deference" in national security matters, but whether Justice Stevens agreed with that formulation is certainly open to question, given some opinions written after 9/11. United States v. Nixon, 418 U.S. 683, 710 (1974). What was important to Justice Stevens in the *Nixon* case was the Court's insistence upon its own "integrity" and "independence" from the executive branch as a source of the Court's own legitimacy and public standing. *See* John Paul Stevens, Five Chiefs: A Supreme Court Memoir 114 (2011).

[58] Judicial opinions sustaining the state secrets privilege during the last three decades contain very little if any sympathy, compassion, or solicitude for the plaintiffs who claim a legal wrong and who are denied a legal remedy because of the privilege. Because the plaintiffs in these cases may not be United States citizens and because the executive branch may challenge the veracity of the allegations of these individuals, it may seem that judges are willing to accept the harsh outcomes resulting from sustaining the state secrets privilege because the plaintiffs disadvantaged by the privilege are not necessarily loyal United States citizens (though they may be). The outcome in the *Reynolds* case belies such a supposition. In *Reynolds*, loyal United States citizens serving the national defense interests and their family members are as disadvantaged by the privilege as any. In contrast, judges seem more open to empathy and sympathy for any defendant who may be disadvantaged by the state secrets privilege. Thus, consider Justice Antonin Scalia's overflowing regard for a defendant who might be harmed by a privilege:

> It seems to us, however, that the effect of our determination with regard to the state secrets privilege is to prevent this issue from proceeding. As noted earlier, we honored the invocation of that privilege because we satisfied ourselves that the in camera

conduct was of such character that one is inclined to ask, as another judge asked in a different case with regard to different judges: "[I]n calmer times, wise people will ask themselves: how could such able and worthy judges have done that?"[59]

We aspire to be a nation of laws and not a nation subject to executive privilege. And for most citizens, day in, day out, we are that. But too often we fall too short of these important aspirations, especially when the executive branch claims that the nation's security is implicated. Although it is true that we will

> affidavit set forth the genuine reason for denial of employment, and that that reason could not be disclosed without risking impairment of the national security. As a result of that necessary process, the court knows that the reason Daniel Molerio was not hired had nothing to do with Dagoberto Molerio's assertion of First Amendment rights. Although there may be enough circumstantial evidence to permit a jury to come to that erroneous conclusion, it would be a mockery of justice for the court—knowing the erroneousness—to participate in that exercise. This is not a case like *Ellsberg v. Mitchell*, in which the court's consideration of the state secrets privilege did not ipso facto disclose to the court the validity of the defense—so that the latter could (at least in the special circumstances of that case) be left to be resolved by subsequent in camera proceedings. Here, by contrast, we know that further activity in this case would involve an attempt, however well intentioned, to convince the jury of a falsehood. (Molerio v. FBI, 749 F.2d 815, 825 (D.C. Cir. 1984))

Note that then Circuit Judge Scalia emphasized that justice would be mocked if a court entered a judgment against a defendant who had not violated the law, but he makes no mention of the converse, namely the injustice inherent in the dismissal of an action in which the defendant violated the plaintiff's rights, but in which the invocation of the privilege barred the plaintiff from having sufficient evidence to prove the relevant factual points. *Id.* A Fourth Circuit panel in *Farnsworth Cannon, Inc. v. Grimes* acknowledged this point:

> Defendant further urges that, when the government asserts a privilege which deprives a defendant of the evidence needed to establish a valid defense, the court should shield the defendant from the effect of the deprivation by dismissing the action. (Understandably, but inconsistently, defendant does not suggest analogous protection for plaintiffs whom an assertion of privilege may deprive of valid causes of action.) (Farnsworth Cannon, Inc. v. Grimes, 635 F.2d 268, 271 (4th Cir. 1980))

Judge Learned Hand also endorsed a neutral hand in the application of evidentiary privileges:

> There certainly is no such excuse. We agree that there may be evidence—"state secrets"—to divulge which will imperil "national security"; and which the Government cannot, and should not, be required to divulge. *Salus rei publicae suprema lex.* The immunity from disclosure of the names or statements of informers is an instance of the same doctrine. This privilege will often impose a grievous hardship, for it may deprive parties to civil actions, or even to criminal prosecutions of power to assert their rights or to defend themselves. That is a consequence of any evidentiary privilege. (United States v. Coplon, 185 F.2d 629, 638 (2d Cir. 1950) (footnotes omitted))

[59] Arar v. Ashcroft, 585 F.3d 559, 630 (2d Cir. 2009) (Calabresi, J., dissenting).

have no order without security, and no liberty without order, it is also true that our security, order, and liberty will be less than what they might be if courts fail in their primary duty to uphold the rule of law, even when the executive claims that the rule of law is incompatible with national security.

The Supreme Court twice failed to fulfill its primary responsibility in the *Reynolds* litigation. In so doing, they put at risk much more than injustice to identified individuals; they put at risk a complicated governing scheme that prizes both security and liberty and that is dependent upon an independent judiciary to fulfill its mandate to check and balance robust executive authority.

The hallmark of a "civilized polity," one federal judge recently stated, is the granting of "redress," and "[i]n the United States, for better or worse, courts are, almost universally, involved."[60] Perhaps in time, federal judges will be less timid and less compromising in adhering to and upholding this basic and valued political principle, even in cases implicating national security.

---

[60] *Id.* at 638.

6

The Evidence Is Secret

The state secrets privilege is the central legal doctrine insulating the executive from meaningful judicial review in a national security case.[1] Because the privilege is the bedrock of the entire era, a study of the contemporary state secrets privilege sheds considerable light on the broader and highly significant theme of the judicial function in national security cases since World War II. This chapter assesses the contemporary state secrets privilege,[2] and in so doing, it briefly outlines the privilege announced by the Supreme Court in *United States v.*

---

[1] The state secrets privilege is a common law rule of evidence that courts have enforced to protect national security secrets. For more details, see David Rudenstine, *The Courts and National Security: The Ordeal of the State Secrets Privilege*, U. of Balt. L. Rev. 37, Part I (2014); *see also* David Rudenstine, *The Irony of a Faustian Bargain: A Reconsideration of the Supreme Court's 1953* United States v. Reynolds *Decision*, 34 Cardozo L. Rev. 1283 (2013). For a selection of recent law review articles on state secrets, see generally Robert M. Chesney, *National Security Fact Deference*, 95 Va. L. Rev. 1361 (2009); Robert M. Chesney, *State Secrets and the Limits of National Security Litigation*, 75 Geo. Wash. L. Rev. 1249 (2007); Laura Donohue, *The Shadow of State Secrets*, 159 U. Pa. L. Rev. 77 (2010); Amanda Frost, *The State Secrets Privilege and Separation of Powers*, 75 Fordham L. Rev. 1931 (2007); Beth George, *An Administrative Law Approach to Reforming the State Secrets Privilege*, 84 N.Y.U. L. Rev. 1691 (2009); Carrie Newton Lyons, *The State Secrets Privilege: Expanding Its Scope Through Government Misuse*, 11 Lewis & Clark L. Rev. 99 (2007); and Christina E. Wells, *State Secrets and Executive Accountability*, 26 Const. Comment. 625 (2010).

[2] See Robert M. Chesney, *State Secrets and the Limits of National Security Litigation*, 75 Geo. Wash. L. Rev. 1249, 1267 n.113 (2007) for a sampling of critical commentary of the state secrets privilege. For two highly controversial cases discussing the states secrets privilege, see Mohamed v. Jeppesen Dataplan, Inc., 614 F.3d 1070 (9th Cir. 2010) and El-Masri v. United States, 479 F.3d 296 (4th Cir. 2007). These cases generated very critical press commentary. *See* Editorial, *Torture Gets a Free Pass*, Boston Globe, Sept. 19, 2010, at 8 ("This standard is far too sweeping because there's a way to honor both the government's need for secrecy and plaintiffs' rights to have their allegations heard"); Editorial, *The ACLU Is Dismissed*, Wall St. J., Sept. 11, 2010, at A12 ("Nor will the ACLU find much solace in the Obama Administration, which has largely preserved the antiterror legal regime established by its predecessor even as it has tinkered with some of the language"); Editorial, *Torture Is a Crime, Not a Secret*, N.Y. Times, Sept. 9, 2010, at 30 (arguing that "the states secrets doctrine is so blinding and powerful that it should only be invoked when the most grave national security matters are at stake . . . . It should not be used to defend against allegations that if true . . . would be 'gross violations of the norms of international law'"); Editorial, *Security Secrets*

Reynolds,[3] which set forth the foundation guidelines for the contemporary privilege. [4] It will also map the expansion of the robust and sweeping contemporary privilege and relate that expansion to the much narrower privilege announced in *Reynolds*.[5]

In summary, this chapter puts forth several claims. The Supreme Court's 1953 *Reynolds* decision set forth a set of doctrinal rules that still guide the application of the state secrets privilege. Those rules had no antecedents in United States[6] law and thus are not a restatement of previously announced state secrets rules.[7] Instead, the Court in *Reynolds* fashioned them out of whole cloth. Moreover, the contemporary state secrets privilege is not a necessary extraction from *Reynolds*,[8] nor are the rules comprising the contemporary state secrets privilege mandated by the Constitution or statute. In other words, the robust and sweeping rules constituting the contemporary privilege are now as much a product of judicial discretion by comparison to the *Reynolds* decision as the rules announced in *Reynolds* were by comparison to earlier state secrets decisions. Thus, just as the *Reynolds* rules constituted a departure from prior state secrets cases, the contemporary state secrets rules are a departure from *Reynolds*.[9] And just as *Reynolds* both reflected and nurtured judicial deference, so do the rules of the contemporary state secrets privilege.

Although the Supreme Court generally initiates and charts the course of important legal doctrine, this was not the case in the development of the contemporary state secrets privilege. Instead, the circuit courts defined the

---

and Justice, Wash. Post, Sept. 13, 2010, at A14 ("The case [Jeppesen] again points out the need for a new law to govern cases in which national security secrets are involved"); Editorial, *Too Much Privilege*, L.A. Times, Dec. 14, 2009, at A26 (stating that the Obama Administration's decision to assert the state secrets privilege was "gravely disappoint[ing]" and urging the Ninth Circuit judges to allow the Jeppesen "case [to] proceed so that these alleged victims of U.S. mistreatment can make their case in court"); Editorial, *Too Many Secrets*, N.Y. Times, Mar. 10, 2007, at 12 ("It is a challenge to keep track of all the ways the Bush Administration is eroding constitutional protections, but one that should get more attention is its abuse of the state secrets doctrine"). *See also* Khaled El-Masri, Editorial, *I Am Not a State Secret*, L.A. Times, Mar. 3, 2007, at 19.

[3] United States v. Reynolds, 345 U.S. 1 (1953).

[4] *See* David Rudenstine, *The Courts and National Security: The Ordeal of the State Secrets Privilege*, U. of Balt. L. Rev. 37, Part I (2014).

[5] *Id.* Part II.

[6] *See* David Rudenstine, *The Courts and National Security: The Ordeal of the State Secrets Privilege*, U. of Balt. L. Rev. 37, 1363–1365 (2014).

[7] *Id.* Part I.

[8] *Id.* Part II.

[9] *Id.* at 1365; *see also* David Rudenstine, *The Irony of a Faustian Bargain: A Reconsideration of the Supreme Court's 1953 United States v. Reynolds Decision*, 34 Cardozo L. Rev. 1283, Part II–III (2013).

boundaries of the contemporary privilege in a handful of decisions,[10] with the Supreme Court assuming a mainly passive role either because a party did not seek review or by denying certiorari in the cases.[11] Now that these rules have been in place for decades with occasional Supreme Court affirmation,[12] it seems that only the Supreme Court has the authority to modify them substantially.

Because the state secrets privilege drew intense attention after September 11,[13] it may be assumed that the contemporary privilege became what it is today only after that epoch-defining moment. But such a view would be a misconception.

[10] *See* Ellsberg v. Mitchell, 709 F.2d 51 (D.C. Cir. 1983), *cert. denied*, 484 U.S. 870 (1987); Fitzgerald v. Penthouse Int'l Ltd., 776 F.2d 1236 (4th Cir. 1985); Halkin v. Helms (*Halkin II*), 690 F.2d 977 (D.C. Cir. 1982); Farnsworth Cannon, Inc. v. Grimes, 635 F.2d 268 (4th Cir. 1980); Halkin v. Helms (*Halkin I*), 598 F.2d 1 (D.C. Cir. 1978).

[11] In addition to the circuit court decisions that initially defined the contemporary privilege, the Supreme Court has had numerous opportunities post–September 11 to revisit the state secrets doctrine. However, in these instances, either the Court has denied certiorari or no appeal has been sought after the circuit court decision. *See* United States v. El-Mezain, 664 F.3d 467 (5th Cir. 2011), *cert. denied*, 133 S. Ct. 525; Mohamed v. Jeppesen Dataplan, Inc., 614 F.3d 1070 (9th Cir. 2010) (en banc), *cert. denied*, 131 S. Ct. 2442; Arar v. Ashcroft 585 F.3d 559 (2d Cir. 2009), *cert. denied*, 130 S. Ct. 3409 (2010); United States v. Stewart, 590 F.3d 93 (2d Cir. 2009); Doe v. C.I.A., 576 F.3d 95 (2d Cir. 2009); United States v. Aref, 533 F.3d 72 (2d Cir. 2008), *cert. denied*, 129 S. Ct. 1582; El-Masri v. United States, 479 F.3d 296 (4th Cir. 2007), *cert. denied*, 552 U.S. 947, 128 S. Ct. 373 (2007); Al-Haramain Islamic Found. v. Bush, 507 F.3d 1190 (9th Cir. 2007); *In re* Sealed Case, 494 F.3d 139, (D.C. Cir. 2007); Marriott Int'l Resorts L.P. v. United States, 437 F.3d 1302 (Fed. Cir. 2006); Sterling v. Tenet, 416 F.3d 338 (4th Cir. 2005), *cert. denied*, 546 U.S. 1093 (2006). *See also* David Rudenstine, *The Courts and National Security: The Ordeal of the State Secrets Privilege*, U. of Balt. L. Rev. 37, app. 3 (2014) and the summary of the Supreme Court decisions that follow in tbl.4 in the article.

[12] *See* General Dynamics Corp. v. United States, 563 U.S. 478 (2011); Tenet v. Doe, 544 U.S. 1 (2005); Webster v. Doe, 486 U.S. 592 (1988).

[13] *See* David Rudenstine, *The Courts and National Security: The Ordeal of the State Secrets Privilege*, U. of Balt. L. Rev. 37, app. 1, tbls.2–3; app. 2, tbl.3. (2014). One scholar summarized the development as follows: "State secrets doctrine catapulted to prominence post-2001, as the executive responded to lawsuits alleging a range of constitutional and human rights violations by refusing to disclose information during discovery and, in some cases, requesting dismissal of suits altogether on national security grounds. More than 120 law reviews followed, and media outlets became outspoken in their criticism of the privilege. In both the Senate and the House, new bills sought to codify what had previously been a common law doctrine. And in September 2009, the Attorney General introduced new procedures for review and created a State Secrets Review Committee." Laura Donohue, *The Shadow of State Secrets*, 159 U. Pa. L. Rev. 77, 78–79 (2010) (footnotes omitted).

This increased attention to *Reynolds* and the state secrets doctrine can be attributed to the number of national security cases reviewed by district and circuit courts post–September 11. While the amount of district court cases citing to Reynolds spiked in the period from the mid-1970s to early 1980s, since 2001, the number of district courts citing to *Reynolds* has been steadily rising. *See* David Rudenstine, *The Courts and National Security: The Ordeal of the State Secrets Privilege*, U. of Balt. L. Rev. 37, app. 1, tbl.1 (2014). While in smaller amounts, the number of circuit courts citing to *Reynolds* mirrors the district courts, with slight spikes of increased citations during the late 1970s and early 1980s, and more steady and increased attention post–2000

The courts of appeals defined the contemporary privilege in the 1970s and 1980s,[14] and those rules continue to form the framework for the contemporary privilege. And although a few judicial decisions in the last few decades have made some alterations in those doctrinal rules,[15] those changes were comparatively minor by comparison to the rules set forth by the courts of appeals in their earlier decisions.

Nonetheless, although the contours of the state secrets privilege were in place for two decades before September 11, there is no question that the post–September 11 state secrets decisions have drawn extensive attention.[16] But that is not because the privilege expanded. Rather, it is because courts applied the privilege to the highly controversial extraordinary rendition cases that arose after September 11. Those cases not only created dissension among judges but also attracted substantial public attention.[17]

Although the national debate over extraordinary rendition did drive the state secrets privilege to center stage,[18] it would be a misjudgment to assume that the privilege will become less robust and sweeping once the intensity of the war on terror diminishes. That is so because the current privilege predated September 11, and the same considerations that generated the privilege also generated the other doctrines that compose the Age of Deference. Thus, the

---

(in particular, the amount of circuit court citations to *Reynolds* increases most consistently after 2003). *Id.* app. 1, tbl.2. Consider also the scant scholarly commentary regarding the state secrets doctrine prior to September 11. *Id.* app. 2, tbl.3. In the forty-seven-year period from 1953 to 2000, only approximately 250 articles were published citing to *Reynolds* (an average of 5.3 articles per year). In 1999, for instance, only sixteen law review articles cited to *Reynolds*. However, following September 11, the heightened attention surrounding national security generated much more scholarly commentary on the state secrets doctrine. During the twelve-year period from 2001 to 2013, approximately 315 law review articles cited to *Reynolds* (an average of 26.25 articles per year). In 2009, the amount of articles citing to *Reynolds* spiked to 45.

[14] *Id.* Part II.A.

[15] Tenet v. Doe, 544 U.S. 1 (2005); Molerio v. FBI, 749 F.2d 815 (D.C. Cir.1984).

[16] *See* David Rudenstine, *The Courts and National Security: The Ordeal of the State Secrets Privilege*, U. of Balt. L. Rev. 37 app. 1, tbls.1–2; app. 2, tbl.3 (2014). *See also* Mohamed v. Jeppesen Dataplan, Inc., 614 F.3d 1070 (9th Cir. 2010) (en banc); El-Masri v. United States 479 F.3d 296 (4th Cir. 2007), *cert. denied*, 552 U.S. 947 (2007); Arar v. Ashcroft, 414 F. Supp. 2d 250 (E.D.N.Y. 2006), *cert. denied*, 560 U.S. 978 (2010).

[17] *See* David Rudenstine, *The Courts and National Security: The Ordeal of the State Secrets Privilege*, U. of Balt. L. Rev. 37, 40 n.24 (2014).

[18] *See* Timothy Bazzle, *Shutting the Courthouse Doors: Invoking the State Secrets Privilege to Thwart Judicial Review in the Age of Terror*, 23 Geo. Mason U. Civ. Rts. L.J. 29 (2012); Amanda Frost, *The State Secrets Privilege and Separation of Powers*, 75 Fordham L. Rev. 1931 (2007); D. A. Jeremy Telman, *Intolerable Abuses: Rendition for Torture and the State Secrets Privilege*, 63 Ala. L. Rev. 429 (2012); *see also* Frank Askin, *Secret Justice and the Adversary System*, 18 Hastings Const. L.Q. 745 (1991); John P. Blanc, *A Total Eclipse of Human Rights—Illustrated by* Mohamed v. Jeppesen Dataplan, Inc., 114 W. Va. L. Rev. 1089 (2012).

privilege and the Age of Deference are intertwined, and courts are unlikely to restructure the privilege before they are willing to reconsider the underpinnings of the Age of Deference.

Although the scope of the privilege will not likely be altered before judges are willing to rethink the exaggerated sense of judicial deference in national security cases, the privilege will likely be invoked less frequently in future cases than it has been in the past because both the executive and the courts, in the wake of the controversy over extraordinary rendition, seem to disfavor the privilege.[19] As a result, a favored evidentiary privilege expanded to protect the nation's security has ironically become a threat to the nation's rule-of-law ideal, thus compromising its utility and making it a legal doctrine of last resort[20] in any effort to insulate the executive from meaningful judicial accountability.[21]

However, disfavoring the privilege does not mean that the judiciary will hold the executive more accountable in national security cases in the future than it has in the past. Courts use numerous legal doctrines[22] to construct a "balloon" that insulates the executive from meaningful judicial review in cases where the executive asserts the nation's security is implicated. When the scope of one doctrine that helps inflate the balloon of insulation is diminished—or squeezed, to follow through with the imagery—with the expectation of increasing meaningful judicial review of the executive, the displaced air merely enlarges the balloon somewhere else, broadening another legal doctrine that insulates the executive. Thus, built into the era of judicial deference is a balloon effect, the consequence of which is that the executive's insulation is more or less constant no matter what modification may be made to any one doctrine of deference.

Nonetheless, the balloon effect should not dampen efforts to reform the state secrets privilege. The current privilege denies arguably wronged individuals judicial relief, erodes checks and balances essential to the constitutional scheme, fails to hold executive unlawful conduct accountable, undermines the national commitment to the rule of law, and threatens the legitimacy of the judiciary. Moreover, not only is the robust and sweeping contemporary privilege unnecessary to the preservation of the nation's security, it may well diminish that security

---

[19] See David Rudenstine, *The Courts and National Security: The Ordeal of the State Secrets Privilege*, U. of Balt. L. Rev. 37, 51 nn.107–109 (2014) and accompanying text.

[20] See David Rudenstine, *The Courts and National Security: The Ordeal of the State Secrets Privilege*, U. of Balt. L. Rev. 37, 51 n.108 (2014).

[21] *But see* Laura Donohue, *The Shadow of State Secrets*, 159 U. Pa. L. Rev. 77, 215–216 (2010), who concluded that the "use of the state secrets privilege is not going to subside." Because Professor Donohue's research for this article ceased in 2008 or 2009, it is possible that the turnabout mentioned earlier in the text had not yet taken hold.

[22] See David Rudenstine, *The Courts and National Security: The Ordeal of the State Secrets Privilege*, U. of Balt. L. Rev. 37, 38 nn. 5–10 (2014).

because it compromises important national values, which are arguably vital to the "soft power" of the United States, contributing to its influence around the globe. Accordingly, guidelines for restructuring the privilege are set forth in Chapter 16.

To take the full measure of the judicially engineered expansion of the state secrets privilege, it is necessary to define the baseline established by the Supreme Court's 1953 decision in *United States v. Reynolds*. That decision announced, for the first time in the history of the United States, a set of rules that federal courts must follow in adjudicating cases in which the executive branch claims the state secrets privilege. Those rules continue, to this day, to provide a skeleton for the contemporary state secrets privilege.[23]

The Court stated that only the government may assert the privilege, and that it should not be "lightly invoked."[24] Moreover, the privilege must be asserted "by the head of the department which has control over the matter" and only after the department head has had "actual personal consideration" of the matter.[25] The Court stressed that a "court itself must determine whether the circumstances are appropriate for the claim of privilege,"[26] and that "[j]udicial control over the evidence in a case cannot be abdicated to the caprice of executive officers."[27] The Court also stated that a court must try to decide whether the privilege should be sustained "without forcing a disclosure of the very thing the privilege is designed to protect."[28] To accomplish the Court's twin goals assuring that it does not abdicate control over the evidence to the "caprice of executive officers,"[29] while not requiring the disclosure of the sensitive information, the Court stated the following guideline:

> It may be possible to satisfy the court, from all of the circumstances of the case, that there is a reasonable danger that compulsion of the evidence will expose military matters which, in the interest of national security, should not be divulged. When this is the case, the occasion for the privilege is appropriate, and the court should not jeopardize the security which the privilege is meant to protect by insisting upon an examination of the evidence, even by the judge alone, in chambers.[30]

[23] David Rudenstine, *The Irony of a Faustian Bargain: A Reconsideration of the Supreme Court's 1953 United States v. Reynolds Decision*, 34 Cardozo L. Rev. 1283, 1389–1391 (2013).

[24] United States v. Reynolds, 345 U.S. 1, 7 (1953).

[25] *Id.* at 8.

[26] *Id.*

[27] *Id.* at 9–10.

[28] *Id.* at 8.

[29] *Id.* at 9–10.

[30] *Id.* at 10.

Lastly, the Court concluded that once a judge was convinced that "military secrets are at stake,"[31] the privilege must be sustained no matter how necessary and vital the information may be to the party seeking access to it or how directly relevant the information may be to matters of general public importance.[32]

The Supreme Court in *Reynolds* characterized the privilege as "well established."[33] Though the doctrine certainly had historical roots that support the claim that it was well established, the privilege had been invoked rarely, and the few reported decisions concerning the privilege were commercial cases between private parties, mainly patent cases. Thus, in support of its claim that the state secrets privilege was "well established," the Supreme Court cited five cases,[34] only one of which was a decision of the Supreme Court—*Totten v. United States*, [35] the so-called *Totten* case—in which the government did not assert a state secrets privilege and the Supreme Court did not even mention the privilege, let alone utilize it as a basis for the decision.[36] Thus, though the general idea of a privilege did have historical roots, the detailed rules the Court announced in *Reynolds* did not; those rules were crafted by the Court and announced in *Reynolds* for the first time.[37]

---

[31] *Id.* at 11.

[32] *Id. See* Robert M. Chesney, *National Security Fact Deference*, 95 Va. L. Rev. 1361, 1377–1378 (2009) for a transcript of *Hepting v. AT&T Corp.*, 539 F.3d 1157, 1158 (9th Cir. 2008), which details an exchange between a circuit judge and a deputy solicitor general in a case involving an alleged state secret in which the line separating judicial "abdication" of its responsibility to exercise some review over the executive's claim that certain information qualified under the privilege from judicial expressions of "utmost deference" is invisible.

[33] United States v. Reynolds, 345 U.S. 1, 6–7 (1953).

[34] The earlier state secrets cases did not establish the rules set forth in *Reynolds. See generally* Cresmer v. United States, 9 F.R.D. 203 (E.D.N.Y. 1949) (Galston, J.); Bank Line Ltd. v. United States, 68 F. Supp. 587 (S.D.N.Y. 1946), 163 F.2d 133 (2d Cir. 1947); Pollen v. Ford Instrument Co., 26 F. Supp 583 (E.D.N.Y. 1939); Firth Sterling Steel Co. v. Bethlehem Steel Co., 199 F. 353 (E.D. Pa. 1912).

[35] Totten v. U.S., 92 U.S. 105 (1875).

[36] *See* David Rudenstine, *The Courts and National Security: The Ordeal of the State Secrets Privilege*, U. of Balt. L. Rev. 37, Part III.D (2014).

[37] Professor Laura K. Donohue argues that scholars, with few exceptions, either before or after the Supreme Court's 1953 decision in *Reynolds*, have not discussed "the history of state secrets in depth," and that failure has resulted in the "proliferation of an Athena-like theory of state secrets: in 1953 it sprung from Zeus's forehead, with little or no previous articulation." *See* Laura Donohue, *The Shadow of State Secrets*, 159 U. Pa. L. Rev. 77, 82–83 (2010). There is an important difference between acknowledging that the common law evidentiary rule authorizing a state secrets privilege had a history both in the United States and the United Kingdom—a history that certainly meant that the Court in *Reynolds* did not invent the concept of a state secret—and the claim that the detailed and convoluted rules announced in *Reynolds* had no antecedents in the United States. The only prior case that seems to have influenced Chief Justice Vinson's shaping of the rules in *Reynolds* was a House of Lords decision: Duncan v. Cammell, Laird & Co., [1942]

In thinking about the *Reynolds* rules in light of the contemporary state secrets privilege, several points are worth emphasizing. First, the *Reynolds* rules tilted in different directions—rules emphasizing that courts must maintain control over application of the rules of evidence and guard against executive abuse of the privilege, and rules directing courts to be so deferential to the executive's claims as to sustain the privilege in some cases without reviewing the disputed document. Nonetheless, within a few decades, the circuit courts effectively eliminated the doctrinal tension these opposing tilts generated by effectively granting the executive de facto absolute control over whether disputed information or documents were covered by the privilege.[38] Second, the *Reynolds* rule made the privilege absolute in nature,[39] meaning that once a court decided that the disputed information or documents were covered by the privilege, the privilege must be sustained no matter how comparatively unimportant the threatened injury to national security might be or how significant the information might be to the allegedly injured party.[40] Third, the Court in *Reynolds* applied the privilege retrospectively to specific and concrete Air Force documents—an investigation report into a plane crash and three witness statements—and although the Court sustained the privilege, it still permitted the case to move forward, which ultimately meant that the plaintiffs were given an opportunity to satisfy their evidentiary burdens with evidence otherwise available to them. Lastly, the Court understood the privilege to be a common law rule of evidence, and not a constitutionally mandated privilege.[41]

As noted, the Court in *Reynolds* gave the executive de facto control over what information was covered by the privilege, made it absolute in character, applied it retrospectively to documents already identified, and, although the Court sustained the privilege, it permitted the action to move forward, effectively treating the privileged evidence as if a witness had died. Without a doubt,

A.C. 624 (H.L.), and the influence of that opinion on the Supreme Court's ruling was limited. Thus, employing Professor Donohue's language, Vinson's rules in *Reynolds* did indeed spring from "Zeus's forehead, with little or no previous articulation." For a detailed discussion of the *Reynolds* decision and the relationship between the *Reynolds* and the *Duncan* cases, see generally David Rudenstine, *The Irony of a Faustian Bargain: A Reconsideration of the Supreme Court's 1953 United States v. Reynolds Decision*, 34 Cardozo L. Rev. 1283 (2013).

[38] David Rudenstine, *The Irony of a Faustian Bargain: A Reconsideration of the Supreme Court's 1953 United States v. Reynolds Decision*, 34 Cardozo L. Rev. 1283, Part II.A.3 (2013).

[39] *Id.* at 1371–1372 (2013).

[40] The *Reynolds* rules invite abuse that courts fail to perceive. Thus, not only was the privilege abused in *Reynolds* itself, but the highly influential opinion in *Halkin II* reaffirmed the error of the *Reynolds* Court and concluded that the disputed documents in *Reynolds* contained military secrets. Halkin v. Helms, 690 F.2d 977, 990 n.53 (1982) ("*Reynolds* itself involved a military secret.").

[41] United States v. Reynolds, 345 U.S. 1, 6 (1953).

the *Reynolds* outcome constituted a major victory for government efforts to expand the veil of secrecy. The Court did not suggest that the privilege could be used to shield innocuous or harmless unlawful conduct or information, or that a ruling sustaining the privilege should result in dismissing an action in which a plaintiff claimed it could satisfy the evidentiary burden without relying on privileged evidence.[42] But that is what the contemporary privilege became in the 1970s and the 1980s—indeed, it became much more than that.

During the last forty years, many distinct doctrinal developments[43] have combined to create a robust and sweeping expansion of the state secrets privilege. The themes that compose the expansion are theoretically distinct from one another, but in practice they are interrelated, reinforce each other, and create a chain of thinking that constitutes a dynamic and breathtakingly expansive state secrets privilege.[44]

The most threatening doctrinal theme to a party arguably wronged by executive officials is that a meritoriously asserted privilege warrants the dismissal of the entire action to avoid an "unacceptable risk"[45] that the litigation will inadvertently expose state secrets. By this reasoning, the privilege is sustained not to guard against the *inevitable* or even the highly likely disclosure of information that satisfies the conditions of the privilege, but to guard against the *possibility* that such information may be disclosed. Thus, it is reasoned that an inquiry during litigation into nonsensitive information, that does not disclose national security information but which is on the "periphery"[46] of sensitive information, may invite lawyers "to probe as close to the core secrets as the trial judge would permit."[47] During such probing, the trial judge, seeking to prevent unintentional disclosure by a witness under aggressive examination, may be disadvantaged because the boundary separating sensitive from nonsensitive

---

[42] *See* David Rudenstine, *The Courts and National Security: The Ordeal of the State Secrets Privilege,* U. of Balt. L. Rev. 37, Part I (2014).

[43] *Id.* Part III.

[44] *Id.* For example, the following themes: unacceptable risks, mosaic doctrine, entanglement, and acknowledging, confirming, denying. *See generally* Kasza v. Browner, 133 F.3d 1159, 1166 (9th Cir. 1998); Bareford v. General Dynamics Corp., 973 F.2d 1138, 1143–1144 (5th Cir. 1992).

[45] *See generally* Mohamed v. Jeppesen Dataplan, Inc., 614 F. 3d 1070 (9th Cir. 2010)(en banc); El-Masri v. United States, 479 F.3d 296, 308 (4th Cir. 2007); Bareford v. General Dynamics Corp., 973 F.2d 1138, 1144 (5th Cir. 1992); Fitzgerald v. Penthouse Int'l, Ltd., 776 F.2d 1236, 1241–1243 (4th Cir. 1985).

[46] Farnsworth Cannon, Inc. v. Grimes, 635 F.2d 268, 281 (4th Cir. 1980) ("Information within the possession of the parties on the periphery of the suppression order would not readily be recognized by counsel, unaware of the specific contents of the affidavit, as being secret or as clearly having been suppressed by the general order of the district court").

[47] *Id.*

information may be so blurred that highly sensitive information is disclosed.[48] Because of this risk of inadvertent disclosure, a judge may dismiss an action before a responsive pleading is filed or discovery is commenced.[49]

The unacceptable risk analysis requires a judge to make a predictive decision regarding how lawyers and a judge will conduct themselves during the course of a trial. Although predictive decisions are vulnerable to the risk of error, judicial rulings applying the unacceptable risk doctrine make little effort to reduce that error by refining the concept of an "unacceptable risk," leaving the possibility open that any risk to any harm is unacceptable.[50] The result is that judges possess broad, unstructured discretion in making these decisions, and because those decisions involve undisclosed information and are predictive in nature, the soundness of the judicial decisions cannot be evaluated.[51]

The unacceptable risk doctrine is a substantial expansion of the state secret rules set forth in *Reynolds*. As noted, the Court in *Reynolds* protected specifically defined and particularized information during the discovery stage of the case and left the action otherwise intact until it became unequivocally plain that the plaintiff was unable to establish a prima facie case without the information covered by the privilege.[52] In contrast, the unacceptable-risk-of-disclosing-state-secrets line of argument is predictive in character, and it results in the dismissal of the entire action.[53]

Courts explain the early dismissal remedy—the limiting or cutting off of litigation "even before any discovery or evidentiary requests have been made in order to protect state secrets"—by claiming that "waiting for specific evidentiary disputes to arise would be both unnecessary and potentially dangerous."[54]

---

[48] *See Jeppesen Dataplan, Inc.,* 614 F.3d at 1082–1083.

[49] *Id.* at 1081.

[50] *See Jeppesen Dataplan, Inc.,* 614 F.3d at 1083; *El-Masri,* 479 F.3d at 305.

[51] David Rudenstine, *The Courts and National Security: The Ordeal of the State Secrets Privilege,* U. of Balt. L. Rev. 37, 59–63 (2014); *See also In re* Sealed Case, 494 F.3d 139, 153 (D.C. Cir. 2007); *Bareford,* 973 F.2d at 1144; Fitzgerald v. Penthouse Int'l, Ltd., 776 F.2d 1236, 1241–1242 (4th Cir.1985); *Farnsworth Cannon,* 635 F.2d at 281.

[52] United States v. Reynolds, 345 U.S. 1, 11–12 (1953).

[53] As the Ninth Circuit has stated "the assertion of privilege will require dismissal because . . . litigating the case to a judgment on the merits would present an unacceptable risk of disclosing state secrets." *Jeppesen,* 614 F.3d at 1079. The Fourth Circuit echoed those words in *El-Masri*: "a proceeding in which the state secrets privilege is successfully interposed must be dismissed if the circumstances make clear that privileged information will be so central to the litigation that any attempt to proceed will threaten that information's disclosure." *El-Masri,* 479 F.3d at 308.

[54] *Jeppesen,* 614 F.3d at 1081. The court in *Jeppesen* also cites to Sterling v. Tenet to support this proposition. Sterling v. Tenet, 416 F.3d 338, 344 (4th Cir. 2005).

The idea that a case should be dismissed to avoid the "unnecessary" taxing of limited judicial resources and to avoid wasteful expenses associated with litigation seems, on its face, totally reasonable. In general, there would be little justification for a judge to indulge litigation that was truly "unnecessary." But whether a legal action in which a state secrets privilege is asserted is "unnecessary" depends entirely—at least in this context—on the capacity of a judge to predict whether the litigation of the claim will risk the inadvertent disclosure of information injurious to national security. Given that a judge would be in a far better position to assess whether additional litigation of a particular action is unnecessary by permitting the action to proceed, judges should dismiss cases to reduce litigation costs only when the circumstances make it certain that further litigation would be wasteful.

But conserving adjudicatory resources is not the major consideration underlying the unacceptable risk doctrine. The primary concern is that any further litigation will present an unacceptable risk that sensitive information will be inadvertently disclosed.[55] Although this is an understandable consideration, the fear of inadvertent disclosure seems greatly exaggerated, since it is difficult to understand how a mere submission of interrogatories or a request for documents could be so "potentially dangerous" as to warrant dismissal of a complaint in which an individual alleges kidnapping and torture. It is equally difficult to understand how a witness being deposed with an attorney (or several attorneys) in the room could inadvertently disclose security information.[56] Moreover, given that judges take almost as hallowed ground the assumption that the judicial function is best performed in a concrete factual context,[57] it is peculiar for the courts to have fashioned a rule that puts a judge in a disadvantaged position by

---

[55] The *Jeppesen* case illustrates the point. Sitting en banc, the court stated that plaintiffs' prima facie case and the defendant's defense "may not inevitably depend on privileged evidence." *Id.* at 1087. Or, to put the matter in a positive mode, the plaintiff may be able to prove a prima facie case without relying upon information covered by the state secrets privilege, and the defendants may be able to mount complete defenses relying on information not covered by the state secrets privilege. Nonetheless, the court dismissed the complaint before a responsive pleading was filed on the ground that "there is no feasible way to litigate" the defendant's liability *"without creating an unjustifiable risk of divulging state secrets." Id.* (emphasis in original).

[56] *But see* General Dynamics Corp. v. United States, 563 U.S. 478 (2011), in which Justice Scalia stated that a former Navy official revealed "military secrets neither side's litigation team was authorized to know," and that copies of the "unclassified deposition were widely distributed and quoted in unsealed court filings until Government security officials discovered the breach a month later." The reliability of Justice Scalia's factual assertions has been called into question by a nationally prominent circuit judge. *See* Richard Posner, *The Incoherence of Antonin Scalia*, The New Republic, Aug. 24, 2012.

[57] *See* Raines v. Byrd, 521 U.S. 811 (1997); Lujan v. Defenders of Wildlife, 504 U.S. 555 (1992); Valley Forge v. Americans United, 454 U.S. 464 (1982); Poe v. Ullman, 367 U.S. 497 (1961).

requiring a predictive decision in a comparatively abstract context.[58] But that is precisely what the courts have done.[59]

There is yet another important turn to the state secrets privilege. In 1972, the Fourth Circuit decided a dispute between a former Central Intelligence Agency (CIA) agent, Victor Marchetti, and the CIA, over the applicability of a secrecy agreement the former agent had signed as a condition of his employment to a book Marchetti had written—*The CIA and the Cult of Intelligence*—that was scheduled to be published by Knopf.[60] The court concluded that the secrecy agreement, which barred Marchetti from disclosing "classified information" that he obtained "during the course of his employment, which was not already in the public domain,"[61] was valid. Moreover, Circuit Judge Haynsworth claimed that the courts should defer to executive branch judgments regarding confidential information; he explained:

> There is a practical reason for avoidance of judicial review of secrecy classifications. The significance of one item of information may frequently depend upon knowledge of many other items of information. What may seem trivial to the uninformed, may appear of great moment to one who has a broad view of the scene and may put the questioned item of information in its proper context. The courts, of course, are ill equipped to become sufficiently steeped in foreign intelligence matters to serve effectively in the review of secrecy classifications in that area.[62]

Thus, Haynsworth cautioned that judges should defer because they were not competent to assess the potential meaning of seemingly meaningless tidbits of information that foreign intelligence officers might assemble into a mosaic that disclosed important information not discernible by examining the individual pieces of the mosaic.[63]

---

[58] A dissent by Circuit Judge Francis D. Murnaghan, Jr. of the Fourth Circuit makes plain the hazards of the unacceptable risk analysis: "Any litigant in the Fourth Circuit whose proof is hampered by the invocation of state secrets can hereafter be turned away from his efforts to obtain justice on the questionable grounds that, for reasons as to which he must remain uninformed, he might stumble intrusively into a protected area. The opportunities for unexplicated imposition of arbitrary fiat under the rule the majority adopts are potentially frightening." Farnsworth Cannon, Inc. v. Grimes, 635 F.2d 268, 282–283 (4th Cir. 1980) (Murnaghan, J., dissenting).

[59] For a discussion of this development, see Beth George, Note, *An Administrative Law Approach to Reforming the State Secrets Privilege*, 84 N.Y.U. L. Rev. 1691, 1697–1699 (2009).

[60] Victor Marchetti, The CIA and the Cult of Intelligence (1974).

[61] United States v. Marchetti, 466 F.2d 1309, 1317 (4th Cir. 1972).

[62] *Id.* at 1318.

[63] *Id.*

Contemporary cases expanding the state secrets doctrine used Haynsworth's statements as a jumping-off point to expand the state secrets privilege, by importing what has become known as the mosaic theory into the privilege,[64] giving rise to the question of the degree to which the mosaic theory should expand the privilege. By comparison to the *Reynolds* decision—which was limited to information that itself presented an unmistakable threat to national security—the utilization of the mosaic theory by the state secrets privilege constitutes an enormous expansion of the scope of the information protected by the privilege. Moreover, as it is now construed by the courts, the idea of the theory—that only experienced individuals steeped in national security can know if seemingly harmless tidbits of information can be disclosed without causing harm—profoundly disables judges from exercising meaningful review over executive judgments.[65] The result is that the inclusion of the mosaic rationale into the state secrets privilege greatly expands the scope of information that is potentially protected by the privilege.

Circuit Judge Harry Edwards gave early expression to the entanglement theme when he explained that the Supreme Court had stated that the state secrets privilege is not "to be lightly invoked," and thus "may not be used to shield any material not strictly necessary to prevent injury to national security," which in turn imposes an obligation on a court to disentangle "nonsensitive information" from "sensitive" information to permit the public release of the nonsensitive information.[66]

Courts have fallen considerably short of that aspiration. Judge Rymer of the Ninth Circuit voiced the practical reality he thinks judges confront in seeking to disentangle sensitive from nonsensitive information: "The government may use the state secrets privilege to withhold a broad range of information. Although 'whenever possible, sensitive information must be disentangled from nonsensitive information to allow for the release of the latter,' courts recognize the inherent limitations in trying to separate classified and unclassified information."[67] Judge Rymer's despairing point was made in even sharper language by Judge Higginbotham of the Fifth Circuit:

> *Fitzgerald* and *Farnsworth Cannon* recognize the practical reality that in the course of litigation, classified and unclassified information cannot always be separated. In some cases, it is appropriate that the

[64] *See generally* C.I.A. v. Sims, 471 U.S. 159, 178 (1985); Kasza v. Brown, 133 F.3d 1159, 1166 (9th Cir. 1998); Halkin I, 598 F.2d 1 (D.C. Cir. 1978).

[65] For a discussion of this development, see Beth George, Note, *An Administrative Law Approach to Reforming the State Secrets Privilege*, 84 N.Y.U. L. Rev. 1691, 1700–1701 (2009).

[66] Ellsberg v. Mitchell, 709 F.2d 51, 57 (D.C. Cir 1983), *cert. denied*, 484 U.S. 870 (1987).

[67] Kasza v. Browner, 133 F.3d 1159, 1166 (9th Cir. 1998) (quoting *Ellsberg*, 709 F.2d at 57).

courts restrict the parties' access not only to evidence which itself risks the disclosure of a state secret, but also those pieces of evidence or areas of questioning which press so closely upon highly sensitive material that they create a high risk of inadvertent or indirect disclosures.[68]

The perspective cautioning disentanglement rests on two lines of analysis. One is the mosaic approach. Pursuant to this perspective, because innocuous information may unintentionally disclose missing pieces of a mosaic that results in insights not previously understood, judges must be mindful not to disentangle, for fear of making an error. The second line of analysis concedes that nonsensitive information may be identified, but it maintains that because this information may be on the "periphery" of sensitive information, judges may err in disentangling the information, thus creating an unacceptable risk.[69]

The judicial paralysis arising from the entanglement theme assumes that judges are not competent to distinguish sensitive from nonsensitive information—even assuming they can distinguish between them—and to police the boundary between these two categories. In short, judicial incompetence stymies judges. However, as discussed later in this chapter, the judicial incompetence theme that streaks through the state secrets privilege is exaggerated to the point of being unpersuasive.

It is one thing for a court to sustain the executive branch's assertion of the state secrets privilege to protect information that is quintessentially military, diplomatic, or intelligence in character. It is quite another for a court to sustain the privilege so that the executive branch is relieved from merely acknowledging the validity or invalidity of information already in the public domain, which is itself not a military, diplomatic, or intelligence secret, which does not form part of a mosaic, and which is not implicated in the examination of a witness in a public trial and does not create an unacceptable risk. Nonetheless, that is what contemporary courts have done. Thus, although in a 1992 opinion Judge Higginbotham was plainly concerned by the "troubling sweep" of the executive's argument based on an "acknowledgment" consideration, he sustained the position: "The government maintains that, even if the data is available from non-secret sources, acknowledgement of this information by government officers would still be damaging to the government, because the acknowledgement would lend credibility to the unofficial data."[70] Or as Judge Higginbotham

---

[68] Bareford v. Gen. Dynamics Corp., 973 F.2d 1138, 1143–1144 (5th Cir.1992).

[69] David Rudenstine, *The Courts and National Security: The Ordeal of the State Secrets Privilege,* U. of Balt. L. Rev. 37, 60 n.139 (2014) and accompanying text.

[70] Barefood v. Gen. Dynamics Corp., 973 F.2d 1138, 1144 (5th Cir. 1992).

wrote in another opinion: "Official acknowledgement by an authoritative source might well be new information that could cause damage to national security."[71]

The previously discussed *Halkin I*[72] case provides a concrete illustration of the "acknowledgment" development and, to appreciate the extraordinary reach of the acknowledgment rationale, it is necessary to examine the *Halkin I* opinion in detail. In this case, the plaintiffs claimed that the National Security Agency (NSA) violated their rights under the Constitution when it conducted warrantless interceptions of their international wire, cable, and telephone communications.[73] The secretary of defense claimed that "admitting or denying the acquisitions would reveal important military and state secrets respecting the capabilities of the NSA for the collection and analysis of foreign intelligence."[74] More specifically, he claimed that "if he were required to identify whose foreign communications were acquired, or to disclose the dates or contents of the acquired communications," the NSA's capabilities would be "jeopardized."[75] The plaintiffs responded "that the state secrets privilege cannot extend to the 'mere fact of interception' of their communications," and argued that "admission or denial of the fact of acquisition of their communications without identification of acquired messages would not reveal which circuits NSA has targeted or the methods and techniques employed."[76]

The Court of Appeals sustained the secretary of defense's position, and it did so by labeling the plaintiffs' position as "naïve," and asserting that a "number of inferences flow from the confirmation or denial of acquisition of a particular individual's international communications."[77] At that point, the court made a series of claims to support its assertion that "a number of inferences flow from the confirmation." The court stated that "the individual himself and any foreign organizations with which he has communicated would know what circuits were used"; "any foreign government or organization that has dealt with a plaintiff whose communications are known to have been acquired would *at the very least* be alerted that its communications *might* have been compromised or that it *might* itself be a target";[78] the "identification of

---

[71] *Id.* (quoting Afshar v. Department of State, 702 F.2d 1125, 1130 (D.C. Cir. 1983)); *see also* Weinberger v. Catholic Action of Hawaii/Peace Educ. Project, 454 U.S. 139, 146 (1981) (stating that "[d]ue to national security reasons, however, the Navy can neither admit nor deny that it proposes to store nuclear weapons at West Loch").

[72] Halkin v. Helms (*Halkin I*), 598 F.2d 1 (D.C. Cir. 1978).

[73] *Id.* at 3.

[74] *Halkin I*, 598 F.2d 1, at 3–4.

[75] *Id.* at 8.

[76] *Id.*

[77] *Id.*

[78] *Id.* (emphasis added).

which plaintiffs' communications were and which were not acquired *could* provide valuable information[79] as to what circuits were monitored and what methods of acquisition were employed";[80] and the disclosures of the identities of the intercepted parties "would enable foreign governments or organizations to extrapolate the focus and concerns of our nation's intelligence agencies."[81]

The circuit court then stated that a "number of inferences flow from the confirmation or denial of acquisition of a particular individual's international communications."[82] The language of this claim—that a "number of inferences flow from the confirmation or denial" of the interceptions—plainly means that the court has concluded that the "inferences" will in fact result from the acknowledgment. But the certainty of that general claim is not supported by the analysis that follows, which is conjectural in character. Moreover, the harm described in the other two sentences is almost identical to the harm that would result if the plaintiffs merely disclosed how it communicated with whom and when. As for the harm described in the two sentences written in conjectural terms, that harm is also identical to the harm that would result from plaintiffs' actual disclosure, except for what the court terms the "methods of acquisition,"[83] and then it is not at all clear why acknowledgment would in fact disclose "methods."

The court also incorrectly assumed that the information that it identified as harmful would be disclosed only if the government was required to confirm or deny the alleged interceptions. The plaintiffs could disclose those facts. The plaintiffs knew how it had communicated, with whom they had communicated, and when it had done so. Thus, while only some of plaintiffs' communications might have been intercepted, plaintiffs' disclosure of this information would have alerted foreign governments and organizations that at least some communications were being intercepted, and it would have identified the means of communications that were subject to interception. Thus, the importance of the government's confirmation or denial of the interceptions boils down to the difference between what information would be disclosed if, on one hand, the government was required to confirm and deny, and on the other hand, the plaintiffs disclosed what information they possessed. Whatever the totality of this information may be, it is certainly much less than the totality of information described by the circuit court.

---

[79] Notice that the court did not state that the disclosure "would" provide such information.
[80] *Id.* at 8 (emphasis added).
[81] *Id.*
[82] *Id.*
[83] *Id.*

The executive consistently claims that confirming, denying, or acknowledging certain information will compromise national security. That may well
be correct with regard to some information in some contexts. But it certainly
is not a convincing position in all contexts, and yet out of deference to the executive, courts seem very willing to defer to such executive assertions. And
when this dynamic is combined with the other three themes—unacceptable
risk, mosaic, and entanglement—the sweeping character of the modern state
secrets privilege is apparent.

In the last decades, courts have extended the *Reynolds* rule from a privilege
that bars a plaintiff from obtaining certain information to a privilege that prevents a defendant from obtaining information the defendant claims may be
helpful. Thus, courts have applied the privilege to information that might help
a defendant mount a valid defense or assist in examining a witness or help in
further discovery. There is nothing inherently troubling in the extension of the
privilege from information sought by a plaintiff to information sought by a defendant. Indeed, such an extension is both logical and appropriate. However,
while the application of the privilege is even-handed, courts have not fairly
allocated the burdens resulting from the privilege's application.

Under the general rules, when the state secrets privilege deprives a plaintiff of
information that may be useful in satisfying a plaintiff's evidentiary burden, the
court in effect directs the plaintiff to proceed as best as the plaintiff is able without the requested information. Indeed, in such circumstances, when a plaintiff
represents that the plaintiff can satisfy its evidentiary burdens by relying solely
upon information in the public domain, the plaintiff's complaint may nonetheless be dismissed if the court decides that the litigation may inadvertently
disclose privileged information.[84] And that is true even if it is likely that the
defendant, as opposed to the plaintiff, might cause the inadvertent disclosure.

Those are far-reaching rules, but they do not necessarily dictate the substance
of a court ruling if the state secrets privilege prevents a defendant from obtaining
information the defendant alleges would be helpful. As noted, when the privilege denies a plaintiff useful information, the court directs the plaintiff to proceed without the information. If that approach were mirrored when the privilege

---

[84] An en banc Ninth Circuit reasoned in *Mohamed v. Jeppesen Dataplan, Inc.*, 614 F.3d 1070,
1090 (9th Cir. 2010), "we do not hold that any of the documents plaintiffs have submitted are subject to the privilege; rather, we conclude that even assuming plaintiffs could establish their entire
case *solely* through nonprivileged evidence—unlikely as that may be—any effort by Jeppesen to
defend would unjustifiably risk disclosure of state secrets." The *Jeppesen* majority cited *El-Masri*,
479 F.3d at 309 (concluding that "virtually any conceivable response [by government defendants
to claims based on factual allegations materially identical to this case's] . . . would disclose privileged information").

disadvantaged a defendant, a court would direct the defendant to do the best the defendant could without the information. But that is not what courts do.[85] Instead, the courts will dismiss the lawsuit because the application of the state secrets privilege has disadvantaged the defendant in defending the action.[86]

Sustaining the state secrets privilege imposes a serious burden, and under current rules the burden falls exclusively on the plaintiff. In other words, no matter which party is denied useful information because of the privilege, the defendant prevails. Although the extension of the privilege to information sought by a defendant is appropriate, the allocation of the burden solely resting on the plaintiff is at odds with basic fairness.

In two opinions, one in 1981[87] and one in 2005,[88] Justice William Rehnquist linked the state secrets privilege to a new justiciability ground. In the 1981 decision *Weinberger v. Catholic Action of Hawaii/Peace Education Project*, the Supreme Court concluded that neither the National Environmental Policy Act nor any regulatory provisions required the Navy to prepare and release an environmental impact statement resulting from the construction of several weapons storage structures capable of storing nuclear weapons. The Court argued that the Act's public disclosure requirements were governed by provisions of the Freedom of Information Act, which generally subordinated the public's interest in ensuring that federal agencies comply with the Act, to the executive's need to protect national security secrets. Furthermore, because national security considerations prevented the Navy from confirming or denying that it proposed to store nuclear weapons at the facility, it was not and it could not be established that the Navy proposed an action that required it to file an environmental impact statement solely for "internal purposes."[89]

Although those reasons constituted sufficient grounds on which to base the result in the case, Justice Rehnquist took a doctrinal step that enlarged the potential scope of the state secrets privilege by turning it from an evidentiary privilege that protected specified information into a new justiciability doctrine. The relevant doctrinal footwork occurred in a short paragraph in

---

[85] For example, see Molerio v. Federal Bureau of Investigation, 749 F.2d 815 (D.C. Cir. 1984); *In re* United States, 872 F.2d 472 (D.C. Cir. 1989). *cert. denied sub nom.*, United States v. Albertson, 493 U.S. 960 (1989); Zuckerman v. General Dynamics Corp., 935 F.2d 544 (2d Cir. 1991); Bareford v. General Dynamics Corp., 973 F.2d 1138, 1143 (5th Cir 1992).

[86] The seeming unfairness of this result is rarely acknowledged by the courts. But see Farnsworth Cannon, Inc. v. Grimes, 635 F. 2d 268, 271–272 (4th Cir. 1980), for a rare acknowledgment.

[87] Weinberger v. Catholic Action of Hawaii/Peace Educ. Project, 454 U.S. 139 (1981).

[88] Tenet v. Doe, 544 U.S. 1 (2005).

[89] *Weinberger*, 454 U.S. at 145–147.

which Rehnquist quoted from a nineteenth-century opinion—*Totten v. United States*[90]—involving a claim by the estate of a Civil War spy against the United States for unpaid compensation, and then cited to the state secrets *Reynolds* opinion as if it were in accord with the quotation from the *Totten* decision:

> Ultimately, whether or not the Navy has complied with [National Environmental Policy Act (NEPA)] "to the fullest extent possible" is beyond judicial scrutiny in this case. In other circumstances, we have held that "public policy forbids the maintenance of any suit in a court of justice, the trial of which would inevitably lead to the disclosure of matters which the law itself regards as confidential, and respecting which it will not allow the confidence to be violated." *Totten v. United States*, 92 U.S. 105, 107, 23 L. Ed.605 (1876). See *United States v. Reynolds*, 345 U.S. 1, 73 S. Ct. 528, 97 L. Ed. 727 (1953). We confront a similar situation in the instant case.[91]

A quarter century later, Chief Justice Rehnquist pushed this doctrinal opening forward another step in *Tenet v. Doe*.[92] In reversing the Ninth Circuit in an espionage case, he argued that the circuit court was "quite wrong" in concluding that the *Totten* ruling did not require the dismissal of the action. Claiming that the Ninth Circuit had construed *Totten* to announce "merely a contract rule," Rehnquist asserted that *Totten* was "not so limited" because it had included a statute that provided: "'[P]ublic policy forbids the maintenance of *any suit* in a court of justice, the trial of which would inevitably lead to the disclosure of matters which the law itself regards as confidential.'"[93] Rehnquist sought to support such a drastic ruling by arguing that the state secrets privilege and the "more frequent use of in camera judicial proceedings simply cannot provide the absolute protection we found necessary in enunciating the *Totten* rule."[94]

Rehnquist's opinion in the *Tenet* case blurred the *Reynolds* state secrets privilege with the *Totten* justiciability ruling. Thus, according to Rehnquist, dismissal—as opposed to protecting the confidentiality of national security information—was required in espionage cases, not to prevent the disclosure of state secrets, but because of the nature of the subject matter. In *Tenet*, Rehnquist surely did not state that all cases involving state secrets were

---

[90] *Totten*, 92 U.S. 105 (1876).
[91] *Weinberger*, 454 U.S. at 146–147.
[92] Tenet v. Doe, 544 U.S. 1 (2005).
[93] *Id.* at 8 (citation omitted).
[94] *Id.* at 11.

henceforth nonjusticiable, but he opened the door to that development, and some years later, two circuit courts walked through the opening and further blurred the distinction between an evidentiary and justiciability ruling.[95]

The brief filed on behalf of the United States in the Supreme Court in the *Reynolds* case strenuously argued in favor of a broad constitutionally mandated executive privilege.[96] Accordingly, it is not possible that the high court overlooked the main argument put forward by the executive. Yet the *Reynolds* opinion did not state that what it terms "the privilege against revealing military secrets"[97] was constitutionally mandated. It does, however, state that both parties make claims that have "constitutional overtones," a phrase that, while having no definite meaning, certainly does not mean that the position of each party is constitutionally based. If it did, Chief Justice Vinson would not have resorted to the ambiguous and unconventional word "overtones."

More importantly, the Vinson opinion makes it perfectly plain that the evidentiary rule it announced in *Reynolds* was not constitutionally based. It did that in the very sentence it used the amorphous phrase "constitutional overtones," when it stated that "we find unnecessary to pass upon" the parties' arguments that have constitutional overtones because there was "a narrower ground for decision." Thus, given that the *Reynolds* majority considered the executive's argument as having only "constitutional overtones," something less than a constitutionally based argument, it stands to reason that the Court's reference to a "narrower ground" was a reference to a ground based on common law. This position is further supported a few sentences later in the opinion when the Court stated that the privilege it was assessing was "well established in the law of evidence." Putting the matter this way was clearly intended by the Court to distinguish the common law character of the privilege from the constitutionally based character of a privilege that was rooted in "inherent executive power" and "protected in the constitutional system of separation of

---

[95] *See id.* at 3; Mohamed v. Jeppesen Dataplan, Inc., 614 F.3d 1070, 1077–1078 (9th Cir. 2010) (en banc); El-Masri v. United States, 479 F.3d 296, 310–311 (4th Cir. 2007). For two circuit court decisions rendered between *Weinberger* and *Tenet* blurring a rule of evidence with a justiciability ruling, see Kasza v. Browner, 133 F.3d 1159, 1166–1167 (9th Cir. 1998) and Weston v. Lockheed Missiles & Space Co., 881 F.2d 814, 815–816 (9th Cir. 1989). *See also* Bareford v. General Dynamics Corp., 973 F.2d 1138, 1144 (5th Cir. 1992); Bowles v. U.S. 950 F.2d 154 (4th Cir. 1991); Guong v. U.S. 860 F.2d 1063 (Fed. Cir. 1988). For a discussion of this development, see Christina E. Wells, *State Secrets and Executive Accountability*, 26 Const. Comment 625, 637–640 (2010); Amanda Frost, *The State Secrets Privilege and Separation of Powers*, 75 Fordham L. Rev. 1931, 1939–1940 (2007); Christopher D. Yamaoka, Note, *The State Secrets Privilege: What's Wrong with It, How It Got That Way, and How the Courts Can Fix It*, 35 Hastings Const. L.Q. 139, 149–150 (2007).

[96] Brief for Petitioner, U.S. v. Reynolds, 345 U.S. 1 (1953), 1952 WL 82378 (1953).

[97] United States v. Reynolds, 345 U.S. 1, 6 (1953).

power," which is how Vinson characterized the executive branch's description of a recordkeeping statute. Moreover, although Vinson did cite the *Totten* case, the result in *Totten* was not based on the Constitution, and the other cases cited by Vinson to support the claim that the privilege was "well established" were all common law–based opinions.[98]

After *Reynolds*, the next judicial development that related to the common law basis of the state secrets privilege was the Supreme Court decision *United States v. Nixon*,[99] involving the special prosecutor's *subpoena duces tecum* of President Nixon's Oval Office tape recordings in the famous Watergate scandal —the case that resulted in Nixon's resignation of the presidency. In that opinion, the Court rejected Nixon's claim that the president was immune from judicial process, or, in the alternative, that the president's claim of executive privilege was an absolute privilege. But the Court concluded for the first time that the president's claim of an executive privilege was constitutionally based, and it reached that conclusion even though the Constitution itself was silent on the matter.

The Court based its conclusion on two grounds. First, the Court concluded that presidential communications in the exercise of Article II powers were constitutionally protected because each of the three branches of government was supreme "within its own assigned area of constitutional duties," and, as a result, certain "powers and privileges flow from the nature of enumerated powers," and the "protection of the confidentiality of Presidential communications has similar constitutional underpinnings." Second, the Court suggested, without explicitly concluding, that the President's claim of executive privilege was also rooted in the doctrine of separation of powers.[100]

It was against these conclusions that the Court then made comments with regard to military and diplomatic secrets, the role of the courts in matters that may involve such secrets, and the state secrets privilege, which gave fresh vitality to an expansive use of the controversial doctrine. The Court did this by first noting that President Nixon did not "place his claim of privilege on the ground"[101] that the communications in dispute involved "military or diplomatic secrets."[102] If the president had made such a claim, the Court reasoned, "the courts have traditionally shown the utmost deference to Presidential responsibilities"[103] and, in support of such "utmost deference," the Court quoted from

[98] *Id.* at 6–7.
[99] United States v. Nixon, 418 U.S. 683 (1974).
[100] *Id.* at 705–706.
[101] *Id.* at 710.
[102] *Id.*
[103] *Id.*

an opinion by Justice Robert Jackson, who actually dissented in the *Reynolds* case.[104] The Court then followed that quote with one from the *Reynolds* case, emphasizing the importance, in matters affecting national security, for the disputed information not to be reviewed even by a judge alone in chambers.[105]

As important as statements in the *Nixon* case may be for indicating that the executive, as a matter of constitutional authority, may in some circumstances withhold certain information from the judiciary, the import of that ruling does not constitutionalize the state secrets evidentiary rules. Those rules encompass much more than the executive's authority merely to withhold information; they encompass a range of doctrines reviewed above, such as the unacceptable risk doctrine, the mosaic doctrine, the entanglement analysis, the resistance to having the executive confirm or deny, remedial expansion, as well as the rules set forth by Chief Justice Vinson in the *Reynolds* opinion. Those aspects of the contemporary state secrets privilege are part and parcel of the common law evidentiary privilege.

Nonetheless, that has not kept the Fourth Circuit from seeking to root the state secrets rules in the Constitution.[106] In *El-Masri v. United States*, the panel stated: "Although the state secrets privilege was developed at common law, it performs a function of constitutional significance, because it allows the executive branch to protect information whose secrecy is necessary to its military and foreign-affairs responsibilities."[107]

This is no academic debate. If the state secrets privilege is a common law privilege, Congress may regulate it; if it is a constitutionally based privilege, Congress may only regulate that part of the privilege that courts conclude are not constitutionally based. In the struggle between those wishing to protect the privilege as currently defined from congressional regulation and those seeking to curtail the privilege, the character of the privilege—whether it is a common law privilege or constitutionally based—makes all the difference.

The expansion of the state secrets privilege beyond the boundaries of the *Reynolds* paradigm was sweeping and swift, and resulted from judicial discretion. Moreover, even assuming that courts in the 1970s and 1980s were

---

[104] *Id.* (citing C & S. Air Lines v. Waterman S.S. Corp., 333 U.S. 103, 111 (1948) ("The President, both as Commander-in-Chief and as the Nation's organ for foreign affairs, has available intelligence services whose reports are not and ought not to be published to the world. It would be intolerable that courts, without the relevant information, should review and perhaps nullify actions of the Executive taken on information properly held secret").

[105] *Nixon*, 418 U.S. at 710–711 (1974) (quoting United States v. Reynolds, 345 U.S. 1, 10 (1953)).

[106] El-Masri v. United States, 479 F.3d 296 (4th Cir. 2007).

[107] *Id.* at 303.

strongly inclined to be deferential towards the executive, they were not re-quired to give the privilege the broad sweep they did. Indeed, if the courts had placed emphasis on the Supreme Court's admonitions in the Reynolds opinion that the privilege not be invoked "lightly,"[108] "that the court itself must deter-mine whether the circumstances are appropriate for the claim of privilege,"[109] and that judicial "control over the evidence in a case cannot be abdicated to the caprice of executive officers,"[110] the expansion of the privilege would have been modest by comparison to what it has become. Thus, there was nothing inevitable or preordained about the extensive expansion of the state secrets privilege during the last four decades; it resulted solely from the exercise of judicial discretion.

In retrospect, the executive's claims for an expansive construction of the state secrets privilege may be dispiriting, but it is not surprising. Indeed, given the constitutional structure of the national government and what might be thought of as the constitutional invitation for the three branches to compete for authority and power, it should be expected that the president, who is com-mander-in-chief and dominates in national security matters, will continually assert authority and press the other two co-equal branches to accede to the executive's requests and demands for more and more unilateral authority.

At the same time, it is disappointing that the Supreme Court has failed to wend its way through the thicket so as to simultaneously respect executive and congressional responsibilities to protect the national security, and not to sur-render so completely its own independence and its responsibility to provide a meaningful check on executive power. But that is what the Supreme Court has done. For decades, it has endorsed a robust and sweeping state secrets privi-lege and even recently—without one member of the Court breaking ranks and criticizing the Court's disposition—reaffirmed its long-standing refusal to re-consider the scope of the privilege.[111]

The fact that the high court's attitude toward the privilege seems so im-penetrable to change, especially given that the privilege is so convincingly criticized, is best understood as a manifestation of a lengthy era of judicial deference. For decades, the Supreme Court has adopted a hands-off attitude toward the executive in national security cases, and although there are notable exceptions to this pattern, those exceptions remain just that—exceptions. The general rule is one of deference, and while the past suggests that now and then a majority of justices will break ranks with tradition, all signals indicate that no

---

[108] United States v. Reynolds, 345 U.S. 1, 7 (1953).
[109] *Id.* at 8.
[110] *Id.* at 9–10.
[111] *See* General Dynamics Corp. v. United States, 563 U.S. 478 (2011).

one currently on the Court will challenge the general rule of deference in the near future. As a result, there is little reason to expect that the Court will any time soon revise the privilege, and moreover, even if the Court did revise the privilege, absent a substantial shift in the Court's deferential disposition, the balloon effect created by the cluster of doctrines of deference would sharply minimize the importance of the restructuring.

Perhaps, in time, individual justices on the Supreme Court will reconsider the Court's deferential disposition in national security cases and write opinions that chart a new course—a course in which the Court functions as a third coequal and independent branch of government that provides meaningful judicial review of executive policies and conduct, even in cases implicating national security.

7

The Law Is Secret

Born in New Mexico in 1971,[1] Anwar al-Awlaki[2] was a United States citizen by birthright. His father, Nasser al-Awlaki, who received advanced degrees from U.S. universities and worked at the University of Minnesota in the mid-1970s, was a prominent member of Yemen's ruling party. When Anwar al-Awlaki was seven years of age, he and his family returned to Yemen, where he remained until 1991, when he entered a university in Colorado. He earned a B.S. in civil engineering in 1994. During the next sixteen years, al-Awlaki became a "radical Muslim cleric"[3] (at least that is how he was often characterized).

During the first weeks of 2010, the Obama administration took the "extraordinary step"[4] of authorizing the CIA[5] to kill al-Awlaki, who was believed to be in Yemen. According to Greg Miller of *The Los Angeles Times*, "[n]o U.S. citizen has ever been on the CIA's target list."[6] The Obama administration took this step because it had concluded that al-Awlaki was a terrorist and had become "operational," which meant that the administration had linked al-Awlaki to two terrorist plots.[7] In one case, al-Awlaki was linked to a U.S. major who killed thirteen individuals at Fort Hood, Texas, in November

---

[1] For a recent account of the United States killing of Anwar al-Awlaki, see Scott Shane, Objective Troy: A Terrorist, a President, and the Rise of the Drone (2015).

[2] Also spelled a-Aulaqi and al-Awlaqi.

[3] Scott Shane, *U.S. Approves Targeted Killing of American Cleric*, N.Y. Times, Apr. 6, 2010, at A12, http://www.nytimes.com/2010/04/07/world/middleeast/07yemen.html.

[4] *Id.*

[5] Greg Miller, *Muslim Cleric Aulaqi is 1st U.S. Citizen on List of Those CIA is Allowed to Kill*, Wash. Post, Apr. 7, 2010, http://www.washingtonpost.com/wp-dyn/content/article/2010/04/06/AR2010040604121.html. Al-Awlaki had previously been on a target list maintained by the U.S. military's Joint Special Operations Command. *Id.*

[6] Greg Miller, *U.S. Citizen in CIA's Cross Hairs*, L.A. Times, Jan. 31, 2010, http://articles.latimes.com/2010/jan/31/world/la-fg-cia-awlaki31-2010jan31.

[7] Dana Priest, *U.S. Military Teams, Intelligence Deeply Involved in Aiding Yemen on Strikes*, Wash. Post, Jan. 27, 2010, http://www.washingtonpost.com/wp-dyn/content/article/2010/01/26/AR2010012604239.html.

2009.[8] In the other case, al-Awlaki was linked to a twenty-three-year-old Nigerian named Umar Farouk Abdulmutallab, who became popularly known as the "Christmas Day bomber,"[9] and who failed to blow up an airliner as it approached Detroit on December 25, 2009. Allegedly Umar Farouk Abdulmutallab told FBI agents that he tracked down al-Awlaki in Yemen and that al-Awlaki discussed "'martyrdom and jihad' with him, approved him for a suicide mission, helped him prepare a martyrdom video, and directed him to detonate his bomb over United States territory."[10] American counterterrorism officials told Scott Shane of the *New York Times* that the United States had concluded that "Mr. Awlaki is an operative of Al Qaeda in the Arabian Peninsula, the affiliate of the terror network in Yemen and Saudi Arabia. They say they believe that he has become a recruiter for the terrorist network, feeding prospects into plots aimed at the United States and at Americans abroad. . . ."[11]

The placing of al-Awlaki on the CIA's kill list in early 2010 was about half a year before the Department of Justice had prepared a secret memorandum of law that addressed all the legal questions implicated in the United States killing a United States citizen outside a combat zone who was not charged with a crime. Indeed, it seems that it was not until that summer of 2010 that lawyers in the Office of Legal Counsel, David Barron and Martin Lederman, commenced work on a secret legal memorandum that addressed the question whether it was or was not lawful for the United States to kill al-Awlaki, "despite his citizenship . . . [and] assuming it was not feasible to capture him."[12] These two lawyers "swiftly completed a short memorandum" that "preliminarily concluded, based on the evidence available at the time, that Mr. Awlaki was a lawful target because he was participating in the war with Al Qaeda and also because he was a specific threat to the country." But within weeks the two lawyers "grew uneasy" because they had not adequately addressed certain issues, particularly whether a United States statute "bars Americans from killing other Americans overseas."

---

[8] Greg Miller, *Muslim Cleric Aulaqi is 1st U.S. Citizen on List of Those CIA is Allowed to Kill*, Wash. Post, Apr. 7, 2010, http://www.washingtonpost.com/wp-dyn/content/article/2010/04/06/AR2010040604121.html.

[9] Al-Aulaqi v. Panetta, 35 F. Supp. 3d 56, 62 (D.D.C. 2014); Leon Panetta, Worthy Fights 386 (2014).

[10] Mark Mazzetti, Charlie Savage, and Scott Shane, *How a U.S. Citizen Came to Be in America's Cross Hairs*, N.Y. Times, Mar. 9, 2013, http://www.nytimes.com/2013/03/10/world/middleeast/anwar-al-awlaki-a-us-citizen-in-americas-cross-hairs.html.

[11] Scott Shane, *U.S. Approves Targeted Killing of American Cleric*, N.Y. Times, Apr. 6, 2010 at A12, http://www.nytimes.com/2010/04/07/world/middleeast/07yemen.html.

[12] Mark Mazzetti, Charlie Savage, and Scott Shane, *How a U.S. Citizen Came to Be in America's Cross Hairs*, N.Y. Times, Mar. 9, 2013, http://www.nytimes.com/2013/03/10/world/middleeast/anwar-al-awlaki-a-us-citizen-in-americas-cross-hairs.html.

Because the two lawyers planned to resign from the Department of Justice and return to their academic positions, they rushed to complete the second secret legal memorandum. This memorandum, which was roughly sixty-three pages in length, set forth the legal justification for killing al-Awlaki and its "reasoning was widely approved by other administration lawyers."[13] The memorandum apparently did not address "whether it would also be permissible to kill citizens, like low-ranking members of Al Qaeda, in other situations."[14]

From the time that the CIA was authorized to target al-Awlaki, it took over a year and a half to locate him. Once that happened, armed drones operated by the CIA took off from a new and secret base in the Arabian Peninsula, crossed into Yemen, and "unleashed a barrage of Hellfire missiles at a car carrying" al-Awlaki and "other top operatives from Al Qaeda's branch in Yemen, including another American citizen," Samir Khan, who was "an editor of Inspire, Al Qaeda's English-language online magazine."[15] And then two weeks later, on October 14, a United States missile "apparently intended for an Egyptian Qaeda operative, Ibrahim al-Banna," killed Awlaki's sixteen-year-old son Abdulrahman al-Awlaki.[16] The day al-Awlaki was killed, President Obama stated that al-Awlaki had taken "the lead role in planning and directing the efforts to murder innocent Americans," that al-Awlaki was "the leader of external operations for Al Qaeda in the Arabian Peninsula," and that his death was "a major blow to Al Qaeda's most active operational affiliate."[17]

---

[13] *Id.* Peter Finn of the *Washington Post* reported that the legal memorandum "involved senior lawyers from across the administration. There was no dissent about the legality of killing Aulaqi, the officials said." Peter Finn, *Secret U.S. Memo Sanctioned Killing of Aulaqi*, Wash. Post, Sept. 30, 2011, https://www.washingtonpost.com/world/national-security/aulaqi-killing-reignites-debate-on-limits-of-executive-power/2011/09/30/gIQAx1bUAL_story.html.

[14] Mark Mazzetti, Charlie Savage, and Scott Shane, *How a U.S. Citizen Came to Be in America's Cross Hairs*, N.Y. Times, Mar. 9, 2013, http://www.nytimes.com/2013/03/10/world/middleeast/anwar-al-awlaki-a-us-citizen-in-americas-cross-hairs.html.

[15] Mark Mazzetti, Eric Schmitt, and Robert F. Worth, *Two-Year Manhunt Led to Killing of Awlaki in Yemen*, N.Y. Times, Sept. 30, 2011, http://www.nytimes.com/2011/10/01/world/middleeast/anwar-al-awlaki-is-killed-in-yemen.html. On September 30, 2011, Peter Finn of the *Washington Post* reported that the killing of Khan was "reminiscent of a 2002 U.S. drone strike in Yemen that targeted" an al-Qaeda operative accused of planning the 2000 attack on the USS *Cole* that also killed a "U.S. citizen who the C.I.A. knew was" in the same vehicle and who was not a target of the attack. Peter Finn, *Secret U.S. Memo Sanctioned Killing of Aulaqi*, Wash. Post, Sept. 30, 2011, https://www.washingtonpost.com/world/national-security/aulaqi-killing-reignites-debate-on-limits-of-executive-power/2011/09/30/gIQAx1bUAL_story.html.

[16] Mark Mazzetti, Charlie Savage, and Scott Shane, *How a U.S. Citizen Came to Be in America's Cross Hairs*, N.Y. Times, Mar. 9, 2013, http://www.nytimes.com/2013/03/10/world/middleeast/anwar-al-awlaki-a-us-citizen-in-americas-cross-hairs.html.

[17] Mark Mazzetti, Eric Schmitt, and Robert F. Worth, *Two-Year Manhunt Led to Killing of Awlaki in Yemen*, N.Y. Times, Sept. 30, 2011, http://www.nytimes.com/2011/10/01/world/middleeast/anwar-al-awlaki-is-killed-in-yemen.html.

Although President Obama did not delay announcing to the public that his administration had intentionally killed a United States citizen outside of a combat zone and to maintain that such a killing was lawful, Obama did not disclose the legal memorandum that set forth the legal reasoning and legal sources he relied upon in offering his legal conclusion that it was lawful for the United States to kill a United States citizen in such circumstances. Nor did he authorize the disclosure of the legal memorandum for months or years thereafter. Indeed, his administration fought tooth and nail in the courts not to disclose the legal memorandum, and it did that while simultaneously publicly insisting time after time that using a drone to kill al-Awlaki in Yemen was lawful. In the end, when the administration finally did agree to disclose a redacted version of the memorandum, it did so only because a few senators took the position that they would oppose the appointment of one of the attorneys who wrote the disputed legal memorandum to a federal appeals court unless the administration agreed to disclose the memorandum.[18]

Although our main focus is on the struggle to convince the courts to order the executive to disclose the memorandum of law that set forth a legal justification for using a drone to kill al-Awlaki,[19] this chapter briefly reviews two other legal initiatives concerning al-Awlaki because they illustrate the context of this important episode how courts utilize different legal doctrines to immunize the executive from meaningful judicial review. In the order of presentation, the first was the lawsuit brought by al-Awlaki's father who sought to restrain the CIA from killing his son. The second, which was brought by al-Awlaki's father as well as a family member of Samir Khan, sought damages for the killing of al-Awlaki, his son, and Samir Khan.[20] The third was an effort by *The New York*

---

[18] For a selection of law review articles discussing targeted killing, see Matthew Craig, *Targeted Killing, Procedure, and False Legitimation*, 35 Cardozo L. Rev. 2349 (2014); Alberto R. Gonzales, *Drones: The Power to Kill*, 82 Geo. Wash. L. Rev. 1 (2013); Stephen I. Vladeck, *Targeted Killing and Judicial Review*, 82 Geo. Wash. L. Rev. Arguendo 11 (2014). *See also* Oren Gross, *The New Way of War: Is There a Duty to Use Drones?*, 67 Fla. L. Rev. 1 (2015). Years after al-Awlaki was killed, what the *New York Times* reporter Scott Shane described as his "inflammatory videos and bomb-making instructions" remained "easily accessible on the Internet" and have "turned up as a powerful influence." In fact, Shane reported: "Killing him, it is clear, only enhanced the appeal of his message to many admirers, who view him as a martyr." As a consequence, Shane reported, pressure "on Internet companies to take down his work is growing, because legal experts say the First Amendment would prohibit the government from ordering restrictions." Scott Shane, *Internet Firms Urged to Limit Work of Anwar al-Awlaki*, N.Y. Times, Dec. 19, 2015.

[19] For a recent study of the Obama administration of the killing of al-Awlaki, see Scott Shane, Objective Troy: A Terrorist, a President, and the Rise of the Drone (2015).

[20] Peter Finn, *Secret U.S. Memo Sanctioned Killing of Aulaqi*, Wash. Post, Sept. 30, 2011, https://www.washingtonpost.com/world/national-security/aulaqi-killing-reignites-debate-on-limits-of-executive-power/2011/09/30/gIQAx1bUAL_story.html. "An administration official

Times and the ACLU to force the executive to disclose the secret legal memorandum setting forth the legal justification relied upon by the Obama administration for killing a citizen outside a war zone who had not been charged with a crime or prosecuted.

In August of 2010, which was eight months after al-Awlaki was placed on the CIA drone kill list and thirteen months before a drone in fact killed al-Awlaki, al-Awlaki's father, Nasser al-Awlaki,[21] commenced an action in the United States District Court in Washington. The complaint sought an injunction enjoining President Obama; Robert M. Gates, the secretary of defense; and Leon E. Panetta, the director of the CIA, from intentionally killing al-Awlaki absent evidence that al-Awlaki presented a "concrete, specific, and imminent threat to life or physical safety, and there are no means other than lethal force that could reasonably be employed to neutralize the threat."[22] In response, the executive made a motion to dismiss the action on five different legal grounds. It asserted that al-Awlaki's father lacked "standing" to bring the action, that the legal claims raised a "political question" that was not justiciable, that the court should dismiss the action as a matter of equitable discretion, that the federal statute the plaintiff relied upon for relief did not authorize relief given these facts, and that the action should be dismissed because it implicated information protected by the state secrets privilege.[23]

Judge John D. Bates presided over the legal effort to restrain the CIA from using a drone to kill al-Awlaki.[24] Earlier in his career Judge Bates had

---

said the CIA did not know Khan was with Aulaqi, but they also considered Khan a belligerent whose presence near the target would not have stopped the attack."

[21] In the legal action al-Awlaki's father spelled his name al-Aulaqi. When he published an op-ed article in the *New York Times*, he spelled it al-Awlaki. For the sake of clarity, the spelling in this chapter is al-Awlaki.

[22] Al-Aulaqi v. Obama, 727 F. Supp. 2d 1, 8 (2010).

[23] *Id.*

[24] *Id.* In outlining his policy regarding the use of drones to kill, President Obama has stated that he proceeds from the Madisonian assumption that "[n]o nation could preserve its freedom in the midst of continual warfare," while recognizing that it is not possible to eradicate the "evil that lies in the hearts of some human beings, nor stamp out every danger to our open society." President Barack Obama, Remarks at the National Defense University (May 23, 2013). https://www.whitehouse.gov/the-press-office/2013/05/23/remarks-president-national-defense-university. But he insisted that what the United States "can do" and "must do" is to "dismantle networks that pose a direct danger to us, and make it less likely for new groups to gain a foothold, all the while maintaining the freedoms and ideals that we defend." *Id.* Against those imperatives, Obama has judged that the "core of al Qaeda in Afghanistan and Pakistan is on the path to defeat" and in its place has emerged "various al Qaeda affiliates" in Yemen, Iraq, Somalia, the Arabian Peninsula, and parts of North Africa which are "lethal yet less capable" than al-Qaeda once was. *Id.*

In responding to these current threats Obama has insisted that his administration has a "strong preference for the detention and prosecution of terrorists" but that "this approach

been an Assistant United States Attorney and a lawyer with Independent Counsel, Kenneth Starr, whose investigation of President Bill Clinton resulted in impeachment proceedings. Thereafter, in 2001, President George W. Bush appointed Bates to the United States District Court, and subsequently John Chief Justice Roberts in 2006 appointed Bates to the Foreign Intelligence Surveillance Court, and in 2013 to the position of director of the Administrative Office of the United States Courts. By the time Judge Bates had to decide the *al-Awlaki* case, he had decided a handful of noteworthy cases that indicated a pronounced disposition to employ flexible legal doctrines to immunize executive branch officials from judicial review. And that is what he did in this case. Judge Bates wrote a fifty-page legal opinion dated December 7, 2010, in which he granted the defendants' motion to dismiss the complaint.

Because our main focus is on the dogged efforts of the Obama administration to preserve the secrecy of the memorandum that set forth the legal reasoning as to why it was lawful for the government to kill al-Awlaki, a United States citizen, in the circumstances of this case, a detailed review of Judge Bates's opinion is unnecessary. But it is worth briefly reviewing the fact that in

is foreclosed" in some locations because they are "distant and unforgiving" and the terrorists hide in "caves and walled compounds" and "train in empty deserts and rugged mountains." *Id.* In some locations the governing authority "only has the most tenuous reach into the territory," and in others the "state lacks the capacity or will to take action." As a result, it is not possible to "deploy a team of Special Forces to capture every terrorist," and even when it may be possible, such a deployment may implicate "profound risks to our troops and local civilians—where a terrorist compound cannot be breached without triggering a firefight with surrounding tribal communities, for example, that pose no threat to us; times when putting U.S. boots on the ground may trigger a major international crisis." *Id.* One consequence of this policy, as characterized by Pulitzer Prize–winning journalist Dana Priest, is that President Obama "has embraced the notion that the most effective way to kill or capture members of al-Qaeda and its affiliates is to work closely with foreign partners, including those that have feeble democracies, shoddy human rights records and weak accountability over the vast sums of money Washington is giving them to win their continued participation in these efforts." Dana Priest, *U.S. Military Teams, Intelligence Deeply Involved in Aiding Yemen on Strikes*, Wash. Post, Jan. 27, 2010, http://www.washington post.com/wp-dyn/content/article/2010/01/26/AR2010012604239.html.

It is within this context that Obama places the highly contentious and debatable use of drones for targeted killing. As he assesses this, Obama concludes that drones "have saved lives," "are legal," "moral," and "wise," in at least some circumstances, especially given the alternatives. President Barack Obama, Remarks at the National Defense University (May 23, 2013), https://www.whitehouse.gov/the-press-office/2013/05/23/remarks-president-national-defense-university. Obama claims that the use of drones outside of Afghanistan is targeted only at al Qaeda and associated forces, and then are used only when capturing an individual terrorist is not possible, and the terrorist presents "a continuing and imminent threat to the American people, and . . . there are no other governments capable of effectively addressing the threat." *Id.* Lastly, Obama asserts that no drone attack outside combat zones will proceed until there is "near-certainty that no civilians will be killed or injured—the highest standard we can set." *Id.*

granting the executive's motion to dismiss the action, Judge Bates relied upon legal doctrines that exhibited exceptional deference to the Obama administration and dismissed the legal proceedings.

Judge Bates devoted twenty pages to assessing whether al-Awlaki's father was able to assert the legal claims on behalf of his son, which in turn required Judge Bates to decide whether al-Awlaki's father satisfied the technical requirements of the law of standing. As already noted, the law of standing is malleable both in terms of its definition and its application, thus vesting a judge with considerable discretion, so that in many factual contexts a judge could decide that a party did or did not satisfy relevant standing requirements. In these circumstances what primarily determines the outcome on the matter is not the details of the law of standing, but other considerations that influence the exercise of a particular judge's discretion, and in the case of al-Awlaki's father's lawsuit seeking to enjoin the targeted killing of his son, it would seem that the dominant factor prompting Judge Bates to conclude that al-Awlaki's father lacked standing was a strong disposition to defer to the executive branch on the grounds of national security.

But Judge Bates did not rest his opinion solely on the law of standing. Judge Bates also decided that al-Awlaki's father presented legal questions that were not appropriate for a court to resolve because they were "political questions" that the Constitution had assigned to the other branches of government to resolve. This doctrine—the so-called political question doctrine—had been, as Judge Bates fully acknowledged, subject to "scathing scholarly attack,"[25] in large part because the doctrine is composed of a set of factors that are easily stated but which are so broad, vague, and open-ended that they defy consistent application. That is at least one major reason why, as another judge, District Judge Rosemary M. Collyer, has observed: "'The political question doctrine has occupied a more limited place in the Supreme Court's jurisprudence than is sometimes assumed. The court has relied on the doctrine only twice in the last 50 years.'"[26] Nonetheless, Judge Bates decided that al-Awlaki's father's complaint did present political questions because the court lacked the "capacity to determine whether a specific individual in hiding overseas, whom the Director of National Intelligence has stated is an 'operational' member of AQAP, see Clapper Decl. #15, presents such a threat to national security that the United States may authorize the use of lethal force against him."[27]

Judge Bates's conclusion that he lacked competence in this matter is not persuasive. Whatever uncertainty may be involved with the concept of "operational,"

---

[25] Al-Aulaqi v. Obama, 727 F. Supp. 2d 1, 45 (2010).

[26] Nasser Al-Aulaqi v. Panetta, 35 F. Supp. 3d 56, 69 (2014).

[27] Al-Aulaqi v. Obama, 727 F. Supp. 2d 1, 52 (2010).

the executive certainly has standards that it uses to decide whether an individual is or is not "operational," and it must also have examples of facts that illuminate its application of the concept to specific facts. Thus, the executive officials could explain such matters to Judge Bates and then detail the evidence it has—and the basis for its evidence—as to why al-Awlaki was in fact "operational."

In reviewing such matters, Judge Bates could certainly exercise—and properly so—some deference with regard to the executive's presentation. But such a review would provide some check on executive authority, while honoring a limited role of courts in matters of national security. The fact that Judge Bates eschewed this doctrinal path in favor of concluding that al-Awlaki's father's complaint presented a political question was the result of an attitude of deference that eliminated any possibility of thoughtful analysis.

A few weeks before a United States drone killed him, al-Awlaki's sixteen-year-old-son, Abdulrahman al-Awlaki Abdulrahman, had left his home in Sana early one morning leaving a note for his mother stating that he was going to go look for his father, "whom he hadn't seen for years." Abdulrahman's note stated that he "missed his father and wanted to find him." The boy asked his mother to "forgive him for leaving without permission."

When the missile allegedly intended for an Egyptian al-Qaeda terrorist operative killed Abdulrahman, he was with his cousin and others "eating dinner at an open-air restaurant in southern Yemen." When Abdulrahman's grandfather visited the site of the drone strike, he was told by the local residents that his grandson's "body was blown to pieces."[28]

Nasser al-Awlaki sought by means of a legal action to obtain damages and an explanation from the Obama administration as to why, as he wrote, "my grandchild is dead."[29] He was joined in the legal action by the mother of Samir Khan. In April of 2014, more than two and one-half years after al-Awlaki was killed, Judge Rosemary M. Collyer, who was appointed to the federal bench by President George W. Bush and to the Foreign Intelligence Surveillance Court by Chief Justice Roberts, dismissed the action for damages.[30]

The defendants supported their motion to dismiss with an argument that the legal questions presented a "political question," that the defendants were protected under a quasi-immunity doctrine, and that even assuming that the defendants had violated the plaintiffs' rights, the plaintiffs were not entitled

---

[28] Nasser al-Awlaki, Opinion, *The Drone That Killed My Grandson*, N.Y. Times, July 17, 2013, http://www.nytimes.com/2013/07/18/opinion/the-drone-that-killed-my-grandson.html?_r=0.

[29] *See* Al-Aulaqi v. Panetta, 35 F. Supp. 3d 56 (D.D.C. 2014).

[30] *Id.*

to a remedy because Congress had not passed a statute authorizing one.[31] Moreover, the United States had filed a "Statement of Interest" in the matter and stated that it reserved the right to raise the state secrets privilege in the event that the judge did not dismiss the complaint on one of the grounds the defendants had asserted. In deciding to dismiss the complaint, Judge Collyer decided that the plaintiffs were not entitled to a remedy in the absence of a statute authorizing one.

Simplifying the legally obscure, the general rule is, as explained previously, that in order for a party to sue executive officials, Congress must have authorized the claim and the award of damages against the federal government. But, in 1971, the Supreme Court ruled in the *Bivens* case that a court may of its own accord grant a damage remedy to an individual whose constitutional rights were violated by the executive branch.[32] In subsequent cases over the next decade the Supreme Court expanded the so-called *Bivens* rule, and thus it looked as if *Bivens* and its progeny were becoming fixtures in American law. But subsequent legal developments proved that assumption false as the Supreme Court in one case after another not only refused to expand and uphold the *Bivens* rule but also curtailed it.[33]

Nonetheless, Judge Collyer's decision not to permit a damage remedy pursuant to the *Bivens* doctrine was not mandated by prior decisions. As the judge stated so plainly in her opinion, the legal question was an open one: "No case has discussed precisely whether a plaintiff can proceed on a *Bivens* action that claims deprivation of life without due process based on the overseas killing by United States officials of a U.S. citizen deemed to be an active enemy."[34] Moreover, although prior cases had made it clear that judges should as a general rule defer to the president and the Congress on national security matters, it was also true that the court had stated in a case involving national security and intelligence that judicial nonintervention was not an absolute rule.[35] Indeed, in 2004, during the second Iraq War, a Supreme Court plurality opinion trumpeted a line that received considerable dissemination that even during wartime the Constitution does not grant the president a "blank check" and that the courts, as a coequal branch of government, retain a vital role in the governing scheme on national security matters.[36] And four years later, a majority drove that point home in insisting that it

[31] *Id.* at 66.

[32] Bivens v. Six Unknown Named Agents of Fed. Bureau of Narcotics, 403 U.S. 388 (1971). See Chapter 11 for a full discussion of the *Bivens* doctrine.

[33] See Chapter 11 for an assessment of these legal developments.

[34] *Al-Aulaqi*, 35 F. Supp. 3d at 74.

[35] Haig v. Agee, 453 U.S. 280, 292 (1981) (cautioning that "matters intimately related to . . . national security are rarely proper subjects for judicial intervention").

[36] Hamdi v. Rumsfeld, 542 U.S. 507, 536 (2004).

retained jurisdiction over petitions for a writ of habeas corpus filed by a detainee at Guantanamo.[37] Furthermore, although Justices Scalia and Thomas had characterized the *Bivens* doctrine as a "relic" and sought to limit *Bivens, Passman,* and *Carlson* to their facts, seven justices disagreed.[38]

In addition to the fact that case law permitted Judge Collyer to provide a *Bivens* remedy, other considerations also argued in favor of a *Bivens* remedy. The facts in this case were exceedingly unusual: the United States deliberately killed a U.S. citizen outside of a combat zone under circumstances that did not suggest that the individual presented an immediate, concrete, and specific threat to other U.S. citizens, property, or significant interests. Or, as one news report sought to place the United States' targeted killing of al-Awlaki in an historical context, it appeared the killing of al-Awlaki was "the first time since the Civil War, the United States government had carried out the deliberate killing of an American citizen as a wartime enemy and without a trial."[39] Thus, although the *Bivens* doctrine required that a court be sensitive to "special factors" that militated against granting a damage remedy, the *al-Awlaki* case may be so unusual that the grant of a *Bivens* remedy in the matter would not open the door to other cases. Moreover, because the estate of al-Awlaki had no remedy other than a damage action, the case fit into that category of cases in which it is either "damages or nothing," as the cautious Justice Harlan wrote when he decided to support the *Bivens* remedy in 1971.[40] And lastly, it did seem as if the underlying claim was meritorious in that the targeted killing of al-Awlaki did not seem to be consistent with the guidelines for the use of drones to kill U.S. citizens as set forth by President Obama.

In dismissing the action, Judge Collyer began her analysis by emphasizing that the matter concerned national defense and the military. Although that is correct, she did not claim that every matter affecting national defense or the military is necessarily immune from a *Bivens* remedy. If that were in fact the controlling legal rule, that would end the discussion. But it is not an absolute controlling rule; it is a consideration, but no more than that. And Judge Collyer recognized that fact.

Judge Collyer next asserted that the "record is replete with evidence" that al-Awlaki was an AQAP leader, that AQAP was affiliated with al-Qaeda, that

---

[37] *See* Boumediene v. Bush, 553 U.S. 723 (2008).

[38] Correctional Servs. Corp. v. Malesko, 534 U.S. 61, 75 (2001) (Scalia, J., concurring).

[39] Mark Mazzetti, Charlie Savage, and Scott Shane, *How a U.S. Citizen Came to Be in America's Cross Hairs,* N.Y. Times, Mar. 9, 2013, http://www.nytimes.com/2013/03/10/world/middleeast/anwar-al-awlaki-a-us-citizen-in-americas-cross-hairs.html.

[40] Bivens v. Six Unknown Named Agents of Fed. Bureau of Narcotics, 403 U.S. 388, 410 (1971) (Harlan, J., concurring).

al-Awlaki was "intimately involved in planning the Christmas Day bombing" in December 2009, and that al-Awlaki praised the actions of "his 'students' " the Christmas Day bomber and the Foot Hood shooter and advocated that others become assassins and suicide bombers.[41] The judge made these claims as if they were findings of facts following a trial. But there had been no trial or evidentiary hearing in the case, and although news reports indicated that the Obama administration thought that al-Awlaki became "operational" and was part of the Christmas Day bombing in December 2009, the plaintiffs in the case did not concede those facts, and those were the critical facts supporting the executive's conclusion that al-Awlaki presented a concrete and imminent threat.

The judge also argued that a *Bivens* damage action would "require the Court to examine national security policy and the military chain of command as well as operational combat decisions regarding the designation of targets and how best to counter threats to the United States." Furthermore, she argued that a *Bivens* remedy would cause the court to raise "fundamental questions regarding the conduct of armed conflict," and that such questions are committed by the Constitution to the president and the Congress.[42] These claims were worded in the most general way and if it were accepted that a *Bivens* action by the al-Awlaki estate would require a court to assess "national security policy" and the "military chain of command" and ask probing questions regarding "the conduct of armed conflict," then a *Bivens* action might well be precluded.

But the judge's claims were far more general and far more encompassing than warranted by the case. The Obama administration publicly stated that the targeted killing of al-Awlaki was lawful, and because of that the central issue in the damage action was whether the targeted killing was indeed lawful. If the killing was lawful, the defendants did not violate al-Awlaki's constitutional rights and his estate was not entitled to damages. If it was not lawful, then the estate might well be entitled to a damage remedy. Framed in this manner— Was the drone killing legal?—the issues raised by the case seem appropriate for adjudication. After all, courts are in fact the ultimate arbiters of what is legal, and given that the Obama administration had a legal memorandum prepared which explained why it was lawful to target al-Awlaki for a drone attack, a legal touchstone prepared by the Obama administration is already in place.

Lastly Judge Collyer claimed that a *Bivens* damage action would raise foreign policy questions because al-Awlaki "was a dual U.S.-Yemeni citizen who was killed in Yemen."[43] What is peculiar about this claim is that it is not at all clear what foreign policy issues would be raised in a damage action not already

---

[41] Al-Aulaqi v. Panetta, 35 F. Supp. 3d 56, 79 (D.D.C. 2014).
[42] *Id.*
[43] *Id.*

raised and discussed by the Obama administration. The administration conceded that it killed al-Awlaki in Yemen, and it claimed that the targeted killing was lawful because al-Awlaki constituted an imminent threat, and because it was not possible to capture him. Under these circumstances the foreign policy questions that might arise in the course of the litigation would seem quite redundant to the considerations already in the news and comparatively minor to the central question of the legality of the killing.

Two months after Judge Collyer dismissed the action, the relatives of the three United States citizens killed in American drone strikes without trial, including Anwar al-Awlaki and his teenage son, Abdulrahman al-Awlaki, decided not to appeal Judge Collyer's dismissal of their lawsuit. In a statement, Nasser al-Awlaki, the father of Mr. Awlaki and the grandfather of Abdulrahman, said that "he had lost faith in the American courts."[44] He added: "A country that believes it does not even need to answer for killing its own is not the America I once knew ... The government has killed a 16-year-old American boy. Shouldn't it at least have to explain why?"[45]

President Obama has emphasized that his "single most important responsibility as President is to keep the American people safe. It's the first thing that I think about when I wake up in the morning. It's the last thing that I think about when I go to sleep at night." He has stated that America's safety in the long run requires the enlistment "of our most fundamental values" such as liberty, justice, equality, and dignity. Indeed, he has argued that "[t]ime and again, our values have been our best national security asset—in war and peace; in times of ease and in eras of upheaval," and he has stated that these values have accounted for the emergence of the United States from a string of tiny colonies to the world's most powerful nation, and that is the reason why "enemy soldiers have surrendered to us in battle," why other nations have become allies, and why America defeated fascism and outlasted communism. In keeping America strong, Obama has insisted that America honor the "rule of law and due process" and that it respects "checks and balances and accountability."[46]

Obama understood that his administration's commitment to these fundamental values and the rule of law would be strengthened if the administration was transparent. But he qualified the importance of transparency by the profound importance of keeping some information secret, information such as "the movement

---

[44] Charlie Savage, *Relatives of Victims of Drone Strikes Drop Appeal*, N.Y. Times, June 3, 2014, http://www.nytimes.com/2014/06/04/us/relatives-of-victims-of-drone-strikes-drop-appeal.html.

[45] Nasser al-Awlaki, Opinion, *The Drone That Killed My Grandson*, N.Y. Times, July 17, 2013, http://www.nytimes.com/2013/07/18/opinion/the-drone-that-killed-my-grandson.html?_r=0.

[46] President Barack Obama, Remarks on National Security (May 21, 2009), https://www.whitehouse.gov/the-press-office/remarks-president-national-security-5-21-09.

of our troops, our intelligence-gathering, or the information we have about a terrorist organization and its affiliates. In these and other cases, lives are at stake."[47] To illustrate how his commitments translated into concrete steps, Obama pointed out that some weeks before he had authorized the disclosure of legal memoranda issued by the Bush administration's Office of Legal Counsel on enhanced interrogation techniques.[48] In releasing the memos he explained that he did so because "the existence" of the enhanced interrogation techniques authorized by the memos "was already widely known, the Bush administration had acknowledged its existence, and I had already banned those methods." Or, in sum, he said that he released the memos because "there was no overriding reason to protect them."[49]

But Obama emphasized that the juxtaposition of security and transparency presented a "delicate balance" and that he "never argued"—never would—"that our most sensitive national security matters should simply be an open book." He continued: "I will never abandon—and will vigorously defend—the necessity of classification to defend our troops at war, to protect sources and methods, and to safeguard confidential actions that keep the American people safe." But, Obama offered: "Whenever we cannot release certain information to the public for valid national security reasons, I will insist that there is oversight of my actions—by Congress *or by the courts*."[50] Such oversight was part of the system of "checks and balances" because "someone must always watch over the watchers—especially when it comes to sensitive administration—information."[51]

It is against these general considerations that we consider the Obama administration's resistance to publicly disclosing the legal memorandum prepared by the Office of Legal Counsel that set forth the legal reasoning Obama claimed justified using a drone to kill al-Awlaki.

As a general idea, the fact that some law is secret is an oxymoron and undemocratic. After all, how are the people to have an effective voice in governing themselves if the laws themselves are secret? And how is the average person to comply with the law if the law itself is secret? And although it is generally assumed that "ignorance of the law is no excuse"—at least generally not an excuse—that generalization is based in part on the idea that the public has some idea of what the law is, and that assumption is implausible if the law is deliberately kept secret. Indeed, the idea that the law be publicly known surely provides one of the

---

[47] *Id.*

[48] To highlight the importance of his commitment to the rule of law while keeping the American people safe, Obama contrasted his approach to the Bush administration's approach. In doing so, he ended waterboarding, promised to close Guantanamo, and pledged to review each of the detainee cases still at Guantanamo. *Id.*

[49] *Id.*

[50] *Id.* (emphasis added).

[51] *Id.*

indispensable supports for the constitutional value that a fair regard for due process requires that a person have notice of the boundary that separates conduct that is lawful from conduct that is not lawful. Absent such clarity, a person might inadvertently cross over the boundary or unintentionally avoid exercising all the rights guaranteed by the Constitution for fear of inadvertently trespassing into criminal conduct.[52]

As odd as it may seem that some law should be secret, there are reasons for this dynamic. Generally the law that is secret is not law embodied in congressional statutes aimed at regulating the conduct of the general public. Instead, secret law that becomes the subject of controversial efforts to make it public is mainly—but not always—executive branch interpretations of the Constitution, statutes, treaties, or international law as that interpretation relates to executive conduct pertaining to national security. And to the extent that the national security initiative is itself secret, a memorandum of law that describes the initiative and sets forth a legal justification for it must also be secret.

Nonetheless, oxymoron or not, the United States today has a body of law pertaining to national security that is secret. For example, after 9/11 the Bush administration claimed that the president had the authority to monitor communications of U.S. citizens with individuals living outside the United States without securing a warrant from the secret FISA court. The Bush administration kept the existence of this NSA surveillance program secret on the ground that its disclosure would undermine the capacity of America's intelligence agencies to gather critical information necessary to protect the nation. In turn, the administration claimed that the legal memorandum prepared by Office of Legal Counsel of the Department of Justice setting forth the legal reasons supporting the assertion of executive authority must be kept secret for the same reason: to protect the effectiveness of the surveillance initiative. And so the surveillance program and the relevant memorandum of law were secret until the surveillance program itself was disclosed, which was later followed by disclosures that detailed the controversy within the Bush administration over the program's legality.[53]

---

[52] One student of the subject, Alan Butler, has observed that "[s]ecret law undermines our system of checks and balances by disabling the democratic oversight by which the public governs its government." Alan Butler, *Standing Up to* Clapper: *How to Increase Transparency and Oversight of FISA Surveillance*, 48 New Eng. L Rev. 55, 87 (2013). Butler also commented: "[c]onstitutional and common law doctrines dating back to the Magna Carta are predicated on the notion that in order that 'a law may be obeyed, it is necessary that it should be known; that it may be known, it is necessary that it be promulgated.'" *Id.* at 86 n.193. Butler, in addition to referencing Jeremy Bentham, *Of Promulgation of the Laws, and Promulgation of the Reasons Thereof,* referenced Lon L. Fuller's *The Morality of Law* (1964) for the proposition that the promulgation of the law "is a central requirement of democracy; the failure to promulgate results in a 'failure to make law.'" *Id.* at 86.

[53] *See* Jack Goldsmith, Power and Constraint: The Accountable Presidency After 9/11, 240 (2012).

This example succinctly highlights the dilemma of secret law. If the surveillance program was necessary to national defense, if it was legal, and if its effectiveness depended on keeping its existence secret, protecting the secrecy of the legal memorandum that described the program and contained legal arguments upholding the program's legality made perfect sense. But if the surveillance program was unlawful, and if it constituted an abuse of executive power in violation of the Constitution, then protecting the secrecy of the legal memorandum deprived the nation of a discussion of important public policy.

Although it may be a surprise, a citizen has no constitutional right to demand that the executive disclose a legal memorandum—whether classified or not—setting forth a controversial and important interpretation of the Constitution or of a statute. Generally, as a matter of constitutional law, the executive has a right to disclose only that information it decides to disclose. There are exceptions such as when a court may subpoena certain documents[54] or if a statute that does not violate the president's constitutional authority grants a right of access to certain information. But neither of these circumstances vests the citizen with a general right to demand certain information from the executive. As a result, in the case of secret law, a citizen's right to demand information depends on the Freedom of Information Act (FOIA).

Quite independently of the effort to enjoin the targeting killing of al-Awlaki and the effort to recover damages for the targeted killing itself, there were two legal efforts—one in Washington and one in New York—to force the Obama administration to make public the legal memorandum it prepared that set forth the legal basis for killing al-Awlaki. Our purposes are amply served by focusing on the New York case aimed at securing the memorandum setting forth the legal reasoning the Obama administration relied upon to kill al-Awlaki.[55]

---

[54] United States v. Nixon, 418 U.S. 683 (1974).

[55] Although not discussed in the text, the *Washington* case reveals the extraordinary extent to which the Obama administration has litigated issues concerning its drone policies and practices. Judge Rosemary M. Collyer, who thirty months later would decide that al-Awlaki's estate had no remedy against senior Obama officials for his death, decided that the Obama administration had no legal duty under the Freedom of Information Act to confirm or deny that the CIA had records sought by the ACLU relevant to the use of drones for killing humans. American Civ. Liberties Union v. DOJ, 808 F. Supp. 2d 280 (D.D.C. 2011). Although the statute establishes a "strong presumption" in favor of disclosure, and although the Obama administration has echoed the importance of transparency, the Freedom of Information Act as construed by the courts, allows a federal agency, including the CIA, to "refuse to confirm or deny the existence of responsive records" when providing such a response would harm an interest protected under the statute by one of its exemptions. *Id.* at 286. A response that refuses to confirm or deny is termed a "Glomar response," which takes its "name from the Hughes Glomar Explorer, an oceanic research vessel at issue in the case that first authorized the government to refuse to confirm or deny the existence of records responsive to a FOIA request." *Id.*

The central issue in the case was not whether the ACLU request fell within one of the FOIA exemptions, thus allowing the CIA to submit a Glomar response, but rather whether the former CIA director, Leon J. Panetta, had "officially admitted that some or all of the requested records exist[ed] so that they are no longer FOIA exempt." *Id.* at 293.

In considering this issue, it is important that the ACLU inquiry be carefully defined. The ACLU did not ask the CIA to admit that it was involved in any way with selecting targets for attacks or in implementing the attacks. Nor did the ACLU inquire as to whether the CIA helped to secure intelligence that was used by others in making the drone attacks effective. Instead, the ACLU requested that the CIA admit that it had some or all of the identified records. In response, the CIA maintained that if it were compelled to respond to the FOIA request as to whether it did or did not have the requested records, its response would "reveal whether or not the CIA was involved or interested in drone strike operations," to which the ACLU argued that Panetta's statements had officially acknowledged that if the CIA was not involved in the drone program it was at least "interested" in the drone program. *Id.*

Under the law at the time, if there had been an official acknowledgment, a party was entitled to its disclosure over an agency's otherwise valid objection that the disputed information was initially exempt from disclosure under the provisions of the statute. As for what constituted an official acknowledgment, the district judge stated that prior decisions had established demanding standards. Thus, to be officially acknowledged: "(1) the information requested must be as specific as the information previously released; (2) the information requested must match the information previously disclosed; (3) the information requested must already have been made public through an official and documented disclosure." *Id.* In short, to satisfy the official acknowledgment standard, the information previously disclosed must have been officially disclosed, as opposed to leaked, and the disclosed information must "match" the information requested.

At the time that the plaintiffs in this case submitted its papers to court, the previously disclosed information it relied upon were statements by Leon J. Panetta, who was, at the time he made the statements, the director of the CIA. Those disclosures were revealing and may have prompted the ACLU lawyers to be hopeful. Thus, on May 18, 2009, Panetta delivered remarks at the Pacific Council on International Policy, and in response to a question concerning the effectiveness of "remote drone strikes" in Pakistan, Panetta stated: "[O]bviously because these are covert and secret operations I can't go into particulars. I think it does suffice to say that these operations have been very effective because they have been very precise in terms of the targeting and it involved a minimum of collateral damage. . . .. I can assure you that in terms of that particular area, it is very precise and it is very limited in terms of collateral damage and, very frankly, it's the only game in town in terms of confronting and trying to disrupt the al-Qaeda leadership." Leon E. Panetta, Remarks at the Pacific Council on International Policy (May 18, 2009), https://www.cia.gov/news-information/speeches-testimony/directors-remarks-at-pacific-council.html. About ten months later, Panetta was quoted in the *Washington Post* commenting on "[r]elentless attacks against al-Qaeda in the Pakistan tribal region" and crediting an "increasingly aggressive campaign," including more frequent strikes and better coordination with Pakistan," for driving the leadership of al-Qaeda into hiding and disrupting its ability to mount attacks. " 'It's pretty clear from all the intelligence we are getting that they are having a very difficult time putting together any kind of command and control, that they are scrambling. And that we really do have them on the run.' " Joby Warrick and Peter Finn, *CIA Director Says Secret Attacks in Pakistan Have Hobbled al-Qaeda*, Wash. Post, Mar. 18, 2010, http://www.washingtonpost.com/wp-dyn/content/article/2010/03/17/AR2010031702558.html. The next day in commenting on a *Wall Street Journal* report that a drone strike had killed a top al-Qaeda leader, Panetta confirmed that "we believe he [the target] was one of those who was involved in providing the explosives for the Khost attack," and added: "No. 1 that we are not going to hesitate to go after them wherever they try to hide, and No. 2 that we are continuing to target their leadership." Siobhan Gorman and Jonathan Weisman, *Drone Kills Suspect in CIA Suicide Bombing*, Wall St. J, Mar. 18, 2010, http://www.wsj.com/articles/

This New York action actually began as two separate actions, one initiated by the ACLU and one initiated by the *New York Times,* which were then consolidated before District Judge Colleen McMahon, who had been appointed to the federal bench by President Clinton. In a lengthy and thoughtful opinion, McMahon's main focus was on the plaintiffs' request that the court order the "disclosure of the precise legal justification for the Administration's conclusion that it is lawful for employees or contractors of the United States Government to target for killing persons, including specifically United States citizens, who are suspected of ties to Al-Qaeda or other terrorist groups," and to do that "far from any recognizable 'hot' field of battle." McMahon noted that the Obama administration "has engaged in public discussion of the legality of targeted killing, even of citizens, but in cryptic and imprecise ways, generally without citing to any statute or court decision that justifies its conclusions."[56]

But as much as Obama did say about the law and the targeted killing of suspected terrorists, McMahon felt that prior decisions prevented her from

SB1000142405274870405900457512812344955I524. And then, two weeks later in a television interview, Panetta stated that "we are engaged in the most aggressive operations in the history of the CIA in that part of the world, and the result is that we are disrupting their leadership. We've taken down more than half of their Taliban leadership, of their Al-Qaeda leadership. We just took down number three in their leadership a few weeks ago." Interview by Jake Tapper with Leon Panetta, CIA director (June 27, 2010).

In assessing whether there had been an official acknowledgment that undermined the CIA's Glomar defense, Judge Collyer provided two lines of analysis. The first stated incorrectly that the ACLU requested that the CIA confirm or deny that "it is or is not involved in the drone strike program." On that score Judge Collyer argued that the "statements cited by Plaintiffs demonstrate that the CIA has carefully and specifically refused to acknowledge any role or interest in such program," and therefore there had been no official acknowledgment that the CIA was in fact involved in the drone strikes. American Civ. Liberties Union v. DOJ, 808 F. Supp. 2d 280, 296 (D.D.C. 2011). Judge Collyer's second line of analysis correctly addressed the ACLU request that the CIA confirm or deny the "existence of CIA records on drone strikes," and with regard to that matter, she concluded that Panetta did not explicitly acknowledge the existence of any CIA records concerning drone strikes. *Id.*

By the time the Court of Appeals decided the appeal in the case, eighteen months had passed since the district court ruling and during that time not only had there had been considerable national discussion of the use of drones, but many within the Obama administration had addressed the matter, including President Obama and his assistant for Homeland Security and Counterterrorism, John Brennan. The appeals court made a critical distinction between a request that would force the CIA to confirm or deny that it was involved in the operation of the drones or that it was "interested" in the drone program, and it insisted it was only the latter issue that was involved in this case. With that distinction in mind and after reviewing the public record, the appeals court concluded that the "CIA asked the courts" to construe the Glomar doctrine "too far—to give their imprimatur to a fiction of deniability that no reasonable person would regard as plausible. 'There comes a point where . . . Court[s] should not be ignorant as judges of what [they]know as men' and women . . . We are at that point with respect to the question of whether the CIA has any documents regarding the subject of drone strikes." ACLU v. CIA, 710 F.3d 422, 431 (D.C. Cir. 2013).

[56] New York Times Co. v. United States DOJ, 915 F. Supp. 2d 508, 515 (S.D.N.Y. 2013).

finding a "way around the thicket of laws and precedents that effectively allow the executive Branch of our Government to proclaim as perfectly lawful certain actions that seem on their face incompatible with our Constitution and laws, while keeping the reasons for its conclusion a secret." McMahon confessed that the "Alice-in-Wonderland nature" of her decision was not lost on her.[57]

Although Judge McMahon's opinion discussed many aspects of the request, the one that was central to her opinion and to the appeal of her decision focused on whether the Obama administration's public discussion of the legality of the drone killing of al-Awlaki constituted a waiver of its right to keep the legal memorandum secret. And central to the resolution of that legal question was the legal standard Judge McMahon felt compelled to apply in deciding whether the administration had or had not waived its right to keep the memorandum out of the public's reach.

McMahon stated that the Second Circuit "has made clear that it is the rare case where the Government waives" its statutory protection to keep information secret and that a "limited exception is permitted only where the government has officially disclosed the specific information the requester seeks." Indeed, Judge McMahon concluded that the Second Circuit had ruled that a waiver is governed by a "strict test" which provides: "Classified information that a party seeks to obtain or publish is deemed to have been officially disclosed only if it (1) '[is] as specific as the information previously released,' (2) 'match[es] the information previously disclosed,' and (3) was 'made public through an official and documented disclosure.' "[58]

The waiver test as set forth by the circuit court that Judge McMahon felt obligated to respect is exceedingly exacting, and in McMahon's opinion the facts in this case did not meet the test. Although McMahon gave many examples as to why the facts of the case did not satisfy the demanding waiver test, one illustrates the demanding challenge the legal test presented.

Attorney General Eric Holder gave a speech at Northwestern University School of Law on March 5, 2012, in which he discussed "the legal considerations that the Executive Branch takes into account before targeting a suspected terrorist for killing." As Judge McMahon commented, the speech, which she characterized as "a far cry from a 'general discussion' of the subject matter," "constitutes a sort of road map of the decision-making process that the Government goes through before deciding to 'terminate' someone 'with extreme prejudice.' " But the judge concluded the "Holder speech is also a far cry from a legal research memorandum." And then she summarized her view of the matter: "The speech mentions relevant doctrines but does not explain the

---

[57] *Id.* at 515–516.

[58] *Id.* at 536.

actual reasoning that led the Government to conclude that the targeted kill-ing of a suspected terrorist complies with the law of war, or accords a suspect due process of law, or does not constitute assassination. In fact, . . . [Holder] did not cite to a single specific constitutional provision (other than the Due Process Clause), domestic statute (other than the AMUF), treaty obligation, or legal precedent. Nor did he address many key matters that are covered by the FOIA requests: for example, Mr. Holder did not address why the Treason Clause was not violated by killing a United States citizen who was engaged in apparently treasonous activities—or, in the alternative, why the Treason Clause simply did not apply." Thus, Judge McMahon concluded, ". . . no lawyer worth his salt would equate Mr. Holder's statements with the sort of robust analysis that one finds in a properly constructed legal opinion addressed to a client by a lawyer."[59] Although Judge McMahon leaves open the possibility that something less than a detailed discussion of every aspect of the legal mem-orandum would satisfy the Second Circuit test, the possibility that the Second Circuit test would ever be satisfied seems most remote.

During the twenty months between Judge McMahon's decision and the deci-sion of the Second Circuit reversing her judgment on August 25, 2014, high-level Obama administration officials made many statements regarding the law per-taining to the use of drones to kill American citizens and the administration dis-closed one important document. The statements were made by John O. Brennan at congressional hearings on his nomination to be director of the CIA; Attorney General Eric Holder in a letter to Senator Patrick J. Leahy, chairman of the Senate Judiciary Committee; and President Obama in an address at the National Defense University. The document was a "16-page, single-spaced DOJ White Paper" ini-tially leaked to Michael Isikoff, a reporter with NBC, on February 4, 2013, and then "officially disclosed by DOJ . . . four days later."[60] These statements and the White Paper prompted the Second Circuit to rule against the executive.

The executive put forth several arguments to the Court of Appeals as to why the legal memorandum, which was prepared by the Office of Legal Counsel, a separate department within the Department of Justice, should remain secret. The disclosure was barred because of the attorney–client privilege and be-cause of what is termed the "deliberative process privilege." The disclosure would "inhibit agencies throughout the government from seeking OLC's legal advice"; the readers of the legal memorandum "might find the reasoning defi-cient" since the "memorandum refers to earlier OLC documents that remain classified." Disclosure was barred because a "logical" or "plausible" connection

---

[59] *Id.* at 537.
[60] N.Y. Times Co. v. United States DOJ, 756 F.3d 100, 110–111 (2d Cir. 2014).

existed between the information in dispute and the protection [of] "intelligence sources and methods from foreign discovery."[61]

The Court of Appeals did not find any of the arguments persuasive. The court accepted that certain matters were indeed protected by the attorney–client privilege and by the deliberative process that seeks to protect discussions and memoranda developed during a period of consultation and evaluation as legal and policy positions are developed. At the same time, the court recognized that the executive could waive any privilege that would otherwise cover the legal memorandum in dispute. In response to the claim that a finding of a waiver would "inhibit" government agencies from seeking the advice of the Office of Legal Counsel, the court concluded that the claim "proves too much," for if it "were upheld, waiver of privileges protecting legal advice could never occur." The court conceded that in some situations the disclosure of a legal analysis could disclose "a planned operation" or "be so intertwined with facts entitled to protection that disclosure of the analysis would disclose such facts,"[62] but the court argued that that was not the situation in this case since the court had already redacted the legal analysis to guard against such a disclosure.

The court dismissed the idea that readers would be confused or misled if only the legal memorandum in dispute were disclosed. The court stated that the legal memorandum is "rather elaborate, and readers should have no difficulty assessing the reasoning on its own terms." The court added that this argument seems like a lawyer's construct solely intended for a courtroom since there was no evidence that the executive had any similar "concern when it released the DOJ White Paper," and that the executive "always has the option of disclosing redacted versions of previous OLC advice."[63]

With regard to a waiver, which was the argument central to the appeals court's opinion, the court claimed that the "numerous statements of senior Government officials discussing the lawfulness of targeted killing of suspected terrorists," which the district judge had characterized as amounting to an "extensive public relations campaign," "establish the context" in which to assess the validity of the waiver even if they "are not themselves sufficiently detailed to establish waiver of the secrecy of the legal analysis in the OLC-DOD Memorandum."[64] The court did not explain what the utility or importance was of what it termed "context," but given its opinion it certainly did not mean that the context of the case was helpful to the executive's claims for secrecy. Indeed, what seems more plausible is that the circuit court was deeply troubled that

---

[61] *Id.* at 114–119.
[62] *Id.*
[63] *Id.* at 117.
[64] *Id.* at 114–115.

the executive could, as Judge McMahon wrote, "proclaim as perfectly lawful certain actions that seem on their face incompatible with our Constitution and laws, while keeping the reasons for its conclusions secret,"[65] and therefore was inclined to find its way through the "thicket of laws and precedents"[66] that Judge McMahon believed barred her from reaching a conclusion that left her feeling that her ruling resonated with a sense of fairness and justice portrayed in *Alice in Wonderland.*

The court's disposition to find a waiver was immensely strengthened by the sixteen-page, single-spaced Department of Justice White Paper that the executive had made public, which it compared to the forty-one-page legal memorandum in dispute, dated July 16, 2010, which it reviewed *in camera.* The panel concluded that the White Paper "virtually parallels" the secret legal memorandum "in its analysis of the lawfulness of targeted killing," and that the "substantial overlap in the legal analyses in the two documents fully establishes that the Government may no longer validly claim that the legal analysis in the Memorandum is a secret."[67]

The Second Circuit decision was a milestone. It capped a lengthy legal struggle in which the executive sought diligently and strenuously to keep the legal memorandum secret. But as forceful as the court was in insisting that the executive had waived the right to keep the legal analysis secret, the panel emphasized that its ruling does not mean that "the entire document must be disclosed;" it "applies only to the portions of the OLC-DOD Memorandum that explain legal reasoning."[68] Moreover, the panel stated that even within the sections setting forth legal analysis the executive claims that certain information should remain secret, and at least to one of the subjects, a subject that remains redacted, the court agreed. Nonetheless, the court overruled the executive's objection that the identity of Yemen as the country in which al-Awlaki was killed should be disclosed and that the role of the CIA in the use of drones should be kept secret since that information had been authoritatively disclosed by officials.

In reaching this result, the Second Circuit panel took a step away from the exceedingly demanding deferential standard the district judge felt compelled to respect and that a prior Second Circuit panel had actually set forth. The panel noted that legal standard required as a condition of waiver that the information in the public domain be as specific as the secreted information, that

---

[65] New York Times Co. v. United States DOJ, 915 F. Supp. 2d 508, 516 (S.D.N.Y. 2013).
[66] *Id.* at 515.
[67] N.Y. Times Co. v. United States DOJ, 756 F.3d 100, 116 (2d Cir. 2014).
[68] *Id.* at 117.

the information released match the secret information, and that the information in the public domain had been made public through an official and documented disclosure. In concluding that legal standard had been satisfied in this case, the panel concluded that the "'matching'" requirement did not require "absolute identity" because such a requirement "would make little sense"; if the exact information was already in the public domain, there would be no need to demand the release of identical but still "secret" information.[69]

It took five years after the disputed legal memorandum was completed and four years after the executive killed al-Awlaki by a drone for a court to order the executive to make public the legal reasoning underlying its claim that the killing of an American citizen outside of a war zone was lawful, and then to do so with redactions. At that point, the executive had at least three choices. It could comply with the decision; it could ask the entire Second Circuit to consider the case en banc; or it could seek Supreme Court review of the court of appeals ruling.

It seems that the Obama administration, which had throughout fiercely opposed disclosing the legal memorandum, was not about to accept the Second Circuit's decision. But by the time of the ruling, President Obama had nominated David Barron to the Court of Appeals for the First Circuit. Barron had been acting head of the Justice Department's Office of Legal Counsel, and the individual who signed the legal memorandum that concluded that "it would be lawful for the government to kill Mr. Awlaki, notwithstanding federal statutes against murdering Americans overseas and protections in the Constitution against unreasonable seizures and depriving someone of life without due process of [the] law." Because of that pending appointment, senators who favored the disclosure of the secret legal memorandum pressured the Obama administration to release "the redacted memo rather than appeal" the court ruling ordering its disclosure by taking the position that they would otherwise block Barron's appointment. In the end, the Obama administration agreed not to appeal the ruling and to disclose the redacted memorandum, which it in fact did after "some delay" as the administration "successfully sought permission from the court to redact additional details."[70]

---

[69] *Id.* The panel's doctrinal step to moderate its deference was even more pronounced in a footnote accompanying its text in which it stated that "a rigid application" of the three-part test for waiver "may not be warranted in view of its questionable provenance," a claim that it explicated in the footnote. *Id.* at 120 n.19.

[70] Charlie Savage, *Court Releases Large Parts of Memo Approving Killing of American in Yemen: Targeting Anwar al-Awlaki Was Legal, Justice Department Said*, N.Y. Times, June 23, 2014, http://www.nytimes.com/2014/06/24/us/justice-department-found-it-lawful-to-target-anwar-al-awlaki.html.

A review of the efforts of the *New York Times* and the ACLU to make public the memorandum of law setting forth the legal reasoning as to why the drone killing of al-Awlaki was lawful is highly revealing. It reveals a strident Obama administration determined to betray its commitment to transparency by hiding behind a veil of national security secrecy the legal reasoning it relied upon to kill al-Awlaki. But just as important, it reveals how exceedingly responsive the judiciary is to executive claims that disclosure will harm national security.

Putting the matter that way is meant more as an observation than a criticism of the New York appeals court. After all, that panel broke ranks with other courts and its own precedent and exhibited a judicial determination and independence in regrettably short supply. But, as the facts set out earlier make plain, it is very difficult to convince a court to rule against the executive when the executive waves the flag of national security, and that is so even in circumstances in which the case in favor of ruling against the executive is exceptionally powerful.[71]

---

[71] A recent court decision made it crystal clear just how determined the Obama administration is to contest every claim to make secret law public and just how solicitous federal courts can be to the executive. Thus, Charlie Savage reported on November 23, 2015, that the United States Court of Appeals—the court that ruled in favor of disclosing the legal memorandum the administration claimed set forth the argument that it was lawful for the United States to kill al-Awalaki—ruled that Justice Department "could continue to conceal internal documents related to targeted killings in the fight against Al Qaeda." Charlie Savage, *Appeals Court Rules on Targeted Killings Can Stay Classified*, N.Y. Times, Nov. 23, 2015.

8

The Court Is Secret

Not only has the post–World War II National Security State created a context for the proliferation of secret evidence and secret law, as well as the judicially crafted legal doctrines that substantially insulate the executive in national security cases from meaningful judicial review, but it has also ushered into existence a secret court. This court breaks with historic tradition by rendering orders and making law in secret and by being nonadversarial in character. Moreover, the emergence of the National Security State and the rise of the Imperial Presidency have so altered political and legal expectations that this secret court—the Foreign Intelligence Surveillance Court (FISC) established by the Congress in 1978 through the Foreign Intelligence Surveillance Act (FISA)[1]—was conceived of and publicly celebrated[2] as an important reform that sought to assure that executive

---

[1] 50 U.S.C. § 1801 et seq.
[2] For example, in his signing statement, President Carter said:

> The bill requires, for the first time, a prior judicial warrant for *all* electronic surveillance for foreign intelligence or counterintelligence purposes in the United States in which communications of U.S. persons might be intercepted. It clarifies the Executive's authority to gather foreign intelligence by electronic surveillance in the United States. It will remove any doubt about the legality of those surveillances which are conducted to protect our country against espionage and international terrorism. It will assure FBI field agents and others involved in intelligence collection that their acts are authorized by statute and, if a U.S. person's communications are concerned, by a court order. And it will protect the privacy of the American people. . . . In short, the act helps to solidify the relationship of trust between the American people and their Government. It provides a basis for the trust of the American people in the fact that the activities of their intelligence agencies are both effective and lawful. It provides enough secrecy to ensure that intelligence relating to national security can be securely acquired, while permitting review by the courts and Congress to safeguard the rights of Americans and others. (Jimmy Carter, Statement on Signing S. 1566 Into Law 1853 (1978), http://www.cnss.org/data/files/Surveillance/FISA/Carter_FISA_Signing_Statement.pdf)

electronic surveillance was consistent with the Constitution and congres-
sionally established boundaries.[3]

Although there were high hopes for the FISA court when it was created, the
secret court has been subject to withering criticism for sorely disappointing the
reformers who promoted it.[4] In fact, to say that many critics consider the court
so inappropriately deferential to the executive that it could be fairly characterized as little more than a "rubber stamp" might well be an understatement, given
that one critic recently took the characterization one step further and asserted
that the court was nothing more than a "kangaroo court with a rubber stamp."[5]

Irony frequently filters through political reforms, but within the context of
legal institutions the ironic history of the FISA court may be in a category by itself.

The background to the FISA statute that created the secret court known as
the Foreign Intelligence Surveillance Court begins as early as 1940, when
President Roosevelt claimed the authority to conduct domestic electronic
surveillance to protect the national security free of judicial and congressional regulation. Roosevelt did this in a memorandum to Attorney General
Robert H. Jackson in which he directed the attorney general to approve the

[3] David S. Kris and J. Douglas Wilson, National Security Investigations & Prosecutions, Vol.
I §3:7 (2d ed. 2012).

> As discussed in Chapter 2, the Church Committee's report detailed the misuse of elec-
> tronic surveillance by the FBI, the CIA, the NSA, and other agencies. The Committee
> identified as one of the "main problems" "the secret surveillance of citizens on the basis
> of their political beliefs, even when those beliefs posed no threat of violence or illegal
> acts on behalf of a hostile foreign power"—a concern that later informed many provi-
> sions of FISA. The Committee also noted that the executive branch had been able to
> abuse electronic surveillance because no judicial or legislative standards existed to
> guide federal agencies . . .. This prompted Congress to consider regulating electronic
> surveillance conducted for national security purposes. At about the same time—and
> for the first time—the executive branch began to urge congressional action in this
> area. (Id. at 106–107)

To be sure, some had reservations about the bill that eventually became the Foreign Intelligence
Surveillance Act. Thus, one careful student of the subject has noted that some groups "such as
the ACLU, worried that if Congress set a wiretap standard too low, it could end up 'authorizing
rather than curtailing intelligence agency abuses.' In other words, would no legislation be better
for civil liberties than bad legislation?" William C. Banks, The Death of FISA, 91 Minn. L. Rev.
1209, 1227–1228, n.121 (2007).

[4] See, e.g., William C. Banks, The Death of FISA, 91 Minn. L. Rev. 1209 (2007); Alan Butler,
Standing Up to Clapper: How to Increase Transparency and Oversight of FISA Surveillance, 48 New
Eng. L. Rev. 55 (2013).

[5] Comment by Russell Tice in Spencer Ackerman, Fisa Chief Judge Defends Integrity of Court
Over Verizon Records Collection, The Guardian (June 6, 2013), http://www.theguardian.com/
world/2013/jun/06/fisa-court-judge-verizon-records-surveillance.

use of "listening devices directed to the conversation or other communications of persons suspected of subversive activities against the Government of the United States, including suspected spies."[6] Although it was uncertain whether "this language was meant to apply to solely domestic subversion," the Supreme Court stated in a 1972 opinion that "electronic surveillance has been used both against organized crime and in domestic security cases at least since 1946," when Attorney General Tom Clark "advised President Truman of the necessity of using wiretaps in 'cases vitally affecting the domestic security.'"[7]

Against that executive practice, two developments prompted the adoption of FISA. The first consisted of a pair of Supreme Court decisions. Although electronic surveillance of telegraph lines was used as early as the Civil War,[8] the question of whether wiretapping of the telegraph or telephone lines violated the Fourth Amendment was not decided by the Supreme Court until 1928. In *Olmstead v. United States*, a majority of the justices concluded that even though the telephone had been invented fifty years earlier,[9] absent a trespass, electronic surveillance was not a search or a seizure within the meaning of the Fourth Amendment. Chief Justice Taft explained:

> The reasonable view is that one who installs in his house a telephone instrument with connecting wires intends to project his voice to those quite outside, and that the wires beyond his house, and messages while passing over them, are not within the protection of the Fourth Amendment. Here those who intercepted the projected voices were not in the house of either party to the conversation.[10]

The consequence of that ruling was to leave the regulation of electronic surveillance to the Congress and the executive. Indeed, the high court all but invited the Congress to enact legislation addressing the matter by making evidence secured from a wiretap inadmissible into evidence in a federal criminal court.[11]

The rule in the *Olmstead* case lasted for a half century, which meant that electronic surveillance of telephone communications was unregulated by the courts

---

[6] Zweibon v. Mitchell, 516 F.2d 594, 673–674 (D.C. Cir. 1975) (en banc). FDR's memo is reprinted in *Zweibon.*

[7] United States v. U.S. Dist. Court (Keith), 407 U.S. 297, 310 n.10 (1972). Or, again as the Court also stated: "Successive Presidents for more than one-quarter of a century have authorized such surveillance in varying degrees, without guidance from the Congress or a definitive decision of this Court." *Id.* at 299.

[8] David S. Kris and J. Douglas Wilson, National Security Investigations & Prosecutions, Vol. I §3:2, 90 (2d ed. 2012).

[9] Olmstead v. United States, 277 U.S. 438 (1928).

[10] *Id.* at 466.

[11] *Id.* at 465–466.

for a century.[12] But in 1967, the Supreme Court changed the rule that the Fourth Amendment did not apply to electronic surveillance absent a trespass and "searches and seizures of tangible property."[13] As the Court wrote in *Katz v. United States*:

> We conclude that the underpinnings of *Olmstead* and *Goldman* have been so eroded by our subsequent decisions that the "trespass" doctrine there enunciated can no longer be regarded as controlling. The Government's activities in electronically listening to and recording the petitioner's words violated the privacy upon which he justifiably relied while using the telephone booth and thus constituted a "search and seizure" within the meaning of the Fourth Amendment. The fact that the electronic device employed to achieve that end did not happen to penetrate the wall of the booth can have no constitutional significance.[14]

Although the Supreme Court concluded for the first time in *Katz* that absent a trespass, electronic surveillance was nonetheless subject to restraints imposed by the Fourth Amendment, it specifically noted that it was expressing no opinion on what, if any, Fourth Amendment safeguards applied to a case involving national security,[15] a circumstance in which the executive asserted that it could engage in electronic surveillance unrestrained by judicial or congressional regulation.[16]

---

[12] It was in the *Olmstead* case that Justice Brandeis penned one of his famous dissents. In this case, he protested against the majority's narrow conception of Fourth Amendment protections. To Brandeis, the idea that the majority narrowed the scope of protection provided by the Fourth Amendment by making a trespass a precondition to its violation missed the entire thrust of the Constitution and of that particular amendment which Brandeis characterized as the "pursuit of happiness." *Id.* at 478. For Brandeis, the grand purpose of the Fourth Amendment was to:

> [P]rotect Americans in their beliefs, their thoughts, their emotions and their sensations. They conferred, as against the government, the right to be let alone—the most comprehensive of rights and the right most valued by civilized men. To protect that right, every unjustifiable intrusion by the government upon the privacy of the individual, whatever the means employed, must be deemed a violation of the Fourth Amendment. (*Id.* at 479)

[13] Katz v. United States, 389 U.S. 347, 352–353 (1967).

[14] *Id.* at 353.

[15] *Id.* at 358 n.23.

[16] Although the executive later argued that the 1968 Omnibus Crime Control and Safe Streets Act "recognized the President's authority to conduct" electronic surveillance in national security matters "without prior judicial approval," the Supreme Court rejected that claim, asserting that the act did not limit or disturb the president's power under the Constitution to protect the nation: "Congress simply left presidential powers where it found them." United States v. U.S. Dist. Court (Keith), 407 U.S. 297, 303 (1972).

Five years after the *Katz* decision, the Supreme Court decided a second and highly important electronic surveillance case. Writing for the Court, Justice Lewis Powell framed the issue as such:

> The issue before us is an important one for the people of our country and their Government. It involves the delicate question of the President's power, acting through the Attorney General, to authorize electronic surveillance in internal security matters without prior judicial approval. Successive Presidents for more than one-quarter of a century have authorized such surveillance in varying degrees, without guidance from the Congress or a definitive decision of this Court. This case brings the issue here for the first time. Its resolution is a matter of national concern, requiring sensitivity both to the Government's right to protect itself from unlawful subversion and attack and to the citizen's right to be secure in his privacy against unreasonable Government intrusion.[17]

The Court ruled that the Fourth Amendment requirement that the executive secure a warrant from a neutral magistrate prior to surveillance applied to domestic national security surveillance. In reaching this result, Powell observed that the rights of citizens "cannot properly be guaranteed if domestic security surveillances may be conducted solely within the discretion of the Executive Branch."[18] Powell also took pains to make certain that the narrowness of the ruling was understood: "this case involves only the domestic aspects of national security. We have not addressed, and express no opinion as to, the issues which may be involved with respect to activities of foreign powers or their agents."[19]

The second development that led to FISA was a report of a congressional committee chaired by Senator Frank Church of Idaho. The Church Committee was established by the Senate by a vote of eighty-two to four on January 27, 1975,[20] and as Frederick A. O. Schwarz Jr., the committee's "chief counsel,"[21] has stated, the "Church Committee . . . conducted the most extensive investigation of a government's secret activities ever, in this country or elsewhere."[22]

The committee report described the conduct of United States intelligence activities since World War II and disclosed to the American public that the intelligence

---

[17] *Id.* at 299.

[18] *Id.* at 316–317.

[19] *Id.* at 321–322.

[20] Frederick A.O. Schwarz Jr., Democracy in the Dark: The Seduction of Government Secrecy 176 (2015).

[21] *Id.* at 1.

[22] *Id.* Later in his study, Schwarz stated that the committee's investigation was the "first—and still the most wide-ranging—investigation of America's secret government." *Id.* at 176.

community "conducted investigations, and otherwise gathered information, in ways that systematically broke the law."[23] Thus, the report concluded that too "many people have been spied upon by too many Government agencies" and the government has "often undertaken the secret surveillance of citizens on the basis of their political beliefs, even when those beliefs posed no threat of violence or illegal acts on behalf of a hostile foreign power." Furthermore, the government has pursued its investigations by using "secret informants," as well as other "intrusive techniques such as wiretaps, microphone 'bugs', surreptitious mail opening, and break-ins." The report noted that the investigations of groups "deemed potentially dangerous—and even of groups suspected of associating with potentially dangerous organizations—have continued for decades, despite the fact that those groups did not engage in unlawful activity."[24] The report shocked the nation.

These two developments produced a strenuous conflict over fundamental political tenets. Until 1978, as one scholar has noted, "no president had ever conceded that the Congress could interpose any set of procedures to confine the constitutional discretion of the president to engage in electronic surveillance to protect the national security."[25] Such assertions of authority were premised on the president's unique political legitimacy and responsibilities within the constitutional scheme, and the belief that a concentration of authority in the presidency was

---

[23] David S. Kris and J. Douglas Wilson, National Security Investigations & Prosecutions, Vol. I §2:2, 39 (2d ed. 2012).

[24] Select Committee on Intelligence Activities Within the United States ("Church Committee"), Intelligence Activities and the Rights of Americans: 1976 US Senate Report on Illegal Wiretaps and Domestic Spying by the FBI, CIA and NSA 10–11 (Red and Black ed. 2007). On January 17, 2014, about seven months after the Snowden disclosures, President Obama publicly acknowledged the intelligence abuses documented by the Church Committee:

> Meanwhile, totalitarian states like East Germany offered a cautionary tale of what could happen when vast, unchecked surveillance turned citizens into informers, and persecuted people for what they said in the privacy of their own homes. . . . In fact, even the United States proved not to be immune to the abuse of surveillance. And in the 1960s, government spied on civil rights leaders and critics of the Vietnam War. And partly in response to these revelations, additional laws were established in the 1970s to ensure that our intelligence capabilities could not be misused against our citizens. In the long, twilight struggle against Communism, we had been reminded that the very liberties that we sought to preserve could not be sacrificed at the altar of national security. (President Barack Obama, Remarks by the President on Review of Signals Intelligence (Jan. 17, 2014), https://www.whitehouse.gov/the-press-office/2014/01/17/remarks-president-review-signals-intelligence)

[25] William C. Banks, The Death of FISA, 91 Minn. L. Rev. 1209, 1211 (2007). As an example of how deeply entrenched this disposition is, consider this. In January of 2007, senior Bush administration officials informed Congress that it would henceforth seek warrants from the FISC for its domestic wiretapping program. But five months later, senior Bush administration officials

required if, as Chief Justice Hughes had written, civil liberties were to be preserved because such liberties "imply the existence of an organized society maintaining public order without which liberty itself would be lost in the excesses of unrestrained abuses."[26] On the other side of the ledger were those considerations Justice Powell referenced in his *Keith* opinion when he wrote:

> There is, understandably, a deep-seated uneasiness and apprehension that this capability will be used to intrude upon cherished privacy of law-abiding citizens. . ... National security cases, moreover, often reflect a convergence of First and Fourth Amendment values not present in cases of "ordinary" crime. . ... Fourth Amendment protections become the more necessary when the targets of official surveillance may be those suspected of unorthodoxy in their political beliefs.[27]

The proposed FISA was sufficiently contentious that the debate over its terms required the attention of both President Ford's and Carter's administrations, and was, in the words of one authority, "the culmination of a multi-branch, multi-year, cross-party initiative directed at bringing the collection of foreign intelligence within a narrowly circumscribed legal framework."[28] More recently, President Obama's Review Group on Intelligence and Communications Technologies characterized the statute as "a carefully designed compromise between those who wanted to preserve maximum flexibility for the intelligence agencies and those who wanted to place foreign intelligence surveillance under essentially the same restrictions as ordinary surveillance activities (at least insofar as the rights of Americans were concerned)."[29]

The 1978 FISA statute, as subsequently amended,[30] is complicated as well as controversial. It sought to provide congressional and judicial oversight of "foreign intelligence surveillance activities while maintaining the secrecy

---

told Congress that the president has the "constitutional authority to decide for himself whether to conduct surveillance without warrants." Michael McConnell, at that time the new director of national intelligence, said that the "president still had the authority under Article II of the Constitution to once again order the N.S.A. to conduct surveillance inside the country without warrants." James Risen, *Administration Pulls Back on Surveillance Agreement, Common Dreams* (May 2, 2007), N.Y. Times, http://www.nytimes.com/2007/05/02/washington/02intel.html?_ r=0.

[26] Cox v. New Hampshire, 312 U.S. 569, 574 (1941).

[27] United States v. U.S. Dist. Court (Keith), 407 U.S. 297, 312–314 (1972).

[28] Laura K. Donohue, *Bulk Metadata Collection: Statutory and Constitutional Considerations*, 37 Harv. J.L. & Pub. Pol'y 757, 783 (2014).

[29] Richard A. Clarke et al., *The NSA Report: Liberty and Security in a Changing World* 21 (2014).

[30] The key amendments were in 1995, 1999, 2006, 2008, and 2011.

necessary to effectively monitor national security threats."[31] The original FISA focused only on electronic surveillance and the collection of foreign intelligence information. Pursuant to the statute, the Department of Justice would apply to the FISC to obtain a warrant authorizing electronic surveillance, and the court would apply a different standard in reviewing the request depending on whether the target was a foreign agent or a U.S. person.[32] The statute "restricted the government's authority to use electronic surveillance *inside the United States* to obtain foreign intelligence from 'foreign powers,'" a term defined to include foreign nations, agents of foreign nations, and "any 'group engaged in international terrorism.'"[33]

---

[31] The Foreign Intelligence Surveillance Act of 1978 (FISA), U.S. Dep't of Justice: Justice Info. Sharing, https://it.ojp.gov/PrivacyLiberty/authorities/statutes/1286 (last updated Sept. 19, 2013); *see also* David S. Kris and J. Douglas Wilson, National Security Investigations & Prosecutions, Vol I. §§4:2, 5:1 (2d ed. 2012). A new court facility with designated judges was required in part because ordinary federal courthouses lacked adequate secure facilities and many federal judges lacked adequate security clearances. Richard A. Clarke et al., The NSA Report: Liberty and Security in a Changing World 22 (2014). FISA also created a new appeals court—the Court of Review—to review FISC orders and decisions. Glenn Greenwald stated in a June 18, 2013 report published in The Guardian that the "primary purpose" of the FISA when initially passed "was to ensure that the US government would be barred from ever monitoring the electronic communications of Americans without first obtaining an individualized warrant from the Fisa court, which required evidence showing 'probable cause' that the person to be surveilled was an agent of a foreign power or terrorist organization." Glenn Greenwald, *Fisa Court Oversight: A Look Inside a Secret and Empty Process*, The Guardian (June 18, 2013), http://www.theguardian.com/commentisfree/2013/jun/19/fisa-court-oversight-process-secrecy.

[32] The term "U.S. person" was defined as U.S. citizens, permanent resident aliens, or U.S. corporations. 50 U.S.C. §1801(i). FISA provided that any federal government agency seeking to use electronic surveillance within the United States for the purpose of advancing foreign intelligence must secure a warrant from the FISC, which would issue only if the government established "'probable cause to believe that the target of the electronic surveillance' is an agent of a foreign power." Richard A. Clarke et al., The NSA Report: Liberty and Security in a Changing World 22 (2014) (quoting 50 U.S.C. §1805). FISA permitted the government to utilize electronic surveillance within the United States not only in circumstances in which probable cause existed to believe that criminal activity was occurring, but probable cause to believe that the "target" of the surveillance was an "agent of a foreign power." *Id.* at 23. It required that information obtained from an electronic intercept "be tied to a specific person or entity, identified as a foreign power or an agent thereof, *before the collection* of the information." Laura K. Donohue, *Bulk Metadata Collection: Statutory and Constitutional Considerations*, 37 Harv. J.L. & Pub. Pol'y 757, 783–784 (2014). To protect political dissidents and to guard against the violation of First Amendment rights more generally, FISA required that probable cause supporting the issuance of an electronic surveillance warrant of U.S. persons—defined as a U.S. citizen or anyone lawfully in the United States—be issued "solely on the basis of otherwise protected First Amendment activities." *Id.* at 766. FISA set forth so-called minimization procedures intended to "restrict the type of information that could be obtained and retained." *Id.* at 784.

[33] Richard A. Clarke et al., The NSA Report: Liberty and Security in a Changing World 21–22 (2014) (quoting 50 U.S.C. §1801(a)).

Since the passage of the original statute, FISA has been amended[34] to address the use of pen registers and trap devices for conducting telephone or email surveillance, physical searches of "premises or property . . . owned, used, possessed by, or . . . in transit to or from a foreign power or an agent of a foreign power," and the obtaining of an order for "third-party production of business records to acquire foreign intelligence information."[35] Although the original statute in retrospect seems more controversial than might have been appreciated at the time when it was characterized as an important reform, the subsequent amendments—especially the post-9/11 amendments—combined with the disclosures made by Edward Snowden have made FISA as well as the FISC the focus of national intense scrutiny and evaluation.

Several factors combine to make it easy to understand why many offer a highly critical assessment of the FISA court.

The tradition is that American courts are open to the public. Thus, courtroom doors are unlocked, and the public and the press are invited to walk in and out and observe the proceedings. Also, many judicial proceedings are televised live. It is assumed that this openness helps assure that the high ideals of the judicial system are promoted, and that this openness encourages judges, lawyers, and parties to conform their conduct to the best traditions of the adversarial system. As the Supreme Court has remarked:

> There can be no blinking the fact that there is a strong societal interest in public trials. Openness in court proceedings may improve the quality of testimony, induce unknown witnesses to come forward with relevant testimony, cause all trial participants to perform their duties more conscientiously, and generally give the public an opportunity to observe the judicial system.[36]

In practice that means that the public and the press may observe as lawyers argue, witnesses testify, and judges rule.[37]

---

[34] As the Review Group noted, FISA changed only "modestly" between 1978 and September 11, 2001. In 1995, Congress expanded FISA to apply to physical searches as well as electronic surveillance; in 1998, FISA was extended to pen register and trap-and-trace orders ("which enable the government to obtain lists of the telephone numbers and e-mails contacted by an individual after the issuance of the order") and to business records, such as documents "kept by common carriers, public accommodation facilities, storage facilities, and vehicle rental facilities." *Id.* at 24.

[35] The Foreign Intelligence Surveillance Act of 1978 (FISA), U.S. Dep't of Justice: Justice Info. Sharing, https://it.ojp.gov/PrivacyLiberty/authorities/statutes/1286 (last updated Sept. 19, 2013).

[36] Gannett Co. v. DePasquale, 443 U.S. 368, 383 (1979).

[37] District Judge Pauley summarized the reasons for public courts:

Moreover, the American judicial tradition is also adversarial, a system that rests on opposing parties each having an opportunity within the rules to present factual and legal matters that advance that party's perspective. The model rests on skepticism regarding human nature and the possibilities of determining the truth, and it assumes that structured legal competitiveness is the most effective way to resolve factual and legal disputes.

In contrast, the FISC is not open to the public, and, except in rare circumstances, the FISC is nonadversarial.[38]

But the suspicions and doubts about the FISC rest on more than the secret, nonadversarial nature of the court. Suspicions and doubts about the court are grounded in the court's annual statistics, and those statistics indicate that the court very rarely denies the executive its requested order (see Table 8.1). These statistics certainly make it understandable why anyone reviewing the court's own report would conclude that the FISA court functions as a rubber stamp.

As much as the FISA court was viewed as a rubber stamp prior to the disclosures made by Edward Snowden in June 2013, Snowden's disclosures strongly reinforced the impression that the FISA court had abdicated its judicial independence by being unduly deferential to the executive. For example, the disclosure of the National Security Agency's (NSA) telephone metadata program reported on June 5, 2013, featured an order signed by FISC Judge Roger Vinson that directed a Verizon Communications subsidiary, Verizon Business Networks Service, "to turn over 'on an ongoing daily basis' to the National Security Agency all call logs

---

Proceedings in Article III courts are public. And the public enjoys a "general right to inspect and copy public records and documents, including judicial records and documents." "The presumption of access is based on the need for federal courts, although independent—indeed, particularly because they are independent—to have a measure of accountability and for the public to have confidence in the administration of justice." (ACLU v. Clapper, 959 F. Supp. 2d 724, 731 (S.D.N.Y. 2013) (citations omitted))

[38] In one rare circumstance, which was in fact adversarial, a news report dated June 13, 2013, in the *New York Times* identifying Yahoo as the adversarial party almost certainly strengthened public suspicions about the FISC. The report, written by Claire Cain Miller, stated:

In a secret court in Washington, Yahoo's top lawyers made their case. The government had sought help in spying on certain foreign users, without a warrant, and Yahoo had refused, saying the broad requests were unconstitutional. The judges disagreed. That left Yahoo two choices: Hand over the data or break the law. So Yahoo became part of the National Security Agency's secret Internet surveillance program, Prism, according to leaked N.S.A. documents, as did seven other Internet companies. Like almost all the actions of the secret court, which operates under the Foreign Intelligence Surveillance Act, the details of its disagreement with Yahoo were never made public beyond a heavily redacted court order, one of the few public documents ever to emerge from the court. The name of the company had not been revealed until now. (Claire Cain Miller, *Secret Court Ruling Put Tech Companies in Data Bind*, N.Y. Times, June 14, 2013, at A1)

Table 8.1 **Traditional FISA Surveillance Orders***

Year	Number of FISA Applications Presented	Number of FISA Applications Approved	Number of FISA Applications Modified	Number of FISA Applications Rejected
1979	199	207	0	0
1980	319	322	1	0
1981	431	433	0	0
1982	473	475	0	0
1983	549	549	0	0
1984	635	635	0	0
1985	587	587	0	0
1986	573	573	0	0
1987	512	512	0	0
1988	534	534	0	0
1989	546	546	0	0
1990	595	595	0	0
1991	593	593	0	0
1992	484	484	0	0
1993	509	509	0	0
1994	576	576	0	0
1995	697	697	0	0
1996	839	839	0	0
1997	749	748	0	0
1998	796	796	0	0
1999	886	880	0	0
2000	1,005	1,012	0	0
2001	932	934	4	0
2002	1,228	1,228	0	0
2003	1,727	1,724	79	4
2004	1,758	1,754	94	0
2005	2,074	2,072	61	0
2006	2,181	2,176	73	1
2007	2,371	2,370	86	4
2008	2,082	2,083	2	1

(continued)

Table 8.1 **Continued**

Year	Number of FISA Applications Presented	Number of FISA Applications Approved	Number of FISA Applications Modified	Number of FISA Applications Rejected
2009	1,329	1,320	14	2
2010	1,511	1,506	14	0
2011	1,676	1,789	30	0
2012	1,789	1,788	40	0
2013	1,588	1,588	34	0

* The statistics set forth in Table 8.1 are drawn from the Electronic Privacy Information Center (EPIC). Foreign Intelligence Surveillance Act Court Orders 1979–2014, epic.org, https://epic.org/privacy/wiretap/stats/fisa_stats.html (last visited Oct. 26, 2015).

'between the United States and abroad' or 'wholly within the United States, including local telephone calls.'"[39] Although the news reports emphasized that the FISC order did not apply to the content of the calls, the order did require that Verizon turn over the telephone numbers of both parties, the "location data, call duration, unique identifiers, and the time and duration of all calls."[40] Moreover, the order gave the appearance that Judge Vinson signed the order without hesitancy or doubt over the legality of the NSA request.

Snowden also made available to the press highly classified documents that disclosed that the executive had been for nearly six years "secretly collecting information on foreigners overseas" from the nation's "largest Internet companies like Google, Facebook and, most recently, Apple, in search of national security threats." Furthermore, the disclosures indicated that the "Internet surveillance program" collected data from online providers, including "e-mail, chat services, videos, photos, stored data, file transfers, video conferencing and log-ins . . . ."[41] Top-secret documents also released by Snowden disclosed that the NSA "is harvesting hundreds of millions of contact lists from personal e-mail and instant messaging accounts around the world, many of them belonging to Americans."[42]

[39] Charlie Savage and Edward Wyatt, *U.S. Secretly Collecting Logs of Business Calls*, N.Y. Times, June 6, 2013, at A16.

[40] Glenn Greenwald, *NSA Collecting Phone Records of Millions of Verizon Customers Daily*, The Guardian (June 6, 2013), http://www.theguardian.com/world/2013/jun/06/nsa-phone-records-verizon-court-order.

[41] Charlie Savage, Edward Wyatt, and Peter Baker, *U.S. Confirms Gathering of Web Data Overseas*, N.Y. Times, June 7, 2013, at A1.

[42] Barton Gellman and Ashkan Soltani, *NSA Collects Millions of E-mail Address Books Globally*, Wash. Post (Oct. 14, 2013), https://www.washingtonpost.com/world/national-security/

The disclosures, especially the report on the telephone metadata surveillance program, hit a raw nerve that triggered a national conversation not only about the proper scope of NSA surveillance, but about whether the FISA court was capable of setting limits on NSA surveillance activities. In fact, the tone of many commentators certainly seemed to indicate that the Vinson order did more than raise that important question; rather, it was thought that the Vinson order established that the FISC was not capable of setting limits to NSA surveillance programs.

It was not just the scope of the NSA surveillance programs and the role of the FISC in approving, for example, the collection of telephone metadata that strengthened the reputation of the FISC as a rubber stamp. That reputation was further strengthened by a *New York Times* report published a month following Snowden's disclosures by Eric Lichtblau, which stated that in "more than a dozen classified rulings, the nation's surveillance court has created a secret body of law giving the National Security Agency the power to amass vast collections of data on Americans while pursuing not only terrorism suspects, but also people possibly involved in nuclear proliferation, espionage and cyberattacks."[43] Lichtblau's report, based on "current and former officials familiar with the court's classified decisions," stated that some rulings were "nearly 100 pages long," and assessed "broad constitutional questions" that established "important judicial precedents, with almost no public scrutiny" that "go far beyond any single surveillance order." Lichtblau pointed out that FISA judges had been persuaded by the executive to give an expansive definition to the concept of "relevance" as that term is used in the statute that governs the surveillance warrants. And his report indicated that the FISC had permitted the expanded scope of the NSA surveillance by utilizing a previously narrowly defined doctrine—termed the "special needs" doctrine—of limited application that permitted screenings at airports, drug testing for railroad workers, or drunken-driving checkpoints to support FISA judge rulings that "the N.S.A.'s collection and examination of Americans' communications data to track possible terrorists does not run afoul of the Fourth Amendment."[44]

Lichtblau's report also highlighted another way in which the FISC had engineered another expansion of the NSA's reach. As Lichtblau wrote: "While President Obama and his intelligence advisers have spoken of the surveillance programs leaked by Snowden mainly in terms of combating terrorism, the court has also interpreted the law in ways that extend into other national

---

nsa-collects-millions-of-e-mail-address-books-globally/2013/10/14/8e58b5be-34f9-11e3-80c6-7e6dd8d22d8f_story.html.

[43] Eric Lichtblau, *In Secret, Court Vastly Broadens Powers of N.S.A.*, N.Y. Times, July 7, 2013, at A1.

[44] *Id.*

security concerns" such as "data on espionage, cyberattacks and other possible threats connected to foreign intelligence' including but not limited to "nuclear proliferation targets." As Lichtblau's report emphasized, the development of this potentially controversial body of law occurred, in contrast to regular judicial proceedings, with the court hearing "only one side of the case—the government," with the court's findings "almost never made public," with only a few known appeals to the specially impaneled FISA Court of Review, and with "no case . . . ever been taken to the Supreme Court."[45]

There was still another report during the weeks following the first Snowden disclosure that further intensified the criticism of the FISC as a rubber stamp. On July 26, 2013, Charlie Savage reported in the *New York Times* that Chief Justice Roberts has used his authority under the FISA statute to designate judges for the FISA court "with conservative and executive branch backgrounds that critics say make the court more likely to defer to government arguments that domestic spying programs are necessary." To support this court-packing charge, Savage claimed that ten out of the then eleven FISA judges had been appointed to the bench by a Republican president, and that six of the eleven had once worked for the federal government, and that since "the chief justice began making assignments in 2005, 86 percent of his choices have been Republican appointees, and 50 percent have been former executive branch officials." In contrast to Roberts's choices, Savage reported that the two previous Chief Justices, Warren E. Burger and William H. Rehnquist, who were also appointed by a Republican president and conservative, made designations to the FISA court that "were more ideologically diverse," with "66 percent of their selections" being Republican appointees and "39 percent [having] once worked for the executive branch."[46]

To illustrate his statistical points, Savage noted that FISA Judge Roger Vinson, who signed that top-secret order directing a Verizon subsidiary to turn over "three months of calling records for all its customers," was appointed to the federal bench by President Ronald Reagan and to the FISA court by Chief Justice Roberts, and had received national attention in 2011 when he struck down "the entirety of President Obama's health care law." When Vinson's term on the FISA court ended in May of 2013, Chief Justice Roberts "replaced him with Judge Michael W. Mosman, who was a federal prosecutor before becoming a judge." As further examples, Savage also noted that then FISA Judge Raymond J. Dearie had been a U.S. Attorney, Judge Reggie B. Walton had been a federal prosecutor "who also worked on drug and crime issues for the White House," and that Judge F. Dennis Saylor IV had been "chief of staff in

[45] *Id.*

[46] Charlie Savage, *Roberts's Picks Reshaping Secret Surveillance Court*, N.Y. Times, July 26, 2013, at A1.

the Justice Department's Criminal Division." And to further solidify his point, Savage noted that the only judge who had been appointed to the federal bench by a Democratic president, Mary A. McLaughlin, "was also a prosecutor."[47]

To provide additional evidence that the chief justice was intentionally using his statutory authority to shape the disposition of the FISA court so that it was sympathetic toward and receptive to executive branch requests to the secret court, Savage noted that the chief justice had used his authority to appoint Republican judges who were thought to be quite conservative to administer the judiciary's important administrative office (Thomas F. Hogan) and to be the presiding judge of the surveillance court (John D. Bates).[48]

The attacks on the FISA court continued and in July of 2013, two former judges who had sat on the FISC made comments that intensified the criticism of the court. Although Judge James Robertson[49] denied that he thought that the FISC judges acted "as 'rubber stamps'" and asserted that the "judges have been scrupulous in pushing back at times against the government, repeatedly sending back flawed warrants,"[50] he also leveled serious criticism at the court—as opposed to the individual judges. In commenting on the fact that FISC lacks an adversarial system, Roberston stated: "Anyone who has been a judge will tell you a judge needs to hear both sides of a case."[51] This view was endorsed by a second former FISC judge, James G. Carr, who wrote in the *New York Times* that Congress should "authorize the FISA judges to appoint, from time to time, independent lawyers with security clearances to serve 'pro bono publico'—for the public's good—to challenge the government when an application for a FISA order raises new legal issues."[52] Carr stated that during his six years of service on the FISC "there were several occasions when I and

---

[47] *Id.*

[48] *Id.*

[49] When Judge Robertson quit the FISC in December 2005, he did so in response to a *New York Times* report submitted by James Risen and Eric Lichtblau, which stated that President Bush had "secretly authorized the National Security Agency to eavesdrop on Americans and others inside the United States to search for evidence of terrorist activity without the court-approved warrants ordinarily required for domestic spying." James Risen and Eric Lichtblau, *Bush Lets U.S. Spy on Callers Without Courts*, N.Y. Times (Dec. 16, 2015), http://www.nytimes.com/2005/12/16/politics/bush-lets-us-spy-on-callers-without-courts.html. Although Judge Robertson gave no reason for his resignation at the time, the *Washington Post* quoted unnamed colleagues as saying he was "concerned that information gained from warrantless NSA surveillance could have then been used to obtain FISA warrants." Carol D. Leonnig and Dafna Linzer, *Spy Court Judge Quits in Protest*, Wash. Post (Dec. 21, 2005), https://www.washingtonpost.com/archive/politics/2005/12/21/spy-court-judge-quits-in-protest/9dfc1009-6854-4f13-aa34-2eac70c251d5.

[50] Associated Press, *Former Judge Admits Flaws with Secret FISA Court*, CBSNews.com (July 9, 2013), http://www.cbsnews.com/news/former-judge-admits-flaws-with-secret-fisa-court.

[51] *Id.*

[52] James G. Carr, Opinion, *A Better Secret Court*, N.Y. Times, July 23, 2013, at A21.

other judges faced issues none of us had encountered before," and although the FISC judges are assisted by a "staff of experienced lawyers," Carr stated that "their help was not always enough given the complexity of the issues."[53]

Robertson also criticized the 2008 amendments to FISA that authorized the court to "approve not simply warrants targeted at individuals, but collection programs aimed at large volumes of data," which he asserted had the consequence of turning FISC "into something like an administrative agency, which makes and approves rules for others to follow."[54] Robertson said that he was " 'frankly

---

[53] *Id.*

[54] Larry Abramson, *Former FISA Judge Questions Court's Approval of Surveillance*, National Public Radio: All Things Considered (July 9, 2013), http://www.npr.org/templates/story/story. php?storyId=200466984. Although Judge Robertson did not explicate his claim that the FISC was acting as if it were an administrative agency, a report in the *Guardian* written by Glenn Greenwald that was published on June 18, 2013, a few weeks before Judge Robertson made his comment before the Privacy and Civil Liberties Oversight Board, most likely illustrates what Judge Robertson meant. *See* Glenn Greenwald, *Fisa Court Oversight: A Look Inside a Secret and Empty Process*, The Guardian (June 18, 2013), http://www.theguardian.com/commentisfree/2013/jun/19/fisa-court-oversight-process-secrecy. For example, in 2008, Congress passed the FISA Amendments Act (FAA) that "legalized much" of President Bush's 2001 secret program to eavesdrop "on the international calls of Americans without any warrants from" the FISC. The 2008 FAA imposed "safeguard" requires that the

> NSA annually submits a document setting forth its general procedures for how it decides on whom it can eavesdrop without a warrant. The Fisa court then approves those general procedures. And then the NSA is empowered to issue "directives" to telephone and internet companies to obtain the communications for whomever the NSA decides—with no external (i.e. outside the executive branch) oversight—complies with the guidelines it submitted to the court. (*Id.*)

Greenwald stated this:

> [O]ffers no real safeguards. That's because no court monitors what the NSA is actually doing when it claims to comply with the court-approved procedures. Once the Fisa court puts its approval stamp on the NSA's procedures, there is no external judicial check on which targets end up being selected by the NSA analysts for eavesdropping. The only time individualized warrants are required is when the NSA is specifically targeting a US citizen or the communications are purely domestic. (*Id.*)

Professor William Banks of Syracuse University stated that as a result of the 2008 FAA, the FISC became "less a court than an administrative entity or ministerial clerk." Nina Totenberg, *Why the FISA Court Is Not What It Used to Be*, National Public Radio (June 18, 2013), http://www.npr.org/ 2013/06/18/191715681/why-the-fisa-court-is-not-what-it-used-to-be. In that regard, on August 15, 2013, the *Washington Post* reported that the NSA "has broken privacy rules or overstepped its legal authority thousands of times each year since Congress granted the agency broad new powers in 2008," and that "[m]ost of the infractions involve[d] unauthorized surveillance of Americans or foreign intelligence targets in the United States." Barton Gellman, *NSA Broke Privacy Rules Thousands of Times per Year, Audit Finds*, Wash. Post (Aug. 15, 2013), https://www.washingtonpost. com/world/national-security/nsa-broke-privacy-rules-thousands-of-times-per-year-audit-finds/ 2013/08/15/3310e554-05ca-11e3-a07f-49ddc7417125_story.html. Although President Obama

stunned'" that the FISC had "created a new body of law broadening the ability of the NSA to use its surveillance programs to target not only terrorists but suspects in cases involving espionage, cyberattacks and weapons of mass destruction."[55] That, he stated emphatically, is "not the bailiwick of judges."[56]

The day after Glenn Greenwald's first report based on the Snowden disclosures appeared in the *Guardian* on June 6, 2013, under the headline "NSA Collecting Phone Records of Millions of Verizon Customers Daily: Top Secret Court Order Requiring Verizon to Hand Over All Call Data Shows Scale of Domestic Surveillance Under Obama," the presiding judge of the FISC, Reggie B. Walton, said that "claims that the body was unduly acquiescent to the government's requests for surveillance orders were 'absolutely false.'"[57] "There is a rigorous review process of applications submitted by the executive branch," he asserted, "spearheaded initially by five judicial branch lawyers who are national security experts and then by the judges, to ensure that the court's authorizations comport with what the applicable statutes authorize."[58]

By itself, Walton's statements would not cause many critics any pause. After all, he is the presiding judge of FISC, and it would be expected that he would

had often emphasized that the NSA was subject to judicial oversight aimed at assuring that the NSA's conduct stayed within lawful boundaries, the presiding FISC judge, Reggie Walton, stated that the "'FISC does not have the capacity to investigate issues of noncompliance,'" and as a result the court is forced to "'rely upon the accuracy of the information that is provided to the Court'" by the government. Carol D. Leonnig, *Court: Ability to Police U.S. Spying Program Limited*, Wash. Post (Aug. 15, 2013), https://www.washingtonpost.com/politics/court-ability-to-police-us-spying-program-limited/2013/08/15/4a8c8c44-05cd-11e3-a07f-49ddc7417125_story.html.

[55] Stephen Braun for the Associated Press, *Foreign Intelligence Surveillance Court System Is Flawed, Former Judge Says*, Huffington Post (July 9, 2013), http://www.huffingtonpost.com/2013/07/09/foreign-intelligence-surveillance-court_n_3567713.html.

[56] Larry Abramson, *Former FISA Judge Questions Court's Approval of Surveillance*, National Public Radio: All Things Considered (July 9, 2013), http://www.npr.org/templates/story/story.php?storyId=200466984. A few weeks before Robertson made his comments before the Privacy and Civil Liberties Oversight Board, Benjamin Wittes, "a Brookings Institution scholar and editor of the influential national-security blog Lawfare," offered a comparable criticism that put the FISC in an unfavorable light when he stated that he was "surprised" by the construction that a FISC judge had given a provision of the FISA—in this case, Judge Roger Vinson broadly construing "relevance" for purposes of §215 of the Patriot Act. "'If that constitutes relevance for purposes of Section 215 [], then isn't all data relevant to all investigations?'" he asked. Spencer Ackerman, *Fisa Chief Judge Defends Integrity of Court over Verizon Records Collection*, The Guardian (June 6, 2013), http://www.theguardian.com/world/2013/jun/06/fisa-court-judge-verizon-records-surveillance.

[57] Spencer Ackerman, *Fisa Chief Judge Defends Integrity of Court over Verizon Records Collection*, The Guardian (June 6, 2013), http://www.theguardian.com/world/2013/jun/06/fisa-court-judge-verizon-records-surveillance.

[58] *Id.* An example of what Judge Walton meant by press reports of statistics indicating that the FISC was a "rubber stamp" is a *New York Times* report filed by Claire Cain Miller dated June

publicly defend the court's integrity. But Walton followed up his general response with a statistical claim that challenged conventional wisdom. In July of
2013, in a letter to Senator Patrick J. Leahy, Walton stated that annual statistics
the FISC provides to Congress, which are "frequently cited to in press reports
as a suggestion that the Court's approval rate of application is over 99 percent,"
fail to "reflect the fact that many applications are altered prior to final submission or even withheld from final submission entirely, often after an indication
that a judge would not approve them."[59]

When Walton wrote that letter, he did not have other statistics that shed any
more light on the conduct of FISC judges. However, ten weeks later, Walton
wrote Senator Leahy a second time,[60] providing new statistics that Walton
thought went some of the distance in establishing that the FISC was far from
being a rubber stamp. "During the three month period from July 1, 2013 through
September 30, 2013," he wrote, "we have observed that 24.4 percent of matters
submitted ultimately involved substantive changes to the information provided
by the government or to the authorities granted as a result of Court inquiry or
action." Walton made it clear that the changes referred to were not "mere typo-
graphical corrections," but he also made it clear he could not represent that the
three-month period was typical, though he had no reason to doubt that it was.[61]

13, 2013, entitled "Secret Court Ruling Put Tech Companies in Data Bind." It stated: "Between
2008 and 2012, only two of 8,591 applications were rejected, according to data gathered by
the Electronic Privacy Information Center." Claire Cain Miller, *Secret Court Ruling Put Tech
Companies in Data Bind*, N.Y. Times, June 14, 2013, at A1.

   [59] Letter from Reggie B. Walton, Presiding Judge, United States Foreign Intelligence Surveillance
Court, to Patrick J. Leahy, Chairman, United States Senate Committee on the Judiciary (July 29,
2013), http://www.leahy.senate.gov/imo/media/doc/Honorable%20Patrick%20J%20Leahy.pdf.

   [60] Letter from Reggie B. Walton, Presiding Judge, United States Foreign Intelligence Surveillance
Court, to Patrick J. Leahy, Chairman, United States Senate Committee on the Judiciary (Oct. 11,
2013), http://www.fisc.uscourts.gov/sites/default/files/Correspondence%20Leahy-11-2013.pdf.

   [61] *Id.* Months later, Walton's reliance on the newly generated statistics to rebut the claim that
FISC was a rubber stamp gained additional support. In February of 2014, a second-year Yale
law student, Conor Clarke, wrote a short article that addressed the question: Was FISC "really a
rubber stamp?" Clarke began his article as such:

> A striking feature of proceedings at the Foreign Intelligence Surveillance Court
> (FISC) is that the executive always wins. Between 1979 and 2012—the first thirty-
> three years of the FISC's existence—federal agencies submitted 33,900 ex parte re-
> quests to the court. The judges denied eleven and granted the rest: a 99.97% rate of
> approval. This "win rate," enviable even to the Harlem Globetrotters, is almost always
> interpreted as evidence that that [sic] the court is failing to do its job. In the media, in
> legal scholarship, and in Congress, there is a widespread sense that a court in which
> the executive always wins can be nothing more than a rubber stamp. (Conor Clarke,
> Note, *Is the Foreign Intelligence Surveillance Court Really a Rubber Stamp? Ex Parte
> Proceedings and the FISC Win Rate*, 66 Stan. L. Rev. Online 125, 125 (2014))

Perhaps Walton is correct. FISC judges may not be rubber stamps, and the FISC is not a "Potemkin court." Perhaps the FISC judges do honor the independence the Constitution grants them and insist on meaningful accountability in reviewing executive requests for surveillance warrants. But it is highly unlikely that Walton will be able to reassure a questioning and skeptical observer that that is the case. [62] The annual statistics, the court's secrecy, the method of appointing judges to the FISA court, all combined with the Snowden disclosures put more of a cloud over the FISC than any chief judge of that court will be able to dispel with a handful of statistics.

To restore public confidence in the FISC requires the enactment of proposed legislative changes. And although the possible restructuring of the FISC is well beyond the purview of this book, the proposed changes that would, at minimum, be required to the enhance the public's trust in the court include a new mechanism for appointing judges to the court so that the chief justice lacks the authority to "pack the court," as Chief Justice Roberts has done; the establishment of an adversarial system that would help judges assess the strength and weaknesses of the executive's allegations both as to the facts and to the law; and the timely disclosure of FISC opinions so that judges felt the pressure or public scrutiny as they decided important matters.

The FISC was the result of scandalous discoveries and reform hopes. It, in turn, has now generated its own scandals and new demands for reform. At the heart of both scandals—the ones in the mid-1970s that resulted in the creation of the FISC and the recent ones that undermined the public's confidence in the FISC—is an effort to control executive surveillance on American citizens. Certainly Congress has an essential role that in imposing on the NSA responsible legislative boundaries and in exercising meaningful oversight to assure that

---

In addition to pointing out that warrant requests are "costly," that the rules governing the issuance of FISC warrants are "clear," that the executive branch lawyers have had extensive experience with the FISC and know what is required to be successful, and that "parties will not bring cases they know they will lose," *Id.* at 128, Clarke then compared the "government's 'win rate'" of 99.97% before the FISC with "the ex parte process by which state and federal law enforcement agencies request warrants under Title III of the Omnibus Crime Control and Safe Streets Act of 1968." Clarke noted that between 1968 and 2012, state and federal agencies made "50,419 requests for Title III wiretaps, and federal courts approved 99.93% of these requests." *Id.* at 130.

[62] Against these developments, the credibility of anyone or any entity that was part of the NSA surveillance program, and that included the judges of the FISC, was tarnished by James R. Clapper, the director of National Intelligence, when the truth of his testimony before the Senate in March of 2013 was undermined by the Snowden disclosures. At the March hearing, Senator Wyden asked Mr. Clapper: "'Does the N.S.A. collect any type of data at all on millions or hundreds of millions of Americans?' 'No, sir,' Mr. Clapper replied. 'Not wittingly.'" Scott Shane and Jonathan Weisman, *Disclosures on N.S.A. Surveillance Put Awkward Light on Previous Denials*, N.Y. Times, June 12, 2013, at A18. In time, Mr. Clapper acknowledged that "his answer had been

the NSA activities remain within constitutional and legislative boundaries. But Congress alone cannot assure that NSA activities remain lawful. The courts have an important role to fulfill in keeping executive surveillance consistent with the law of the land. Unfortunately, the courts have severely undermined their own legitimacy, and whether the FISC, or some reformed version of the FISC, can redeem itself and regain the public's trust cannot be answered in the absence of meaningful reform legislation and sufficient disclosures by the FISC that establish that it is in fact insisting upon meaningful judicial accountability.[63]

problematic, calling it 'the least untruthful' answer he could give." Michael V. Hayden, the former director of both the NSA and the CIA, said: " 'There's not another country in the world where that question would have been asked and answered in a public session.' " Id.

[63] Although President Obama certainly did not characterize the FISC as a "rubber stamp," he gave a speech in January of 2014 on government electronic surveillance that certainly did help fan the fires of FISC critics. In commenting on the importance of protecting individual privacy and the need to impose lawful but sensible restraints on government electronic surveillance, he stated:

> But all of us understand that the standards for government surveillance must be higher [than it is for surveillance by private corporations]. Given the unique power of the state, it is not enough for leaders to say: Trust us, we won't abuse the data we collect. For history has too many examples when that trust has been breached. Our system of government is built on the premise that our liberty cannot depend on the good intentions of those in power; it depends on the law to constrain those in power.

President Barack Obama, Remarks by the President on Review of Signals Intelligence (Jan. 17, 2014), https://www.whitehouse.gov/the-press-office/2014/01/17/remarks-president-review-signals-intelligence. And although he emphasized that it was important to get "the details right," which might have suggested that he was not about to offer details, Obama went on to offer reform recommendations that were in fact detailed. These suggestions applied not only to the NSA but also to the FISC. Obama made it clear that the FISC needed to be more transparent than it had been and he did that in two ways. He reminded the nation that during the last several months his administration had "declassified over 40 opinions and orders of the Foreign Intelligence Surveillance Court." He also stated that "going forward, I'm directing the Director of National Intelligence, in consultation with the Attorney General, to annually review for the purposes of declassification any future opinions of the court with broad privacy implications, and to report to me and to Congress on these efforts." Moreover, Obama stated that to "ensure that the court hears a broader range of privacy perspectives, I am also calling on Congress to authorize the establishment of a panel of advocates from outside government to provide an independent voice in significant cases before the Foreign Intelligence Surveillance Court." Id. Obama's actions and recommendations surely were not as extensive as many of the recommendations offered by critics of the NSA or the FISC. Nonetheless, except for the efforts of Presidents Ford and Carter in supporting the FISA legislation and the creation of the FISC in the first place, the fact that Obama distanced himself from the "trust us" school of thought, recognized that intelligence abuses had occurred, and took executive action to change intelligence operations and FISC procedures is rare if not unique by comparison to prior presidential statements or conduct, and surely gave further support to the assessment of the FISC as a court that amounted to little more than a "rubber stamp" that was sorely in need of serious reform.

9

Secret Court Shoots Foot

Although the telephone metadata program certainly had "its roots in counter-terrorism efforts that originated in the immediate aftermath of the September 11 attacks,"[1] the details of the origins and development of the program—a program that President Obama stated in an address to the nation on January 17, 2014, had "generated the most controversy these past few months"—are uncertain. The program collects, as the president stated, "phone numbers and the times and the lengths of calls," and it does not "involve the content of phone calls, or the names of people making calls." The statutory authorization of the so-called bulk collection of telephone records—the statutory authorization expired in November 2015—was section 215 of the 1978 Foreign Intelligence Surveillance Act [FISA] as amended. [2]

James Risen and Eric Lichtblau were the first to disclose the program in their important news report in the *New York Times* dated December 16, 2005, a report which admitted that "the newspaper delayed publication for a year."[3] The lead sentence of the newspaper report stated: "Months after the Sept. 11 attacks, President Bush secretly authorized the National Security Agency to eavesdrop on Americans and others inside the United States to search for

---

[1] Privacy and Civil Liberties Oversight Board, Report on the Telephone Records Program Conducted Under Section 215 of the USA PATRIOT Act and on the Operations of the Foreign Intelligence Surveillance Court 9 (2014).

[2] President Barack Obama, Remarks by the President on Review of Signals Intelligence (Jan. 17, 2014). On Friday, November 27, 2015, the *Wall Street Journal* reported that the NSA will "follow through on a plan to cease collecting bulk telephone records on Sunday [Nov. 29, 2015], the Office of the Director of National Intelligence said Friday." The report stated that Congress voted on June 2 "to ban the NSA from collecting telephone record in bulk, ending a practice adopted following the Sept. 11, 2001, terror attacks. The law that ended the program, the USA Freedom Act, gave the NSA 180 days to transition into a new system, and that period expires Sunday." Damian Paletta, *NSA to End Phone Program Despite Calls for Extension*, Wall St. J., Nov. 27, 2015.

[3] James Risen and Eric Lichtblau, *Bush Lets U.S. Spy on Callers Without Courts*, N.Y. Times, Dec. 16, 2005.

evidence of terrorist activity without the court-approved warrants ordinarily required for domestic spying, according to government officials." Although the report suggested that only a small number of Americans were subject to the program, that information may have been inaccurate at the time, and it bears no relationship to the enormous reach of the program in recent years.

It was this program, along with others it seems, that required periodical reauthorization that resulted in the dramatic confrontation on March 10, 2004, between, on the one hand, Attorney General John Ashcroft, while he was hospitalized, and Department of Justice officials, and, on the other, President Bush's White House Counsel Alberto Gonzales and Chief of Staff Andrew Card. The program was up for reauthorization and the Department of Justice officials refused to sign off on the program as it was then defined. In time, adjustments were made to the program, as the Privacy and Civil Liberties Oversight Board stated in a report, and "the NSA collected bulk telephony metadata based upon presidential authorizations issued every thirty to forty-five days."[4] That all changed on May 24, 2006, the day that a FISA judge for the first time "granted an application by the government to conduct the telephone records program under Section 215."[5] The ten-page FISA court order, now declassified but redacted to delete information the executive considers too sensitive to make public, was signed by FISA Judge Malcolm J. Howard.[6]

Judge Howard graduated from the U.S. Military Academy at West Point in 1962. He served two tours of duty in Vietnam and was a federal prosecutor and a special counsel to President Nixon during the Watergate investigations. In 1987, President Reagan nominated Howard to the federal bench, and he was commissioned in 1988. In May of 2005, Chief Justice Rehnquist designated Howard as a FISA judge, about one year before he signed the order authorizing the NSA to collect bulk telephone metadata.

Given the singularity and significance of Judge Howard's decision, his order is remarkably bare bones. Indeed, it is an order—nothing more. It is not, in any way, a memorandum of law that discusses the numerous statutory and constitutional issues.

Four paragraphs appearing on pages two and three of the redacted order conclude that the application of the FBI director satisfies the requirements of the statute, and it does this mainly by reproducing the requirements of the statutes. For example, paragraph three states: "There are reasonable grounds to believe that

---

[4] Privacy and Civil Liberties Oversight Board, Report on the Telephone Records Program Conducted Under Section 215 of the USA PATRIOT Act and on the Operations of the Foreign Intelligence Surveillance Court 9 (2014).

[5] Id.

[6] In re F.B.I. for an Order Requiring Prod. of Tangible Things from Redacted, No. BR 06-05, 2006 WL 7137486 (Foreign Intel. Surv. Ct. Aug. 18, 2006).

the tangible things sought are relevant to authorized investigations (other than threat assessments) being conducted by the FBI under guidelines approved by the Attorney General under Executive Order 12333 to protect against international terrorism, which investigations are not being conducted solely upon the basis of activities protected by the First Amendment to the Constitution of the United States. [50 U.S.C. §1861 (c)(1)]."[7] After the next paragraph, Judge Howard concluded: "WHEREFORE, the Court finds that the application of the United States to obtain the tangible things, as described in the application, satisfies the requirements of the Act, and therefore, IT IS HEREBY ORDERED, pursuant to the authority conferred on this Court by the Act, that the application is GRANTED."[8] And with those few words, the NSA was able to launch the massive collection of bulk telephone metadata that may affect every U.S. citizen in the United States.[9]

Pages four through ten of Judge Howard's order did set forth various requirements as to how the program was to function. But without diminishing their significance, they are, by comparison to what Judge Howard authorized in paragraphs one through four, mere details.

What Judge Howard authorized and what fifteen different Foreign Intelligence Surveillance Court [FISC] judges have authorized thirty-five subsequent times was a program in which "specified United States telecommunications providers [were required] to turn over to the FBI and the NSA 'on an ongoing daily basis,' for a period of approximately 90 days, 'all call detail records' or 'telephony meta-data' created by [the provider] for communications (i) between the United States and abroad; or (ii) wholly within the United States, including local telephone calls."[10] By "all call detail records" or "telephony meta-data," the order literally meant all records.

---

[7] *Id.* at *1.

[8] *Id.*

[9] Judge Howard did not write on a blank slate. A few years earlier, the chief judge of the FISA court, Colleen Kollar-Kotelly, who was nominated to the D.C. Superior Court by President Reagan, and to the U.S. District Court by President Clinton, wrote an eighty-seven-page opinion, which has been declassified and redacted, so that the names of the parties, the docket number, and the date of the opinion are not available, addressing the NSA collection of bulk metadata.

No. PR/TT at 84–85 (Foreign Intel. Surv. Ct.). In the opinion, she addressed numerous statutory and constitutional questions. As a result, when the executive submitted its application to Judge Howard, it submitted a memorandum of law justifying its request. In its January 2014 report, the Privacy and Civil Liberties Oversight Board stated that the government "relied heavily on the" reasoning of Judge Kollar-Kotelly's memorandum. Privacy and Civil Liberties Oversight Board, Report on the Telephone Records Program Conducted Under Section 215 of the USA PATRIOT Act and on the Operations of the Foreign Intelligence Surveillance Court (2014).Thus, Judge Howard not only had access to the government's memorandum but also access to Judge Kollar-Kotelly's opinion.

[10] Richard A. Clarke et al., *The NSA Report: Liberty and Security in a Changing World* 49 (2014).

By any measure, the judicial endorsement of the telephone metadata program was a remarkable development involving complex legal questions. And yet no judge on the FISA court bothered to write an opinion that carefully assessed the issues. In fact, according to the Privacy and Civil Liberties Oversight Board, the "first judicial opinion explaining the FISA court's legal reasoning in authorizing the bulk records collection" was not prepared until some weeks after the *Guardian* published an article disclosing the previously secret program, and then made public in a redacted form shortly thereafter on August 29, 2013.[11]

That opinion was written by FISC Judge Claire V. Eagan, and the public record offers only limited evidence as to why the Eagan opinion was made public. But given the intense national controversy triggered by the Snowden disclosures over the NSA surveillance programs and the FISA court in approving them, the decision to disclose the Eagan opinion so quickly after it was prepared was certainly not premised on the assumption that the opinion would provide yet another basis for criticizing the FISC. Moreover, because opinions and orders written by FISC judges are generally secret, there was no expectation that Eagan's opinion or the opinion of any other FISC judge would be made public. As a result, the decision to make the opinion public must have been based on the judgment that the opinion's quality—its reasoning, its thorough review of relevant law, its sensitivity to the interplay of values and conflicting legal considerations—would reflect favorably on the FISC and the FISC judges, and thus help strengthen the standing of the FISC at a time when it was publicly criticized. In other words, the facts that are known suggest that the public disclosure of the Eagan opinion was part of an orchestrated campaign to strengthen the legitimacy of the FISC in the wake of the severe criticism leveled at it in the wake of the disclosures by Edward Snowden.[12] Indeed, that is precisely the surmise of the *New York Times*, which reported that while "other judges had routinely reauthorized the program every 90 days with only brief reiteration of the court's legal analysis . . . Judge Eagan wrote the lengthier memorandum apparently for the purpose of public release."[13]

Because Eagan's opinion seems to have been intended to showcase the excellence of the FISC judges as they grappled with controversial national issues, it provides an unusual opportunity to assess the quality of the FISC judges.

---

[11] Privacy and Civil Liberties Oversight Board, Report on the Telephone Records Program Conducted Under Section 215 of the USA PATRIOT Act and on the Operations of the Foreign Intelligence Surveillance Court 9 (2014).

[12] *In re* F.B.I. for an Order Requiring Prod. of Tangible Things from Redacted, No. BR 13-109, 2013 WL 5741573, at *1 (Foreign Intel. Surv. Ct. Aug. 29, 2013).

[13] Charlie Savage, *Extended Ruling by Secret Court Backs Collection of Phone Data*, N.Y. Times, Sept. 17, 2013 at A1.

Judge Claire V. Eagan, who was appointed to the federal bench by President George W. Bush in 2001, upon the recommendation of Oklahoma Senators James Inhofe and Don Nickles, and to the FISC by Chief Justice Roberts in 2013, assessed the legality of the telephone metadata program under the Fourth Amendment to the Constitution and §215 of the USA PATRIOT Act.[14] The opinion is twenty-nine double-spaced pages, and although the length of an opinion is not necessarily indicative of its quality or potential influence,[15] a twenty-nine-page opinion is a comparatively short opinion given the complexity of the issues Judge Eagan had to resolve.[16] Indeed, Judge Eagan's Fourth Amendment analysis occupies fewer than sixty lines of text and five footnotes spread out over four pages. [17] By comparison to her twenty-nine-page opinion,

---

[14] *In re* F.B.I. for an Order Requiring Prod. of Tangible Things from Redacted, No. BR 13-109, 2013 WL 5741573 (Foreign Intel. Surv. Ct. Aug. 29, 2013).

[15] For example, see Justice Holmes's remarkably influential dissents in Lochner v. New York, 198 U.S. 45 (1905) and Abrams v. United States, 250 U.S. 616 (1919).

[16] For comparison, see Klayman v. Obama, 957 F. Supp. 2d 1 (D.D.C. 2013) *vacated and remanded*, No. 14-5004, 2015 WL 5058403 (D.C. Cir. Aug. 28, 2015); Am. Civil Liberties Union v. Clapper, 959 F. Supp. 2d 724 (S.D.N.Y. 2013) *vacated and remanded*, 785 F.3d 787 (2d Cir. 2015).

[17] One of the five footnotes merely quotes the Fourth Amendment. *In re* F.B.I. for an Order Requiring Prod. of Tangible Things from Redacted, No. BR 13-109, 2013 WL 5741573, at *2 n.9 (Foreign Intel. Surv. Ct. Aug. 29, 2013). Another dismisses the claim that the telephone metadata constitutes "property" belonging to the individual telephone subscriber on the ground the information was "obtained from telephone company equipment," thus depriving the telephone user of the claim that "his 'property' was invaded or that police intruded into a 'constitutionally protected area.'" *Id.* at *2 n.10. A third note simply pointed out what the governing statute provided, namely that a "service provider" was authorized to challenge the business records order on the ground that it "infringed on its own Fourth Amendment rights." *Id.* at *2 n.13. That leaves two footnotes in which Eagan did address substantive constitutional matters. In note 11, Eagan dismisses the idea that the NSA collection of bulk telephone metadata implicates the "Fourth Amendment expectation of privacy in call detail records similar to the data sought in this matter." *Id.* at *2 n.11. In reaching this conclusion she acknowledges that the "Court is aware that additional call detail data is obtained via this production than was acquired through the pen register acquisition at issue in *Smith [v. Maryland]*" decided by the Supreme Court in 1979. *Id.* Nonetheless, she argues that court decisions which were not binding on her—and here she refers to three circuit opinions (the ninth, tenth, and D.C. Circuits) rendered between 1990 and 2009—have considered this important question and concluded that what she terms "call detail records" did not give rise to a protectable Fourth Amendment expectation of privacy. *Id.* at *2 n.9. In note 12 of her opinion, Eagan provides case citations to support an alternative reason as to why the individual telephone user has no Fourth Amendment expectation of privacy in the data "transmitted" to a third party. *Id.* at *2 n.11. In the text, Eagan states that the Smith decision of 1979 "found that once a person has transmitted this information to a third party (in this case, a telephone company), the person 'has no legitimate expectation of privacy in [the] information.'" *Id.* at *2. In note 12, she embellishes the claim by reference to other Supreme Court decisions, one decided in 1976 (a year before Smith) and one decided in 1984 (seven years after Smith). *Id.* at *2 n.12.

two regular district judges who covered the same issues as Eagan and reached opposite conclusion from each other—one upheld the program and one invalidated it—wrote opinions that ran sixty-eight pages and fifty-four pages,[18] while the United States Court of Appeals for the Second Circuit recently concluded that the NSA metadata program was not authorized by the relevant statute, rendering an opinion of ninety-seven pages.[19]

In reviewing the request for an order, Eagan wrote that she "considered whether the Fourth Amendment to the U.S. Constitution imposed any impediment to the government's proposed collection,"[20] and decided that there were no impediments. Eagan then turned to whether the requested order permitting the collection of telephone metadata was authorized by section 215 and concluded that it was.[21]

The legal issues presented by the claim that the metadata program violates the Fourth Amendment are complex and that is so no matter how the issues are resolved. And yet Eagan's analysis of whether the telephone metadata program violates the Fourth Amendment occupies fewer than sixty lines of text and five footnotes spread out over four pages of her twenty-nine-page memorandum.

Central to Judge Eagan's brevity is her premise that the 1977 Supreme Court decision in *Smith v. Maryland* controlled the outcome in this case. In that criminal case, the defendant argued that the Fourth Amendment was violated by the "use of a pen register on telephone company equipment to capture" the telephone numbers the suspect was calling from his home phone in order to determine whether the suspect was the individual who was harassing and threatening another person.[22] The court majority in *Smith* rejected the defendant's argument. In concluding that she thought that the *Smith* decision "controlled"[23] and "compels"[24] the outcome in the NSA telephone metadata case, Eagan, in 2013, relied upon the high court's 1977 sociological assumption that "[a]ll subscribers realize . . . that the phone company has facilities for making permanent records of the number they dial . . ." and that "once a person has transmitted this information" to a telephone company, the telephone user has

---

[18] *Klayman*, 957 F. Supp. 2d 1; *Am. Civil Liberties Union*, 959 F. Supp. 2d 724.

[19] *Am. Civil Liberties Union*, 785 F.3d 787.

[20] *In re* F.B.I. for an Order Requiring Prod. of Tangible Things from Redacted, No. BR 13-109, 2013 WL 5741573 *1 (Foreign Intel. Surv. Ct. Aug. 29, 2013).

[21] Given that the available evidence indicates that Chief Justice Roberts has made it a practice to appoint to the FISC only judges whom he believes will uphold executive programs and warrant requests, Judge Eagan's opinion provides additional evidence of the success of the chief justice's court-packing strategy.

[22] *In re* F.B.I. for an Order Requiring Prod. of Tangible Things from Redacted, No. BR 13-109, 2013 WL 5741573, at *1 (Foreign Intel. Surv. Ct. Aug. 29, 2013).

[23] *Id.* at 9.

[24] *Id.* at 3.

"no legitimate expectation of privacy in [the] information" and "assumes the risk that the company will provide that information to the government."[25]

Eagan added one last point before closing out her analysis. Because Fourth Amendment rights are personal to the individual, the fact that a telephone metadata program collects data on millions of subscribers does not in any way strengthen the privacy claim against executive surveillance. She put the matter as follows: "Put another way, where one individual does not have a Fourth Amendment interest, grouping together a large number of similarly-situated individuals cannot result in a Fourth Amendment interest springing into existence *ex nihilo*."[26]

If it were beyond reasonable debate that the majority opinion in *Smith* required a lower court judge to uphold the constitutionality of the telephone metadata program, then a short discussion of the Fourth Amendment issue would be appropriate. But that is not the case here.

Judge Eagan's claim that the 1979 *Smith* decision compelled her decision was dependent on two important considerations. Eagan had to accept the *Smith* court's conclusion as still valid—that information obtained via a pen register did not implicate protectable constitutional privacy expectations. Eagan also had to ignore the fact that the NSA telephone metadata program collected much more information than was collected by the pen register in *Smith*.

The soundness of each conclusion is dubious. The controlling force of *Smith* is dependent on the merits of Justice Harry Blackmun's reasoning in *Smith*, and that reasoning rests on several doubtful sociological assumptions, which he summarized as follows:

> [W]e doubt that people in general entertain any actual expectation of privacy in the numbers they dial. All telephone users realize that they must "convey" phone numbers to the telephone company, since it is through telephone company switching equipment that their calls are completed. All subscribers realize, moreover, that the phone company has facilities for making permanent records of the numbers they dial, for they see a list of their long-distance (toll) calls on their monthly bills . . . Although most people may be oblivious to a pen register's esoteric functions, they presumably have some awareness of one common use: to aid in the identification of persons making annoying or obscene calls . . . Telephone users, in sum, typically know that they must convey numerical information to the phone company; that the phone company has facilities for recording this information; and that the phone company

---

[25] *Id.* at 9.
[26] *Id.* at 2.

does in fact record this information for a variety of legitimate business purposes. Although subjective expectations cannot be scientifically gauged, it is too much to believe that telephone subscribers, under these circumstances, harbor any general expectation that the numbers they dial will remain secret . . . [E]ven if petitioner did harbor some subjective expectation that the phone numbers he dialed would remain private, this expectation is not one that society is prepared to recognize as "reasonable" . . . This Court consistently has held that a person has no legitimate expectation of privacy in information he voluntarily turns over to third parties . . . In so doing, petitioner assumed the risk that the company would reveal to police the numbers he dialed.[27]

In sum, Blackmun made several assumptions: (1) telephone users have no expectation of privacy in the telephone numbers they dial; (2) telephone users know that the telephone companies know what numbers they dial; (3) telephone users know that the telephone companies have facilities for making permanent records of numbers dialed; (4) telephone users realize that one use of telephone companies maintaining records is to aid police in investigating obscene and annoying callers; and (5) telephone users surrender any expectation of privacy and thus run the risk that a telephone company will turn over pen register information to the police when they voluntarily give pen register information to a telephone company.

In making these five assumptions, Blackmun offered no evidence to support the validity of these assumptions. Moreover, the dissenting justices convincingly questioned their validity. For example, Justice Potter Stewart pointed out that when the court extended Fourth Amendment protections to electronic communications in *Katz v. United States*, it commented on the "vital role that the public telephone has come to play in private communication[s]" and then added that the "role played by a private telephone is even more vital" now than it was when *Katz* was decided.[28] Moreover, Stewart argued that the numbers dialed from a private telephone are "not without content," and Stewart doubted—thus directly challenging Blackmun's sociological assertion—that there are many telephone users "who would be happy to have broadcast to the world a list of the local or long distance numbers they have called" because such information "could reveal the identities of the persons and places called, and thus reveal the most intimate details of a person's life."[29]

Justice Thurgood Marshall's dissent took aim at another weakness in Blackmun's opinion. Blackmun assumed that telephone users have a

[27] Smith v. Maryland, 442 U.S. 735, 742–744 (1979).
[28] *Id.* at 746 (Stewart, J., dissenting).
[29] *Id.* at 748.

meaningful choice in deciding to use telephones and thus can be said to have surrendered their privacy expectation. As Marshall wrote: "It is idle to speak of 'assuming' risks in contexts where, as a practical matter, individuals have no realistic alternative."[30] But Marshall does not stop his analysis at that point. He argues that "to make risk analysis dispositive in assessing the reasonableness of privacy expectations would allow the government to define the scope of Fourth Amendment protections."[31] As an example, he argued that "law enforcement officials, simply by announcing their intent to monitor the content of random samples of first-class mail or private phone conversations, could put the public on notice of the risks they would thereafter assume in such communications."[32] And to rebut the majority's sociological assumption that the public has no privacy expectation in information collected by pen registers, Marshall made a point that reflected his personal experience as a civil rights leader: "The prospect of unregulated governmental monitoring will undoubtedly prove disturbing even to those with nothing illicit to hide. Many individuals, including members of unpopular political organizations or journalists with confidential sources, may legitimately wish to avoid disclosure of their personal contacts."[33]

When Stewart and Marshall wrote their opinions, they sharply questioned *Smith*'s assumptions, and the persuasiveness of their perspectives only became stronger as the telephone and other forms of electronic communications became increasingly indispensable to daily American life between the time of the *Smith* opinion and 2013, when Judge Eagan wrote her opinion. But that transformation is lost on Eagan. Indeed, it is not that Eagan recognizes the transformation but rejects its legal significance—she simply ignores it.

Eagan's failure to engage the assumptions underlying her opinion was not the only significant or even the most important shortcoming of her discussion of the constitutional law issues. In 2012, the Supreme Court decided that the "attachment of a Global-Positioning-System (GPS) tracking device to an individual's vehicle, and subsequent use of that device to monitor the vehicle's movements on public streets" constituted a search within the meaning of the Fourth Amendment.[34] The majority opinion written by Justice Scalia

---

[30] *Id.* at 750 (Marshall, J., dissenting).

[31] *Id.*

[32] *Id.*

[33] *Id.* at 751.

[34] United States v. Jones, 132 S. Ct. 945, 947 (2012). Justice's Scalia's opinion in *Jones*, which insists that the 2012 GPS tracker dispute in *Jones* violated the Fourth Amendment because of 1791 conceptions of what constituted trespass, seems remarkably stilted and artificial, if not mysterious, until Scalia's approach is set alongside the Supreme Court's decision in *Smith* and

avoided the question of whether the collection of data transmitted by a GPS tracking device violated constitutional privacy expectations by claiming that attaching a GPS tracking device to the defendant's car was a trespass and thus constituted a search. In contrast, five justices made it clear that attaching a GPS tracking device to a personal vehicle implicated constitutional privacy expectations not because of a trespass but because the data yielded by the GPS, in the words of one justice, "generates a precise, comprehensive record of a person's public movements that reflects a wealth of detail about her familial, political, professional, religious and sexual associations," which the government can "store" and "efficiently mine for information years into the future."[35] In addition to privacy arguments, these justices argued that the GPS tracking devices chilled "associational and expressive freedoms" and opened the door to possible abuse.[36]

Justice Samuel Alito, writing for himself and Justices Ruth Bader Ginsburg, Stephen Breyer, and Elena Kagan, criticized the majority for deciding the case on the basis of "18th century tort law," because such an approach is "unwise," "strains the language of the Fourth Amendment," "has little support in current Fourth Amendment case law," and "is highly artificial."[37] Alito argued that the better approach was for the court to follow the "*Katz* expectation-of-privacy test," which he conceded is "not without its own difficulties."[38] Alito argued that grounding the Fourth Amendment protections in privacy expectations allows the doctrine to take account of technological developments and accepts that "[d]ramatic technological change may lead to periods in which popular expectations are in flux and may ultimately produce significant changes in popular attitudes."[39] In this case, and in the absence of congressional action, which Alito thinks would be more effective in identifying "the best solution to privacy concerns," Alito thought that the "best

contemporary NSA electronic surveillance. If Scalia had concluded that the GPS tracker violated the Fourth Amendment because of reasonable expectations of privacy, that reasoning might have signaled a reconsideration of the *Smith* decision that rested on the assertion that the pen register in that case did not clash with reasonable expectations of privacy. That consequence, in turn, would have provided a precedent for asserting that reasonable expectations of privacy are violated by various executive branch electronic surveillance programs, which the executive states are warranted by national security considerations. And to the extent that Justice Scalia favored granting the executive what Justice O'Connor termed a "blank check" on security matters, he would seek in his opinion writing to avoid a legal ground—in this case a reasonable expectation of privacy—that could be asserted as a basis for the judiciary to impose limits on security surveillance.

[35] *Id.* at 955–956 (Sotomayor, J., concurring).

[36] *Id.* at 956.

[37] *Id.* at 958 (Alito, J., concurring).

[38] *Id.* at 962.

[39] *Id.*

that we can do in this case is to apply existing Fourth Amendment doctrine and to ask whether the use of GPS tracking in a particular case involved a degree of intrusion that a reasonable person would not have anticipated."[40]

Alito's rationale, in the eyes of four justices, had plain implications for the constitutionality of the telephone metadata collection program. Alito tied protectable privacy expectations to evolving societal standards and acknowledged that those standards were susceptible to change because of technological advancements. In making these comments, Alito referenced "new devices that permit the monitoring of a person's movements," "closed-circuit television video monitoring," "automatic toll collection systems" on toll roads, "devices affixed to cars that keeps a central location informed of a car's location," and "[p]erhaps most significant, cell phones and other wireless devices."[41]

Eagan did not discuss Alito's opinion, which represented four votes on the high court. She also did not discuss Justice Sonia Sotomayor's opinion, even though Sotomayor's views were aligned with Alito's and together the two opinions represented a majority of the justices on the Supreme Court. Sotomayor stated that she concurred in Scalia's opinion because in this case the "Government usurped Jones' property for the purpose of conducting surveillance on him, thereby invading privacy interests long afforded, and undoubtedly entitled to, Fourth Amendment protection."[42] But she quickly added that the Fourth Amendment also protects against searches that violate the "subjective expectation of privacy that society recognizes as reasonable." It also protects individuals in—and here she is quoting the historic *Katz* case—"[s]ituations involving merely the transmission of electronic signals without trespass would *remain* subject to *Katz* analysis."[43] But that is not all. Sotomayor accepts, as did Alito, that "the same technological advances that have made possible nontrespassory surveillance techniques will also affect the *Katz* test by shaping the evolution of societal privacy expectations."[44] And then Sotomayor recognizes that the data transmitted by the GPS monitoring constitute a "precise, comprehensive record of a person's public movements that reflects a wealth of detail about her familial, political, professional, religious, and sexual associations," which the executive may store and as Sotomayor wrote, "efficiently mine them for information years into the future."[45] For Sotomayor, not only does data collection

---

[40] *Id.* at 964.
[41] *Id.* at 963.
[42] *Id.* at 954 (Sotomayor, J., concurring).
[43] *Id.* at 955.
[44] *Id.*
[45] *Id.* at 955–956.

violate the Fourth Amendment, it "chills associational and expressive freedoms."[46]

Unexpectedly, and quite significantly in terms of the telephone metadata program, Sotomayor then takes another step and states that it may be "necessary to reconsider the premise that an individual has no reasonable expectation of privacy in information voluntarily disclosed to third parties."[47] Sotomayor argues that this controversial premise is "ill suited to the digital age, in which people reveal a great deal of information about themselves to third parties in the course of carrying out mundane tasks," and she doubts that "people would accept without complaint the warrantless disclosure to the Government of a list of every Web site they had visited in the last week, or month, or year . . . I would not assume that all information voluntarily disclosed to some member of the public for a limited purpose is, for that reason alone, disentitled to Fourth Amendment protection."[48]

It is one thing for a judge to disagree with what five members of the Supreme Court stated in recent opinions that are relevant, but not controlling, to that judge's statement as to what the law is. In such a situation it is expected that a judge would offer a fair summary of the relevant views of Supreme Court members and also provide a statement as to why those views are not being followed. But it is quite another to write an opinion—as Judge Eagan did—that fails to discuss the relevant views of a majority of the justices on the Supreme Court. From that perspective, Judge Eagan's opinion fails to measure up to reasonable professional expectations, let alone exemplary ones, that might reassure the public that the judges on the FISA court are sensitive to the complexity of the issues they confront and will assess them in a persuasive manner.

Judge Eagan addressed the question of whether the telephone metadata surveillance program was authorized by section 215 of the USA PATRIOT Act. By comparison to the three-and-one-half-page discussion of the constitutional law issues, this discussion filled sixteen pages. In the first of three sections she argued that the language of section 215, especially by comparison to similar statutes used to obtain communications for use in a criminal investigation, must be interpreted to provide the "government with more latitude at the production stage . . . by not requiring specific and articulable facts or meeting a materiality standard."[49] For Eagan, a lower production standard granted

---

[46] *Id.* at 956.

[47] *Id.* at 957.

[48] *Id.*

[49] *In re* F.B.I. for an Order Requiring Prod. of Tangible Things from Redacted, No. BR 13-109, 2013 WL 5741573, at *5 (Foreign Intel. Surv. Ct. Aug. 29, 2013).

more latitude and was appropriate given that the "government's interest is significantly greater when it is attempting to thwart attacks and disrupt activities that could harm national security, as opposed to gathering evidence on domestic crimes."[50] She also asserted that a lower standard was appropriate because "post-production checks in the form of mandated minimization procedures" aimed at protecting the privacy of individuals were imposed and that those checks were enhanced by what Eagan terms a "structured adversarial process."[51]

Eagan's next six pages addressed the key issue of "relevance." The 2005 version of section 215 that Eagan construed provided that the FISC should issue orders "only if the government provides 'a statement of facts showing that there are reasonable grounds to believe that the tangible objects sought are relevant' to an authorized investigation intended to protect 'against international terrorism or clandestine intelligence activities.'"[52] Noting that Congress did not define the term *relevance*,[53] Eagan argues that the meaning of the term *relevance*, which determines the scope of the metadata collection plan, depends "on the conclusion that bulk collection is *necessary* for NSA to employ tools that are likely to generate useful investigative leads to help identify and track terrorist operatives."[54] In other words, *relevance* must be defined broadly to enhance the possibility that information that will be obtained will be useful in identifying and tracking potential terrorists. Against that premise Eagan argues that because "known and unknown international terrorist operatives are using telephone communications, and because it is necessary to obtain the bulk collection of a telephone company's metadata to determine those connections between known and unknown international terrorist operatives as part of authorized investigations,"[55] "the whole production is relevant to the ongoing investigation out of necessity."[56]

Sensitive to the argument that her ruling, as well as all of the FISC rulings since FISC Judge Howard's ruling in 2006, were not authorized by section 215, and that Congress never intended to authorize a massive telephone metadata bulk collection programs for Americans making international and domestic calls, Eagan argues that Congress is presumed to have been aware of the FISC

---

[50] *Id.* at *17.

[51] *Id.*

[52] Richard A. Clarke et al., The NSA Report: Liberty and Security 37 (2014) (quoting 50 U.S.C. §1861(b)(2)(A)).

[53] *In re* F.B.I. for an Order Requiring Prod. of Tangible Things from Redacted, No. 13-109, 2013 WL 5741573, at *18 (Foreign Intel. Surv. Ct. Aug. 29, 2013).

[54] *Id.*

[55] *Id.* at *6.

[56] *Id.* at *7.

rulings pursuant to section 215 when "Congress subsequently re-authorized Section 215 without change in 2011."[57] Eagan concedes that the classification of FISC orders and opinions would mean that FISC rulings and orders were not "widely available to Members of Congress for scrutiny," and because of that, the presumption of ratification upon reauthorization "would be easily overcome."[58] But Eagan claims that is not the case here because of unusual efforts made by the "Executive Branch and relevant congressional committees . . . to ensure that *each* Member of congress knew or had the opportunity to know how Section 215 was being implemented under this Court's Orders."[59]

The weakness of Eagan's reasoning as she argued that the telephone metadata program fell within the meaning of section 215 was highlighted by the Privacy and Civil Liberties Oversight Board, "an independent bipartisan agency within the executive branch established by the Implementation Recommendations of the 9/11 Commission Act of 2007."[60] In concluding that "Section 215 does not provide an adequate legal basis to support" the metadata program, the Board offered five reasons in support.[61] The Board claimed that section 215 was "designed to enable the FBI to acquire records that a business has in its possession, as part of an FBI investigation, when those records are relevant to the investigation,"[62] but that the telephone records acquired under the program have "no connection to any specific FBI investigation at the time of their collection."[63] As is, the FISC definition of the word *relevant*, "circular, unlimited in scope, and out of step with the case law from analogous legal contexts involving the production of records."[64] The telephone metadata program obligates the telephone companies to "furnish new calling records on a daily basis as they are generated (instead of turning over records already in their possession)" and that obligation is "lacking foundation in the statute and . . . is inconsistent with FISA as a whole."[65] The statute "permits only the FBI to obtain items for use in its investigations; it does not authorize the NSA to collect anything."[66]

---

[57] *Id.* at *8.

[58] *Id.*

[59] *Id.* at *9.

[60] Privacy and Civil Liberties Oversight Board, Report on the Telephone Records Program Conducted Under Section 215 of the USA PATRIOT Act and on the Operations of the Foreign Intelligence Surveillance Court 2 (2014).

[61] *Id.* at 10.

[62] *Id.*

[63] *Id.*

[64] *Id.* It should be noted that this citation is drawn from a sentence in the Privacy Report that is partially redacted.

[65] *Id.*

[66] *Id.*

The contention that Congress ratified the FISC construction of section 215 when it reauthorized the statute is unpersuasive because the FISC construction of the section is contrary to the "plain meaning of [the] law, and cannot save an administrative or judicial interpretation that contradicts the statute itself."[67] Furthermore, to condone the so-called ratification-by-means-of-reauthorization rationale in this context would constitute a new application of the rationale, and such a new application would "undermine the public's ability to know what the law is and hold their elected representatives accountable for their legislative choices."[68]

---

[67] *Id.*

[68] *Id. See also* Richard A. Clarke et al., The NSA Report: Liberty and Security in a Changing World 48–71 (2014). Subsequent to Judge Eagan's opinion upholding the legality of the telephone metadata bulk collection program, the opinions of three other FISC judges addressing the same issues were disclosed to the public. Each upholds the legality of the program. Judge Eagan's memorandum dated August 29, 2013, and published in redacted form on September 17, 2013, was followed about two weeks later by a memorandum by FISC Judge Mary A. McLaughlin. *In re* Application of the F.B.I. for an Order Requiring the Production of Tangible Things from Redacted, No. BR 13-158 (Foreign Intel. Surv. Ct. Oct. 11, 2013). McLaughlin noted that this was the first time, she "entertained an application requesting the bulk production of call details records" and that she conducted "an independent review of the issues." But following that review, she "agrees with and adopts Judge Eagan's analysis as the basis for granting the Application." McLaughlin concluded, as Eagan did, that the "re-enactment of section 215 without change in 2011 triggered the doctrine of ratification through re-enactment." *Id.* at *2. McLaughlin also agreed with Eagan that "the production of call detail records . . . does not constitute a search under the Fourth Amendment." But unlike Eagan, McLaughlin does acknowledge that the 2012 Supreme Court decision in *United States v. Jones* does bear on the Fourth Amendment issue, but then argues that the majority decision written by Justice Scalia "does not point to a different result here." *Id.* at *4. FISC Judge Rosemary M. Collyer was the next FISC judge to address the lawfulness of the telephone metadata program, and she did so in a thirty-one-page "Opinion and Order" dated March 20, 2014. *In re* Application of the F.B.I. for an Order Requiring the Production of Tangible Things, No. BR 14-01 (Foreign Intel. Surv. Ct. March 20, 2014). In this case, a party whose identity is redacted and who was subject to a FISC order compelling the disclosure of telephone metadata challenged a production order. In the end, Judge Collyer upheld the order, and she did so by focusing solely on whether the metadata program violated the Fourth Amendment. She reasoned, as did Eagan, that the Supreme Court's decision in Smith controlled the outcome in the matter. Collyer repeated Smith's two assumptions from the 1970s: (1) that no protectable privacy expectation existed in metadata; and (2) an individual surrenders whatever privacy expectation may be present when the individual voluntarily turns information over to a third party, as in the case of a bank or a telephone company. Collyer acknowledge that the 2012 Supreme Court decision in Jones was relevant to her analysis but concludes that Justice Scalia's decision in Jones left the law as it was—an individual has no protectable privacy expectation in metadata. A few months later, another FISC judge issued yet another memorandum reviewing the legality of the telephone metadata program. In an opinion dated June 19, 2014, Judge James B. Zagel, appointed to the federal bench by President Reagan, followed in the footsteps of Judges Eagan, McLaughlin,

Because prior cases and the relevant statues did not compel Judge Eagan's reasoning, the question arises as to why Judge Eagan reasoned as she did. Judge Eagan's opinion suggests the answer.

Eagan makes it clear that in order to prevail, the executive was not required to establish that the telephone metadata program was an effective tool in obtaining foreign intelligence about international terrorism, and thus effective in protecting the national security. Yet she notes[69] that the executive has demonstrated through its "written submissions and oral testimony that this production has been and remains valuable for obtaining foreign intelligence information regarding international terrorist organizations."[70] Moreover, although Judge Eagan had no reason to comment on whether the *Guardian* news reports disclosing the telephone metadata program did or did not harm the nation's security, at the end of her opinion, Eagan quotes NSA Director General Keith Alexander, who stated that the Snowden disclosures seriously harmed the effectiveness of the telephone metadata program and thus "have caused 'significant and irreversible damage to our nation.'"[71]

---

and Collyer and upheld the legality of the bulk collection program. *In re* Application of the F.B.I. for an Order Requiring the Production of Tangible Things from Redacted, No. BR 14-96, 2014 WL 5463290 (Foreign Intel. Surv. Ct. June, 19, 2014). In doing so, Judge Zagel stated that he "fully agree[s] with and adopt[s] the constitutional and statutory analyses" contained in Eagan and McLaughlin's opinions, and concurs in the conclusion that "under the controlling precedent of *Smith v. Maryland* . . . the production of call detail records in this matter does not constitute a search under the Fourth Amendment." Judge Zagel added that he also adopted "the analysis put forth by Judge Eagan," of the claim the telephone metadata program violated the section 215 and "in particular, I note her discussion on the issue of relevance," which he then quoted. *Id*. at *2. Judge Zagel noted, as had Judge Collyer in her opinion, that in recent months four district judges assessed the legality of the collection program and that three of the four upheld the legality of the program. With regard to Judge Leon's opinion, which concluded that the telephone metadata program violated the Fourth Amendment, Judge Zagel stated that he agreed with Judge Collyer that Judge Leon erred in concluding that "*Smith v. Maryland* is inapplicable to the collection of bulk telephony metadata." *Id*. at *10. Judge Zagel concluded by observing the obvious: "Courts must follow the law as it stands until the Congress or the Supreme Court changes it." *Id*. at *11. What Zagel's observation failed to acknowledge was a point that Judge Leon had emphasized: that in *Jones v. United States*, five members of the Supreme Court indicated that the continued vitality of the *Smith* decision was undermined by advances in technology, the massive amount of information new technology collected, the fact that individuals today had no choice but to surrender personal data to third parties, and that privacy expectations evolved with the evolution of technology. As a result, Judge Zagel, as did Judge Collyer, ignored the obvious, that *Smith* may not be controlling, and adopted a stance that it was not for them to make new law.

[69] *In re* F.B.I. for an Order Requiring Prod. of Tangible Things from Redacted, No. BR 13-109, 2013 WL 5741573, at *1 (Foreign Intel. Surv. Ct. Aug. 29, 2013).

[70] *Id*. at *2.

[71] *Id*. at *9.

Judge Eagan's opinion indicates that she considered the telephone meta-data program an important and effective investigative device protecting the national security, and that its disclosure inflicted irreparable harm on the nation. Putting aside the merits of her legal judgments, Judge Eagan's opinion suggests that her estimation of the importance of the telephone metadata program to national security probably greatly influenced her legal conclusion that the metadata program was lawful.

As for the usefulness of the telephone metadata program, Eagan's conclusion regarding the effectiveness of the telephone metadata program in protecting the nation from attack stands in marked contrast to the conclusion reached by the Privacy and Civil Liberties Oversight Board. That board concluded:

> The threat of terrorism faced today by the United States is real. The Section 215 telephone records program was intended as one tool to combat this threat—a tool that would help investigators piece together the networks of terrorist groups and the patterns of their communications with a speed and comprehensiveness not other-wise available. However, we conclude that the Section 215 program has shown minimal value in safeguarding the nation from terrorism. Based on the information provided to the Board, including classified briefings and documentation, we have not identified a single instance involving a threat to the United States in which the program made a concrete difference in the outcome of a counterterrorism investiga-tion. Moreover, we are aware of no instance in which the program di-rectly contributed to the discovery of a previously unknown terrorist plot or the disruption of a terrorist attack. And we believe that in only one instance over the past seven years has the program arguably con-tributed to the identification of an unknown terrorism suspect. Even in that case, the suspect was not involved in planning a terrorist attack and there is reason to believe that the FBI may have discovered him without the contribution of the NSA's program.[72]

The Oversight Board was not alone in reaching a fundamentally different conclusion regarding the utility of the telephone bulk collection program. The President's own Review Group reached a comparable conclusion. "Our review suggests that the information contributed to terrorist investigations by the use of section 215 telephony meta-data was not essential to preventing

---

[72] Privacy and Civil Liberties Oversight Board, Report on the Telephone Records Program Conducted Under Section 215 of the USA PATRIOT Act and on the Operations of the Foreign Intelligence Surveillance Court 11 (2014).

attacks and could readily have been obtained in a timely manner using conventional section 215 orders. Moreover, there is reason for caution about the view that the program is efficacious in alleviating concern about possible terrorist connections, given the fact that the meta-data captured by the program covers only a portion of the records of only a few telephone service providers."[73]

Judge Eagan's opinion as to why the metadata program was lawful was not compelling, trenchant, or incisive. Her analysis, neither nuanced nor exhaustive, skimmed the surface of the constitutional issues, and, to the extent that the opinion was disclosed so as to reassure Americans about the competence of FISA judges, it constituted a shot in the foot.

[73] Richard A. Clarke et al., The NSA Report: Liberty and Security in a Changing World 57 (2014).

PART THREE

JUDICIAL DEFERENCE

10

NSA Surveillance

The Injury Is Speculative

Decades before a publicly available Internet became a reality, and long before Edward Snowden disclosed the extraordinary intrusiveness of the National Security Agency's surveillance programs, Supreme Court Justice William O. Douglas incorporated themes from George Orwell's *1984* into an opinion speculating on the capacity of constitutionally based freedoms to guard against oppressive state orthodoxy:

> The time may come when no one can be sure whether his words are being recorded for use at some future time; when everyone will fear that his most secret thoughts are no longer his own, but belong to the Government; when the most confidential and intimate conversations are always open to eager, prying ears. When that time comes, privacy, and with it liberty, will be gone. If a man's privacy can be invaded at will, who can say he is free? If his every word is taken down and evaluated, or if he is afraid every word may be, who can say he enjoys freedom of speech? If his every association is known and recorded, if the conversations with his associates are purloined, who can say he enjoys freedom of association? When such conditions obtain, our citizens will be afraid to utter any but the safest and most orthodox thoughts; afraid to associate with any but the most acceptable people. Freedom as the Constitution envisages it will have vanished.[1]

We live in a world Douglas worried would one day come. It is a world in which what Justice Louis Brandeis characterized as "the most comprehensive of rights and the right most valued by civilized men," the "right to be let alone" is

---

[1] Z. T. Osborne, Jr., v. United States, 385 U.S. 323, 353 (1967).

seriously endangered by the government's surveillance capacity.[2] And because that right "to be let alone" is intimately tied to the individual's freedom of belief and of expression, Douglas's observation brings to mind the memorable words of Supreme Court Justice Robert Jackson: "If there is any fixed star in our constitutional constellation, it is that no official, high or petty, can prescribe what shall be orthodox in politics, nationalism, religion, or other matters of opinion or force citizens to confess by word or act their faith therein. If there are any circumstances which permit an exception, they do not now occur to us."[3] Although the national security surveillance state does not directly dictate what is "orthodox," it strips away the privacy that shields the mind's spontaneity and thus stunts both belief and expression.

The Supreme Court is in a position to push back against the surveillance programs aimed at protecting national security. By upholding claims that surveillance by the National Security Agency, the FBI, or the Army of United States citizens violated the Constitution, the high court would be placing a boundary around executive surveillance. Such outcomes might not by themselves be adequate to curb an aggressive and sweeping surveillance state, but they might prompt the Congress to exercise a more demanding oversight role, and they might stimulate public discussion of the issues, which might result in public opposition to such surveillance. Together these efforts might more effectively rein in intrusive and ineffective surveillance initiatives than can be imagined today.[4]

But the Supreme Court has rendered no such outcomes. Indeed, it has utilized different doctrines as a basis for dismissing such legal actions.[5] Thus, over the decades a majority of justices on the Supreme Court have turned a deaf ear to requests that the judiciary use its authority to make the executive's surveillance intrusiveness judicially accountable and to assure that it functions within lawful boundaries. Relying mainly on the legal doctrine of "standing," a doctrine the high court has shaped and reshaped over the decades that requires that a party have a sufficient stake in the dispute to warrant the exercise of judicial jurisdiction, the Court has dismissed challenges to government surveillance on the ground that the grievant lacked standing.[6]

---

[2] Olmstead v. United States, 277 U.S. 438, 478 (1928).

[3] W. Va. State Bd. of Educ. v. Barnette, 319 U.S. 624, 647 (1943).

[4] See Malcolm Gladwell, Tipping Point (2002), for an effective presentation of the argument that seemingly minor changes can tip the scales in a complicated and dynamic matrix in a direction not previously considered possible.

[5] For an example of this, see Halkin v. Helms, 598 F.2d 1, 3 (1978), in which the D.C. Circuit Court dismissed the action on the basis of state privilege.

[6] The law of standing has changed substantially over the last half century, and the legal literature on the subject is vast. For three law review articles that together offer important insights into the multiple issues, see Heather Elliott, *The Functions of Standing*, 61 Stan. L. Rev. 459 (2008);

As a result, it may be thought that the Court has assigned itself a seat on the sidelines as the executive engages in surveillance of citizens in the name of assuring order and security. But a sideline seat is not a neutral seat. By using the standing doctrine to prohibit judicial oversight of national security surveillance activities, the high court has permitted the executive a comparatively free and unaccountable hand that functions in secrecy to shape its surveillance activities. And given these developments it is only Congress that might possibly monitor and curtail executive surveillance programs, and given Congress's past record on this matter there is little basis to support a belief that Congress would diligently and demandingly exercise these responsibilities.[7]

The jurisdiction of the federal courts is limited to what the Constitution terms "cases" and "controversies"—terms the Constitution does not define, but which Chief Justice Earl Warren described decades ago as "those two words [which] have an iceberg quality, containing beneath their surface simplicity submerged complexities which go to the very heart of our constitutional form of government."[8] There is nothing inherent in either word—"case" or "controversy"—that necessarily defines them. But since the adoption of the Constitution, courts have developed several doctrines that help define what a case or a controversy is, and although these doctrines cut across the entire swath of federal court litigation, what we do know is that the words prohibit federal courts from providing an "advisory" opinion—another technical term—that means to offer a legal opinion to a perhaps highly important question merely because an individual, in the absence of a dispute, has posed it. That, the courts will not do. Something more is required, and what that "more" is is subject to debate and hardly a static, concrete concept.

In *Flast v. Cohen*, Chief Justice Earl Warren wrote that the words "cases" and "controversies" embody "two complementary but somewhat different limitations. In part, those words limit the business of federal courts to questions presented in an adversary context and in a form historically viewed as capable of resolution through the judicial process. And in part those words define the role assigned to the judiciary in a tripartite allocation of power to assure that the federal courts will not intrude into areas committed to the other branches of

---

Cass R. Sunstein, *Standing Injuries*, 1993 Sup. C. Rev. 39 (1993); Louis L. Jaffe, *The Citizen as Litigant in Public Actions: The Non-Hohfeldian or Ideological Plaintiff*, 116 U. Pa. L. Rev. 1033 (1968).

[7] Theoretically the FISA court, a secret court established in 1978 as a reform measure to curb executive surveillance on Americans, is in a position to provide meaningful oversight on executive surveillance activities. But as reviewed in Chapter 8, the history of that court is riddled with a profound irony as that reform effort now needs reforming itself if it is to be effective in fulfilling its purposes.

[8] Flast v. Cohen, 392 U.S. 83, 94 (1968).

government."[9] More recently, the court has elevated Warren's second purpose over his first in asserting that the law of standing is "built on a single basic idea—the idea of separation of powers."[10] Basically the notion of separation of powers is that each coequal branch should not improperly interfere with the functioning of the other two branches, and for the courts that means that courts must find a pathway that fulfills their primary function of resolving disputes without inappropriately sapping the dynamic energies of the two politically accountable branches.

Finding the proper balance is said to be essential to courts defining the proper role for themselves—a politically unaccountable branch of government—in a democratic society.[11] In addition to this core function, standing requirements help assure that the courts decide matters that are rooted in concrete situations, which it is assumed illuminates what is at stake and the possible consequences of different rulings. By requiring that a party have a stake in the outcome—termed an "injury" in the cases—it is assumed that the issues will be sharply defined and effectively presented, thus helping judges understand the different layers of meaning a case may embrace.

But a statement of the broad purposes underlying standing does little to define the specific and detailed requirements of standing. And because judges have such discretionary authority in shaping the law of standing, and because membership of the high court changes over time, the Supreme Court's definition of the law of standing has not only changed but more recent changes are often at odds with prior decisions. Thus, as members of the Supreme Court have become more hostile to, for example, the use of courts to vindicate the rights of minorities and political dissenters, the justices closed the courthouse door to litigants by increasing standing requirements. [12]

---

[9] *Flast,* 392 U.S. at 95.

[10] Allen v. Wright, 468 U.S. 737, 752 (1984).

[11] Warth v. Seldin, 422 U.S. 490, 498 (1975).

[12] Thus, in 1992, and on behalf of a divided court, Justice Scalia departed from the established standing elements of many earlier cases and set forth what is often considered a brief summary of contemporary minimal standing requirements: "First, the plaintiff must have suffered an injury in fact—an invasion of a legally protected interest which is (a) concrete and particularized, and (b) actual or imminent, not conjectural or hypothetical. Second, there must be a causal connection between the injury and the conduct complained of—the injury has to be fairly traceable to the challenged action of the defendant, and not the result of the independent action of some third party not before the court. Third, it must be likely, as opposed to merely speculative, that the injury will be redressed by a favorable decision." Lujan v. Defenders of Wildlife, 504 U.S. 555, 560–561 (1992). As is evident, the meaning of this standard is uncertain at critical points. For example, a person "must have suffered an injury in fact" which certainly means that the injury has already been experienced and is in the past, and yet Scalia leaves open the possibility, as he must unless he and his colleagues are prepared to sweep aside considerable past precedent, that an injury not yet experienced but one that is likely to occur because it is

Because the law of standing is complicated, not linear, and hardly consistent, it is a great leap from the 1960s when the Supreme Court relaxed standing requirements to the early 1970s and thereafter when the Court enhanced the requirements. The purpose of the following discussion is not to detail and systematize the law of standing over the last half century. Nor is it to claim that all of the changes in the law of standing can be traced to judicial deference in national security cases. But it is to claim that the Supreme Court has used its discretionary authority to redefine the law of standing with special rigor in cases involving executive surveillance so as to insulate the executive surveillance programs from judicial accountability, and that such a development has great importance for individual privacy and executive transparency.

During the 1960s, the Warren Court gave a fresh impulse to federal courts being available to protect constitutional rights. It did this in part by relaxing standing requirements; this relaxation made it possible for individuals to test the boundaries separating protected from unprotected conduct by claiming that not knowing the location of that boundary would "chill" the exercise of those rights. Relaxed standing requirements also served to impute fresh legitimacy to the idea that citizens should be able to bring government to account in the courts to assure that government complies with the law.[13]

Lastly, and closely related to the idea of citizens functioning as private attorney generals, relaxed standing requirements responded to the idea that a grievance that was widely shared—in the law known as a "generalized grievance"—was still a noteworthy grievance that did not undermine the concreteness of a dispute, did not mean that a party would not vigorously litigate a matter, and did not threaten the vitality of the democratic process by improperly expanding the roles of the courts. Indeed, the granting of standing to an individual whose interest in the lawsuit was that of a citizen furthers democratic values by allowing the individual in mass contemporary society, whose life is so frequently entangled with larger and invisible forces, to participate in the governing and lawmaking processes in a manner that resonates

---

imminent is sufficient. Or consider that the phrase "fairly traceable" was certainly deliberately used instead of the phrase "directly causes" to permit judges considerable leeway as they assess the relationship between a plaintiff's injury and a defendant's conduct. Or lastly, the idea that a judicial order will "likely" redress the injury as opposed to "will redress" the injury was surely adopted to leave judges discretion in deciding whether the requested relief will in fact redress the injury.

[13] During the years that the Supreme Court altered the law of standing, Professor Louis L. Jaffe of the Harvard Law School argued for the importance of what became known as citizen standing. Louis L. Jaffe, *The Citizen as Litigant in Public Actions: The Non-Hohfeldian or Ideological Plaintiff*, 116 Harv. L. Rev. 1033 (1968).

with the iconic citizen as represented by Norman Rockwell exercising his right to speak at a New England town hall meeting.[14]

Three cases decided in the 1960s illustrate how the Supreme Court, a politically insulated governing institution within a democratic republic, may undermine that familiar critique that it is a countermajoritarian governing body, by defining standing requirements so as to strengthen democratic values by enhancing citizen participation in government.

The famous *Baker v. Carr*[15] decision is a stunning example of the Supreme Court not only validating the legitimacy of a generalized grievance but doing so in a case that made an inestimable contribution to democratic values and changed the nation's political landscape.[16] In that case, the plaintiffs alleged that the malapportionment of the state legislature denied the plaintiffs equal protection of the laws by "virtue of the debasement of their votes."[17] In other words, they claimed the less populated rural areas had disproportionate political influence in the state legislature compared to the more populated urban areas. *Baker* is best known for its refusal to dismiss the action on the ground that the so-called Equal Protection Clause claim was in fact a Guarantee Clause claim "masquerading under a different label,"[18] and that the Guarantee Clause claim should be dismissed on the ground that the case presented a "political question" in that the Constitution had delegated the claim to the Congress to resolve.

In framing the standing question, the Court made no reference to separation of powers or the role of courts in a democratic society or the possibility that a relaxed standing requirement would sap the vitality of the politically accountable branches. Nor did the Court state that the essential inquiry was whether the plaintiff had suffered what the contemporary court insists is the primary requirement of standing, namely, an "injury." Instead, Justice Brennan

---

[14] In sharp contrast to this understanding of the law of standing, Supreme Court Justice Antonin Scalia wrote a law review article that has influenced conservative jurists who favor demanding standing requirements that have the effect of closing the courthouse door on individuals seeking redress for possible violations on federal rights. In the article, entitled "The Doctrine of Standing as an Essential Element of the Separation of Powers," Justice Scalia stated his theses as follows: "My thesis is that the judicial doctrine of standing is a crucial and inseparable element of that principle, whose disregard will inevitably produce—as it has during the past few decades—an overjudicialization of the process of self-governance. More specifically, I suggest that courts need to accord greater weight than they have in recent times to the traditional requirement that the plaintiff's alleged injury be a particularized one, which sets him apart from the citizenry at large." XVII Suffolk L. Rev. 881, 881–882 (1983).

[15] Baker v. Carr, 369 U.S. 186 (1962).

[16] Reynolds v. Sims, 377 U.S. 533 (1964).

[17] *Baker*, 369 U.S. at 188.

[18] *Id.* at 297.

stated that the standing objection asked whether the complaining party adequately "alleged such a personal stake in the outcome of the controversy as to assure that concrete adverseness which sharpens the presentation of issues upon which the court so largely depends for illumination of difficult constitutional questions?"[19] A "personal stake" is a much different requirement from an "injury," and indeed a party may have a profound personal stake in the outcome without having being harmed or injured in a manner that is distinctive to that particular individual. Moreover, the purpose of the "personal stake" requirement was to assure that the case was presented to the Court with "concrete adverseness," which would help illuminate the "difficult constitutional questions," not to protect the democratic process from erosion resulting from judicial decisions. In framing the requirements of standing in these words, Justice Brennan emphasized that the plaintiffs in the case were "entitled to a hearing and to the District Court's decision on their claims" because, and here Justice Brennan quotes Chief Justice John Marshall, the "very essence of civil liberty certainly consists in the right of every individual to claim the protection of the laws, whenever he receives an injury."[20]

Baker changed the law of standing and three years later the Supreme Court did that again in *Dombrowski v. Pfister.*[21] In that case, the plaintiff initiated a civil rights action against the Louisiana governor, police and law enforcement officials, and the Chairman of the Legislative Joint Committee on Un-American Activities in Louisiana, requesting declaratory and injunctive relief restraining them from "prosecuting or threatening to prosecute" the plaintiffs for "alleged violations of the Louisiana Subversive Activities and Communist Control Law and the Communist propaganda Control Law."[22] The complaint alleged that the statutes "on their face violate the First and Fourteenth Amendment guarantees securing freedom of expression, because overbreadth makes them susceptible of sweeping and improper application abridging those rights."[23] As is apparent, the plaintiffs in this action had not yet been prosecuted, and despite their alleged fears, may never have been prosecuted. Moreover, if they had been prosecuted, they would have been able to assert as a defense that the First Amendment to the Constitution provided a complete and total defense. Under these circumstances, the Court could have concluded that the plaintiffs had not yet suffered an injury, that they might never suffer an injury, and that if and when they were indeed prosecuted they could at the time have the Court

---

[19] *Id.* at 204.

[20] *Id.* at 206 (quoting Marbury v. Madison, 1 Cranch 137, 163 (1803)).

[21] Dombrowski v. Pfister, 380 U.S. 479 (1965).

[22] *Id.* at 482.

[23] *Id.*

decide whether the prosecution violated the Constitution. Nonetheless, the Court ruled that the plaintiffs had standing to bring this preemptive lawsuit to define the boundaries of their protected speech. The Court stated: "Because of the sensitive nature of constitutionally protected expression, we have not required that all of those subject to overbroad regulations risk prosecution to test their rights. For free expression—of transcendent value to all society, and not merely to those exercising their rights—might be the loser. For example, we have consistently allowed attacks on overly broad statutes with no requirement that the person making the attack demonstrate that his own conduct could not be regulated by a statute drawn with the requisite narrow specificity."[24] *Dombrowski* concluded that an individual who claimed that possible government conduct chilled the exercise of constitutional rights presented a case that satisfied Article III requirements.

In *Flast v. Cohen*,[25] the high court snapped a forty-five-year pattern, first announced in *Frothingham v. Mellon*,[26] of not allowing individuals to challenge congressional acts solely on the basis of their interest as a federal taxpayer.[27] In *Flast*, a taxpayer attacked a federal spending law that helped finance "instruction in reading, arithmetic, and other subjects in religious schools, and to purchase textbooks and other instructional materials for use in such schools" on the ground that such expenditures violated the Establishment and Free Exercise Clauses of the First Amendment.[28] On behalf of eight members for the Court, Warren concluded that the taxpayer did have standing because the plaintiff satisfied two essential nexus requirements. First, the plaintiff's status as a taxpayer had a "logical link" between that status and the congressional enactment under the taxing and spending clause of Article I, section 8 of the Constitution. Second, the taxpayer in *Flast* challenged the congressional expenditure on the ground that it violated a specific constitutional provision intended to limit the exercise of the congressional power at issue. However the nexus requirement as set forth by Chief Justice Warren is viewed, what is certain about the outcome in *Flast* is that the Court permitted a person to sue whose grievance was widely shared and whose financial interest in the outcome was certainly not the reason for commencing and prosecuting the lawsuit. The parties who brought this action brought it to enforce the constitutional provisions that barred the Congress from using its authority to establish

---

[24] *Id.* at 486.

[25] Flast v. Cohen, 392 U.S. 83 (1968).

[26] Frothingham v. Mellon, 262 U.S. 447 (1923).

[27] *Flast*, 392 U.S. at 85.

[28] *Id.* at 85–86.

a religion and they claimed that the spending law that provided financial assistance to religious schools did just that.

Surely the reasons prompting the rules set forth in *Baker, Dombrowski*, and *Flast* are varied and complicated, but the historical context in which this transition took place cannot be ignored.

Justice Douglas got to the nub of the matter when he wrote: "The judiciary is an indispensable part of the operation of our federal system. With the growing complexities of government it is often the one and only place where effective relief can be obtained. If the judiciary were to become a super-legislative group sitting in judgment on the affairs of the people, the situation would be intolerable. But where wrongs to individuals are done by violations of specific guarantees, it is abdication for courts to close their doors."[29] In Justice Douglas's view, the judiciary had an increased, and increasingly, meaningful role in considering individual claims against the government. In making this important point, Douglas, unfortunately and quite characteristically, did not exhaust himself by elaborating in his opinion the qualities of an appropriate standing doctrine. He simply insisted that there was a broad spectrum separating judicial abdication, on the one hand, and judicial usurpation, on the other, and that the Court should construct the rules of standing to allow individuals to challenge government conduct in response to the fact that individual lives had over the decades become increasingly intertwined with the government.[30]

---

[29] *Id.* at 111 (Douglas, J., concurring). Even Chief Justice Warren Burger, who disliked the Warren Court's opening of the courthouse doors to a broad range of claims and who helped engineer the curtailment of the relaxed law of standing, recognized the historical context of the relaxation even as he implemented a curtailment: "As our society has become more complex, our numbers more vast, our lives more varied, and our resources more strained, citizens increasingly request the intervention of the courts on a greater variety of issues than at any period of our national development." United States v. Richardson, 418 U.S. 166, 179 (1974).

[30] As important as these developments were, they left the Court's traditional reluctance to resolve the merits of a legal dispute involving war unchanged. Thus, the very same Court that decided these cases refused, in 1967, to grant certiorari in a case in which petitioners, who were drafted into the United States Army and "ordered to a West Coast replacement station for shipment to Vietnam," brought suit to prevent the "Secretary of Defense and the Secretary of the Army from carrying out those orders, and requested a declaratory judgment that the present United States military activity in Vietnam is 'illegal.'" Mora v. McNamara, 389 U.S. 934, 934 (1967) (Stewart, J., dissenting). And then, over three dissenting votes filed by Justices Douglas, Harlan, and Stewart, the Court in 1970 denied the application of the state of Massachusetts to adjudicate, in the words of Justice Douglas, the "constitutionality of the United States' participation in the Indochina war." Commonwealth of Massachusetts v. Laird, 400 U.S. 886, 886 (1970) (Douglas, J., dissenting). In his dissent, Douglas argued that Massachusetts had at least as much of a stake in the outcome as the plaintiff in the Flast case as well as others in which the Court had found that a party had standing. *Id.* at 889. He also argued that the case presented no "political question," as that term was defined in *Baker v. Carr. Id.* at 897.

Douglas understood an important development in American life and related it to his conception of the responsibilities of federal courts. President Roosevelt's New Deal and the emergence of a powerful national government, that had an increasing reach into the far corners of individual American lives, combined with the political imperatives of the Cold War that the United States narrow the gap between its political ideals and its political and social reality, made it important that America do more than it had done to make its national ideals a reality. That, in turn, required that the courts open their doors to at least the possibilities that they would use their authority to adjudicate significant claims rooted in constitutional values advanced by individual citizens, who were seeking a voice in a governing structure that was ever more complicated, remote, and well beyond the influence of the ordinary citizen. That was what Douglas advocated and that is what *Baker, Dombrowski,* and *Flast* represented.

Baker, Dombrowski, and *Flast* were decided by the Warren Court, and that Court came to an end shortly after Richard Nixon was sworn in as president in January 1969. Abe Fortas and Earl Warren resigned from the Court within months of Nixon becoming president, and two years later Black and Harlan also resigned from the Court. That gave President Nixon four appointments to the Court, and those appointments ended the Warren Court's jurisprudence and ushered in the new conservativism in the high court that has continued for over four decades.

Two surveillance cases separated by forty-one years are bookends for this conservative period and illuminate the issues inherent in the law of standing. One case, decided in 1972, arose from the domestic disturbances of the 1960s; the other, decided in 2013, emerged from the post-9/11 war on terrorism. The high court divided four to five in each case. No justice who sat on the 1972 case was alive when the 2013 case was decided.

Sometime in the early 1960s, "the United States Government, acting through the armed forces and primarily the Army, began a massive program of investigation and surveillance of the thoughts, habits, attitudes, political activities and associations of individual American citizens."[31] At the height of the surveillance program in the late 1960s, known as "Operation CONUS," "thousands of agents of the United States Army Intelligence Command were involved,"[32] some of whom were used as "undercover agents to infiltrate civilian

---

[31] Amicus Brief filed by Unitarian Universalist Association Council for Christian Social Action, United Church of Christ American Friends Service Committee National Council of Churches of Christ for Respondents at 5, Laird v. Tatum, 408 U.S. 1 (1972), No. (71-288) 1972 WL 135681 (U.S.) (Appellate Brief).

[32] *Id.*

groups and open confidential files."[33] These undercover agents moved "as a secret group among civilian audiences, using cameras and electronic ears for surveillance" for the purpose of collecting data that was "distributed to civilian officials in state, federal, and local governments and to each military intelligence unit and troop command under the Army's jurisdiction (both here and abroad); and these data are stored in one or more data banks."[34] Or, as Professor Donohue observed: "Army intelligence agents attended meetings and submitted reports," reports that also drew from "open sources and law enforcement databases,"[35] to headquarters, describing the name of the organization, date of the gathering, speakers, attendees, and whether a disorder occurred.

Ultimately Operation CONUS maintained files "on more than 100,000 political activists." Some of these individuals were nationally prominent figures such as "Senators Adlai Stevenson III, J. William Fulbright, and Eugene McCarthy, Congressman Abner Mikva, singer Joan Baez, and civil rights leader Martin Luther King."[36] The Army reports contained information that "ranged from targets' political views to their sex lives and financial conditions."[37] It also maintained files on the "membership, ideology, programs, and practices of virtually every political activist group in the country, including groups such as the Southern Christian Leadership Conference, Clergy and Laymen United Against the War in Vietnam, the American Civil Liberties Union, Women's Strike for Peace, and the National Association for the Advancement of Colored People."[38]

Captain Pyle, who had been part of the Military Intelligence initiative, disclosed the Army surveillance program in an article published in *The Washington Monthly* in January 1970. Within a few weeks of the publication, the secretary of the Army received approximately thirty congressional inquiries concerning the surveillance program, and some individuals filed an action in the United States District Court in Washington, D.C. which became known as *Laird v. Tatum*. During the months following the publication of the Pyle article, Senator Sam J. Ervin, Jr., who chaired the Constitutional

---

[33] Laura K. Donohue, *Criminal Law: Anglo-American Privacy and Surveillance*, 96 J. Crim. L. & Criminology 1059, 1089 (2006). *See also* Laird v. Tatum, 408 U.S. 1, 25 (1972) (Douglas, J., dissenting) ("The Army uses undercover agents to infiltrate these civilians groups and to reach into confidential files of students and other groups").

[34] *Laird*, 408 U.S. at 25 (Douglas, J., dissenting).

[35] Laura K. Donohue, *Criminal Law: Anglo-American Privacy and Surveillance*, 96 J. Crim. L. & Criminology 1059, 1089 (2006).

[36] *Id.* at 1088.

[37] *Id.* at 1089.

[38] *Laird*, 408 U.S. at 25 (Douglas, J., dissenting). *See also* Laura K. Donohue, *Criminal Law: Anglo-American Privacy and Surveillance*, 96 J. Crim. L. & Criminology 1059, 1088–1089 (2006).

Rights Subcommittee of the Senate Judiciary Committee, investigated the Army Surveillance program.[39] By the time the *Laird* case was presented to the Supreme Court, Senator Ervin's subcommittee had gathered considerable information about the program, which he summarized in an amicus brief he and Lawrence M. Baskir, who at the time was chief counsel for Ervin's subcommittee, signed and submitted.[40]

---

[39] Senator Ervin later chaired a Senate committee that investigated the Nixon administration following the break-in at the Watergate complex in Washington, D.C.

[40] Baskir later held different positions in and out of government while serving as editor-in-chief of the *Military Law Reporter* and before becoming a judge of the United States Federal Court of Claims. The Ervin and Baskir brief set forth an authoritative description of the Army Surveillance program and when it is compared to Chief Justice Warren Burger's summary of the program in his majority opinion in *Laird v. Tatum*, the degree to which the Chief Justice sanitized his version of the program is evident.

> Sometime in the 1960's, prompted by an increase in civil violence, the United States Government, acting through the armed forces and primarily the Army, began a massive program of investigation and surveillance of the thoughts, habits, attitudes, political activities and associations of individual American citizens. This Army program took the form of the development and maintenance of investigative files in manual and computerized systems. It was an expansion of pre-existing investigative operations of the armed forces, such as personal background investigations, and was in many aspects inseparable from these other functions. The program was ostensibly developed in connection with the increased use of the Army to put down civil violence. Although there is little evidence available to support the contention, it has been explained as an effort to "predict" situations in which the use of military force would be required.
>
> At the height of the program in the late 1960's, thousands of agents of the United States Army Intelligence Command were involved. In addition, numerous other investigative personnel and other sources of military manpower from the Continental Army Command, the Navy and the Air Force were employed. According to Army documents, the responsibility of these investigators was to gather information on persons and organizations engaged in various activities associated with racial problems, antiwar, antidraft, and other controversial public issues. Intelligence activities have been conducted in public places, on college campuses, at high schools, in churches, and at private meetings. Persons subjected to this program have ranged from leaders of active organizations, to ordinary members, the curious and the passerby. Individuals expressing support or sympathy with subjects of the surveillance have also come under investigation. Subjects have included numerous Congressmen and United States Senators and family members of a Senator, state and local officials, a member of this Court, newspaper reporters, clergymen, and thousands of other Americans. Although no total number can be estimated, it is not an exaggeration to talk in terms of hundreds of thousands of individuals, organizations, events, and dossiers.
>
> The information gathered on these citizens has included their participation or presence at political events, their political views, their relationships with other political activities, their travel, their family associations, finances, education, and other types of personal data. Once a person becomes the subject of investigation, the data gathered about him and his activities is unlimited. Information for the Army dossiers

Plaintiffs' suit challenging the Army surveillance program was initiated by four individuals and nine unincorporated organizations "engaged in lawful political activity, including but not limited to union organizing, public speaking, peaceful assembly, petitioning the government, newspaper editorializing, and educating the public about political issues."[41] They claimed that the surveillance program exceeded the mission requirements of the Army, constituted an impermissible burden on the litigants and others, and exercised "*present inhibiting effect* on their full expression and utilization of their First Amendment rights of free speech, etc. The baleful effect, if there is one, is thus a present inhibition of lawful behavior and of First Amendment rights."[42] The plaintiffs sought a "declaratory judgment that the Army's present conduct is unconstitutional or otherwise illegal," as well as an injunction "forbidding future similar activity, and the destruction of all such data hitherto illegally obtained."[43]

has been obtained by observation of public activities, by covert infiltration, by electronic devices, tape-recorders, cameras, and by videotape, as well as by requesting data from other governmental agencies and from private sources. The Army analyzed and attempted to categorize and label individuals according to their utterances and the way they exercised their rights of free speech, assembly, association, and petition.

The bulk of investigative activity by the Army's own personnel occurred at the field level. Agents collected information and filed "spot reports," "agent reports," and "summaries of investigation." Most of this data was forwarded up the chain of command but record copies were kept in data centers at every level of command. Manual files were maintained at every level. At least four and possibly more computer systems were employed to store, analyze, and retrieve, the information collected. Many files were microfilmed and integrated with other files on persons who were suspected of violations of security and espionage laws. These were located at the headquarters of the Intelligence Command (Fort Holabird), the Continental Army (Fort Monroe), the Third Army Corps (Fort Hood), and in the Pentagon. More than one computer data bank was maintained in some of these locations.

Information gathered in this program and political analyses produced as part of it were indiscriminately shared and exchanged by the Army and were distributed to other military record systems, and to other federal, state, and local agencies maintaining investigative files. Although subsequent to the filing of this lawsuit, many of the Army computer systems and other collections of data were ordered destroyed, much of the data still exists in files maintained by the Department of the Army, the Defense Department, and the other federal, state, and local agencies to which it was regularly sent. The Department of the Army has been unwilling or unable to ensure the complete elimination of the information collected under this program from its own and other governmental records. (Laird v. Tatum, 408 U.S. 1 (No. 71-288) (1972), Amicus Brief filed on behalf of Unitarian Universalist Association Council for Christian Social Action, United Church of Christ, American Friends Service Committee, National Council of Churches of Christ, 1972 WL 135681)

[41] Reply Brief for Respondents at 7, Laird v. Tatum, 408 U.S. 1 (1972), No. (71-288).
[42] Tatum v. Laird, 444 F.2d 947, 954 (D.C. Cir. 1971) (emphasis in original).
[43] *Id.* at 948.

In the district court the plaintiffs offered to provide testimony to support their allegations, including a witness who had "infiltrated a coalition of church groups in Colorado."[44] But the district judge denied the request and dismissed the action on the basis of pleadings, affidavits, and oral argument. The appeals court reversed, concluding that the plaintiffs had standing, that the matter was "ripe," and that the case was justiciable. In doing so, the Court handed the executive a rare defeat because the ruling held out the possibility that the district judge might decide the merits of the case, that is, provided that the district judge did not dismiss the action on the ground that the matter could not be litigated because of the state secrets privilege.

Although the Court of Appeals ruled against the executive, its opinion contained several paragraphs that sought to explain, if not provide some justification for, the Army surveillance program. In "recent years," the panel noted, the "Army and the National Guard have been called upon to act to preserve domestic peace against violent protests leading to civil disorders," many of which were aimed at "military functions and installations themselves, as in ransacking Selective Service offices, barring troop and supply trains by prostrate bodies on the tracks, unlawful attempts to enter military bases or demonstrations thereon, and harassment of defense-oriented businesses."[45] In these missions, the Army confronted "[r]iotous mobs protesting matters unrelated to military operations" as in Detroit, Newark, and other of our large cities. The panel emphasized that during just 1967–1968, "the National Guard was called upon eighty-three times and the Army four times to quell cases of civil disorder."[46] And to make sure that all understood that the military was used to quell disturbances that challenged values across the political spectrum, the panel noted that "in the period beginning with the use of the Army paratroops at Little Rock in 1957 the Army has been called upon under related constitutional and statutory provisions to preserve civil peace in order that certain groups might exercise their constitutional rights."[47]

The appeals panel related the Army's role in quelling civil disorders to its surveillance activities. "To quell disturbances or to prevent further disturbances the Army needs the same tools and, most importantly, the same information to which local police forces have access." And because the Army is often sent into unfamiliar territory, "their need for information is likely to be greater than that of the hometown policeman."[48] "So," the panel concluded,

[44] Amicus Brief for A Group of Former Army Intelligence Agents at 5, Laird v. Tatum, 408 U.S. 1 (1972), No. (71-288).

[45] Tatum v. Laird, 444 F.2d 947, 952 (D.C. Cir. 1971).

[46] Id.

[47] Id.

[48] Id.

"we take it as undeniable that the military, *i.e.*, the Army, need a certain amount of information in order to perform their constitutional and statutory missions."[49]

In finding that the plaintiffs had standing to bring the case and that the matter was ripe for adjudication, the circuit panel stated that the plaintiffs presented a "unique argument."[50] Their contention emphasized that the "*present existence of this system of gathering* and distributing information . . . constitutes an impermissible burden" on them and others in that it "exercises a *present inhibiting effect* on their full expression and utilization of their First Amendment rights of free speech, etc. The baleful effect, if there is one, is thus a present inhibition of lawful behavior and of First Amendment rights."[51] The panel ended this analysis by concluding that "it is the operation of the system itself which is the breach of the Army's duty toward appellants and other civilians," and that because of the "overbreadth" of the surveillance system ("the collection of information not reasonably relevant to the Army's mission to suppress civil disorder"), and because it was not likely that "a better opportunity will later arise to test the constitutionality of the Army's action, the issue can be considered justiciable at this time."[52]

The Supreme Court granted the executive's request for review. The executive's brief argued that the plaintiffs' claim "lacks sufficient focus and concreteness to present the constitutional issue in an 'adversary context' as required by the 'Case' or 'Controversy' language in Article III of the Constitution. In addition, we argue that the named respondents, who readily admit that they are themselves insulated from any chilling effect, have no standing to maintain the present suit as 'private attorneys general' on behalf of other members of the public at large."[53]

The plaintiffs' brief argued that the matter was justiciable and asserted: "Stripped of technicalities, the question before the court is whether the Army may abridge First Amendment rights by an unconstitutional program in excess of its statutory authority while remaining immune from judicial review."[54] To that question, as to whether the Army's alleged unlawful conduct was immune from judicial review, the plaintiffs claimed that the answer must be "no," and then quoting from the Civil War *Milligan* opinion, the plaintiffs' brief stated that liberty dies under the heel of martial law, that "'republican government

---

[49] *Id.* at 953.

[50] *Id.* at 954.

[51] *Id.*

[52] *Id.* at 956.

[53] Brief for Petitioners at 14, Laird v. Tatum, 408 U.S. 1 (1972), (No. 71-288).

[54] Brief for Respondents at 26, Laird v. Tatum, 408 U.S. 1 (1972), (No. 71-288).

is a failure, and there is an end of liberty regulated by law,' for 'civil liberty and this kind of martial law cannot endure together.'"[55]

A divided Court, voting five to four, with the new Chief Justice Warren Burger writing the majority, concluded that an action challenging the legality of the Army's intelligence-gathering and distributing system directed at "lawful and peaceful civilian political activity"[56] should be dismissed because the plaintiffs lacked standing. Although Chief Justice Burger acknowledged that the Supreme Court had found in "recent years . . . in a number of cases that constitutional violations may arise from the deterrent, or 'chilling,' effect of governmental regulations that fall short of a direct prohibition against the exercise of First Amendment rights,"[57] he distinguished those cases and stated that what the plaintiffs "appear to be seeking is a broad-scale investigation, conducted by themselves as private parties armed with the subpoena power of a federal district court and the power of cross-examination, to probe into the Army's intelligence-gathering activities, with the district court determining at the conclusion of that investigation the extent to which those activities may or may not be appropriate to the Army's mission."[58] And Burger's sarcasm did not stop there. He went on to characterize the plaintiffs as having ridiculous ambitions, asserting that if the plaintiffs' claims were "[c]arried to its logical end, this approach would have the federal courts as virtually continuing monitors of the wisdom and soundness of Executive action . . . it is not the role of the judiciary, absent actual present or immediately threatened injury resulting from unlawful governmental action."[59]

Burger exaggerated. The plaintiffs did not request the federal courts to become "virtually continuing monitors of the wisdom and soundness of executive action."[60] Rather, the plaintiffs put forth exactly what Burger claimed they did not put forth and that he conceded would be sufficient to satisfy the requirements of standing and to warrant judicial review, namely an "actual present or immediately threatened injury." And that is what the four dissenters thought the plaintiffs claimed. As Justice Brennan wrote, quoting a circuit

[55] *Id.*

[56] Laird v. Tatum, 408 U.S. 1, 2 (1972). For contemporary discussions of the Supreme court's decision, see George C. Christie, *Government Surveillance and Individual Freedom: A Proposed Statutory Response to* Laird v. Tatum *and the Broader Problem of Government Surveillance of the Individual,* 47 N.Y.U. L. Rev. 871 (1972); Note, Laird v. Tatum, *The Supreme Court and a First Amendment Challenge to Military Surveillance of Lawful Civilian Political Activity,* 1 Hofstra L. Rev. 244 (1973).

[57] Laird v. Tatum, 408 U.S. at 10.

[58] *Id.* at 14.

[59] *Id.* at 15.

[60] *Id.*

court judge, the plaintiffs contend that the "present *existence of this system of* gathering and distributing information, allegedly far beyond the mission requirements of the Army, constitutes an impermissible burden" on the plaintiffs, which in turn "exercises a *present inhibiting effect* on their full expression and utilization of the First Amendment rights of their First Amendment rights" of free speech.[61]

The plaintiffs in the *Laird* case challenged the legality of an Army surveillance program targeting domestic civilians it considered political dissidents on the ground that the surveillance program chilled the political rights of the people. Chief Justice Burger mischaracterized the plaintiffs' claims and reshaped the law of standing to insulate the Army and its surveillance program from judicial review.[62]

---

[61] *Id.* at 38 (Brennan, J., dissenting).

[62] Only two years later, the Court decided two important standing cases that constituted a frontal assault on the law of standing as presented in the *Flast* and *Baker* cases. In *Schlesinger v. Reservists Committee to Stop the War*, 418 U.S. 208 (1974), the plaintiffs included "present and former officers and enlisted members of the reserves" who opposed the United States military involvement in Vietnam who sought a declaration that the so-called Incompatibility Clause of the Constitution rendered members of Congress ineligible to hold a commission in the Armed Forces Reserve. Schlesinger v. Reservists Committee to Stop the War, 418 U.S. 208, 210 n.1 (1974). They claimed that they had a sufficient stake in the outcome because of their status as citizens and taxpayers. Although there did not seem to be any sunlight between their effort and the successful efforts of the plaintiffs in *Flast* and *Baker*, a majority of six justices concluded that their interest in the outcome was no different from that of any other individual and thus concluded that the plaintiffs lacked standing. Unlike his opinion in the *Laird* case, which ridiculed the plaintiffs, Burger stated that the court had "no doubt about the sincerity" of the military reservists and the "depth of their commitment" to the overall goals. *Schlesinger*, 418 U.S. at 225. The second case decided that day, June 25, 1974, was far more important as revealing the Court's willingness to insulate the executive from judicial accountability and by so doing help develop the National Security State. The Constitution requires that "a regular Statement and Account of the Receipts and Expenditures of all public money shall be published from time to time." U.S. Const. art. I § 9, cl. 9. Because the expenditures of the Central Intelligence Agency were not public, the plaintiffs initiated a lawsuit to enforce the plain wording of the Constitution and to secure at least a partial disclosure of the CIA expenditures. The purpose of the suit was not mysterious, as Justice Douglas stated: "The public cannot intelligently know how to exercise the franchise unless it has a basic knowledge concerning at least the generality of the accounts under every head of government." United States v. Richardson, 418 U.S. 166, 201 (1974) (Douglas, J., dissenting). Chief Justice Burger wrote for a five-person majority, concluding that the plaintiffs lacked standing. Burger was hardly an even-handed assessor of the claim. Indeed, he even had the audacity to assert that the plaintiffs, who brought the suit just so that they could learn how public funds were spent, totally failed to make any "claim that appropriated funds are being spent in violation of a 'specific constitutional limitation upon the . . . taxing and spending power . . . '" *Id.* at 175 (majority opinion). In Burger's mind the plaintiffs merely viewed the federal courts "as a forum in which to air [their] generalized grievances about the conduct of government," and that if the high court granted them standing it would mean that the "Founding Fathers intended to set up something in the nature of an Athenian democracy or a New England town meeting to oversee

Many important Supreme Court decisions are decided by a five-to-four vote, as was this case. But the vote in this case was distinctive because it illustrates how important Supreme Court decisions may, simultaneously, be the result of an historical accident and personal intention.

The Supreme Court decided *Laird v. Tatum* three and one-half years after Richard Nixon was sworn in as president. Nonetheless, the seeds for the outcome in the case were sown years before. During the 1968 presidential campaign Nixon more or less declared war on the Supreme Court, as a prominent historian of the Nixon presidency wrote: "By 1968, Nixon had become almost as critical of the Warren Court as he was of the Johnson Administration,"[63] and he was "promising as President, to appoint judges who would reverse some of the basic decisions of the past fifteen years."[64] Because Nixon's attacks on the Warren Court left little to the imagination, Johnson was concerned that if Nixon won the presidency he would appoint individuals to the Supreme Court who would be hostile to the Great Society reforms, and try to do to them what a majority of the justices did to New Deal legislation in 1935 and 1936.[65] At the same time, Chief Justice Warren, who had a personal dislike of Nixon, feared that if Nixon were elected president his appointments to the high court would try to undo decisions he considered central to his legacy. As a result, when Chief Justice Warren advised Johnson in June of 1968—just one-half year before Johnson's term ended—that he wished to resign, Johnson acted quickly. He immediately announced that he was nominating his old friend and confidant, Supreme Court Justice Abe Fortas, to the Chief Justiceship,[66] and that he was nominating Homer Thornberry, "a Texas jurist and old friend,"[67] to Fortas's seat.

Many considered these nominations troubling and warned Johnson. In fact, Johnson was told that Fortas would confront stiff opposition and not likely be

the conduct of the National Government by means of lawsuits in federal courts." *Id.* at 179. Four justices dissented—Douglas, Brennan, Stewart, and Marshall. Though Douglas made it a point that he was not deciding the merits of the issues presented, from the vantage point of today he did understand the impact of the decision on future developments when he stated that the long-term consequences of the decision were to give secrecy a "new sanctity," and that by keeping secret "vast operations of government" the Court was contributing to a serious "crisis in confidence" that would result from the fact that the public would be uninformed about "secret plans concerning this Nation or other nations." *Id.* at 199–202. (Douglas, J., dissenting).

[63] II Stephen Ambrose, Nixon: The Triumph of a Politician 1962–1972, 159 (1989).

[64] *Id.*

[65] Robert Dallek, Lyndon B. Johnson: Portrait of a President 346 (2004).

[66] When Nixon learned of Warren's announcement, he immediately issued a statement that because of the Court's importance in American life the position of chief justice should be filled by the next president.

[67] Robert Dallek, Lyndon B. Johnson: Portrait of a President 346 (2004).

confirmed as chief justice, and that Senate Republicans would oppose Thornberry as a "Johnson crony." As things turned out, those preaching restraint were correct. Johnson gravely miscalculated. Fortas was charged with "breaching the tradition of separation of powers by secretly counseling Johnson on policy matters after joining the Court and of taking money for a course he taught at American University from former clients with business before the court,"[68] and his nomination was "sunk." And once Fortas's nomination to succeed Warren failed, there was no seat for Thornberry to occupy. Johnson's effort to make Abe Fortas chief justice and Harold Thornberry an associate justice had completely backfired.

But there was more to this episode. In the spring of 1969 Fortas was forced to resign from the Court because of a scandal, and weeks later Warren retired. Nixon had been president for less than a year, and he had the opportunity to replace two liberal justices with two conservative ones. Nixon appointed Warren E. Burger to succeed Warren (sworn in on June 23, 1969), and after Lewis Powell declined Nixon's offer to appoint him to fill Fortas's seat, and after the Senate rejected Haynsworth and then Carswell to fill Fortas's seat on the Court, Nixon nominated Harry Blackmun (sworn in on June 9, 1970).

Fifteen months later, Hugo Black, after serving thirty-four years on the Supreme Court, resigned and died a week later. A few days before Black died, John Harlan resigned from the Court because of illness and died that December. Black and Harlan's resignations allowed Nixon to appoint Powell—who now relented and accepted the appointment—to Black's seat and William Rehnquist, who at the time was an assistant attorney general, to Harlan's seat. They were sworn in on January 7, 1972, ten weeks before the Supreme Court heard oral argument in *Laird v. Tatum*, and, as a result, their participation in the case determined the outcome.

Apart from the historical accident that permitted Nixon to appoint four justices to the Supreme Court within the first term of his presidency, there was another aspect of *Laird v. Tatum* that made the circumstances, resulting in a narrow majority of five votes, unique.

Although the available evidence leaves the issue unresolved, the circumstantial evidence certainly suggests that Justice Rehnquist, while serving in the Department of Justice, advised the Nixon administration on the legality of the Army surveillance program. Thus, on March 19, 1971, a few weeks before the D.C. Circuit issued its decision in the *Laird* case and more than a half year before there was an opening on the Supreme Court to which Rehnquist was appointed, Rehnquist gave "remarks" on the Army surveillance program at the National Conference of

[68] *Id.* at 347.

Law Reviews in Williamsburg, Virginia, which Senator Ervin later included in the published version of his subcommittee report. A review of those remarks indicates that Rehnquist was keenly aware of the Army surveillance program. Indeed, the entire thrust of his remarks was to discuss the recent public disclosure of the "activities of the Army Intelligence Service in collecting, over a period of several years, a vast amount of information which that service considered to be relevant to civil disturbances and potential civil disturbances,"[69] to defend the necessity and legality of the surveillance program, and to assert that the courts should dismiss the lawsuit challenging the surveillance program because the matter was not appropriate for judicial resolution.

In his remarks, Rehnquist noted the testimony of Assistant Secretary of Defense Robert Froehlke before the Ervin committee. Rehnquist observed that Froehlke "freely conceded that much of the lower level Army activity in this area had been undertaken with insufficient guidance from the civilian officials in the Executive Branch," and that such "lower level Army activity" resulted in surveillance activities and data collection that was "useless for any legitimate law enforcement purpose and offensive to the traditions of a country which has always recognized the right of political dissent."[70] Rehnquist insisted that the surveillance of the peaceful meetings held for the purpose of expressing "public disapproval of some governmental policy, such as the Vietnam War," had been "emphatically repudiated" by the Nixon administration.[71]

But Rehnquist did not state the Nixon administration would cease all Army surveillance programs. Instead, Rehnquist stated that the Nixon administration would not favor "a continuation of some of the types of surveillance conducted by the Army in the past, or the conducting of investigative activity that was not reasonably related to the prevention of crime or the apprehension of criminal suspects."[72] That quite plainly left open the possibility that the Nixon administration permitted the Army to continue with some version of the surveillance program that it had previously employed and some version of its investigative activity that was related to the prevention of crimes or the apprehension of criminals.[73]

---

[69] Federal Data Banks, Computers, and the Bill of Rights: Hearings Before the Subcommittee on Constitutional Rights on Federal Data Bank, Computers, and the Bill of Rights of the Committee on the Judiciary United States Senate, 92nd Cong. 1 (1971) (statement of William H. Rehnquist, Assistant Attorney General, Office of Legal Counsel, Department of Justice, Privacy, Surveillance, and the Law).

[70] *Id.*

[71] *Id.* at 1592.

[72] *Id.* at 1596.

[73] At another point in his remarks, Rehnquist seems to suggest that the Army no longer gathered information on "potential civil disturbances": "The responsibility for gathering information

Rehnquist asserted that surveillance and the use of federal troops to quell civil disorder was not only lawful but important. His prime example focused on the three large demonstrations in Washington, D.C., against the Vietnam War between 1968 and 1970. Rehnquist stated that during these protests most demonstrators did nothing more than demonstrate their "support for peace in Vietnam."[74] But he insisted that in the November 1969 and May 1970 demonstrations, "there were isolated instances of destruction of federal property and other related offenses."[75] Because of the size of these demonstrations and the likelihood of unlawful conduct, "any law enforcement agency [would] seem foolish, indeed, if it did not do what it could to apprise itself of the plans of the demonstrators, and to make adequate personnel available during the demonstration to assure the protesters that their right to protest would be preserved, and to assure the rest of the public that anyone who violated the law would be apprehended and punished."[76] In pressing the case for surveillance, Rehnquist accepted that a surveillance program implicated a mosaic of values that included security and privacy, that it was not possible to advance both values simultaneously, and that some choice had to be made. He argued that having to elevate one value above another was not uncommon in the law and as examples he cited the law that granted the press substantial protection when sued for libel or the law that protected executive officials from damage claims resulting from their conduct. Thus, Rehnquist argued that the elevation of surveillance above privacy in the context of the executive using surveillance in connection with the deployment of federal troops to preserve civil disorder did not mean that such surveillance programs were unchecked. He emphasized that surveillance programs were subject to effective congressional and executive branch oversight.

That left unaddressed how Rehnquist assessed the possibility of judicial oversight of the Army surveillance program. On that point he did not seem equivocal: "I believe that no legitimate interest of any segment of our population would be served by permitting individuals or a group of individuals to prevent by judicial action, the government's gathering information."[77] Rehnquist argued that because the Army surveillance activities did not present any threat of a legal sanction and because "no effort has yet been made to seek imposition of legal penalties on the basis of the information obtained,"[78] the case for "judicial supervision" is weak by comparison to "where the government seeks to impose

on potential civil disturbances resided now in the Department of Justice, rather than in the Department of the Army." *Id.* at 1593.

[74] *Id.* at 1592.
[75] *Id.* at 1592.
[76] *Id.* at 1593.
[77] *Id.* at 1593.
[78] *Id.* at 1594.

sanction on an individual who refuses to divulge information voluntarily, or where criminal penalties or disabilities are sought against an individual on the basis of information collected."[79] In offering these judgments Rehnquist stated that he did not think the courts would in fact uphold any claim restraining legitimate law enforcement surveillance,[80] but he was nonetheless deeply concerned that lawyers would use and abuse the discovery process to the disadvantage of legitimate law enforcement purposes.[81] Moreover, he thought the judicial process was "ill suited to regulation of detailed and continuing investigative activities of law enforcement agencies, where frequently time is of the essence."[82]

Ten months later Rehnquist was on the Supreme Court sitting in judgment of the plaintiff's claims in *Laird v. Tatum*. Many at the time thought that Rehnquist would and should recuse himself from participating in the case as a judge because of his past involvement in the matter. As one student of the Rehnquist recusal issue put it, plaintiffs assumed that Justice Rehnquist would recuse himself from participating in the *Laird v. Tatum* case in keeping with "'Lord Coke's venerable maxim that 'no man should be a judge of his own case.'"[83] Moreover, Rehnquist's presumed participation in approving of the Army's surveillance activities when he was in charge of the Office of Legal Counsel would have made him a possible "deponent had the *Tatum* case gone forward" and that Rehnquist "should reasonably have been expected" to be deposed if not a witness.[84]

But Rehnquist did not recuse himself. What he did do was cast the fifth and decisive vote in the case. Because plaintiffs had been cautioned against making such a recusal motion in the belief that it might offend some justices,[85] it was only after the Court's ruling in *Laird v. Tatum* that the plaintiffs made a motion that he should disqualify himself from participation in the case.[86]

---

[79] *Id.* at 1594.

[80] "The threat of ultimate judicial restraint of legitimate law enforcement activity is not great." *Id.* at 1594. Rehnquist in part based this judgment on his conclusion that the claim that Army or law enforcement surveillance was not a justiciable claim when not "accompanied" by a "threat of compulsion, and when no use has yet been made of the information in order to seek imposition of any legal sanction on a person." *Id.* at 1595.

[81] *Id.* at 1594.

[82] *Id.* at 1594.

[83] Jeffrey W. Stempel, *Rehnquist, Recusal, and Reform*, 53 Brook. L. Rev. 589, 592–593 (1987).

[84] *Id.* at 592.

[85] *Id.* at 592 n.16. "Why did the [*Tatum*] plaintiffs wait until they had lost before moving to disqualify Justice Rehnquist? They said they feared offending the Court needlessly when it seemed possible he would not participate without having to be asked. Senator [Sam] Ervin had urged caution on them, saying he was sure the Justice would recognize the need to disqualify himself."

[86] Laird v. Tatum, Rehnquist memorandum denying the motion that he disqualify himself. Laird v. Tatum, 409 U.S. 824 (1972). Plaintiffs' lawyers later explained that they had been

At that point, Rehnquist refused. And after his refusal Rehnquist submitted a memorandum published in the Supreme Court reports in which he offered an explanation of his decision.

In this memorandum, he stated that his statement appears to be the first of its kind since "neither the Court nor any Justice individually appears ever to have" submitted such a memorandum. In the first seven pages of the memorandum, Rehnquist reviewed prior twentieth-century cases in which the issue of recusal arose and which to Rehnquist seemed to support his decision not to recuse himself. And yet when he completed the analysis he stated that he would concede that "fair minded judges might disagree about the matter" and that he regarded the "question as a fairly debatable one."[87]

It is at that point that Rehnquist makes clear what tipped his decision not to recuse himself. As he put it, in a case in which the Court is divided five to four, a recusal would have resulted in the "affirmance of the judgment below . . . [as a result of] an equally divided Court."[88] Or, as Rehnquist also stated, when the Court is equally divided, thus leaving the lower court ruling as the law in the case, "the principle of law presented by the case is left unsettled," and while such a result "is obviously not a reason for refusing to disqualify oneself where in fact one deems himself disqualified," Rehnquist wrote that he believed "it is a reason for not 'bending over backwards' in order to deem one self disqualified."[89]

As weighty as that consideration might be if the lower court had decided a substantive legal issue of national importance that would reverberate across the land, that was hardly the situation at the case at hand, in that the lower court had decided a standing issue in a factual setting that Rehnquist himself characterized as unusual if not rare. Indeed, because Rehnquist's reasons for not recusing himself were so unconvincing, it seems highly likely that Rehnquist was motivated not to recuse himself because he favored having the case dismissed for lack of standing. And Rehnquist wanted that result so as to insulate the executive surveillance program from judicial review.[90]

Laird, decided in 1971, involving Army surveillance, is one of the two bookends; *Clapper*, decided in 2013, involving NSA surveillance, is the other.

---

cautioned not to make this motion before the case was argued before the Supreme Court on the assumption that Rehnquist would disqualify himself and that such a motion might be considered by some on the court as offensive. Jeffrey W. Stempel, *Rehnquist, Recusal, and Reform*, 53 Brook. L. Rev. 589, 592 n.16 (1987).

[87] Laird v. Tatum, 409 U.S. 824, 838–837 (1972).

[88] *Laird*, 409 U.S. at 837–838.

[89] *Id.*

[90] Rehnquist's refusal to recuse himself was an issue that arose during his confirmation hearings to be chief justice.

In the wake of the September 11 attacks, President George W. Bush authorized what is known as the President's Surveillance Program, a program that contained several initiatives, one of which was the monitoring of international telephone calls and international email of Americans and others inside the United States in search for evidence of terrorist activity without securing court-approved warrants ordinarily required for domestic spying. Although the ostensible targets of the monitoring were individuals outside the United States believed to be affiliated with al-Qaeda, the program was designed to intercept communications with individuals in the United States, and it was that linkage that made the legality of the program controversial. Indeed, it was the continued authorization of this program in March 2004 that gave rise to dramatic confrontation at the hospital bedside of Attorney General John Ashcroft between, on the one hand, Ashcroft, Deputy Attorney General James Comey, and other Department of Justice officials, who questioned the legality of the program, and, on the other, White House Counsel Alberto Gonzales and White House Chief of Staff Andrew Card, who advocated for the continuation of the program. After a brief interruption the surveillance program continued.

Two *New York Times* reporters, James Risen and Eric Lichtblau, learned of the surveillance program in 2004 and prepared a report that was ready for publication before the 2004 presidential election. But after a meeting with President Bush and some senior administration officials during which they argued that the disclosure of the program would undermine its utility and injure national security, the leadership of the *New York Times* decided against publishing the report. As a result, the existence of the program became public only on December 16, 2005, when the *New York Times* published the Risen and Lichtblau report under the headline "Bush Lets U.S. Spy on Callers Without Courts," and then—at that point—the Times published the report only because Risen was about to disclose the warrantless surveillance program in a published book. The *Times* report ignited a storm of protest against the program, which was in turn followed by the publication of additional reports by Risen and Lichtblau that gave rise to additional criticism of the Bush Administration's antiterrorist programs as well as criticism of the *Times* and the press in general for destroying effective antiterrorist programs that kept the nation safe.[91]

The warrantless surveillance program, slightly modified by President Bush in the wake of the confrontation between White House representatives and the Department of Justice, continued until February 1, 2007, when the Protect

---

[91] James Risen and Eric Lichtblau, *Bush Lets U.S. Spy on Callers Without Courts*, N.Y. Times, Dec. 16, 2005, http://www.nytimes.com/2005/12/16/politics/bush-lets-us-spy-on-callers-without-courts.html?_r=0.

America Act of 2007 became effective. This Act authorized the continuation of the surveillance program until early 2008, when the adoption of the 2008 amendments to Foreign Intelligence Surveillance Act (FISA) extended the surveillance program until 2012. Although the bill was adopted by a lopsided majority in the House and the Senate, it was controversial, subject to a fili-buster led by Senators Russ Feingold and Chris Dodd, and received national media attention. The *Clapper* case was an outgrowth of these developments, and it was commenced the day the 2008 amendments became effective.

In essence, the plaintiffs' challenge to the federal surveillance procedure claimed that the amendments to the FISA put the plaintiffs in a position in which they risked having sensitive communications monitored by the government or in which they were forced to incur financial and professional costs to avoid being monitored. In March of 2011, a Second Circuit panel composed of Judges Calabresi, Sack, and Lynch decided that lawyers, journalists, and human rights researchers, whose work required international communications with individuals who "they believe are likely targets of surveillance" by the United States pursuant to 2008 amendments to FISA, had legal standing to challenge the facial constitutionality of Section 702 of the Foreign Intelligence Surveillance Act of 1978.[92]

A year and a half later, on February 26, 2013, the Supreme Court decided this case—now styled as *Clapper v. Amnesty International*—by a five-to-four vote in which the Court concluded that the individuals who claimed that the procedures set forth in the 2008 FISA amendments violate the "Fourth Amendment, the First Amendment, Article III of the Constitution, and the principle of separation of powers because they 'allow[] the executive branch sweeping and virtually unregulated authority to monitor the international communications . . . of law-abiding U.S. citizens and residents,'"[93] did not have standing to contest the constitutionality of the procedures.[94]

Justice Alito wrote for Chief Justice Roberts and Justices Scalia, Thomas, and Kennedy, while Justice Breyer's dissent was joined by Justices Ginsburg, Sotomayor, and Kagan. The thrust of Alito's argument was that the plaintiffs'

---

[92] Six months later the Second Circuit denied a hearing en banc, with four judges writing a dissent. Section 702 was added to FISA by Section 101 (a)(20) of the FISA Amendments Act of 2008, and codified at 50 U.S.C. §1881a. Amnesty Int'l USA v. Clapper, 638 F.3d 118, 121 (2d Cir. 2011).

[93] Amnesty Int'l USA v. Clapper, 638 F.3d 118, 121 (2d Cir. 2011).

[94] For law review commentary on the Clapper opinion, see Andrew C. Sand, *Standing Uncertainty: An Expected-Value Standard for Fear-Based Injury in* Clapper v. Amnesty International USA, 113 Mich. L. Rev. 711 (2015); Amanda Marianm McDowell, *The Impact of* Clapper v. Amnesty International USA on the Doctrine of Fear-Based Standing, 49 Ga. L. Rev. 247 (2014); and Neil M. Richards, *The Dangers of Surveillance*, 126 Harv. L. Rev. 1934 (2013).

claims that their communications would be monitored by the government by means of section 1881a procedures (as opposed to procedures set forth in another statute) were mere speculation and conjecture, and that they were engaged in nothing more than an effort to "manufacture standing by choosing to make expenditures based on hypothetical future harm that is not certainly impending."[95] In keeping with recent efforts by justices who wish to close the courthouse door on certain claims,[96] Justice Alito raised the standing bar in the *Clapper* case by claiming that it was "well established"[97] that to satisfy the standing requirements a party had to have been already injured or facing a threatened injury that "must be 'certainly impending.'"[98] The legal requirement of "certainly impending" was of recent origin and fell far short of qualifying as being "well established."[99] Moreover, the "certainly impending" requirement is only used in some cases—not all—and is thus inconsistent with many cases in which standing has been accepted.

In raising the standing bar to "certainly impending," Alito emphasized that the Court's inquiry into standing has been "especially rigorous" when deciding the merits of a dispute that "would force" the Court to decide whether "an action taken by one of the other two branches of the Federal Government was unconstitutional."[100] And then, most notably, Alito pointed out that the "especially rigorous" approach the Court employs in cases involving other co-equal branches becomes even more demanding when the "Judiciary has been requested to review actions of the political branches in the fields of intelligence gathering and foreign affairs."[101] In other words, the requirements of standing become more demanding when a case implicates separation of powers considerations, and those more demanding requirements only become more demanding when a case implicating separation of powers also implicates matters affecting intelligence or foreign affairs.

Alito's description of the pertinent law of standing may seem reasonable in the abstract. But when he applied the rules to the facts of the *Clapper* case,

---

[95] Clapper v. Amnesty Int'l USA, 133 S. Ct. 1138, 1143 (2013).

[96] Erwin Chemerinsky, The Conservative Assault on the Constitution, 201–238 (2010).

[97] *Clapper*, 133 S. Ct. at 1143.

[98] *Id.*

[99] *Id.* In a 1993 law review article published twenty years before Alito wrote his opinion in the *Clapper* case, law professor Cass R. Sunstein concluded that the claim that the Constitution requires an "injury in fact," whether "certainly impending" or not, was "an extraordinarily novel development," and contrary to the Supreme Court's assertions, it "has no basis in the text or history of the constitution." Cass R. Sunstein, *Standing Injuries*, 1973 Sup. C. Rev. 37, 38 (1993).

[100] *Clapper*, 133 S.Ct. at 1147.

[101] *Id.*

the drastic lengths that Alito and the majority were willing to go to deny the plaintiffs' standing becomes fully apparent.

Alito argues that the plaintiffs' fears of surveillance are premised on each of five implausible eventualities occurring. First, Alito stated that the government must decide to "target the communications of non-U.S. persons with whom" the plaintiffs communicate.[102] Alito did not explain why he thought this doubtful. One plaintiff, Scott McKay, was a lawyer, who represented a non-U.S. person who was tried and acquitted of terrorism charges in 2004, and, who, in addition to facing criminal charges after September 11, was named as a defendant in several civil cases, and who also represented a detainee before Military Commissions in Guantanamo Bay, Cuba. McKay stated that his professional duties required him to communicate with people outside the United States, and that prior to 2008, the government had "intercepted some 10,000 telephone calls and 20,000 email communications" involving just one of his clients. Another plaintiff, Sylvia Royce, stated in her affidavit that she represented a prisoner held at Guantanamo Bay as an enemy combatant, that in her capacity as his lawyer she spoke with the prisoner's brother who lived in Germany, and she had been told that the government had threatened her client that his "family members would be arrested and mistreated if he did not cooperate."[103] The fact that these two lawyers would fear that their communications with persons they contacted in their professional capacity would be subject to electronic surveillance would seem not only plausible, but sensible and likely.

Second, even assuming that the executive monitored the communications with whom the plaintiffs communicated, Alito argued that it was purely speculative that the executive would do so under the statute the plaintiffs challenged in this action—section §1881a of the amended FISA—as opposed to "utilizing another method of surveillance."[104] On its surface, the claim may seem perfectly reasonable. But that reasonableness quickly vanishes upon the most superficial inspection.

Alito's opinion itself sets forth the facts that provide the fatal blow. In 2007, the FISC issued orders that restricted the issuance of an order authorizing the monitoring of communications in or out of the United States to circumstances in which there was "probable cause to believe that one participant to the communication was a member or agent of al Qaeda or an associated terrorist organization."[105] The impact of these orders was to subject "any electronic surveillance that was then occurring under NSA's program to the approval of

---

[102] *Id.* at 1148.
[103] *Id.* at 1157.
[104] *Id.* at 1148.
[105] *Id.* at 1144.

the Foreign Intelligence Surveillance Court." At that point a FISC judge "narrowed the FISC's authorization of such surveillance,"[106] and, as Alito wrote in his opinion, the "executive," in response, "asked Congress to amend FISA so that it would provide the intelligence community with additional authority to meet the challenges of modern technology and international terrorism."[107]

Congress consented and amended FISA—the new section 1881a—to permit "a new and independent source of intelligence collection authority, beyond that granted in traditional FISA,"[108] which was much less demanding than the previous standard and which Alito summarized: section 1881a does not require the government "to demonstrate probable cause that the target of the electronic surveillance is a foreign power or agent of a foreign power," and section 1881a does not require the government "to specify the nature and location of each of the particular facilities or places at which the electronic surveillance will occur."[109] As is evident, section 1881a made it easier for the government to engage in electronic surveillance than it had been.

Against that background, the plaintiffs' claim that the executive utilized section 1881a to monitor their communications was not only plausible but realistic. After all, why would the government utilize a more demanding avenue for obtaining authorization to monitor communications when a less demanding avenue was available? Or, as Justice Breyer stated: ". . . compared with prior law, §1881a simplifies and thus expedites the approval process, making it more likely that the Government will use §1881a to obtain the necessary approval."[110] Although Alito claimed the plaintiffs merely assumed that the executive utilized section 1881a procedures, he offered no reason or explanation as to why he thought the government would avoid utilizing section 1881a when it was adopted in response to the executive's requests and it is widely understood to constitute a set of standards that were more relaxed by comparison to others for obtaining a judicial warrant.

Alito's third factor focused on the Foreign Intelligence Surveillance Court, and his claim was that the plaintiffs assume that the Article III judges who serve on that court will "conclude that the Government's proposed surveillance procedures satisfy §1881a's many safeguards and are consistent with the Fourth Amendment."[111] Alito is correct; plaintiffs assumed that the FISA court judges would approve the executive's surveillance request. But that assumption is not

[106] *Id.*
[107] *Id.*
[108] *Id.*
[109] *Id.*
[110] *Id.* at 1159 (Breyer, J., dissenting).
[111] *Id.* at 1148 (majority opinion).

only reasonable but almost certainly the fact. As Justice Breyer's respectful dissent disclosed, the executive "rarely files requests [to the FISA court] that fail to meet the statutory criteria"; in 2011, the government submitted 1,676 requests, withdrew two requests, and had the remaining 1,674 approved (30 with "some modification"); and given the communications plaintiffs describe, there is "no reason" to believe that the court would decline to approve the requests.[112] In response to Justice Breyer, Alito offered no reason and no statistics to support the premise that a FISA judge would deny a government request.

Alito's fourth and fifth points in support of his claim that plaintiffs' allegations constitute nothing more than a "highly speculative fear" were similarly unpersuasive. What Alito stated is that it is mere speculation that the government would succeed in intercepting the communications of the targeted individual and that even assuming the government did succeed, it is mere speculation that the government would actually intercept a communication between a target and one of the plaintiffs. Again, to the extent that Alito stakes out a claim that plaintiffs offer no specific evidence that the government would in fact be successful in intercepting a target's communications and that the interception would intercept one of the plaintiffs' communication, he is on solid ground. The plaintiffs offered no such evidence. But then, how could they? The entire electronic surveillance program was secret. What they claimed was that based on the government's past conduct, based on the government's capacities, and based on the government's motivation to engage in broad electronic surveillance, it is not only reasonable, not only likely, but it is very likely that the government will succeed in intercepting the target's communications and because of the frequency of the plaintiffs' communications that the government will intercept the plaintiffs' communications. Given what was known at the time, those allegations seem completely sensible and compelling, so much so that they, along with the other factors assessed earlier, make Alito's opinion seem contrived. Thus, Justice Breyer, relying upon the same information available to Justice Alito, spelled out the compelling case as to why there was no

---

[112] *Id.* at 1159 (Breyer, J., dissenting). "Of course, to exercise this capacity the Government must have intelligence court authorization. But the Government rarely files requests that fail to meet the statutory criteria." *Id.* In 2011, of the 1,676 applications to the intelligence court, two were withdrawn by the government, and the remaining 1,674 were approved, 30 with some modification. Letter from Ronald Weich, Assistant Attorney General, to Joseph R. Biden, Jr., 1 (Apr. 30, 2012), http://www.justice.gov/sites/default/files/nsd/legacy/2014/07/23/2011fisa-ltr.pdf. "As the intelligence court itself has stated, its review under §1881a is 'narrowly circumscribed.' *In re* Proceedings Required by §702(i) of the FISA Amendments Act of 2008, No. Misc. 08–01, 3 (Aug. 17, 2008). There is no reason to believe that the communications described would all fail to meet the conditions necessary for approval. Moreover, compared with prior law, §1881a simplifies and thus expedites the approval process, making it more likely that the Government will use § 1881a to obtain the necessary approval." *Clapper*, 133 S. Ct. at 1159 (Breyer, J., dissenting).

doubt that the government had the capacity and the will to intercept the communications in question.[113]

When the five-person majority in *Clapper* decided that the plaintiffs lacked standing, it stated: "we have repeatedly reiterated that 'threatened injury must be *certainly impending* to constitute injury in fact,' and that '[a]llegations of *possible* future injury' are not sufficient."[114] The phrase "certainly impending" suggests that the injury must be so imminent as to be practically inevitable. Yet, a year and a half later, those same five justices, joined by the four justices who thought that the plaintiffs in *Clapper* had standing, concluded that an antiabortion group had standing to challenge the constitutionality of an Ohio statute that prohibited "certain 'false statements'[made] during the course of a political campaign."[115] And that was true, even though the antiabortion group's claim of injury was hypothetical and conjectural as opposed to "certainly impending," in that it was uncertain when an occasion would again arise which would cause the group to make such statements that might make it susceptible to a claim that it violated the Ohio law; it was uncertain that the group would make such

---

[113] In his dissent, Justice Breyer stated:

> Fourth, the Government has the *capacity* to conduct electronic surveillance of the kind at issue. To some degree this capacity rests upon technology available to the Government. See D. Kris and J. Wilson, National Security Investigations & Prosecutions, Vol. I §16:6, 562 (2d ed. 2012) ("NSA's technological abilities are legendary"); *id.*, §16:12, at 572–577 (describing the National Security Agency's capacity to monitor "*very* broad facilities" such as international switches). *See, e.g.,* Lichtblau and Risen, *Spy Agency Mined Vast Data Trove, Officials Report*, N.Y. Times, Dec. 24, 2005, A1 (describing capacity to trace and to analyze large volumes of communications into and out of the United States); Lichtblau and Shane, *Bush is Pressed Over New Report on Surveillance*, N.Y. Times, May 12, 2006, at A1 (reporting capacity to obtain access to records of many, if not most, telephone calls made in the United States); Priest and Arkin, *A Hidden World, Growing Beyond Control*, Wash. Post, July 19, 2010, at A1 (reporting that every day, collection systems at the National Security Agency intercept and store 1.7 billion e-mails, telephone calls and other types of communications). *Cf.* Statement of Administration Policy on S. 2248, *supra*, at 1156 (rejecting a provision of the Senate bill that would require intelligence analysts to count "the number of persons located in the United States whose communications were reviewed" as "impossible to implement" (internal quotation marks omitted)). This capacity also includes the Government's authority to obtain the kind of information here at issue from private carriers such as AT & T and Verizon. See 50 U.S.C. §1881a(h). We are further told by *amici* that the Government is expanding that capacity. See Brief for Electronic Privacy Information Center et al. as 22–23 (National Security Agency will be able to conduct surveillance of most electronic communications between domestic and foreign points). (Clapper, 133 S. Ct. at 1158 (Breyer, J., dissenting))

[114] *Id.* at 1147 (majority opinion).
[115] Susan B. Anthony List et al. v. Driehaus, 134 S. Ct. 2334, 2338 (2014).

a statement even if the occasion did arise; and it was uncertain that the group would be prosecuted if it made such a statement.

In reaching this result, the unanimous Court did not overrule or modify *Clapper*. Rather, it argued that *Clapper* authorized two different standards for deciding whether a party satisfied the requirements of standing. One standard was the "certainly impending" standard applied in the *Clapper* case.[116] The other standard was much more lenient and simply required that there existed a "substantial risk that the harm will occur."[117] The *Clapper* majority did not explain why it employs two standards as opposed to one, or when it would employ one standard as opposed to the other, or why it employed the more demanding standard in *Clapper*. What is known is that Justice Alito and four other members of the high court employed the more demanding standard when the legality of a NSA surveillance program was challenged and the far less demanding standard when an antiabortion group sought the assistance of the courts, and they did not explain themselves.

After *Clapper* will anyone have standing to challenge, in a civil action, the constitutionality of government surveillance? It seems most unlikely.

On its face, Alito's opinion stands for the view that these plaintiffs offering these allegations fail to satisfy the standing requirement, leaving open the possibility that some other plaintiffs making similar legal claims but supported by other allegations would have standing. But that impression seems seriously misleading. Although Alito does not preemptively shut the courthouse to such lawsuits challenging surveillance activities by the government, in no place in his opinion does he actually state or imply or suggest that the courthouse door is open. Indeed, Alito's explanation of the shortcomings of plaintiffs' allegations indicate that, to satisfy the standing requirements, a plaintiff must be in possession of facts that a plaintiff is almost certainly not going to possess. In other words, when Alito's standing requirements are understood against the background of the secrecy of the government's surveillance programs and the secrecy of the FISA court as well as the breadth of the state secrets privilege, it is plain that Alito and the four justices of the Supreme Court who joined his opinion are prepared to dismiss on standing grounds any attack by an individual on a government surveillance program outside of a criminal action against a particular individual. And although Alito does not make this statement

---

[116] As Alito's opinion makes plain, the certainly impending standard itself has three distinct levels of difficulties. The least demanding standard is applied in cases not involving a coequal branch of government and not involving national security. The middle-level standard is applied to cases involving a coequal branch of government but not involving security. The most demanding construction of certainly impending is applied to cases involving a coequal branch of government and national security. *See Clapper*, 133 S. Ct. at 1143.

[117] The *Clapper* opinion noted the "substantial risk" standard. *Id.* at 1150, n.5.

unequivocally, he comes close when he says that the Court has "often found a lack of standing in cases in which the Judiciary has been requested to review actions of the political branches in the fields of intelligence gathering and foreign affairs."[118] In fact, Alito cites not one case—and for that matter Justice Breyer is also unable to identify one case in his dissent—in which the Supreme Court granted standing to plaintiffs seeking declaratory and injunctive relief in a civil action based on claims that the government's surveillance program violated the Constitution.[119]

The Court's stance on standing masks a fundamental calculation. The Court not only raised the bar on standing to a point that prevents anyone from surmounting it, but it presented its reasons for doing so as responsive to democratic considerations. Because the Court is an undemocratic government institution within a governing structure that emphasizes democratic values, the Court presents its ruling as advancing democratic values by closing the courthouse door. No one can definitively state that the justices do not embrace that outlook in a case such as *Clapper*. But when *Clapper* is read against the sweep of cases over the last four or five decades, it would be naïve to think that judicial respect for democratic values was the only, or perhaps main, consideration driving the outcome. The justices find ways of undermining judicial review of executive conduct in national security cases not simply because the Court is mindful of democratic values or protective of national security, but because

---

[118] *Id.* at 1147.

[119] Justice Alito's hostility to the plaintiffs' effort to use the courts to protect constitutional rights from NSA violation, as evidenced by his opinion, is only moderately disguised by comparison to Chief Justice Burger's more frankly hostile opinions in *Laird v. Tatum* and *United States v. Richardson*, or by comparison to an opinion in the *Clapper* case submitted by Chief Judge Dennis Jacobs of the United States Court of Appeals for the Second Circuit from a denial of rehearing en banc. The Jacobs's opinion is an undisguised assault in tone and substance on the *Clapper* plaintiffs and their attorneys. Because the Jacobs opinion may well express in plain words the views usually expressed in repressed legal formulations of many conservative jurists, including Justice Alito and the four members of the Supreme Court who composed the majority of five in the *Clapper* case, it is worthy of brief quotation. Jacobs describes the individuals who initiated the *Clapper* case as an "assortment of lawyers, journalists and activists, and organizations representing such people." Amnesty Int'l USA v. Clapper, 667 F.3d 163, 201 (2d Cir. 2011). The affidavits submitted by the plaintiffs in support of their claims "employ all the lawyer's arts to convey a devious impression." *Id.* And then, as if there were any doubt about his disposition, Jacobs wrote: "At the risk of being obvious, the purpose of this lawsuit is litigation for its own sake—for these lawyers to claim a role in policy-making for which they were not appointed or elected, for which they are not fitted by experience, and for which they are not accountable. As best I can see, the only purpose of this litigation is for counsel and plaintiffs to act out their fantasy of persecution, to validate their pretensions to policy expertise, to make themselves consequential rather than marginal, and to raise funds for self-sustaining litigation. In short, counsel's and plaintiffs' only perceptible interest is to carve out for themselves an influence over government policy—an interest that the law of standing forecloses." *Id.* at 203.

the justices have decided that it is far more important to uphold national security than it is to permit parties to unearth executive conduct that may have violated the Constitution or the criminal law.

In other words, the very governing body most responsible for upholding the law adopts a position that implies that national security requires it to tolerate unlawful conduct. It does so because it thinks that security is essential to a regime committed to the rule of law and the toleration of unlawful executive conduct is essential to upholding security, which in turn means, from this perspective, that shaping legal doctrine to insulate unlawful conduct is essential to upholding the rule of law.

Such reasoning is part of the same gene pool as Chief Justice Hughes's comment that the power to wage war is the power to wage war successfully.[120] The essence of Hughes's thinking was that during wartime, the end may justify the means. But Hughes offered that calculation as one that was conceivable during wartime, not at other times. Moreover, as Chief Justice Earl Warren observed, the opposite "truism," that the end does not justify the means, has "at least as respectable a lineage," even during wartime.[121] Thus, while it may be arguable which of the two truisms should be honored when the nation is engaged in a world war that threatens its survival, the idea that the end warrants discarding the rule of law in circumstances a far cry from a world war constitutes a seriously distorted assessment of the relevant fundamental considerations, especially since there is nothing inherently contradictory in protecting the nation's security and adhering to the rule of law.

[120] See Chief Justice Hughes's opinion in Home Bldg. & Loan Ass'n. v. Blaisdell, 290 U.S. 398, 426 (1934).

[121] Earl Warren, The Bill of Rights and the Military, 37 N.Y.U. L. Rev. 181, 192 (1962).

11

Rights without Remedies

On September 26, 2002, Maher Arar, a dual citizen of Syria and Canada, arrived at JFK airport in New York City while en route from Tunisia to Montreal, and was then detained by U.S. authorities because of information received from Canadian officials regarding Arar's possible terrorist links. For twelve days, Arar alleged, he was in the custody of U.S. officials who mistreated him. At that point he was removed to Syria via Jordan, pursuant to an intergovernment understanding that he would be interrogated under torture by Syrian officials. A little more than one year later, on October 5, 2003, Arar was released into the custody of Canadian Embassy officials in Damascus. After an investigation, the Canadian government compensated Arar approximately $9.75 million (U.S. dollars) in exchange for withdrawing a lawsuit against the Canadian government. Arar's lawsuit for damages in the U.S. courts was dismissed on the ground that the law did not authorize the courts to grant him a damage remedy.[1]

In the *Arar* case, an individual who federal officials suspect of being a terrorist is arguably kidnapped and tortured, yet has no judicial remedy for damages because the Congress has not authorized the courts to grant one and the federal courts refuse to fashion one. Could it be that an individual who was detained for months on a pretext that he was a potential witness in a criminal proceeding would be without a remedy against the high officials who allegedly ordered the abuse of the "material witness" law in a national security context, and that he would be without such a remedy but because of a second and quite different legal doctrine? Or is it possible that an individual, who was identified as a person of interest in a national security investigation—a designation that resulted from the implementation of discriminatory policies designed and implemented by high officials based on race, religion, and national origin—and who was then abused and harshly treated during confinement following 9/11, could have his case dismissed against the senior officials for still a third and different doctrine of deference?

---

[1] *See* Arar v. Ashcroft, 585 F.3d 559 (2d Cir. 2009). For a comment on the *Arar* case, see Comment, 123 Harv. L. Rev. 1787 (2010).

The answer to these questions is yes. There are three interrelated doctrines, quite apart from the state secrets privilege and the law of standing, that may cause an action to be dismissed even though an individual has been injured. These doctrines—and they concern whether an injured party may be entitled to a damage remedy, whether a defendant public official may have a quasi-immunity defense, or whether the plaintiff's complaint contains sufficient factual claims—mainly developed outside of a national security context and, as a consequence, they implicate considerations other than national security ones. But as exemplified by the *Arar* case, the three doctrines may have a dramatic and salient impact on cases arising in a national security context in that courts deny relief to individuals who may have been egregiously harmed, courts fail to hold accountable executive officials who arguably committed unlawful conduct and thus encourage a dynamic of future unlawful conduct, and courts undermine the system of checks of balances central to the governing plan. We consider the three interlocking doctrines in this chapter and the next.

The first of these doctrines involves the important question whether an individual has a claim for damages against executive officers who may have violated that person's constitutional rights.

The case, *Bivens v. Six Unknown Named Agents of Federal Bureau of Narcotics*,[2] had the most mundane origins. The claimant alleged that on the morning of November 26, 1965, federal narcotics agents entered his apartment, "manacled" him "in front of his wife and children," "threatened to arrest the entire family," "searched the apartment from stem to stern," and arrested him. Not quite two years later, the claimant, without the assistance of a lawyer, filed a legal action in federal court seeking $15,000 in damages and alleging that the arrest and search "were effected without a warrant," that "unreasonable force was employed in making the arrest," and that the arrest was made without probable cause. The claimant asserted that he suffered "great humiliation, embarrassment, and mental suffering as a result of the agents' unlawful conduct."[3] The district court dismissed the complaint because the judge concluded that it failed to state a claim upon which relief may be granted. The circuit court affirmed the dismissal, and it was that order

---

[2] 403 U.S. 388 (1971). For a very incisive and thoughtful law review article that importantly revises conventional wisdom on the utility of the Bivens remedy, and, in the notes, provide, very useful leads to the vast legal literature the Bivens decision sparked, see Alexander A. Reinert, *Measuring the Success of* Bivens *Litigation and its Consequences for the Individual Liability Model*, 62 Stan. L. Rev. 809 (2010).

[3] *Bivens*, 403 U.S. at 389–390.

that the Supreme Court reviewed and reversed,[4] thus turning an invisible case into a national landmark.

In support of the circuit court judgment dismissing the action, the executive did not argue that the claimant should be without a remedy. Rather, the executive argued that the right asserted by the claimant—primarily a right of privacy—was the creation of state and not federal law, and that the claimant could recover relief for the violation of such a right under state law in state court.[5] In sum, the plaintiff had a state law remedy, not a federal law remedy.

In rejecting the executive's position and in reversing the lower court, Justice Brennan made several points.[6] First, Justice Brennan characterized

---

[4] *Id.* at 390.

[5] *Id.*

[6] The rule in the *Bivens* case permitted the awarding of money damages against federal officials, even though Congress had not passed a statute authorizing such relief. This judge-made rule was prompted at least in part by a Supreme Court decision a decade before in *Monroe v. Pape*, which authorized federal courts to award money damages against state officials who violated the federal rights of individuals. Monroe v. Pape, 365 U.S. 167 (1961). *Monroe* represented three shifts in thinking. First, built into the constitutional framework is a struggle for power between the states and the national government. Throughout the history of the republic there have been major moments when the arrangements between these governing entities fundamentally shifted, as was true during the Civil War period and the New Deal era of the 1930s. After World War II, when the standing of the United States in world affairs and its confrontation with the Soviet Union required that the United States put an end to Jim Crow laws and the system of legally mandated race segregation, the Supreme Court rendered its historic decision in *Brown v. Board of Education*, which thrust the federal courts into engineering profound changes in the nation's public schools, which were administered by state and local officials. Brown v. Board of Educ., 347 U.S. 483 (1954). Thus, the Brown decision fundamentally reworked the relationship between federal courts and state and local governments by assigning federal judges the task of overseeing the desegregation of mandatorily segregated public schools. Second, during the balance of the Fifties and Sixties, the Supreme Court rendered one decision after another declaring new federal constitutional rights, a development that resulted in the era being named the "Warren Court" after its chief justice, Earl Warren. For the most part these rights involved judicial orders that required the state and local officials to either refrain from doing something or that compelled them to do something. In other words, these orders did not impose money damages on state or local officials; rather, they were prohibitory or mandatory injunctions. Third, although money damages were considered the preferred form of relief by comparison to injunctive relief, the federal courts had been for decades granting injunctive relief against state and local officials to protect federal rights but rarely granting money damages. In *Monroe*, the Supreme Court stated that a federal remedy for damages for the violation of federal rights against state officials was supplementary to any remedies theoretically available in state court under state law, which in this particular case meant that an individual could sue law enforcement officials for money damages in federal court, even though the same individual might have an adequate remedy in state court under state law. Monroe, 365 U.S. at 183. It is hard to think that the majority rule in *Bivens* was not a judicial responsive to the asymmetry the Monroe decision created between the damage liability of federal officials on the one hand and state and local officials on the other.

the implication of the executive's argument as providing that the Fourth Amendment did nothing more than provided federal agents with a defense in state court if sued under state tort law. In other words, the executive claimed that the only purpose of the Fourth Amendment was to allow federal agents to prevail in a lawsuit in which a party claimed that the agents had violated a person's rights under state tort law, provided the agents were able to prove that their conduct did not violate the restrictions of the Fourth Amendment.[7] Instead, Brennan insisted that the Fourth Amendment is more than a defense to a state law damage action; it is "an independent limitation upon the exercise of federal power." Or, to track the executive's argument, the Fourth Amendment proscribes the conduct of federal agents, even though that same conduct if engaged in by a private party would not be "condemned by state law."[8]

Second, the interests protected by state law "regulating trespass and the invasion of privacy" and those protected by the Fourth Amendment's guarantee "against unreasonable searches and seizures, may be inconsistent or even hostile." A person may lock the door against a private party intruder or call the police for assistance, and a private party "will not normally be liable in trespass" if granted entrance onto private property by the owner. In contrast, a person claiming entrance under the guise of federal authority "stands in a far different position."[9] Private resistance to federal authority will be futile, may constitute a crime, and will not be aided by local police.

Third, federal courts must have the authority to grant a remedy for the violation of a constitutional right. Because the Fourth Amendment guarantees rights against the government, and because damages are historically an "ordinary remedy for an invasion of personal interests in liberty," Brennan asserted that it "should hardly seem a surprising proposition" that damages may be obtained "for injuries consequent upon a violation of the Fourth Amendment by federal officials."[10] That, he insisted, should certainly be the case in a nation that long ago embraced John Marshall's aspiration: "The very essence of civil liberty certainly consists in the right of every individual to claim the protection of the laws, whenever he receives an injury."[11]

---

[7] *Bivens*, 403 U.S. at 390–391. The executive conceded to the Court that it was its policy to remove such actions from the state courts to the federal courts pursuant to the appropriate removal statute, which only seems to make its legal position awkward. Nonetheless, the executive urged the Court to dismiss the complaint so that the claimant could file a new action in state court asserting state law grounds, which the defendants would then remove to the federal court. *Id.* at 391.

[8] *Id.* at 394, 392.

[9] *Id.* at 394.

[10] *Id.* at 396, 395.

[11] *Id.* at 398 (citing Marbury v. Madison, 5 U.S. 137, 163 (1803)).

In many respects Justice Harlan's concurring opinion in *Bivens* penetrated the entangled issues more effectively than Justice Brennan's opinion. The executive had claimed that a federal court was barred from awarding Bivens a damage remedy absent a federal statute authorizing it. At the same time, Harlan asserted that neither the executive nor any of the three judges who dissented in the *Bivens* case took the position that Bivens's right to be "free from the type of official conduct prohibited by the Fourth Amendment" was dependent "on a decision by the State in which he resides to accord him a remedy." Harlan noted that such an extreme position would be "incompatible with the presumed availability of federal equitable relief" under proper circumstances. Having established that point—a point that was not disputed—Harlan made the obvious but important point that the "interest which Bivens claims—to be free from official conduct in contravention of the Fourth Amendment—is a federally protected interest."[12] In short, the issue raised by the case was not whether *Bivens* had a federal right—everyone agreed that he did—but "whether the power to authorize damages as a judicial remedy for the vindication of a federal constitutional right is placed by the Constitution itself exclusively in Congress' hands."[13]

Once Harlan had put the spotlight on whether the Constitution granted Congress exclusive authority to authorize a judicially imposed damage remedy or whether the federal courts possessed concurrent authority, Harlan presented three convincing assertions. First, it was undisputed that federal courts had previously granted "damages in the absence of explicit congressional action authorizing the remedy" by implying such a remedy in a statutory scheme or in the name of federal common law, and that such courts had even gone one step further and had generated "substantive rules governing primary behavior in furtherance of broadly formulated policies articulated by statute or Constitution." Against those accepted claims, Harlan maintained that it would be "at least anomalous" to then conclude that federal courts are "powerless to accord a damages remedy to vindicate social policies which, by virtue of their inclusion in the Constitution, are aimed predominately at restraining the Government as an instrument of the popular will."[14]

Second, if "explicit congressional authorization is an absolute prerequisite to the power of a federal court to accord compensatory relief regardless of the necessity or appropriateness of damages as a remedy simply because of the status of a legal interest as constitutionally protected," then such statutory authority is similarly a prerequisite to the exercise of equitable remedial discretion in favor of constitutionally protected interests. And on that score Harlan claimed that since it was thought that a federal statute granting the federal

---

[12] *Id.* at 400 (Harlan, J., concurring).
[13] *Id.* at 401–402.
[14] *Id.* at 403–404.

courts jurisdiction was sufficient statutory authority to warrant the grant of equitable relief, then, he argued, it seemed to him "the same statute is sufficient to empower a federal court to grant a traditional remedy at law."[15]

Third, prior Supreme Court decisions had made it "clear" that if the Congress had granted the federal courts jurisdiction over a particular subject matter and had not explicitly restricted the remedial authority of the federal courts, then the scope of the courts' power to grant injunctive relief was to be determined by history and tradition and that the "reach" of the courts' "inherent equitable powers" was "broad indeed."[16]

Brennan and Harlan agreed on many points. The interests guaranteed by the Fourth Amendment were independent from any protected by state privacy and trespass laws. A federal remedy—whether it was equitable in nature or money damages—was supplemental to any remedy otherwise provided for by state law, and it was required if the Fourth Amendment was to restrain the conduct of federal officers and provide a remedy to an allegedly wronged individual. The courts, in the absence of a statute explicitly prohibiting the courts from granting such relief, had inherent authority to grant both an equitable and a damage remedy. In every such case courts should be aware of whether any "special factors" counsel "hesitation in the absence of affirmative action by Congress" authorizing the grant of a damage remedy.[17]

In the wake of *Bivens*, "many" lower federal courts had cited "*Bivens* as authorizing implied actions for money damages based on constitutional rights other than the fourth amendment."[18] Nonetheless, when a woman sought damages against a member of Congress, claiming that he discharged her because of her sex, the Fifth Circuit Court of Appeals, sitting en banc, concluded that in the absence of congressional authorization she was not entitled to a damage remedy under the Due Process Clause of the Fifth Amendment.[19] It was that

---

[15] *Id.* at 405.

[16] *Id.* at 404.

[17] *Id.* at 396 (majority opinion). The Bivens decision gave rise to academic discussions over the usefulness of the Bivens rule, which imposed liability on individual federal officials who could assert a defense of qualified immunity (a doctrine discussed in the next chapter) as opposed to a legal rule that imposed liability on the United States. The latter rule would require a congressional enactment that waived sovereign immunity. The impact of the individual liability model on individual federal officials adopted by the Court in Bivens is moderated because the "federal government, like most states and municipalities, usually indemnifies employees for the damages awarded in constitutional tort actions." Alexander A. Reinert, *Measuring the Success of* Bivens *Litigation and its Consequences for the Individual Liability Model*, 62 Stan. L. Rev. 809, 811 n.2.

[18] Davis v. Passman, 571 F.2d 793, 795 (5th Cir. 1978) (en banc) (refusing to find a damage remedy for an alleged violation of the Fifth Amendment).

[19] *Id.* at 801.

decision that prompted the Supreme Court to consider—after an eight-year hiatus—the exportability of *Bivens*'s Fourth Amendment reasoning to other constitutional provisions.

In *Davis v. Passman*, in a five-to-four vote, Justice Brennan concluded that a "damages remedy can . . . be implied directly under the Constitution when the Due Process Clause of the Fifth Amendment is violated."[20] In support of that conclusion, Justice Brennan offered several arguments. First, damages were an appropriate remedy in this case because there was in this case "no other alternative forms of judicial relief." As Justice Brennan wrote, quoting Justice Harlan: "it is damages or nothing."[21] Second, although a suit against a member of Congress for conduct taken in his official capacity raises "special concerns counseling hesitation," Brennan concluded that those considerations were "coextensive with the protections afforded by the Speech or Debate Clause," and thus did not bar the Court from authorizing a damage action, though they might, after further consideration by the lower court, prompt a court to sustain the Speech and Debate Clause privilege in the case, thus immunizing the congressman from liability.[22] Third, there is "no *explicit* congressional declaration" barring a person allegedly discriminated against from recovering damages, and the Court concluded that there is "no evidence . . . that Congress meant . . . to foreclose alternative remedies available to those not covered by the statute." Fourth, Brennan did not perceive a ruling permitting a damage remedy in this case as causing a "deluge" of claims flooding into the federal courts.[23] But even more importantly, even if the ruling did result in an increase of filings in the federal courts, Justice Brennan thought that Justice Harlan completely answered that concern in his concurrence in *Bivens*:

> Judicial resources, I am well aware, are increasingly scarce these days. Nonetheless, when we automatically close the courthouse door solely on this basis, we implicitly express a value judgment on the comparative importance of classes of legally protected interests. And current limitations upon the effective functioning of the courts arising from budgetary inadequacies should not be permitted to stand in the way of the recognition of otherwise sound constitutional principles.[24]

[20] Davis v. Passman, 442 U.S. 228, 230 (1979).

[21] *Id.* at 245 (quoting Bivens v. Six Unknown Named Agents of Fed. Bureau of Narcotics, 403 U.S. 388, 410 (1971) (Harlan, J., concurring)).

[22] *Id.* at 246.

[23] *Id.* at 246–248.

[24] *Id.* at 248 (quoting Bivens v. Six Unknown Named Agents of Fed. Bureau of Narcotics, 403 U.S. 388, 411 (1971) (Harlan, J., concurring)).

A year after the Court decided *Davis*, the Court expanded the *Bivens* doctrine again. In *Carlson v. Green*, the Court, by a vote of seven to two, concluded that the mother of a federal prisoner who died while in prison, allegedly because of treatment at the hands of prison officials who arguably violated his rights guaranteed by the Eighth Amendment to the Constitution that he not be subjected to cruel and unusual punishment, could maintain a claim for damages under *Bivens* against the appropriate federal prison officials.[25] In reaching this result, Justice Brennan's majority opinion stated that the right of an individual to recover damages against federal officials in federal court in the absence of any statute conferring such a right "may be defeated in a particular case ... in two situations." First, when the party sued demonstrates "special factors counseling hesitation in the absence of affirmative action by Congress," and second, when the defendant establishes that "Congress has provided an alternative remedy which it explicitly declared to be a *substitute* for recovery directly under the Constitution and viewed as equally effective."[26]

Justice Rehnquist—whose refusal to recuse himself in the *Laird*[27] case protected executive surveillance initiatives from judicial accountability—was not a member of the Court in June of 1971 when the Court decided *Bivens*; he was sworn in six months later in early January of 1972. But he was on the Court when the *Davis* case was decided, and although he dissented from Brennan's majority opinion in that case, he did so by joining each of three dissenting opinions written by Burger, Stewart, and Powell, but without penning his own views. But in the *Carlson* case, Rehnquist wrote his own long dissent. Although Rehnquist was alone in his opinion, it took issue with the *Bivens* ruling along lines adopted by later *Bivens* critics, and because of that, it deserves a brief review.

Rehnquist did not equivocate in his criticism of the *Bivens* rule in which the Court, without congressional authorization, implied a damage remedy:

> In my view, it is "an exercise of power that the Constitution does not give us" for this Court to infer a private civil damages remedy from the Eighth Amendment or any other constitutional provision. The creation of such remedies is a task that is more appropriately viewed as falling within the legislative sphere of authority.[28]

---

[25] Carlson v. Green, 446 U.S. 14, 24 (1980).

[26] *Id.* at 18–19.

[27] Laird v. Tatum, 408 U.S. 1 (1972). See Chapter 10 for a discussion of the circumstances resulting in Rehnquist's appointment to the Supreme Court and his refusal to recuse himself in the Laird case.

[28] *Carlson*, 446 U.S. at 34 (Rehnquist, J., dissenting) (quoting Bivens v. Six Unknown Named Agents of Fed. Bureau of Narcotics, 403 U.S. 388, 428 (1971) (Black, J., dissenting)).

Rehnquist viewed *Bivens* and its inferring a damage remedy in response to alleged violations of constitutional rights as nothing more than a highly inappropriate trespass by the Court upon a "domain" reserved to Congress.[29] If that approach meant that a party would be without relief in federal or state court, Rehnquist would accept that result. If that meant that federal officials would be subject to rules of liability that varied from one state to another—which would be the consequence of insisting that a damage remedy in federal court for the violation of a federal constitutional right by a federal official in the absence of a congressional statute explicitly authorizing such a remedy was solely dependent on a remedy being available under state law in state court—Rehnquist would accept that. If that meant that federal courts could grant complicated injunctions to cure constitutional violations but not a damages remedy, even though damage relief was the traditional form of relief and far less disruptive as compared to exceptional equitable relief, Rehnquist not only accepted that but advocated it.

Carlson constituted the Supreme Court's farthest extension of the *Bivens* doctrine. Three years later, in a pair of cases decided on the same June day in 1983, the high court distinguished *Bivens* and unanimously refused to infer a damage remedy. In each case Justice Brennan, the author of the majority opinions in *Bivens*, *Davis*, and *Carlson*, was part of the majority, signaling that at least from his perspective the rulings in these cases were consistent with *Bivens* and presented no threat to the soundness of that ruling.[30] But the Court's decision in

[29] *Id.* at 35, 38.

[30] In *Chappell v. Wallace*, enlisted military personnel alleged that "because of their minority race" their superior officers had "failed to assign them desirable duties, threatened them, gave them low performance evaluations, and imposed penalties of unusual severity." Chappell v. Wallace, 462 U.S. 296, 297 (1983). The Court decided that the plaintiffs could not maintain a suit to "recover damages from superior officers for injuries sustained as a result of violations of constitutional rights in the course of military service." In reaching this outcome, the Court asserted that the "need for special regulations in relation to military discipline, and the consequent need and justification for a special and exclusive system of military justice" constituted "special factors counseling hesitation" as provided for in *Bivens*. *Id.* at 300. The Court made it clear that Congress had "established a comprehensive internal system of justice to regulate military life, taking into account the special patterns that define the military structure" and that the system "provides for the review and remedy of complaints and grievances" such as those presented in this case. *Id.* at 302. In the second case, *Bush v. Lucas*, an aerospace engineer employed by a facility operated by the National Aeronautics and Space Administration who objected to his reassignments "made a number of public statements, including two televised interviews, that were highly critical of the agency." Bush v. Lucas, 462 U.S. 367, 369 (1983). After a complicated set of administrative and judicial proceedings, the engineer's case presented a distilled legal question to the Supreme Court: whether the engineer was entitled to recover a damage remedy for a violation of rights guaranteed by the First Amendment in the absence of a statute that expressly authorized a court to award such a remedy. And to that question, the Court answered no: because Congress had already established an elaborate and intricate

United States v. Stanley[31] in 1987 foreshadowed a set of decisions that in 2001 provided a basis for Justice Scalia to characterize the *Bivens* doctrine as a "relic" that should be limited to the "precise circumstances" involved in the *Bivens, Davis,* and *Carlson* cases.[32]

The facts in *Stanley* cried out for a remedy. In February 1958, an Army master sergeant, James B. Stanley, who "volunteered to participate in a program ostensibly designed to test the effectiveness of protective clothing and equipment as defenses against chemical warfare," was "secretly administered [four] doses of lysergic acid diethylamide (LSD)" within one month. The Army gave Stanley these four LSD doses pursuant to a "plan to study the effects of the drug on human subjects." In an action for damages against the United States and individual officials, Stanley claimed that the LSD exposure caused him to suffer "hallucinations and periods of incoherence and memory loss," "impaired [] his military performance," and caused him to wake "from sleep at night and, without reason, violently beat his wife and children, later being unable to recall the entire incident." Stanley also asserted that he was discharged from the Army in 1969, and that one year later his marriage "dissolved because of the personality changes wrought by the LSD."[33]

Seventeen years after the 1958 secret experiment and six years after his 1969 discharge from the Army, the Army sent Stanley a letter dated December 10, 1975, "soliciting his cooperation in a study of the long-term effects of LSD on 'volunteers who participated' in the 1958 tests." As Justice Scalia wrote in the Court's majority opinion, "[t]his was the Government's first notification to Stanley that he had been given LSD during his time in Maryland."[34]

The central question presented to the Supreme Court, as summarized by Scalia, was whether Stanley "can proceed with his *Bivens* claims notwithstanding the decision in *Chappell*."[35] On that question the Court divided five to four in concluding that because of the existence of "special factors counseling hesitation,"

administrative scheme to regulate the government's relationship with its employees, "Congress is in a better position to decide whether or not the public interest would be served by creating it." *Id.* at 390. There was nothing in the *Chappell* or *Lucas* decisions that suggested that the *Bivens-Davis-Carlson* trilogy was in danger of being sharply curtailed. *Chappell* concerned the military and the Supreme Court, as a general rule, refused to decide cases that intruded into internal military affairs. *Lucas* concerned the relationship between the government and its employees, and since Congress had provided a remedial alternative to aggrieved employees apart from damage actions in federal courts, the Supreme Court could, consistent with the *Bivens* line of cases, conclude that a *Bivens* damage remedy would not be authorized in this context.

[31] United States v. Stanley, 483 U.S. 669 (1987).

[32] Correctional Servs. Corp. v. Malesko, 534 U.S. 61, 75 (2001).

[33] *Stanley*, 483 U.S. at 671.

[34] *Id.* at 671–672.

[35] *Id.* at 678.

factors such as the "'unique disciplinary structure of the Military Establishment and Congress' activity in the field,'"[36] Stanley was not entitled to a *Bivens* remedy for "injuries that 'arise out of or are in the course of activity incident to service.'"[37] In reaching this result, Justice Scalia emphasized that the Court in *Bivens* limited the availability of remedy to cases in which special factors were absent or to cases in which Congress had not created an alternative remedy, and that subsequent to *Bivens* the Court had solidified these conditions as central to the *Bivens* doctrine and thus warranting dismissal if either were present.

Scalia's opinion astonished Justice O'Connor. In her view, the Army's conduct was "beyond the bounds of human decency," and in her dissent, O'Connor stated that she would permit Stanley's *Bivens* action to go forward because the alleged Army conduct in this case is "so far beyond the bounds of human decency that as a matter of law it simply cannot be considered a part of the military mission."[38]

Justice Brennan also dissented, and his dissent was joined by two other members of the Court. By quoting from a 1959 Army report, Justice Brennan made it clear that the Army intentionally and knowingly deviated from its basic premise that "the basic American principle of dignity and welfare of the individual will not be violated"[39] when it commenced its secret LSD program, and that it sought to justify the betrayal of such a basic moral principle on the ground of "national security," and sought to protect the government from any legal liability resulting from the secret LSD experiment by assuring that the secrecy of the program remains intact. Thus, Brennan concluded, the "Government of the United States treated thousands of its citizens as though they were laboratory animals, dosing them with this dangerous drug without their consent." Brennan asserted that if the majority's ruling was required by the Constitution, the decision "would expose a tragic flaw in that document," but he argued that the Constitution requires no such result. Instead, the majority "disregards the commands of our Constitution, and bows instead to the purported requirements of a different master, *military discipline*."[40] As a result, the government initially invoked national security to conceal its actions, and when its experiments resulted in damage lawsuits, it claimed that government officials "remain free to violate the constitutional rights of soldiers without fear of money damages" in order to preserve military discipline, and the Court's ruling in this case institutionalizes this unlawful conduct by immunizing it from judicial review.[41]

---

[36] *Id.* at 683 (quoting Chappell v. Wallace, 462 U.S. 296, 304 (1983)).

[37] *Id.* at 684.

[38] *Id.* at 709 (O'Connor, J., concurring in part and dissenting in part).

[39] *Id.* at 688 (Brennan, J., concurring in part and dissenting in part).

[40] *Id.* at 686.

[41] *Id.* at 689.

Surely the Army's conduct in *Stanley*, as Justice O'Connor suggested, constituted the boot's heel on decency. And just as surely, the five-person majority decision in *Stanley* betrayed constitutional aspirations, which perhaps at the Constitution's most fundamental level seek to assure that the state's interactions with its citizens respect their individual dignity. Nonetheless, *Stanley* need not have been understood as putting an end to the *Bivens* doctrine as constructed by the Court's decisions in *Bivens, Davis,* and *Carlson*, since the *Stanley* case might be understood as reflecting the Court's deferential stance toward the military. But whatever doubts remained about the vitality of the *Bivens* doctrine after *Stanley* vanished the next year, when the Court announced its judgments in *Schweiker v. Chilicky.*

In *Schweiker,* three individuals, who were "wholly dependent" upon their Social Security disability benefits, had those benefits wrongfully terminated in 1981 and 1982.[42] After a hiatus of seven to nineteen months the benefits were restored retroactively. At that point the individuals initiated a lawsuit seeking injunctive and declaratory relief as well as damages for "emotional distress and for loss of food, shelter and other necessities" caused by the termination of benefits for which they were eligible. The legal question the Court addressed was whether a *Bivens* remedy "should be implied for alleged due process violations in the denial of social security disability benefits."[43]

In deciding that no *Bivens* remedy should be implied, the majority concluded that the "special factors counseling hesitation" included "appropriate judicial deference to indications that congressional inaction has not been inadvertent," and that in this case the "design of a Government program suggests that Congress has provided what it considers adequate remedial mechanisms for constitutional violations that may occur in the course of its administration."[44] In reaching this result, the majority claimed that this case, as well as in *Bush v. Lucas*[45]—a case that involved the relationship between the federal government and its employees—the fact that the statute does not provide a distinct remedy for alleged unconstitutional conduct did not mean that the statute failed to provide an adequate remedy for the constitutional wrong.[46] The Court made it clear that "Congress is the body charged with making the inevitable compromises required in the design of a massive and complex welfare benefits program,"[47] and that in this case, Congress's compromises were clear.

---

[42] Schweiker v. Chilicky, 487 U.S. 412, 418 (1988).

[43] *Id.* at 419, 420.

[44] *Id.* at 423.

[45] Bush v. Lucas, 462 U.S. 367 (1983).

[46] *Schweiker,* 487 U.S. at 427–428.

[47] *Id.* at 429.

Justice Brennan, the architect of the *Bivens* doctrine, dissented and he was joined by Justices Marshall and Blackmun. When he wrote his dissent, Brennan surely understood that the six-person majority in *Schweiker* meant that the future of the *Bivens* doctrine would be in the hands of those who wanted to relegate the doctrine to the dustbin. Such a perspective helps explain the force of Brennan's dissent, in which he criticized the Court's result by pointing out that the Court "not for a moment suggest[s] that the retroactive award of benefits to which respondents were always entitled remotely approximates full compensation for such trauma."[48] Brennan further claims that there was no evidence that Congress ever intended to preclude a *Bivens* remedy for individuals whose constitutional rights were violated or that Congress understood the remedy it provided to be an adequate substitute for violations of constitutional rights. Indeed, Brennan went one step further and asserted that he did not believe that legislators of what he terms "normal sensibilities" would "wish to leave such traumatic injuries unrecompensed," and that he found it "inconceivable that Congress meant by mere silence to bar all redress for such injuries."[49] As Brennan understood the situation of the plaintiffs, the restoration of the disability awards "fails miserably to compensate disabled persons illegally stripped of the income upon which, in many cases, their very subsistence depends."[50]

Brennan also took aim at how the majority in his view had distorted the "special factors" test to include congressional silence:

> The mere fact that Congress was aware of the prior injustices and failed to provide a form of redress for them, standing alone, is simply not a "special factor counseling hesitation" in the judicial recognition of a remedy. Inaction, we have repeatedly stated, is a notoriously poor indication of congressional intent, all the more so where Congress is legislating in the face of a massive breakdown calling for prompt and sweeping corrective measures.[51]

[48] *Id.* at 431 (Brennan, J., dissenting).

[49] *Id.* at 432.

[50] *Id.* at 437.

[51] *Id.* at 440. In 1994, the Court once again retreated from an expansive construction of *Bivens* but for a reason that made the decision in *FDIC v. Meyer* of potentially limited significance. In that case, an employee of a savings and loan association who was terminated allegedly by a representative of the Federal Deposit Insurance Corporation (FDIC) in violation of due process brought a damage action against the FDIC, a federal agency, as opposed to an individual. A unanimous Court refused to recognize a *Bivens* claim for damages against federal agencies because if it did it would be "creating a potentially enormous financial burden for the Federal Government," a rationale that is not applicable to any entity other than a federal agency. FDIC v. Meyer, 510 U.S. 471, 486 (1994).

The hostility of the conservative members of the Court to the *Bivens* remedy expressed itself again in a 2001 ruling. In *Correctional Services Corp. v. Malesko,* the question decided by the high court was whether a prisoner had a *Bivens* damage claim against a "private corporation operating a halfway house under contract with the Bureau of Prisons" for conduct that caused him injury.[52] In denying the *Bivens* claim, the Court relied upon two reasons. The prisoner had a potential tort claim under state law that he did not assert because of what the Court termed a "strategic choice,"[53] a characterization the dissent convincingly claims was wide of the mark since the plaintiff was without the assistance of counsel when he initially filed his action against the private corporation. Second, the majority argued that because the main purpose of *Bivens* was to deter individual federal officers from committing constitutional violations, it would not authorize a damage claim against a private corporate entity, even though it was entirely plausible that such an action would "discourage future harms."[54] The majority's hostility to *Bivens* was made particularly evident in Scalia's concurrence, which Thomas joined, in which he termed *Bivens* a "relic" that should be limited, along with *Davis* and *Carlson,* "to the precise circumstances that they involved."[55]

The four justices in dissent understood the *Malesko* decision as a definitive effort by the majority to limit *Bivens, Davis,* and *Carlson* to their facts. As Justice Stevens wrote, it is "apparent . . . that the driving force behind the Court's decision is a disagreement with the holding in *Bivens* itself." From Stevens's perspective the Court's ruling was thus "improper"[56] because "Congress has effectively ratified the *Bivens* remedy," and because "our law for over 30 years should be accorded full respect by the Members of this Court, whether or not they would have endorsed that rule when it was first announced," for it is the Court's "primary duty" to "apply and enforce settled law, not to revise that law to accord with our own notions of sound policy."[57]

The *Bivens* doctrine took another body blow six years later. *Wilkie v. Robbins*[58] was a tangled dispute between a Wyoming landowner and employees of the Bureau of Land Management (BLM). Because careless federal authorities failed to record an easement before the grantor sold a commercial ranch to Frank Robbins and thus lost an easement to use and maintain a road across the property, BLM officers "mounted a seven-year campaign of

---

[52] *Correctional Servs. Corp. v. Malesko,* 534 U.S. 61, 63 (2001).
[53] *Id.* at 74.
[54] *Id.* at 71.
[55] *Id.* at 75 (Scalia, J., concurring).
[56] *Id.* at 82 (Stevens, J., dissenting).
[57] *Id.* at 83.
[58] *Wilkie v. Robbins,* 551 U.S. 537 (2007).

relentless harassment and intimidation to force Robbins to give in" and grant federal authorities a new easement. In response, Robbins commenced a lawsuit to "end the incessant harassment and intimidation," claiming that the "Fifth Amendment's Takings Clause forbids government action calculated to acquire private property coercively and cost free."[59] Robbins asserted a damage claim relying on the *Bivens* line of cases.

Justice Souter's majority opinion denied Robbins's claim, asserting that allowing Robbins to assert a *Bivens* claim would "invite claims in every sphere of legitimate governmental action affecting property interests," and that in the end a "*Bivens* cure would be worse than the disease."[60] Justice Ginsburg, joined by Stevens, dissented and in so doing took aim at a central tenet underlying the majority opinion, that the judiciary should stay its remedial hand out of respect for Congress's superior competence in assessing and weighing the public policy choices involved in providing a damage remedy against federal officials. What she wrote was that the *Bivens* rule was "hardly an obscure part of the Court's jurisprudence. If Congress wishes to codify and further define the *Bivens* remedy, it may do so at anytime. Unless and until Congress acts, however, the Court should not shy away from the effort to ensure that bedrock constitutional rights do not become 'merely precatory.'"[61]

The most recent case in the line, decided in 2012 by a lopsided vote of eight to one, nailed tight the lid on *Bivens*'s coffin. In this case, a prisoner incarcerated in a federal facility operated by a private company filed a pro se complaint against several employees, alleging that they deprived him of adequate medical care and thus deprived him of his rights guaranteed by the Eighth Amendment.[62] This case seemed to be exactly like the *Carlson* case except that the federal authorities had contracted with a private company to operate the prison. But that distinction was enough to persuade the majority of eight to deny Pollard a *Bivens* remedy.[63] As Ginsburg wrote in her dissent, if Pollard had been incarcerated in a federal- or state-operated facility, "he would have a federal remedy for the Eighth Amendment violations he alleges," and because of that he should have one in this case.[64]

Bivens rectified a peculiar gap in the remedies available to a federal judge when a judgment was against a federal official, not only in cases implicating national security but others as well. Historically a party was able to secure an injunction only if damages were inadequate, and yet courts had turned these

[59] *Id.* at 568, 569 (Ginsburg, J., concurring in part and dissenting in part).

[60] *Id.* at 561 (majority opinion).

[61] *Id.* at 585 (Ginsburg, J., concurring in part and dissenting in part).

[62] Minneci v. Pollard, 132 S. Ct. 617 (2012).

[63] *Id.* at 626.

[64] *Id.* at 626–627 (Ginsburg, J., dissenting).

traditional rules on their head and granted injunctions against executive officials while taking the position that they could not grant damages against the same officials unless Congress authorized such damages, which Congress had not. And that was the case, even assuming that the award of damages was the only remedy that was meaningful to a party. The decision in *Bivens* corrected this defect in the law of remedies, and once the decision was announced it became clear that the damage awards authorized in the Fourth Amendment *Bivens* context could be applied by courts to other legal contexts, which is just what the Court did during the next decade.

However, as the Supreme Court's membership changed and became increasingly circumspect with regard to courts enforcing constitutional rights against the executive, a new Court majority not only failed to further extend the *Bivens* doctrine, it began to curtail it. A dominant reason offered by the Court for cabining the *Bivens* doctrine is that Congress has primary responsibility for authorizing courts to grant a remedy and in the absence of a statute authorizing such relief, the Court should stay its hand. Relying upon that attitude, the Court beginning in the 1980s characterized *Bivens* and its progeny as a departure from the more cautious judicial stance and thus began an unbroken trend in refusing to imply a damage remedy against federal officials for the deprivation of constitutional rights.

This is a peculiar rationale. There is no question that Congress retained the authority to pass a statute essentially stating that the federal courts should not grant a damage remedy for the violation of a federal constitutional right against a federal official. The effect of such a statute would be to prohibit the courts from implying a remedy going forward absent a congressional enactment that specifically authorized such relief. But Congress did not do that after the Court decided the *Bivens* case, nor did the Congress enact such a statute that affirmatively authorized an individual's right to damages against executive officers after the Supreme Court decided the *Davis* and *Carlson* cases.[65] Given these circumstances, a sensible conclusion for the Court to have reached was just the opposite of the one it did reach: that in the absence of congressional action, the *Bivens* doctrine was appropriate. The fact that the Court did just the opposite seems, under the circumstances, to mean that the Court is more focused on using its discretion to close the courthouse door to cases in which an individual alleges that the executive violated a constitutional right than it is on exhibiting respect toward Congress.

---

[65] But James E. Pfander and David Baltmanis have argued that Congress has because of other legislation approved by implication of a *Bivens* damage action. James E. Pfander and David Baltmanis, *Rethinking* Bivens: *Legitimacy and Constitutional Adjudication*, 98 Geo. L. J. 117 (2009).

By and large these developments occurred without regard to cases implicating national security concerns. But after 9/11 that changed, especially with regard to damage claims against senior executive officials. In those cases, the contraction of the *Bivens* doctrine simply gave the federal courts one more alternative—in addition to, for example, the state secrets privilege, the quasi-immunity defense, enhanced pleading rules—to utilize as a basis for dismissing a case without having to decide the merits of the case. As such, the contraction of the *Bivens* doctrine became yet one more expression of the Supreme Court's eagerness to shape and apply doctrines that insulated senior executive officials from meaningful judicial review.[66]

---

[66] One prominent and thoughtful scholar on the general subject of remedies restated the general rule that the "dictum of *Marbury* v. *Madison* [5 U.S. (1 Cranch) 137 (1803)] notwithstanding, there is no right to an individually effective remedy for every constitutional violation." Richard H. Fallon, Jr., *Some Confusions About Due Process, Judicial Review, and Constitutional Remedies*, 93 Columbia L. Rev. 309, 311 (1993). The dictum Fallon referred to is the very famous statement by Chief Justice John Marshall that: "The very essence of civil liberty certainly consists in the right of every individual to claim the protection of the laws, whenever he receives an injury . . . The government of the United States has been emphatically termed a government of laws, and not of men. It will certainly cease to deserve this high appellation, if the laws furnish no remedy for the violation of a vested legal right." Marbury v. Madison, 5 U.S. (1 Cranch) 137, 163 (1803). But Fallon went on to observe the "ultimate commitment of the law of due process remedies—analogous to that of procedural due process—is to create schemes and incentives adequate to keep government, overall and on average, tolerably within the bounds of law." Richard H. Fallon, Jr., *Some Confusions About Due Process, Judicial Review, and Constitutional Remedies*, 93 Colum. L. Rev. 309, 311 (1993). Not everyone would endorse Fallon's lenient remedial guideline, which is to create a legal remedial regime that keeps the government "overall and on average, tolerably within the bounds of law." But even accepting Fallon's low bar for the goals of a remedial scheme, the degree of deference courts exhibit toward the executive in national security cases means that the federal judiciary has even failed to satisfy Fallon's standard to keep the government "overall and on average, tolerably within the bounds of law."

12

Still More Obstacles Close
the Courthouse Door

Once the *Bivens* doctrine burst onto the legal stage in 1971, it enjoyed a decade of modest expansion that held out the promise of further development before some justices on the Supreme Court so devalued the importance of providing individuals with a meaningful remedy that they not only preferred to curtail the *Bivens* doctrine but to overrule it. But they never garnered the necessary votes, and as a consequence the *Bivens* doctrine is curtailed but still holds out the promise of providing a remedy to arguably wronged individuals in some limited circumstances.

While the direct confrontational battle over the scope of the *Bivens* remedy was underway, some justices took an indirect route to neutralize the impact of the *Bivens* doctrine. This second line of attack aimed at neutralizing *Bivens* relied upon the development of a doctrine that immunized senior executive officials from damages claims. Indeed, the justices who supported the development of this legal doctrine endorsed the idea of absolute immunity for senior executive officials, as had been granted the president, which would have more or less left executive officials in the same position they would have been in as if the high court had never decided the *Bivens* case.[1] But they failed in this endeavor, and the Court debate then turned to the definition of the quasi-immunity doctrine.

At first, the critics of the *Bivens* doctrine were unsuccessful in shaping the doctrine of quasi-immunity to provide as much protection to executive

---

[1] The two positions are not precisely the same. There is a difference between not being subject to a damage remedy and having a defense of absolute immunity to such a claim. If a party is not subject to a damage remedy, then the claim for damages is dismissed because of the failure to state a claim upon which relief may be granted. If a party has an absolute immunity defense, the claim for damages will not be dismissed until it is established that the claim for relief in a particular case falls within the parameters of the absolute immunity defense.

officials as they favored, but as case law developed in the 1980s, the *Bivens* critics were remarkably successful in redefining the concept of quasi-immunity so as to provide executive officials with an immunity that is in fact close to absolute immunity.[2] Thus, although the high court presents the immunity doctrine as qualified, just as it presents the state secrets privilege as qualified, the gap between an absolute immunity defense and a qualified immunity defense is quite narrow and thus affords defendants a formidable defense.

America's commitment to the idea of a society ruled by law, not by individuals, requires that an injured individual deprived of a legal right by a public official be entitled to a legal remedy. At the same time the nation has an interest in having its public officers not be intimidated in discharging their duties by the threat of damage lawsuits. These values are in conflict with one another, and it is within this conflict that that the legal doctrines defining an official's immunity are shaped.

Two nineteenth-century Supreme Court opinions illustrate this tension. In 1882, the Court made it clear that "[n]o man in this country is so high that he is above the law. No officer of the law may set that law at defiance with impunity. All the officers of the government, from the highest to the lowest, are creatures of the law and are bound to obey it."[3] At the same time, the Court recognized that because it is important that government officials exercise their authority without intimidation or apprehension, it is troubling if the vigorous discharge of legal duties may result in the legal imposition of a damage award in favor of

---

[2] Apart from the immunity of federal officials, there is the question of the liability of state and local officials from damage claims. In a case that arose from the shooting of students by Ohio State Guardsmen at Kent State University following President Nixon's announcement that he had widened the Vietnam War by invading Cambodia, the Court considered the scope of immunity available to the Ohio governor, as well as others, who had been sued for damages by the estates of three of the killed students. Scheuer v. Rhodes, 416 U.S. 232 (1974). A nineteenth-century statute authorized federal courts to award damages against state and local officials for violating federal constitutional and statutory rights. That statute made no reference whatsoever to any form of immunity for public officials, and if the Supreme Court had followed its admonition set forth by then Associate Justice Rehnquist that the "plain language of [the law] marks the beginning and end of our inquiry," U.S. R.R. Ret. Bd. v. Fritz, 449 U.S. 166, 176 (1980), the Supreme Court would not have utilized its common law authority to have crafted a doctrine of quasi-immunity that protected public officers from damage liability arising from their unlawful acts. Instead, it would have deferred to Congress and stated that the important question of whether state officials should be protected from damage claims by an immunity doctrine is a matter for the Congress to decide, not the Court. In Wood v. Strickland, the Supreme Court conceded that although the "language of §1983 is silent with respect to immunities," it went on to claim that it had no basis for believing that Congress "intended to eliminate the traditional immunity of legislators from civil liability for acts done within their sphere of legislative action." Wood v. Strickland, 420 U.S. 308, 316–317 (1975).

[3] United States v. Lee, 106 U.S. 196, 220 (1882).

an individual claiming to have been injured by the discharge of those duties. In addition to the fear that such a dynamic would make such officers unduly cautious in discharging their duties, there was a concern that the possibility of liability would deter some individuals from being willing to accept the responsibilities and risks of public office.

In response, the Court, without guidance or authorization from the legislature, exercised its discretionary authority to create an immunity doctrine that protected public officials from liability in some circumstances. In setting forth this doctrine, the Court acknowledged that difficulties may arise in "applying these principles to particular cases, in which the rights of the citizen may have been materially impaired by the inconsiderate or wrongful action" of a department head. But the Court surmised that a legal standard that made department heads more potentially vulnerable to legal liability "would seriously cripple the proper and effective administration of public affairs as intrusted to the executive branch of the government" and must be rejected.[4]

Judge Learned Hand elegantly captured the tension among these interfacing values in *Gregoire v. Biddle*:

> It does indeed go without saying that an official, who is in fact guilty of using his powers to vent his spleen upon others, or for any other personal motive not connected with the public good, should not escape liability for the injuries he may so cause; and, if it were possible in practice to confine such complaints to the guilty, it would be monstrous to deny recovery. The justification for doing so is that it is impossible to know whether the claim is well founded until the case has been tried, and that to submit all officials, the innocent as well as the guilty, to the burden of a trial and to the inevitable danger of its outcome, would dampen the ardor of all but the most resolute, or the most irresponsible, in the unflinching discharge of their duties. Again and again the public interest calls for action which may turn out to be founded on a mistake, in the face of which an official may later find himself hard put to it to satisfy a jury of his good faith. There must indeed be means of punishing public officers who have been truant to their duties; but that is quite another matter from exposing such as have been honestly mistaken to suit by anyone who has suffered from their errors. As is so often the case, the answer must be found in a balance between the evils inevitable in either alternative. In this instance it has been thought in the end better to leave unredressed the wrongs

---

[4] Spalding v. Vilas, 161 U.S. 483, 498 (1896).

done by dishonest officers than to subject those who try to do their duty to the constant dread of retaliation.[5]

With these rival considerations in mind, and during the same years as the nine Supreme Court justices struggled over the viability of the *Bivens* doctrine, the high court sought to be the biblical Solomon by qualifying both an individual's right to a remedy and the legal liability of a public official and leaving the resolution of the competing values to courts to figure out one case at a time.

The Court first addressed the issue of executive official immunity in *Butz v. Economou*[6] in 1978. Writing for a bare majority of five, Justice Byron White stated that the case "concerns the personal immunity of federal officials in the Executive Branch from claims for damages arising from their violations of citizens' constitutional rights." The claimant in the case filed suit against "a number of officials in the Department of Agriculture claiming that they had instituted an investigation and an administrative proceeding against him in retaliation for his criticism of that agency."[7] As Justice White wrote, the "single submission" by the United States is that "all of the federal officials sued in this case are absolutely immune from any liability for damages even if in the course of enforcing the relevant statutes they infringed respondent's constitutional rights and even if the violation was knowing and deliberate."[8]

Four justices endorsed the executive's request for absolute immunity. If they had captured one more vote, the granting of absolute immunity would have more or less nullified the potentiality of *Bivens* liability. But the four failed to capture a fifth vote and thus dissented.

What Justice White wrote for the majority was that he was "quite sure" that the request for absolute immunity was "unsound" and he "consequently reject[ed] it." And then with the scope of immunity the Court had provided state officials in mind, Justice White wrote: "in the absence of congressional direction to the contrary, there is no basis for according to federal officials a higher degree of immunity from liability when sued for a constitutional infringement as authorized by *Bivens* than is accorded state officials when sued for the identical violation under §1983."[9] Accordingly, Justice White concluded that it is

[5] Gregoire v. Biddle, 177 F.2d 579, 581 (2d Cir. 1949).
[6] Butz v. Economou, 438 U.S. 478 (1978).
[7] *Econonomou*, 438 U.S. at 480.
[8] *Id.* at 485.
[9] *Id.* at 500.

[N]ot unfair to hold liable the official who knows or should know he is acting outside the law, and that insisting on an awareness of clearly established constitutional limits will not unduly interfere with the exercise of official judgment. We therefore hold that, in a suit for damages arising from unconstitutional action, federal executive officials exercising discretion are entitled only to the qualified immunity specified in *Scheuer,* subject to those exceptional situations where it is demonstrated that absolute immunity is essential for the conduct of the public business.[10]

In amplifying the meaning of quasi-immunity, White emphasized that federal officials will not be liable for "mere mistakes in judgment, whether the mistake is one of fact or one of law." But White made it clear that federal officials may not with "impunity discharge their duties in a way that is known to them to violate the United States Constitution or in a manner that they should know transgresses a clearly established constitutional rule."[11]

White defended this standard by arguing that this standard would permit the federal courts to terminate quickly insubstantial lawsuits, even ones containing "artful pleading."[12] Cases that fail to state a compensable claim should not survive a motion to dismiss, and others may be disposed of on a summary judgment motion, thus avoiding a trial.

A mere four years later, the high court, troubled by the practical litigation consequences of its ruling in *Butz,* once again tried its hand at defining the scope of immunity for senior executive officials. In *Harlow v. Fitzgerald,*[13] which was made public the same day that the Court granted the president absolute immunity,[14] the majority concluded that the subjective element of

---

[10] *Id.* at 506–507.

[11] *Id.* at 507.

[12] *Id.*

[13] Harlow v. Fitzgerald, 457 U.S. 800 (1982).

[14] In 1982, a divided Supreme Court concluded that the president of the United States should be entitled to "absolute immunity from damages liability predicated on his official acts." Nixon v. Fitzgerald, 457 U.S. 731, 749 (1982). Justice Powell's majority opinion walked a wavering line as to the basis for that ruling. On the one hand, he suggested that the ruling was based on the Constitution and the doctrine of separation of powers. Emphasizing the president's "unique position in the constitutional scheme," Powell wrote: "We consider this immunity a functionally mandated incident of the President's unique office, rooted in the constitutional tradition of the separation of powers and supported by our history." *Id.* At the same time, Powell stated that the Court had no reason at that time to decide whether Congress could authorize "a damages action against the President of the United States." *Id.* at 748 n.27. If the majority had concluded without qualification that the president's absolute immunity was constitutionally based, there would have been no reason to even entertain the suggestion that Congress could override the president's immunity by permitting damage liability. Thus, the reservation of the legal question regarding Congress's potential authority to impose damage liability on the president indicates that Powell's

the good-faith defense had made it difficult for trial judges to dismiss insubstantial actions prior to trial, especially since some judges have considered an official's subjective good faith as a factual question a jury must decide. As a result, the majority concluded that "substantial costs attend the litigation of the subjective good faith of government officials,"[15] entailing among things a "broad-ranging discovery and the deposing of numerous persons, including an official's professional colleagues."[16]

Indeed, in reaching this result, Justice Powell quoted extensively from a concurring opinion written by District Judge Gerhard Gesell—a judge whose conduct in nationally prominent trials such as the Pentagon Papers case in 1971, or the criminal trial of John D. Ehrlichman, former President Richard Nixon's chief adviser on domestic affairs, in 1974, earned him a reputation as being anything but highly deferential to the executive[17]—in which he stated that the courts "should not close our eyes to the fact that with increasing frequency in this jurisdiction and throughout the country plaintiffs are filing suits seeking damage awards against high government officials in their personal capacities based on alleged constitutional torts," and each such suit "results in these officials and their colleagues being subjected to extensive discovery into traditionally protected areas, such as their deliberations preparatory to the formulation of government policy and their intimate thought processes and communications at the presidential and cabinet levels." Gesell thought that such discovery was "wide-ranging, time-consuming, and not without considerable cost to the officials involved."[18]

Because of the considerations set forth by Gesell, the majority in *Harlow* rewrote the quasi-immunity standard so that "bare allegations of malice should not suffice to subject government officials either to the costs of trial or to the burdens of broad-reaching discovery."[19] Instead, Powell argued

---

reasoning for the majority walked a wavering line tilting toward both a constitutional rule as well as a common law rule. The ambivalence of Powell's opinion prompted Chief Justice Burger to write a concurring opinion in which he stated that in his mind there was no doubt that presidential immunity was constitutionally based and is "mandated by the constitutional doctrine of separation of powers." *Id.* at 758 (Burger, C. J., concurring). Granting the president absolute immunity left undecided the scope of immunity that should be granted to other members of the executive branch. The issues fell into two basic categories: whether the immunity of such officials should be absolute or qualified; and if the immunity should be qualified, what the scope of that qualified immunity should be.

[15] *Harlow*, 457 U.S. at 816.

[16] *Id.* at 817.

[17] Bruce Lambert, *Judge Gerhard Gesell Dies at 82; Oversaw Big Cases*, N.Y. Times (Feb. 21, 1993), http://www.nytimes.com/1993/02/21/us/judge-gerhard-gesell-dies-at-82-oversaw-big-cases.html?pagewanted=all.

[18] Halperin v. Kissinger, 606 F.2d 1192, 1214 (1979).

[19] *Harlow*, 457 U.S. at 817–818.

that government officials "performing discretionary functions generally are shielded from liability for civil damages insofar as their conduct does not violate clearly established statutory or constitutional rights of which a reasonable person would have known." In offering this standard, Powell thought the courts would be able to avoid "excessive disruption of government and permit the resolution of many insubstantial claims on summary judgment."[20]

It did not take long for the Court to become dissatisfied with how the *Butz* and *Harlow* opinions had resolved the competing values raised by the quasi-immunity doctrine. Just three years after the *Harlow* opinion, the high court once again restated the quasi-immunity doctrine in *Mitchell v. Forsyth*.[21]

In 1970, the FBI learned that a group opposed to the Vietnam War was planning on blowing up the heating tunnels linking federal office buildings in Washington, D.C., and had also discussed the possibility of kidnapping President Nixon's national security advisor, Henry Kissinger. Acting on the basis of that information, Attorney General John Mitchell authorized a warrantless wiretap—the purpose of which was the "gathering of intelligence in the interest of national security"—on the telephone of a college professor who was a member of the antiwar group. During the course of the six-week tap, the FBI intercepted three innocuous conversations the college professor had with Keith Forsyth. Forsyth learned of the intercepted conversations in 1972 when, as a criminal defendant facing unrelated charges, he requested the prosecutor to disclose government electronic surveillance to which he had been subjected. In providing that information to Forsyth, the prosecutor submitted an affidavit sworn to by then Attorney General Richard Kleindienst "averring that the surveillance to which Forsyth had been subjected was authorized 'in the exercise of [the president's] authority relating to the national security.'"[22]

Shortly after Forsyth learned of the intercepted conversations, the Supreme Court ruled in the *Keith* case that the Fourth Amendment to the Constitution prohibits warrantless wiretaps in cases involving "domestic threats to the national security."[23] On the basis of that ruling, Forsyth filed a damage action against Mitchell and several others, alleging that the surveillance to which he had been subjected violated his constitutional and statutory rights, thus entitling him to compensatory and punitive damages.[24]

---

[20] *Id.* at 818. Only Justice White seemed not to endorse the quasi-immunity standard announced in *Harlow v. Fitzgerald.*

[21] Mitchell v. Forsyth, 472 U.S. 511 (1985).

[22] *Forsyth,* 472 U.S. at 513–514.

[23] United States v. United States District Court (Keith), 407 U.S. 297, 322 (1972).

[24] *Mitchell,* 472 U.S. at 515.

Mitchell's argument, as summarized by White, was as follows:

> [T]he national security functions of the Attorney General are so sen-
> sitive, so vital to the protection of our Nation's well-being, that we
> cannot tolerate any risk that in performing those functions he will
> be chilled by the possibility of personal liability for acts that may be
> found to impinge on the constitutional rights of citizens.[25]

By the time Mitchell made that claim he had already been named a defendant
in what Justice White termed a "significant number of lawsuits stemming from
his authorization of warrantless national security wiretaps."[26] Thus, there did
seem some factual basis to the claim that the lawsuits could distract an attorney general from his responsibilities and perhaps even deter the aggressive
pursuit of responsibilities.

Nonetheless, White on behalf of a majority of the justices did not hesitate:
"We conclude that the Attorney General is not absolutely immune from suit
for damages arising out of his allegedly unconstitutional conduct in performing his national security functions."[27] In reaching this result, Justice White
argued that Mitchell's status as a cabinet officer "is not in itself sufficient to
invest him with absolute immunity" because the "considerations of separation
of powers that call for absolute immunity for state and federal legislators and
for the President of the United States do not demand a similar immunity for
Cabinet officers or other high executive officials." Alternatively, White contended that Mitchell's claim for absolute immunity because of the "nature of
the functions he was performing in this case" also fails because "the situations
in which we have applied a functional approach to absolute immunity questions provide scant support for blanket immunization of his performance of
the 'national security function.'" That was so, White argued, because a grant
of absolute immunity in national security matters that are carried out in secret
would mean that high-ranking officers will not be intimidated from abusing
their power.[28]

Finally, White claimed that "most of the officials who are entitled to absolute immunity from liability for damages are subject to other checks that help to
prevent abuses of authority from going unredressed." In sharp contrast, White
pointed out that "[s]imilar built-in restraints on the Attorney General's activities in the name of national security . . . do not exist." While acknowledging the

[25] *Id.* at 520.
[26] *Id.* at 522 n.6.
[27] *Id.* at 520.
[28] *Id.* at 522.

singular importance of activities aimed at preserving and promoting the safety of the nation, White stated that the high court "cannot accept the notion that restraints are completely unnecessary." "The danger that high federal officials will disregard constitutional rights in their zeal to protect the national security is sufficiently real to counsel against affording such officials an absolute immunity."[29]

White concluded that the quasi-immunity doctrine was more than sufficient to provide the attorney general with adequate protection to allow him to discharge his responsibilities aggressively. Thus, White emphasized that the attorney general will be immune "so long as his actions do not violate 'clearly established statutory or constitutional rights of which a reasonable person would have known.' "[30] White conceded that in some circumstances the attorney general may have to "pause to consider whether a proposed course of action can be squared with the Constitution and laws on the United States," but White continued that was the entire point of the legal standard—to prompt a high-ranking official to pause and consider the lawfulness of the proposed conduct. And then to give the screw one more turn on Mitchell's argument, White wrote: "We do not believe that the security of the Republic will be threatened if its Attorney General is given incentives to abide by clearly established law."[31]

Having resisted the national security's siren call for absolute immunity, White suddenly surrendered much that he seemed so earnest to capture. White had already made it clear in his opinion that he understood that history was replete with incidents in which benevolent and benign government officials " 'view with suspicion those who most fervently dispute its policies" and acting under the "vague concept" of "domestic security," are prone to abuse their power and to engage in unlawful conduct.[32] As a result, it was important, White argued, that abused citizens have a remedy against such officials.

But, in his discussion of whether a government official who had asserted a defense of quasi-immunity should be entitled to an interlocutory appeal, Justice White gave back just about all the ground the prior portion of his opinion had seized. Interlocutory appeals are generally disfavored because of a desire to protect limited judicial resources from being depleted by piecemeal litigation. Nonetheless, Justice White stated that the concept of quasi-immunity was not merely a defense to liability but a concept that provided a complete and total "immunity from suit." For Justice White, the importance of providing a senior official with a quasi-immunity defense would be greatly diminished

---

[29] *Id.* at 522, 523.

[30] *Id.* at 524 (quoting Harlow v. Fitzgerald, 457 U.S. 800, 818 (1982)).

[31] *Id.* at 524.

[32] *Id.* at 523 (quoting United States v. United States District Court (Keith), 407 U.S. 297, 313–314 (1972)).

if an executive was subjected to the rigorous demands of judicial discovery procedures.[33] In other words, as Justice White assessed the situation, even if a defendant who asserts a quasi-immunity defense prevails after trial, the values of the quasi-immunity defense are defeated by forcing the executive official to submit to discovery and to go to trial. The consequence of White's reasoning was to arm trial judges with a rationale that permitted dismissal of an action before any discovery took place or before a trial upon a motion for summary judgment. Thus, when Justice White in the *Mitchell* case characterized the quasi-immunity defense as favoring summary judgment over the demands of trial, he opened the door to the possibility that the Court would use the phrase "immunity from suit" as a basis for reshaping legal doctrine so as to foreclose discovery altogether, even in circumstances in which the law regulating official conduct was clearly established.[34]

---

[33] *Id.* at 526.

[34] Characterizing quasi-immunity as not merely a defense but as an immunity from suit that offered a defendant protection in certain situations, not only from a trial but from discovery, was foreshadowed by the Court's decision in the *Harlow* case. As already noted, the Court's focus in *Harlow* was on refashioning the quasi-immunity defense so that "insubstantial claims should not proceed to trial." Harlow v. Fitzgerald, 457 U.S. 800, 815–816 (1982). To that end, the Court in *Harlow* excised the "subjective good faith of government officials" from the quasi-immunity defense and reframed the defense as rising or falling on whether the conduct in question did or did not "violate clearly established statutory or constitutional rights of which a reasonable person would have known." *Id.* at 816, 818. In making this judgment, the Court was focused on the importance of avoiding trial by having matters disposed of on summary judgment:

> Reliance on the objective reasonableness of an official's conduct, as measured by reference to clearly established law, should avoid excessive disruption of government and permit the resolution of many insubstantial claims on summary judgment. On summary judgment, the judge appropriately may determine, not only the currently applicable law, but whether that law was clearly established at the time an action occurred. If the law at that time was not clearly established, an official could not reasonably be expected to anticipate subsequent legal developments, nor could he fairly be said to "know" that the law forbade conduct not previously identified as unlawful. Until this threshold immunity question is resolved, discovery should not be allowed. If the law was clearly established, the immunity defense ordinarily should fail, since a reasonably competent public official should know the law governing his conduct. Nevertheless, if the official pleading the defense claims extraordinary circumstances and can prove that he neither knew nor should have known of the relevant legal standard, the defense should be sustained. But again, the defense would turn primarily on objective factors. (*Id.* at 818–819)

As is clear, the Court in *Harlow* was focused on making sure the government officials were not unnecessarily subject to trial in circumstances in which the relevant law governing the pertinent conduct was not clearly established. And although discovery was to be delayed until this preliminary matter was resolved, there was no suggestion in the opinion that discovery would be delayed beyond the resolution of this narrow legal question. In other words, the refashioned

The last turn of the screw that made a quasi-immunity defense a de facto absolute immunity claim for senior executive officials occurred in 2011, in a post-9/11 case entitled *Ashcroft v. al-Kidd*.[35]

The United States may legally detain a person who is a suspect, but for whom it lacks probable cause to charge with a crime. However, what is less well known is that the United States may also detain a person to assure the availability of that person as a witness in a legal proceeding involving others. The pertinent federal statute authorizes judges to "order the arrest of [a] person" whose testimony is "material in a criminal proceeding . . . if it is shown that it may become impracticable to secure the presence of the person by subpoena." But if a person is taken into custody pursuant to the material witness statute, that person is entitled, as Justice Scalia wrote in his opinion, to "the same constitutional right to pretrial release as other federal detainees, and federal law requires release if their testimony 'can adequately be secured by deposition, and if further detention is not necessary to prevent a failure of justice.' "[36]

In March of 2003, the FBI took Abdullah al-Kidd into custody while he was at the ticket counter at Dulles Airport waiting to board a plane to Saudi Arabia. Al-Kidd, an African American, was born in Kansas in 1972. He converted to Islam and changed his birth name while attending the University of Idaho, where he was a highly regarded football running back. Al-Kidd was detained by FBI agents "on a material witness warrant issued in Idaho in the case of Sami Al-Hussayen, who had been indicted for visa fraud and making false statements to the government, but was never convicted of those charges or any of the other subsequently added charges." The FBI affidavit in support of the material warrant application placed al-Kidd in a suspicious light by asserting that at the moment of his arrest, al-Kidd was about to take a "one-way, first class flight (costing approximately $5,000.00) to Saudi Arabia,"[37] and that al-Kidd had received payments from Al-Hussayen and his associates when the FBI knew or should have known that al-Kidd "had worked for the same charitable organization as Al-Hussayen and had received a salary for his work."[38]

When the FBI agents arrested al-Kidd at the ticket counter, he was placed in handcuffs and interrogated at an airport police station for one to two hours without being given his *Miranda* rights and without a lawyer present. The day

---

quasi-immunity defense was aimed at avoiding trials unless the relevant law was clearly established, not at avoiding discovery to determine the relevant details of an official's conduct, assuming that the relevant law was clearly established.

[35] Ashcroft v. al-Kidd, 563 U.S. 731, 131 S. Ct. 2074 (2011).

[36] *Al-Kidd*, 563 U.S. at 2079 (quoting 18 U.S.C. §3144).

[37] Brief for Respondent at 2, Ashcroft v. al-Kidd, 563 U.S. 731, 131 S. Ct. 2074 (WL 219561) (2011) (No. 10-98).

[38] *Id.* at 4.

after his arrest, al-Kidd was brought before a federal magistrate judge in Virginia without the assistance of appointed counsel. The magistrate judge told al-Kidd that he was entitled to a "release hearing in Virginia," but that he might be "better served going to Idaho for the hearing,"[39] an outcome the government attorney endorsed by representing that al-Kidd "would be brought to Idaho as quickly as possible." As it turned out, the phrase "as quickly as possible" in this case meant fifteen nights of confinement in "jails in Virginia, Oklahoma and Idaho," where al-Kidd was "placed in high-security wings with convicted criminals, strip-searched and routinely shackled." Al-Kidd was released after fifteen days "but was required to live with his in-laws, report regularly to the government and remain within a four-state area." In the end, the government did not call al-Kidd to testify as a witness at Al-Hussayen's trial, which did not commence for more than one year after al-Kidd's arrest. Nor was al-Kidd ever accused of any criminal activity. And even after Al-Hussayen's trial ended, the government did not make a motion to vacate the conditions of al-Kidd's supervision; the obligation fell to al-Kidd.[40]

In the brief filed in the Supreme Court, al-Kidd's lawyers stated that al-Kidd's "core allegation" was that the attorney general and others "authorized the systematic use of the material witness statute to detain and investigate suspects whom the government lacked probable cause to charge with a crime, and not to secure testimony from witnesses."[41] The brief charged the defendants of using the material witness statute to detain and investigate suspects rather than to secure testimony, and it argued that such a use constituted an abuse of the statute and resulted in the deprivation of rights guaranteed by the Fourth Amendment.[42]

In support of his position, al-Kidd argued that the FBI affidavit filed in support of the material warrant request was deceptive and misleading. Thus, al-Kidd pointed out that the FBI affidavit made no mention of the fact that al-Kidd was married with two children and that al-Kidd's parents, wife, and children were citizens and residents of the United States. Al-Kidd further pointed out that the FBI affidavit did not state that the FBI had attempted to locate al-Kidd prior to seeking the arrest warrant, nor did it state that al-Kidd had in fact cooperated with the FBI prior to his arrest. Indeed, al-Kidd "had voluntarily talked with the FBI on several occasions prior to his arrest and had never failed to show up to these pre-arranged meetings."[43] Moreover, the FBI's statement

---

[39] *Id.* at 4–5.
[40] *Id.* at 5.
[41] *Id.* at 1.
[42] *Id.* at 11–12.
[43] *Id.* at 3.

that al-Kidd had a one-way, first-class ticket to Saudi Arabia was incorrect; Al-Kidd had a "round-trip, coach-class ticket that cost $1,700"[44] to Saudi Arabia, where he planned to "study Arabic and Islamic law on a scholarship at a Saudi university."[45] In contrast to al-Kidd, who was arrested as a material witness in the Al-Hussayen case, "another witness . . . was permitted simply to relinquish his passport and postpone his trip to Saudi Arabia."[46]

And then to add additional weight to the accusation that high officials within the justice department deliberately and knowingly set in motion a policy to use the material witness statute as a pretext for detaining individuals who were criminal suspects, but for whom there was no probable cause to arrest, al-Kidd's lawyers pointed out that while al-Kidd remained in detention, FBI Director Robert Mueller made the following statements before Congress about the government's antiterrorism efforts:

> I am pleased to report that our efforts have yielded major successes over the past 17 months. Over 212 suspected terrorists have been charged with crimes, 108 of whom have been convicted to date. Some are well-known—including Zacarias Moussaoui, John Walker Lindh and Richard Reid. But, let me give you just a few recent examples:
>
> . . . Khalid Shaikh Mohammed was located by Pakistani officials and is in custody of the US at an undisclosed location. Mr. Mohammed was a key planner and the mastermind of the September 11th attack. . . .
>
> . . . Abdullah al-Kidd, a US native and former University of Idaho football player, was arrested by the FBI at Dulles International Airport en route to Saudi Arabia. The FBI arrested three other men in the Idaho probe in recent weeks. And the FBI is examining links between the Idaho men and purported charities and individuals in six other jurisdictions across the country.[47]

In reassuring the Congress that the FBI was aggressively pursuing suspected terrorists, Mueller impliedly concluded that the FBI abused the material witness law. The FBI did not detain al-Kidd as a witness, but it had arrested him along with "three other men in the Idaho probe," and the FBI was "examining

---

[44] Ashcroft v. al-Kidd, 563 U.S. 731, 131 S. Ct. 2074, 2088 (2011) (Ginsburg, J., concurring in the judgment).

[45] Al-Kidd v. Ashcroft, 598 F.3d 1129 (9th Cir. 2010).

[46] Brief for Respondent at 3, Ashcroft v. al-Kidd, 563 U.S. 731, 131 S. Ct. 2074 (WL 219561) (2011) (No. 10-98).

[47] *Id.* at 6.

links" between the arrested suspects and "purported charities and individuals in six other jurisdictions across the country."[48]

Even Attorney General John Ashcroft made statements within weeks of 9/11 conceding that the Department of Justice would abuse the material witness law as a preventative detention provision allowing for detention and investigation without probable cause to arrest for a crime. Ashcroft stated that "[a]ggressive detention of lawbreakers and material witnesses is vital to preventing, disrupting or delaying new attacks" and that this policy would "form one part of the department's concentrated strategy to prevent terrorist attacks by taking suspected terrorists off the street."[49]

In the end, the Supreme Court concluded that Ashcroft and other senior officials did not violate al-Kidd's Fourth Amendment rights. In reaching this result, Justice Scalia wrote:

> Because al-Kidd concedes that individualized suspicion [of him] supported the issuance of the material-witness arrest warrant; and does not assert that his arrest would have been unconstitutional absent the alleged pretextual use of the warrant; we find no Fourth Amendment violation. Efficient and evenhanded application of the law demands that we look to whether the arrest is objectively justified, rather than to the motive of the arresting officer.[50]

In other words, although al-Kidd claimed that the attorney general used the material witness statute as a pretext for detaining him, it is improper to inquire into the motives behind the policy because al-Kidd conceded that the material witness warrant in his case was in fact based on facts pertaining to al-Kidd that supported a finding of individualized suspicion, and because al-Kidd failed to allege that his arrest violated the requirements of the Fourth Amendment.

Without assessing the merits of Scalia's argument, what is clear is that it was sufficient to dispose of the case. In other words, putting aside the persuasiveness of Scalia's opinion, it was more than adequate to decide the case.

But Scalia did not stop at that point. He unnecessarily went further to discuss the quasi-immunity doctrine. After stating the previously established rule that federal officials are immune from money damages "unless a plaintiff pleads facts showing (1) that the official violated a statutory or constitutional right, and (2) that the right was 'clearly established' at the time of the

---

[48] *Id.*

[49] *Id.* at 8.

[50] Ashcroft v. al-Kidd, 563 U.S. 731, 131 S. Ct. 2074, 2083 (2011).

challenged conduct,"[51] Scalia stated that although the Court does not "require a case directly on point," legal precedent must have placed the disputed right "beyond debate."[52]

Prior cases had not explicated the term "clearly established," but the term "clearly established" is certainly not the same as "beyond debate," and it is plausible that a "right" may well be considered "clearly established" while still debatable by a minority of judges. In contrast, if a small number of judges continue to debate whether a "right" is "clearly established," it would seem a foregone conclusion that such a "clearly established" right is not "beyond debate." In short, Justice Scalia unnecessarily expanded the scope of the quasi-immunity doctrine by insisting that the disputed right be not merely "clearly established," but "beyond debate."

The claim in favor of a powerful quasi-immunity defense immunizing federal officials from damage claims is dependent on two considerations. First, it is more important for the public good that such officials not be intimidated from exercising the authority granted to them by law by the threat of a damage judgment than it is that individuals who were harmed, perhaps irreparably, by such officials be granted a damage remedy. The weighing of the competitive benefits and disadvantages of immunizing officials and providing relief to harmed individuals does not lend itself to being broken down into concrete and measurable factors that are comparable to one another and thus may indeed be weighed to determine which was on balance more important to the welfare of society. Both certainly have value, but since they run against each other, the combustion that results from a collision between the two results in a zero-sum analysis. The more the law permits a damage recovery on behalf of an individual, the more intimidated officials may be in exercising their authority, and the greater the immunity protection granted officials, the less likely that the law provides an injured individual with a remedy. Second, it is claimed that high-ranking public officials need to be protected from the demands and distractions of litigation so that they can devote their energy and their concentration to discharging their responsibilities.[53]

When considered in isolation, the fact that the Supreme Court has used its discretionary authority to fashion a federal common law quasi-immunity defense protecting federal officials may be understood as nothing more than an

---

[51] *Id.* at 2080.

[52] *Id.* at 2083.

[53] Although it was claimed in the *al-Kidd* litigation that a high-ranking official is often sued in a personal capacity after leaving public office (see the amicus brief filed by six former attorneys general of the United States, 2008 WL 4154531), there seems to be little to no support for the claim. *See* Motion for Leave to File Brief for *Amici Curiae* Ibrahim Turkmen, et al., 2008 WL 4805227 (Oct. 31, 2008), at 23.

isolated judgment balancing off assuring an effective executive against providing remedies to individuals. But when the judicial construction of the quasi-immunity doctrine is understood as a reaction to the *Bivens* doctrine and then in the context of judicially crafted legal doctrines designed to grant a broad immunity to the executive in national security cases, the high court's embrace of the quasi-immunity doctrine takes on a different coloration. For example, when the Court retreated from the *Bivens* doctrine it argued that the judicial construction of federal common law as represented by *Bivens* was an inappropriate judicial initiative. This position rested on the idea that Congress makes law, not the courts, and that in the absence of a statute authorizing the courts to grant a damage remedy the court should refrain from crafting a remedy. If this analysis were applied to the executive's claim of quasi-immunity, the Supreme Court should have reached the opposite result. Instead of exercising its own common law powers to fashion a quasi-immunity defense, the Court should have stayed its hand on the ground that Congress makes the nation's law.

There is a second perspective from which to consider the Court's quasi-immunity doctrine that suggests that the Court's immunity doctrine results more from an ideological springboard than a careful assessment of the comparative public benefits. As indicated, the quasi-immunity defense protects an official from liability unless the law establishing the alleged violated right is concrete, clear, and beyond debate, a remarkably high standard since so much law, including the scope of individual rights, is subject to debate. But then such a high bar may seem reasonable if the balance between providing a remedy and encouraging the exercise of lawful authority to its fullest is assessed in isolation.

But if the context is broadened, the Court's rationale for its immunity rule is highly questionable. For example, in a 2010 decision concerning the providing of material support such as legal representation to groups the secretary of state identified as terrorist, the Court rejected a challenge to the federal statute on the ground that it was unconstitutionally vague.[54] The doctrine of unconstitutional vagueness emphasizes that an individual should not have to guess as to the location of the boundary distinguishing between what is lawful and unlawful. Instead, the law should provide a clear guide so that every person may fully exercise the entire spectrum of the rights granted by the Constitution and not be intimidated from exercising rights to their fullest on the ground that a statute is so vaguely worded that the average person could not decide what is or is not lawful conduct.

---

[54] Holder v. Humanitarian Law Project, 561 U.S. 1, 7–8 (2010).

But when the high court upheld that statute in that 2010 case, it did so on the ground that the federal statute was sufficiently certain that a person of average intelligence should be able to determine what was and was not lawful.[55] Although in isolation this standard could be severely assessed on the ground that it left in place a vague statute of uncertain meaning, thus undermining the primary value of encouraging individuals to exercise their rights to the fullest, the regrettable weakness of the standard takes on a rare clarity when it is compared to the quasi-immunity doctrine. Under the immunity doctrine, in order to encourage federal officials to fully exercise their authority, the Supreme Court immunizes them unless the law they allegedly violated is beyond debate, a much higher and more demanding standard than that employed under the vagueness doctrine.

Thus, if the high court considers it just as important for individuals to exercise their rights to the fullest as it does government officials to exercise their authority to the fullest—and no reason arises suggesting that these interests are not of equal significance—the Court should have invalidated the material support statute unless it could be said that the boundary distinguishing between lawful and unlawful conduct was beyond debate, which it was not.

The fact that the Court did not apply the standard to protect individual rights as it does to the exercise of federal power suggests that the immunity doctrine rests on more than a balance of federal power versus individual remedies and is driven by a more broadly based ideological commitment to depressing the scope of rights and remedies while immunizing executive power from accountability.

Reshaping the immunity doctrine for senior executive officials so as to blunt the impact of the *Bivens* doctrine was only one of two assaults on providing a remedy to individuals harmed by policies adopted by senior executive officers. On May 18, 2009, the Supreme Court decided *Ashcroft v. Iqbal*[56] by a vote of five to four. *Iqbal* is a prime example of how the contemporary Supreme Court expands and strengthens the iron curtain protecting senior executive officials from meaningful judicial accountability. But it is more than that; it is a dramatic illustration of how the Court grants relief in excess of the relief the executive requested.[57]

Iqbal was arrested in November 2001 "on charges of conspiracy to defraud the United States and fraud in relation to identification documents" and

---

[55] *Id.* at 20.

[56] Ashcroft v. Iqbal, 556 U.S. 662 (2009).

[57] The Supreme Court did the same thing in the nineteenth-century *Totten* case, discussed in Chapter 3. The Court granted relief much more sweeping in scope than the relief the United States requested.

detained at the Metropolitan Detention Center in Brooklyn. Iqbal claimed that he was designated a person of "high interest . . . solely because of his race, religion, or national origin," and that because of that designation he was placed in "Administrative Maximum Special Housing Unit for over six months while awaiting the fraud trial,"[58] a confinement designed to prevent the prisoners from "communicating with the general prison population or the outside world."[59] Iqbal alleged that on the day he was transferred to the special unit, prison guards "picked him up and threw him against the wall, kicked him in the stomach, punched him in the face, and dragged him across the room."[60] He also claimed that prison guards denied his requests for medical care, subjected him to "unjustified strip and body cavity searches," "verbally berated him as a 'terrorist,' and 'Muslim killer,'" denied him "adequate food," "turned on [the] air conditioning during the winter and heating during the summer," and "interfered with his attempts to pray and engage in religious study."[61]

Some months after Iqbal pled guilty to criminal charges, served a term of imprisonment, and was returned to his native Pakistan, he filed a federal action seeking damages against "34 current and former federal officials and 19 'John Doe' federal corrections officers."[62] But it was his claims against senior executive officials—John Ashcroft, the then attorney general, and Robert Mueller, the then director of the FBI—that were central to the Supreme Court case.

Iqbal claimed that Ashcroft and Mueller "were at the very least aware of the discriminatory detention policy and condoned it (and perhaps even took part in devising it), thereby violating his First and Fifth Amendment rights,"[63] and making them potentially liable for damages to Iqbal pursuant to the *Bivens* doctrine. In other words, Iqbal claimed that at minimum Ashcroft and Mueller knew that their subordinates implemented an unlawful policy that discriminated on the basis of race, religion, and national origin, that this policy was the immediate cause of his designation and treatment, and that they did not stop it. Moreover, Iqbal claimed that both Ashcroft and Mueller may have done more than simply condone the discriminatory policy initiated by others; they may have actually devised and directed its implementation.

The district judge denied Ashcroft and Mueller's request to have Iqbal's action dismissed and the Court of Appeals affirmed the denial of the motion to dismiss.[64] The three-member circuit court panel was unanimous, but one

---

[58] *Id.* at 688 (Souter, J., dissenting).
[59] *Id.* at 667 (majority opinion).
[60] *Id.* at 688–689 (Souter, J., dissenting).
[61] *Id.* at 689.
[62] *Id.* at 668 (majority opinion).
[63] *Id.* at 688 (Souter, J., dissenting).
[64] *Id.* at 689.

judge, José Cabranes, wrote a concurrence. Because the Supreme Court eventually discussed it, and because the Cabranes concurrence actually spells out the tension in values embedded in the case with a clarity absent from the Supreme Court majority opinion, the Cabranes opinion deserves a summary.

Cabranes first noted that prior Supreme Court decisions regarding the sufficiency of a plaintiff's allegations are "less than crystal clear and fully deserve reconsideration by the Supreme Court." In so doing, he compliments Judge Newman, who wrote the majority opinion for the panel which Cabranes joined, for writing a "careful and comprehensive" opinion that "seeks to hew closely to the relevant Supreme Court and Second Circuit precedents." Next, Cabranes claims that the "relevant pleading standards," which the panel concluded Iqbal satisfied, "reflects the uneasy compromise . . . between a qualified immunity privilege rooted in the need to preserve 'the effectiveness of government as contemplated by our constitutional structure,' and the pleading requirements" of the Federal Rules of Civil Procedure.[65]

It is an "uneasy compromise"[66] for Cabranes because the conclusion that Iqbal satisfies the pleading requirements means—from Cabranes's perspective—that Ashcroft and Mueller "will have to submit to discovery, and possibly to a jury trial . . . . at a time when Ashcroft and Mueller were trying to cope with a national and international security emergency unprecedented in the history of the American Republic."[67] Or as Cabranes stated in his concluding paragraph:

> But a detached observer may wonder whether the balance struck here between the need to deter unlawful conduct and the dangers of exposing public officials to burdensome litigation—a balance compelled by the precedents that bind us—jeopardizes the important policy interest Justice Stevens aptly described as "a national interest in enabling Cabinet officers with responsibilities in [the national security] area to perform their sensitive duties with decisiveness and without potentially ruinous hesitation."[68]

Cabranes argued for making the pleading requirements more demanding so that even high officials who acted unlawfully were shielded from accountability on the assumption that such a rule would better protect national security.

---

[65] Iqbal v. Hasty, 490 F.3d 143, 178 (2d Cir. 2007) (Cabranes, J., concurring).

[66] *Id.*

[67] *Id.* at 179.

[68] *Id.* (citing Mitchell v. Forsyth, 472 U.S. 511, 541 (1985) (Stevens, J., concurring in judgment).

The case presented to the Supreme Court asked whether Ashcroft and Mueller should be subject to the rigors of discovery and trial or whether they should be entitled to having the complaint dismissed at this preliminary stage. Justice Alito framed the central question this way: "Did respondent [Iqbal], as the plaintiff in the District Court, plead factual matter that, if taken as true, states a claim that petitioners deprived him of his clearly established constitutional rights?"[69]

The parties' presentation of the case to the Supreme Court agreed about two central considerations. First, the case was presented to the Supreme Court on the "uncontested assumption" that the *Bivens* case "allows personal liability based on a federal officer's violation of an individual's rights under the First and Fifth Amendments."[70] This was odd, to say the least, since the Supreme Court had for the previous three decades sharply curtailed the *Bivens* doctrine, so much so that it seemed *Bivens* was all but limited to the facts of the three cases in which the Court had endorsed *Bivens* claims. Moreover, Ashcroft was a former attorney general and was likely aware that the high court had sharply limited the liability of federal officials under the *Bivens* doctrine. The oddity of the concession notwithstanding, Ashcroft and Mueller did concede that they could be liable under a *Bivens* rationale.

Second, Ashcroft and Mueller conceded that they "would be liable [to Iqbal] if they had 'actual knowledge' of discrimination by their subordinates and exhibited 'deliberate indifference' to that discrimination."[71] Thus, these two senior government officials did not claim that their liability depended upon their devising and ordering the discriminatory policy that Iqbal claimed resulted in his treatment. Nor did they argue that they could be held "only liable for his or her own misconduct."[72] Instead, they conceded that they could be held liable even if the discriminatory policy was devised and implemented by their subordinates, provided that they became aware of the policy and failed to take appropriate action to end it. Or as Justice Souter stated the matter: Ashcroft and Mueller conceded in this case that "a supervisor's knowledge of a subordinate's unconstitutional conduct and deliberate indifference to that conduct are grounds for *Bivens* liability."[73]

Since Iqbal sought to recover against Ashcroft and Mueller "on a theory" that they "at least knowingly acquiesced (and maybe more than acquiesced) in the discriminatory acts of their subordinates," Iqbal and the two defendants shared common ground on this important issue, an important matter since, as

[69] Ashcroft v. Iqbal, 556 U.S. 662, 666 (2009).
[70] *Id.* at 687.
[71] *Id.* at 690 (Souter, J., dissenting).
[72] *Id.* at 677 (majority opinion).
[73] *Id.* at 691 (Souter, J., dissenting).

Justice Souter stated in dissent, if Iqbal can "show this, he will satisfy Ashcroft and Mueller's own test for supervisory liability."[74]

As is obvious, both concessions by Ashcroft and Mueller were significant because together they enhanced Iqbal's chances of prevailing, since Iqbal's success required a valid *Bivens* claim and possibly some degree of supervisory liability. Furthermore, the Supreme Court will not normally put aside concessions made by a party. That is so because the presence of a concession usually means that the conceded issue has not been briefed and argued by the parties, thus depriving the justices of any advantage careful exploration of the issues may yield. Moreover, putting aside a concession is unfair to the party who may benefit from it, in that that party may have refrained from addressing the broader question in reliance on the concession.

The high court followed its normal rule with regard to Iqbal's *Bivens* claim. The Court noted that although causes of action not authorized by an act of Congress are "disfavored," the majority respected the 1971 decision in *Bivens*, but then repeated recent Court statements that the Court is "reluctant to extend *Bivens* liability 'to any new context or new category of defendants.'" Against those postulates, the Court noted that Iqbal asserted a claim under the First and the Fifth Amendments to the Constitution, but that the Court had previously not recognized *Bivens* claims arising from the First Amendment. However, Ashcroft and Mueller had not "press[ed] this argument" in this case, and as a consequence Alito stated that the Court would "assume, without deciding," that Iqbal's First Amendment claim is "actionable."[75]

But the majority departed from its usual practice of respecting concessions that would have caused it to respect Ashcroft and Mueller's second concession. In making this departure, the majority noted that Iqbal correctly conceded that "Government officials may not be held liable for the unconstitutional conduct of their subordinates under a theory of *respondeat superior*," but then jumped to the conclusion that because "vicarious liability is inapplicable to *Bivens* and §1983 suits, a plaintiff must plead that each Government-official defendant, through the official's own individual actions, has violated the Constitution." In the context of the *Iqbal* case, the majority concluded that a claim of discrimination on the basis of race, religion, and national origin requires evidence of a discriminatory "purpose rather than knowledge" of the fact that subordinates may be acting in a discriminatory manner. Or to the put the matter slightly differently, the requirement of a discriminatory purpose requires that a party prove that the course of action was taken " 'because

---

[74] *Id.*

[75] *Id.* at 675 (majority opinion) (quoting Correctional Servs. Corp. v. Malesko, 534 U.S. 61, 68 (2001)).

of,' not merely 'in spite of,' [the action's] adverse effects upon an identifiable group." And then with regard to Iqbal's detention and identification as a person of high interest, Iqbal must "plead sufficient factual matter to show that petitioners adopted and implemented the detention policies at issue not for a neutral, investigative reason but for the purpose of discriminating on account of race, religion, or national origin." Accordingly, Alito wrote that a "plaintiff must plead that each Government-official defendant, through the official's own individual actions, has violated the Constitution," or as Alito phrased the standard two paragraphs later: "each Government official, his or her title notwithstanding, is only liable for his or her own misconduct."[76]

The majority's doctrinal turn here was extraordinary. It rejected an explicit concession. It did away with "*Bivens* supervisory liability entirely."[77] It adopted a legal rule not advanced by the executive and not briefed or argued by the parties. And in so doing it ignored the broad spectrum that existed between the rule it laid down and the rule of respondeat superior. In short, the majority ignored the sound stopping points between the extremes and granted high-level executive officials new insulation from liability.

At this point, the majority turned its attention to assessing the sufficiency of Iqbal's pleadings. The relevant Federal Rule provided that a complaint must set forth a "short and plain statement of the claim showing that the pleader is entitled to relief."[78] In explicating these few and simple words, Alito concedes that a party is not required to provide detailed factual allegations while insisting that an "unadorned, the-defendant-unlawfully-harmed-me accusation" is required. An unadorned set of claims that is insufficient is one that provides "'labels and conclusions,'" presents "'a formulaic recitation of the elements of a cause of action,'" or "tenders 'naked assertion[s]' devoid of 'further factual enhancement.'"[79] In other words, while the contemporary practice rules marked a "notable and generous departure from the hyper-technical, code-pleading regime of a prior era," the rules do not "unlock the doors of discovery for a plaintiff armed with nothing more than conclusions."[80]

Alito sought to explicate these vague terms and phrases in his next paragraph, when he insisted that to survive a motion to dismiss, a complaint must "contain sufficient factual matter, accepted as true, to 'state a claim to relief that is plausible on its face.'"[81] In explaining the phrase "plausible on its face,"

---

[76] *Id.* at 676–677.

[77] *Id.* at 693 (Souter, J., dissenting).

[78] *Id.* at 677–678 (majority opinion) (quoting Fed. R. Civ. P. 8(a)(2)).

[79] *Id.* at 678 (quoting Bell Atlantic Corp. v. Twombly, 550 U.S. 544, 555–557 (2007)).

[80] *Id.* at 678–679.

[81] *Id.* at 678 (quoting Bell Atlantic Corp. v. Twombly, 550 U.S. 544, 570 (2007)).

Alito claimed that he relied upon the distinction between plausible and prob-able on the one hand and plausible and possible on the other. A requirement that a complaint contain factual allegations that were plausible on their face was not as demanding as would be a requirement that the factual allegations establish that the defendant was probably—as opposed to plausibly—liable for the misconduct alleged, but it was more demanding than a requirement that the allegations merely establish that the defendant was possibly responsi-ble for the alleged misconduct. Thus, a complaint that merely pleads facts that "are 'merely consistent with' a defendant's liability,"[82] or "do not permit the court to infer more than the mere possibility of misconduct" is one that merely establishes the possibility of the defendant's liability, and that. Alito asserts, is insufficient.[83] Or, as Alito characterized his thinking: "Threadbare recitals of the elements of a cause of action, supported by mere conclusory statements, do not suffice."[84]

Try as he did, Alito failed to clarify what factual allegations are required to satisfy the legal requirements for pleading. He stated that pleadings that "are no more than conclusions, are not entitled to the assumption of truth" and that "legal conclusions . . . must be supported by factual allegations," while conceding that a court must consider whether a complaint that includes "well-pleaded factual allegations" gives rise "to an entitlement to relief."[85] In sum, Alito time and time again fell back on vague phrases that shed no light on what he said was legally required of a pleading.[86]

So how did Iqbal's complaint compare to the legal standard Alito set forth? The complaint alleged that Ashcroft and Mueller "'knew of, condoned, and will-fully and maliciously agreed to'" subject Iqbal to the discriminatory policy and practices. It also alleged that Ashcroft was the "'principal architect'" of the in-vidious policy.[87] In retrospect it would seem that Iqbal's complaint made legally

---

[82] *Id.* at 678 (quoting Bell Atlantic Corp. v. Twombly, 550 U.S. 544, 557 (2007)).

[83] *Id.* at 679.

[84] *Id.* at 678.

[85] *Id.* at 679.

[86] A recent and very thoughtful study of the Iqbal decision reports the following: "Many scholars have criticized *Iqbal* and *Twombly* for altering the meaning of the Federal Rules outside of the traditional procedures contemplated by the Rules Enabling Act. Almost all commentators agree that *Iqbal* and *Twombly* mark a break from the liberal pleading doctrine enunciated in 1957 by Conley v. Gibson." Alexander A. Reinert, *Measuring the Impact of Plausibility Pleading*, 101 Virginia L. Rev. 2117, 2118 (2015). Professor Reinert concluded "on an analysis of more decisions than any prior research has canvassed in detail," that the post-Iqbal era has significantly increased dismissal rates by comparison to the pre-Iqbal era. *Id.* at 2218. Professor Reinert's article also provides a guide to recent law review literature on the subject.

[87] *Id.* at 669 (quoting First Amended Complaint and Jury Demand at ¶¶ 96, 10, Ashcroft v. Iqbal, 556 U.S. 662 (2009) (No. 04 CV 1809 (JG)(JA))).

sufficient allegations against Ashcroft and Mueller. That conclusion seems especially warranted given that Iqbal's allegations seemed totally plausible if not highly likely, and that absent some rudimentary discovery, Iqbal was stymied in presenting detailed allegations regarding Ashcroft and Mueller, given that discussions, conduct, emails, notes, and memoranda that might detail the allegations were and are confidential. But to Alito, these allegations were "bare assertions" that amounted to "nothing more than a 'formulaic recitation of the elements' of a constitutional discrimination claim."[88] Accordingly, Alito wrote that the "allegations are conclusory and not entitled to be assumed true."[89]

As stunning as all of that is, there is still one more side to the *Iqbal* majority opinion that sheds still more light on how determined the majority was to shape the law to protect high officers from damage actions. Thus, it is one thing for a majority to do what the majority did in *Iqbal* because its doctrinal crafting was essential to the outcome. It is quite another when the Court unnecessarily makes new law that it need not have made in order to decide the case at hand, which was the situation in *Iqbal*.

The majority in *Iqbal* concluded that the key allegations against Ashcroft and Mueller were "conclusory and not entitled to be assumed as true." That conclusion by itself was sufficient to dispose of the matter. Thus, when the majority not only reached that conclusion but went further and rejected Ashcroft and Mueller's concession regarding the scope of their potential liability, the majority underlined its determination to protect executive officials by shaping the law well beyond what the executive asserted it should be.[90]

The unrelenting eagerness of the majority in *Iqbal* to protect high-level officials from judicial accountability is particularly revealed in one other aspect of the opinion. Iqbal argued that the Supreme Court's construction of Federal Rule of Civil Procedure 8, which sets forth the "notice" pleading standard, "should be tempered" by the important fact that a trial judge could—and in this case had been instructed by the Court of Appeals to—" 'cabin discovery in such a way as to preserve' " Ashcroft and Mueller's "defense of qualified immunity 'as much as possible in anticipation of a summary judgment motion.' "[91]

---

[88] *Id.* at 681 (quoting Bell Atlantic Corp. v. Twombly, 550 U.S. 544, 570 (2007)).

[89] *Id.*

[90] Justice Souter made this point in his dissent when he wrote that as a matter of sheer logic, even if the majority accepted "Ashcroft and Mueller's concession and asked whether the complaint sufficiently alleges knowledge and deliberate indifference, it presumably would still conclude that the complaint fails to plead sufficient facts and must be dismissed." *Id.* at 694 (Souter, J., dissenting).

[91] *Id.* at 684 (majority opinion) (quoting Brief for Respondent at 27, Ashcroft v. Iqbal, 556 U.S. 662 (2009) (No. 07-1015)).

The majority rejected that position, and it did so for reasons that deserve to be quoted:

> If a Government official is to devote time to his or her duties, and to the formulation of sound and responsible policies, it is counterproductive to require the substantial diversion that is attendant to participating in litigation and making informed decisions as to how it should proceed. Litigation, though necessary to ensure that officials comply with the law, exacts heavy costs in terms of efficiency and expenditure of valuable time and resources that might otherwise be directed to the proper execution of the work of the Government. The costs of diversion are only magnified when Government officials are charged with responding to, as Judge Cabranes aptly put it, "a national and international security emergency unprecedented in the history of the American Republic."[92]

Whether potential discovery demands on an attorney general or the director of the FBI will so infringe on their time as to present a threat to the nation's security is an empirical claim that is predictive in nature. And given that, one might understandably be inclined to favor taking a cautious approach and guard the national security by protecting the time and energies of individuals whose responsibilities at least partially pertain to national security issues. But before deciding to endorse such an approach—or at least deciding what the reasons were for the *Iqbal* Supreme Court to decide the issue the way it did— it is worth recalling the Supreme Court's reasoning in Paula Corbin Jones's sexual harassment case against President Bill Clinton.[93]

In that dispute, Jones accused Clinton of violating her federal rights when he was governor of Arkansas. Clinton argued, among other things, that the presidency was a "unique" office within the republic,[94] and that the litigation of the dispute would impose "burdens" on him as president that would "hamper the performance of his official duties,"[95] which included his duties as commander-in-chief and as head of the nation's intelligence agencies, and, as a result, the matter should be stayed until he left office. The argument presented by Clinton is the same as that presented by Alito in the *Iqbal* case. The difference between the cases was that in the *Clinton* case the office holder was the president, whereas in the *Iqbal* case the office holders were an attorney general and FBI director—important offices, but certainly not as significant as the presidency.

---

[92] *Id.* at 685 (quoting Iqbal v. Hasty, 490 F.3d 143, 179 (2007) (Cabranes, J., concurring)).
[93] Clinton v. Jones, 520 U.S. 681 (1997).
[94] *Id.* at 697.
[95] *Id.* at 701.

And yet the Supreme Court in the *Clinton* case unanimously decided that Jones's civil complaint against Clinton could proceed while Clinton was president on the ground that the distractions of litigation did not present a threat to national security.[96] The justices in that case did not credit the president's claim that discovery and trial would necessarily interfere with the performance of his duties as president. And that was true, even though Justice Stevens wrote that the Court did not dispute the claim that the presidency was a unique office that imposed enormous responsibilities on the holder of that office. In fact, Stevens quoted President Lyndon Johnson, who observed: "Of all the 1,886 nights I was President, there were not many when I got to sleep before 1 or 2 a.m., and there were few mornings when I didn't wake up by 6 or 6:30."[97] But the Court was unmoved as it pushed aside Clinton's argument that the litigation might interfere with his national security responsibilities and affirmed its "confidence in the ability of our federal judges to deal" with the matter constructively.[98]

The Court's resolution of this issue—the degree to which discovery and possible trial interfere with the discharge of a high official's duties—in these two cases is inconsistent with one another. In *Clinton* the Court concluded the interference was acceptable; in *Iqbal* the interference was unacceptable. One expects judges to be consistent, and when they are not the expectation is that the inconsistency will be acknowledged and explained. Nonetheless, three justices who decided in the *Clinton* case that discovery and trial did not burden the president—Justices Scalia, Kennedy, and Thomas—reached just the opposite conclusion in the *Iqbal* case, and they did not write a word acknowledging or explaining the inconsistency.

---

[96] *Id.* at 705–707.

[97] *Id.* at 698 (quoting Lyndon Baines Johnson, The Vantage Point: Perspectives of the Presidency 1963–1969, at 425 (1971)).

[98] *Id.* at 709.

13

Guantanamo

The Supreme Court Blinks

Weeks after the attacks on the United States on September 11, 2001, Abu Bakker Qassim, a Muslim Uighur and a native of China's western semiautonomous Xinjiang province, was turned over by the Pakistani military to United States authorities in return for a bounty of $5,000 that the United States had offered for each terrorist. In June 2002, he was transferred to the Guantanamo Naval Bay Base in Cuba, where he was detained as an enemy combatant.[1] In late 2004 or early 2005, U.S. military authorities determined that Abu Bakker Qassim was not an enemy combatant, but the authorities did not inform Abu Bakker of this conclusion. On March 10, 2005, not knowing that the United States did not consider him a threat to national security, Abu Bakker Qassim petitioned for a writ of habeas corpus. At that point, the United States requested that the district judge stay the proceedings pending a decision by the District of Columbia Court of Appeals. On April 13, 2005, District Judge James Robertson, "also ignorant"[2] that the military had concluded that Qassim was not an enemy combatant, granted the United States the requested stay of judicial proceedings. On July 14, 2005, Qassim and his lawyers met for the first time, and at that meeting Qassim was imprisoned in a "box" and "chained to the floor."[3] It was at that meeting that Qassim's "counsel were informed by their clients" that the military authorities had "found them not to be enemy combatants."[4] On December 22, 2005, District Judge Roberston concluded that the United States' detention of Qassim at

---

[1] Qassim v. Bush, 407 F. Supp. 2d 198, 199 (D.D.C. 2005).
[2] *Id.*
[3] The Rule of Law Oral History Project, The Reminiscences of P. Sabin Willet, Columbia Center for Oral History 8 (Columbia University, 2011).
[4] *Qassim*, 407 F. Supp. 2d at 199.

Guantanamo was unlawful,[5] but that as a federal judge, he had "no relief to offer" Qassim. [6] On Friday, May 5, 2006, after five and one-half years of captivity, Qassim and a handful of other Uighurs imprisoned at Guantanamo were transferred to Albania, and the United States filed "an emergency motion to dismiss" Qassim's appeal to the circuit court, scheduled to be heard on Monday, May 8, as "moot."[7] The Court of Appeals granted the motion.

When the United States began to capture individuals "in connection with military operations in Afghanistan or in other counterterrorism operations overseas"[8] following the attacks on September 11, 2001, it had to decide where to incarcerate them. In response, it developed many sites, including some secret sites that became known as "black sites," located in Afghanistan, Thailand, and Eastern Europe, as well as a publicly disclosed site at the Guantanamo Bay Naval Base.[9] Guantanamo was selected because Department of Justice lawyers assumed that U.S. courts would not exercise jurisdiction over a petition for the writ of habeas corpus filed by alleged alien enemies detained at Guantanamo who challenged the legality of their confinement.[10] What that meant as a practical matter was that no federal court would review any claim put forth by an

---

[5] *Id.* at 201.

[6] *Id.* at 203.

[7] Qassim v. Bush, 466 F.3d 1073, 1074 (D.C. Cir. 2006).

[8] Dep't of Justice, Dep't of Def., Dep't of State, Dep't of Homeland Security, Office of the Dir. of Nat'l Intelligence, Joint Chiefs of Staff, Guantanamo Review Task Force, Final Report (Jan. 22, 2010).

[9] Dana Priest disclosed the CIA use of "secret" facilities in Thailand, Afghanistan, and Eastern Europe, where the CIA interrogated "some of its most important al Qaeda captives." These sites were known as " 'black sites' in classified White House, CIA, Justice Department and congressional documents," and were known "to only a handful of officials in the United States and, usually, only to the president and a few top intelligence officers in each host country." Dana Priest, *CIA Holds Terror Suspects in Secret Prisons*, Wash. Post, Nov. 2, 2005.

[10] In his dissent in *Boumediene*, Justice Scalia stated that the "President relied on our settled precedent in *Johnson v. Eisentrager*, 339 U.S. 763 (1950), when he established the prison at Guantanamo Bay for enemy aliens. Citing that case, the President's Office of Legal Counsel advised him 'that the great weight of legal authority indicates that a federal district court could not properly exercise habeas jurisdiction over an alien detained at [Guantanamo Bay].' Memorandum from Patrick F. Philbin and John C. Yoo, Deputy Assistant Attorneys General, Office of Legal Counsel, Dep't of Defense (Dec. 28, 2001). Had the law been otherwise, the military surely would not have transported prisoners there, but would have kept them in Afghanistan, transferred them to another of our foreign military bases, or turned them over to allies for detention." Boumediene v. Bush, 553 U.S. 723, 828 (2008) (Scalia J., dissenting).

individual imprisoned at Guantanamo—a total of 779 individuals[11]—who claimed not to be an enemy combatant.[12]

In 2004, the Supreme Court turned the executive's apple cart of expectations upside down. In *Rasul v. Bush*, the Court decided that a statute granted the district courts jurisdiction over habeas petitions filed by imprisoned aliens at Guantanamo who were accused of being enemy combatants. At the time of the *Rasul* decision, there was no question that a federal court would have jurisdiction over a habeas petition filed by a U.S. citizen challenging the legality of confinement at Guantanamo. Nor was there any question that a federal court would have jurisdiction over a habeas petition filed by an alien imprisoned within the United States. But those accepted postulates left undecided whether a federal court would exercise jurisdiction over a habeas petition filed by an alien accused of being an enemy combatant incarcerated at Guantanamo, which was not within the United States, but over which the United States exercised de facto sovereignty. Justice Stevens framed the question as follows: "whether the habeas statute confers a right to judicial review of the legality of executive detention of aliens in a territory over which the United States exercises plenary and exclusive jurisdiction, but not 'ultimate sovereignty.'"[13] His answer was that the statute did confer such jurisdiction.[14]

Although *Rasul* rejected the executive's position, the opinion itself was cautious, if not clinical. It certainly was "no trumpet of liberty, no ringing

---

[11] The executive uses the term *detainee*, not *prisoner*, to describe the individuals incarcerated at Guantanamo. During the Vietnam War, the United States used the term *prisoner of war* or *POW*—not *detainee*—to describe American soldiers detained by North Vietnam. Perhaps John McCain, who was the Republican Party nominee for president in 2008, is the most famous of the Vietnam War POWs. Presumably, the executive in part avoided the use of the term *prisoner* because it refused to categorize the aliens incarcerated at Guantanamo as *prisoners of war*, as such a designation would entitle them, as a matter of law, to certain protections the executive did not extend to them. *See* Ronald Dworkin, *Why It Was a Great Victory*, N.Y. Rev. Books, Aug. 14, 2008. Alternatively, the use of the word *detainee*, as opposed to *prisoner*, to describe those captured and incarcerated at Guantanamo was little more than an effort to sanitize the precise nature of the Guantanamo confinement by the United States.

[12] During 2002, 632 individuals were imprisoned; during 2003, another 117 individuals were imprisoned; between 2004 and 2006, an additional 29 individuals were imprisoned; and during 2007 and 2008, another 6 individuals were imprisoned. Dep't of Justice, Dep't of Def., Dep't of State, Dep't of Homeland Security, Office of the Dir. of Nat'l Intelligence, Joint Chiefs of Staff, Guantanamo Review Task Force, Final Report 1 (Jan. 22, 2010).

[13] Rasul v. Bush, 542 U.S. 466, 475 (2004).

[14] Justice Stevens wrote: "We therefore hold that §2241 confers on the District Court jurisdiction to hear petitioners' habeas corpus challenges to the legality of their detention at the Guantanamo Bay Naval Base." *Rasul*, 542 U.S. at 484.

endorsement of the importance of due process, no memorable restatement of the significant linkage between a vital democracy and a strong separation of powers doctrine." In fact, one can pore over this "dry as sand" opinion without finding any "lofty phrases" or "uplifting sentences."[15] In essence, the six-to-three majority "said nothing about what should happen next. It left until another time and another case what process should be followed to determine whether the government could continue to imprison"[16] the accused enemy combatants at Guantanamo. The result in *Rasul* was important but limited.[17]

Congress subsequently amended the statute to deny the federal courts jurisdiction over such petitions. But in *Hamdan v. Rumsfeld*,[18] the Supreme

[15] David Rudenstine, *American Preeminence, Separation of Power and Human Rights: The Guantanamo Detainee Case*, in Guantanamo Bay and the Judicial-Moral Treatment of the Other 15, 17 (Clark Butler ed., 2007).

[16] *Id.* at 16.

[17] Jack Goldsmith of Harvard Law School has a very different perspective on the *Rasul* case, as well as the *Hamdan* and *Boumediene* cases discussed later in the text. For Goldsmith, the Supreme Court should have dismissed the habeas petition in *Rasul* on the ground that the Court lacked jurisdiction because the petitioner was an "alien enemy who at no relevant time and in no stage of his captivity has been within [the United States] territorial jurisdiction." Jack Goldsmith, Power and Constraint: The Accountable Presidency After 9/11 163 (2012). The language Goldsmith quoted was from Justice Jackson's opinion in *Johnson v. Eisentrager*, 339 U.S. 763, 768 (1950), a case Goldsmith considered controlling. In *Eisentrager*, the Court dismissed a habeas petition filed by German nationals confined by U.S. military authorities in Germany following conviction by a military commission for having engaged in military activity against United States forces in China after Germany surrendered. Goldsmith wishes to characterize the Court's opinion in *Eisentrager* as standing for the proposition that a United States court will not exercise jurisdiction over a habeas petition filed by "an alien enemy who, at no relevant time and in no stage of his captivity" has been within the United States. *Id.* at 768. If that is what Justice Jackson wrote in Eisentrager, then the distance between exercising jurisdiction over an enemy alien within the United States and without would be—to use Justice Jackson's words—"how much farther we must go" if the Court is to exercise jurisdiction over a habeas petition filed by an enemy alien who was outside the United States. *Id.* at 767. But that is not what Jackson wrote in *Eisentrager*. Rather, Jackson emphasized that the petitioners were in United States custody in Germany and had never been within the "territorial jurisdiction" of the United States. *Id.* at 768. More tellingly, in the central paragraph in *Eisentrager*, Justice Jackson emphasized the distinction between being within the United States and being in a United States territory, and that the Court might well have jurisdiction over a habeas petition filed by an enemy alien imprisoned in a United States territory. *Id.* at 777. Because Justice Jackson accepted that the Court had jurisdiction over a habeas petition arising within the United States or a territory of the United States, he left open the question that *Rasul* raised: whether the Guantanamo Bay Naval Base was a territory "over which the United States is sovereign." *Id.* at 778. Thus, for all of Goldsmith's suggestions that the outcome in *Rasul* was flatly inconsistent with *Eisentrager*, the fact is that the language of *Eisentrager* invited the *Rasul* question and tilted in favor of the outcome in *Rasul*.

[18] Hamdan v. Rumsfeld, 548 U.S. 557 (2006).

Court concluded that Congress had withdrawn such jurisdiction only prospectively, and it did not intend to withdraw jurisdiction over cases then pending in the federal courts. In the same opinion, the Court's majority concluded, as Justice Breyer summarized the matter, that "Congress has denied the President legislative authority to create military commissions of the kind at issue here,"[19] that the charge against the detainee was not authorized by the law of war, and that the commission's procedures violated the Uniform Code of Military Justice.[20]

In the wake of the *Hamdan* decision, Congress passed legislation that withdrew federal court jurisdiction over pending habeas petitions filed by those incarcerated at Guantanamo. In 2008, the constitutionality of that statute was presented to the Court in *Boumediene v. Bush,* the most controversial and important of the three post-9/11 Supreme Court decisions. The question presented by *Boumediene,* as framed by Justice Kennedy for the slim five-justice majority, was whether the individual aliens alleged to be enemy combatants imprisoned at Guantanamo "have the constitutional privilege of habeas corpus, a privilege not to be withdrawn except in conformance with the Suspension Clause, Art. I, §9, cl. 2."[21] Justice Kennedy then stated that the "petitioners do have the habeas corpus privilege," and because a statute, termed the Detainee Treatment Act of 2005, that "provides certain procedures for review of the detainees' status" is not "an adequate and effective substitute for habeas corpus . . . §7 of the Military Commissions Act of 2006 . . . operates as an unconstitutional suspension of the writ,"[22] which can only be suspended by Congress, and then "in Cases of Rebellion or Invasion."[23] Reaching this result, Justice Kennedy observed that the "privilege of habeas corpus entitles the prisoner to a meaningful opportunity to demonstrate that he is being held pursuant to 'the erroneous application or interpretation' of relevant law."[24] Justice Kennedy explained the words "meaningful opportunity" as follows: "And the habeas court must have the power to order the conditional release of an individual unlawfully detained—though release need not be the exclusive remedy and is not the appropriate one in every case in which the writ is granted."[25] Thus, Justice Kennedy insisted that the habeas court must have the "power to order the conditional release,"

---

[19] *Id.* at 636 (Breyer, J., concurring).

[20] The plurality also concluded that the military commission's procedures did not satisfy the four Geneva Conventions signed in 1949. *Hamdan,* 548 U.S. at 626–635 (plurality opinion).

[21] Boumediene v. Bush, 553 U.S. 723, 732 (2008).

[22] *Id.* at 733.

[23] U.S. Const. art. I, §9, cl. 2.

[24] *Boumediene,* 553 U.S. at 779.

[25] *Id.*

while also qualifying that assertion with cautionary words that "release need not be the exclusive remedy" and may not be "appropriate" in "every case." Nonetheless, a few pages later, Kennedy emphasized that the "writ must be effective" and that the "habeas court must have sufficient authority to conduct a meaningful review of both the cause for detention and the Executive's power to detain."[26]

The *Boumediene* decision was praised and condemned. For example, the prominent legal philosopher Ronald Dworkin spoke for many when he stated that *Boumediene* was "one of the most important Supreme Court decisions in recent years" because it made it possible for the Guantanamo prisoners to argue that "the administration has no factual or legal ground for imprisoning them." In contrast, Senator John McCain expressed what many others thought when he termed the *Boumediene* decision "one of the worst" in the nation's history.[27] Despite these strong disagreements, no one could contest the fact that the *Boumediene* decision itself did not free one person incarcerated at Guantanamo.[28] Thus, for all of the verbal fireworks over the decision—including Justice Scalia's demagoguery in predicting that the Court's ruling "will almost certainly cause more Americans to be killed"[29]—*Boumediene* did not order the release of anyone imprisoned at Guantanamo. At the same time, Kennedy's opinion suggests that lengthy incarcerations at Guantanamo—in some cases "six years have elapsed without" meaningful oversight—combined with the absence of any claim by the executive that it "cannot respond to habeas actions,"[30] had caused the Court to move away from its posture of excessive deference in these cases, and to hold out for the possibility of the Court ordering the conditional release of detainees in some cases.[31]

---

[26] *Id.* at 783.

[27] Ronald Dworkin, *Why It Was a Great Victory*, The New York Review, Aug. 14, 2008.

[28] *Id.*

[29] *Boumediene*, 553 U.S. at 828.

[30] *Id.* at 794.

[31] One of the more unexpected and bizarre attacks on the rule of law that occurred during the administration of President George W. Bush arose as a result of the Supreme Court's decisions concluding that the federal courts had jurisdiction of habeas petitions filed by Guantanamo prisoners challenging the legality of their detention. This episode involved a senior Pentagon official in charge of military detainees suspected of terrorism, Charles Stimson, who stated he was "dismayed that lawyers at many of the nation's top firms were representing prisoners at Guantanamo Bay, Cuba, and that the firm's corporate clients should consider ending their business ties." Neil A. Lewis, *Official Attacks Top Law Firms Over Detainees*, N.Y. Times, Jan. 13, 2007. A few weeks later, Stimson, whose statements were sorely criticized, announced his resignation.

Over the last decade and a half, the Guantanamo prisoners[32] have generated a few hundred habeas petitions,[33] raising many complex and entangled issues.[34] However, a review of all those matters is not required to gain a perspective on the role of the Supreme Court in Guantanamo litigation in upholding the rule of law. That is because among the Guantanamo prisoners were a small number not considered enemy combatants, and thus not a threat to U.S. security, whose efforts to win their release through the courts provide a dramatic

---

[32] Although the word *detainment* may be used to describe the imprisonment of Uighurs at Guantanamo, it is more of a public relations term than it is an apt description of their condition or status. *Imprisonment* is the more appropriate term, and in that regard, consider the following comment by Justices Holmes and Jackson. Quoting Justice Holmes in an immigration case, Justice Robert Jackson wrote:

> [I]t was said that he should be regarded, as if he had been stopped and kept at the limit of our jurisdiction, still it would be difficult to say that he was not imprisoned, theoretically as well as practically, when to turn him back meant that he must get into a vessel against his wish and be carried to China ... But we need not speculate upon niceties ... But, on the question whether he is wrongly imprisoned, we must look at the actual facts. *De facto* he is locked up until carried out of the country against his will. (Shaughnessy v. Mezei, 345 U.S. 206, 220 n.3 (1953) (Jackson, J., dissenting))

In his dissent involving the detainment of an alien on Ellis Island, Justice Jackson addressed a similar point in these words:

> Government counsel ingeniously argued that Ellis Island is his "refuge" whence he is free to take leave in any direction except west. That might mean freedom if only he were an amphibian! Realistically, this man is incarcerated by a combination of forces which keeps him effectively as a prisoner, the dominant and proximate of these forces being the United States immigration authority. It overworks legal fiction to say that one is free in law when by the commonest of common sense he is bound. Despite the impeccable legal logic of the Government's argument on this point, it leads to an artificial and unreal conclusion. (*Id.* at 220)

[33] Linda Greenhouse, who covered twenty-nine Supreme Court terms as the *New York Times* Supreme Court correspondent and studiously followed the Guantanamo litigation, stated that the Guantanamo detainees filed "[s]ome 200 petitions" in the federal courts. Linda Greenhouse, *Guantanamo Dreams*, N.Y. Times, Dec. 24, 2014.

[34] The literature on the detainees held by the United States at the Guantanamo Bay Naval Base is extensive. For a general introduction into the web of highly entangled issues, see Jess Bravin, Terror Courts: The Rough Justice at Guantanamo Bay (2013); Joseph Margulies, Guantanamo and the Abuse of Presidential Power (2006); and Louis Fisher, Military Tribunals & Presidential Power: American Revolution to the War on Terrorism (2005). For an account of the life of a Guantanamo prisoner, see Guantanamo Diary by Mohamedou Ould Slahi (edited by Larry Siems) (2015). In his review of *Guantanamo Diary*, published in the *New York Times* on January 25, 2015, Scott Shane wrote of Mohamedou Ould Slahi's effort to secure his release through American courts:

> A federal judge who reviewed Mr. Slahi's habeas petition in 2010, James Robertson, concluded that the government's evidence was "so attenuated, or so tainted by coercion

window on the strength of the Supreme Court's allegiance to the rule of law. After all, if the Supreme Court cannot uphold the rule of law on behalf of individuals the executive concedes are not enemy combatants and should never have been incarcerated in Guantanamo in the first place, there is no reason to expect the Court to be more vigorous in upholding the rule of law in cases in which there may be strong reasons to consider the individual seeking legal redress a threat to U.S. security.

Twenty-two Guantanamo prisoners were Uighurs, who were imprisoned at Guantanamo in 2002 and remained prisoners from four to eleven years, even though the Bush administration had concluded possibly as early as 2003 that these individuals were not enemy combatants and presented no national security threat to the United States. The Uighurs claimed that their imprisonment was unlawful and sought judicial relief. After the initial impulse to argue that the Uighurs were in fact enemy combatants, the Bush administration decided that they were not and that they did not present a threat to U.S. security. Nonetheless, the Bush administration—as well as the Obama administration—took the position that the Uighurs had to remain imprisoned because they could not be returned to China for fear of being tortured or executed, the administration would not release them into the United States, and no third country had agreed to admit them. Against these dead ends, the Uighurs sought, in federal court, an order of conditional release into the United States. Because the Uighurs presented no national security threat, they presented a very strong claim for relief. Indeed, no other individual detained

---

and mistreatment, or so classified, that it cannot support a criminal prosecution." The judge said the government's fear that Mr. Slahi could rejoin Al Qaeda if freed "may indeed be well founded," but that such concerns did not justify his continued imprisonment. Judge Robertson ordered his release. Despite President Obama's vow to close the prison, his administration challenged that decision. An appeals court overturned the release order, and Mr. Slahi, age 44, remained at Guantánamo, where he has been held without trial for more than 12 years. (Scott Shane, *From Inside Prison, a Terrorism Suspect Shares His Diary*, N.Y. Times, Jan. 25, 2015, at C1)

In November of 2015, Mr. Slahi's case was before U.S. District Judge Royce Lamberth, who "chided" President Obama for "pledging to close the Guantanamo detention facility while allowing the process for clearing detainees to drag on for years with no resolution in sight." Mr. Slahi was seeking to force the executive to "schedule his transfer" since he had been cleared for a transfer to a country that would accept him in accordance with the established process. Judge Lamberth, frustrated with the executive's lawyer, summed up what he thought the executive's position was, which was that Mr. Slahi had "no rights." The judge, exasperated with President Obama's failure to fulfill his promise and to effectively transfer detainees cleared for transfer, concluded that he did not think the president cared enough to do what he said he would do: "Obviously, if the president cared, he could get this done in a year." Jess Bravin, *Federal Judge Chides Obama Administration Over Guantanamo*, Wall St. J., Nov. 24, 2015.

at Guantanamo presented a stronger claim. Accordingly, the Uighurs' cases present an effective window for assessing the Supreme Court's role in providing meaningful judicial relief in all of the detainee cases.

China's far western province Xinjiang, which "lies along the ancient Silk Road,"[35] is the "traditional home"[36] to the Uighur, a "Turkic-speaking people who converted to Islam in the 1300s." When the Communist government of China took control of the region in 1949, the government began to resettle Han Chinese people in Xinjiang in an effort to consolidate its authority. Over time, the resettlement initiative resulted in a "dramatic shift in demographics in the region," which in turn caused the Uighur population to feel "slighted" and economically discriminated against, which provided a foundation for a "violent opposition movement."[37]

Because of political unrest and increasing violence, some Uighurs fled their traditional homeland for "a Uighur village in Afghanistan."[38] In October 2001, when the United States began its attacks on Afghanistan in the wake of 9/11, the Uighurs fled the "bombing campaign, crossing into Pakistan."[39] At the time, the United States was offering a bounty of $5,000 to Pakistani villagers for each terrorist they turned over. As a result, in late 2001, "Pakistani villagers lured the Uighurs to a mosque, where they were . . . arrested by Pakistani security forces,"[40] who turned them over to United States forces for the bounty.[41]

---

[35] Bill Delahunt and Sabin Willett, *Innocent Detainees Need a Home*, Boston Globe, Apr. 1, 2009.

[36] Adam Wolfe, *China's Uighurs Trapped at Guantanamo*, Asia Times, Nov. 4, 2004.

[37] *Id.* The relationship between the Uighur minority and the Chinese government continues to be a source of tension. For example, a December 26, 2015, report in the *New York Times* disclosed that China would expel a French journalist for writing an article about ethnic violence in China's northwest corner in part because the news report suggested that "attacks in Xinjiang, often carried out by members of the Muslim Uighur minority, had 'nothing in common' with the Paris killings and stemmed from China's own hard-line policies toward the Uighurs." Michael Forsythe, *China Says It Will Expel French Journalist*, N.Y. Times, Dec. 26, 2015.

[38] Bill Delahunt and Sabin Willett, *Innocent Detainees Need a Home*, Boston Globe, Apr. 1, 2009. There is some dispute over these camps, such as whether the Uighurs received weapon training at the camps and what the relationship was between the camps and the Taliban and al-Qaeda.

[39] *In re Guantanamo Bay Detainee Litig.*, 581 F. Supp. 2d 33, 35 (D.D.C. 2008) *rev'd and remanded sub nom.*, Kiyemba v. Obama, 555 F.3d 1022 (D.C. Cir. 2009) *vacated*, 559 U.S. 131 (2010) and *judgment reinstated as amended*, 605 F.3d 1046 (D.C. Cir. 2010); Bill Delahunt and Sabin Willett, *Innocent Detainees Need a Home*, Boston Globe, Apr. 1, 2009.

[40] Bill Delahunt and Sabin Willett, *Innocent Detainees Need a Home*, Boston Globe, Apr. 1, 2009.

[41] According to U.S. District Judge Urbina, local villagers "handed the petitioners over to Pakistani officials," who in turn handed the petitioners over "to the U.S. military for $5,000 a head." *In re* Guantanamo Bay Detainee Litig., 581 F. Supp. 2d 33, 35 (D.D.C. 2008) *rev'd and remanded sub nom.*, Kiyemba v. Obama, 555 F.3d 1022 (D.C. Cir. 2009) *vacated*, 559 U.S. 131 (2010) and *judgment reinstated as amended*, 605 F.3d 1046 (D.C. Cir. 2010).

In May of 2002, the United States transported the Uighurs to Guantanamo,[42] and sometime during that year, the United States "listed the East Turkestan Islamic Movement as a terror group, a classification that some believed was a concession to China in exchange for China's support of the American-led anti-terrorist campaign."[43] The twenty-two Uighurs incarcerated in Guantanamo "were never charged with any wrongdoing,"[44] and by late 2003, "the Pentagon [had] quietly decided that 15 Chinese Muslims detained at the military prison in Guantanamo Bay, Cuba, could be released."[45]

Following the Supreme Court decision in *Rasul v. Bush* in June of 2004,[46] which concluded that a federal statute granted the U.S. district courts jurisdiction to entertain a petition for writ of habeas corpus filed on behalf of detainees held at Guantanamo, the Pentagon established a military tribunal, formally termed the Combatant Status Review Tribunals (CSRT), to

[42] Bill Delahunt and Sabin Willett, *Innocent Detainees Need a Home*, Boston Globe, Apr. 1, 2009. U.S. District Judge Robertson stated that the United States transferred the Uighurs to Guantanamo in June of 2002. Qassim v. Bush, 407 F. Supp. 2d 198, 199 (D.D.C. 2005). In an opinion for the United States Court of Appeals in al-Qaeda, 532 F.3d 834 (D.D.C. 2008), Judge Garland, with these circumstances in mind, provided the following summary of facts:

> Parhat is a Chinese citizen of Uighur heritage . . . The Uighurs are from the far-western Chinese province of Xinjiang, which the Unighurs call East Turkistan. According to Parhat, he fled China in May 2001 because of "oppression and torture imposed on [Ui] gh[u]r people by the Chinese Government." "This oppression," he said, "included harassment, forced abortions for more than two children, high taxes, the taking away of land, and the banishing of educated people to remote areas." Parhat arrived at a Uighur camp in Afghanistan in June 2001. . . . In mid-October 2001, U.S. aerial strikes destroyed the camp where Parhat had been living. Thereafter, according to his undisputed testimony, Parhat and seventeen [according to many other sources the total number of Uighurs detained at Guantanamo was twenty-two] other unarmed Uighurs fled the camp, eventually crossing into Pakistan. Local villagers took the Uighurs in, gave them food and shelter, and then—in approximately December 2001—handed them over to Pakistan officials who turned them over to the U.S. military. In June 2002, the U.S. transferred Parhat to the U.S. Naval Base at Guanatanamo Bay, Cuba, where he remains imprisoned. In 2003, a military officer of the Criminal Investigation Task Force (CITF), US Department of Defense (DOD), who was charged with reviewing Parhat's case, "'recommend[ed] the release of Paraht under a conditional release agreement.'" (*Id.* at 837)

Judge Garland's opinion concluded that Parhat's classification as an enemy combatant was invalid. In June 2009, roughly seven years after he arrived at Guantanamo, the United States transferred Parhat to Bermuda.

[43] Alexa Olesen, *China Demands Return of Gitmo Detainees*, Associated Press, May 9, 2006.
[44] Brief for Petitioner at 3, Qassim v. Bush, 466 F.3d 1073 (D.C. Cir. 2006) (No. 05-892).
[45] Robin Wright, *Chinese Detainees Are Men Without a Country*, Wash. Post, Aug. 24, 2005.
[46] Rasul v. Bush, 542 U.S. 466 (2004).

determine whether two Uighurs, Abu Bakker Qassim and Adel Abdu' Al-Hakim, were enemy combatants. In late 2004 or early 2005, the military tribunal held hearings in each case and on March 26, 2005, the tribunal concluded that both of the Uighurs "should no longer be classified as enemy combatants,"[47] an odd finding since the Pentagon had not formally concluded that the Uighurs were enemy combatants. But putting aside the phraseology, the United States did not inform these two Uighurs until months later—July of 2005—that they had been "cleared" and were no longer considered enemy combatants.[48] Moreover, because the Bush administration "balked at allowing them to enter the United States, even under restricted supervision," and because the "State Department has also been unable to find another country to take them in,"[49] the Uighurs "languish[ed] at Guantanamo, imprisoned and sometimes shackled, with most of their families unaware whether they are even alive," and with "no end in sight."[50]

On March 10, 2005, at a time when Qassim and Al-Hakim did not know that the CSRT had concluded that they were not enemy combatants, the two Uighurs filed petitions for writs of habeas corpus. Four days later, the executive requested that the matter be stayed until the appeals court resolved issues raised by other Guantanamo prisoners. In response to an inquiry raised by the petitioners' attorney as to whether "it alleged that Petitioners were enemy combatants," the executive "never responded." Instead, on March 29, the executive filed a brief which misled the district court as to the petitioners' status. Instead of stating what the Uighurs' status was in fact, the executive's brief obfuscated the status of the Uighurs by providing a statement describing what it considered a typical Guantanamo case: "[a] factual record for a petitioner

---

[47] Qassim v. Bush, 407 F. Supp. 2d 198, 199 (D.D.C. 2005); Brief for Petitioner at 5, Qassim v. Bush, 466 F.3d 1073 (D.C. Cir. 2006) (No. 05-892); Robin Wright, *Chinese Detainees Are Men Without a Country*, Wash. Post, Aug. 24, 2005. An important distinction must be drawn between Uighurs being a threat to the United States and a threat to China. The U.S. military authorities responsible for reviewing the Uighurs' claims arising from Guantanamo concluded that the Uighurs did not threaten the United States. A recent news report emphasizes the threat that Uighurs present to China. Edward Wong and Adam Yu, *ISIS Extends Recruitment Efforts to China With New Chant*, N.Y. Times, Dec. 9, 2015.

[48] Qassim v. Bush, 407 F. Supp. 2d 198, 199 (D.D.C. 2005); Brief for Petitioner, Qassim v. Bush, 466 F.3d 1073 (D.C. Cir. 2006) (No. 05-892); Robin Wright, *Chinese Detainees Are Men Without a Country*, Wash. Post, Aug. 24, 2005.

[49] Robin Wright, *Chinese Detainees Are Men Without a Country*, Wash. Post, Aug. 24, 2005. According to the same report, seven other Uighurs were classified by military authorities as "enemy combatants." In time, the appropriate U.S. authorities withdrew this designation.

[50] *Id.* Sabin P. Willett, a Boston lawyer who volunteered to represent two Uighurs, told a judge in a judicial proceeding in which he sought his clients' release, that one Uighur "'had a leg shackle[d] that was chained to a bolt in the floor'" and that he was shackled in a "'box with no windows.'" *Id.*

in a Guantanamo Bay detainee case typically has consisted of the record of proceedings before the combatant Status Tribunal that confirmed petitioner's status as an enemy combatant properly subject to detention."[51] Because the executive knew when it submitted this paper to the court that it had determined that the Uighurs were not enemy combatants, the purpose of this obscure language must have been to mislead the court into thinking that the Uighurs were enemy combatants, so as to induce the judge to stay the proceedings.[52] The strategy was effective; the judge stayed the proceedings.

Days later, the executive informed the Uighurs that the tribunal had determined that they were not enemy combatants, but it did not inform the district judge or petitioners' attorney. Because the two petitioners "were unable to contact anyone," it was another two months before the petitioners' attorney learned from one of the petitioners, who was at the time chained to the floor in an isolation cell, of the "noncombatant findings."[53]

In December of 2005, District Judge Robertson concluded that the continued detention of Qassim and Al-Hakim was unlawful. In his opinion, he noted that because the CSRT had decided nine months earlier that the two petitioners were "no longer enemy combatants," there was no justification for their continued detention, and thus their "indefinite imprisonment at Guantanamo Bay is unlawful."[54] At that point the judge turned to the question of a remedy and asked: "The question in this case is whether the law gives me the power to do what I believe justice requires."[55] Because the parties agreed that the petitioners could not be returned to China without risking torture or death, and because the executive "cannot find, or has yet not found, another country that will accept the petitioners," the judge concluded that the "only way to comply with a release order would be to grant the petitioners entry into the United States."[56] At that point in the opinion, the judge decided that ordering the petitioners released into the United States was "beyond the competence or the authority of this Court" because such an order had "national security and diplomatic implications."[57]

[51] Brief for Petitioner at 5, Qassim v. Bush, 466 F.3d 1073 (D.C. Cir. 2006) (No. 05-892).

[52] *Id.* at 6.

[53] *Id.* at 6.

[54] Qassim v. Bush, 407 F. Supp. 2d 198, 201 (D.D.C. 2005).

[55] *Id.*

[56] *Id.* at 202.

[57] *Id.* at 203. As stated in other footnotes, Professor Jack Goldsmith has suggested that the federal courts have improperly interfered with the executive's imprisonment of alleged enemy combatants at Guantanamo. It is far from clear what support Goldsmith has for such a view. Certainly this case is of no support. Here, the court found that the Uighurs were not enemy combatants and that their continued imprisonment was unlawful, but that the court did not have the authority to grant the petitioners a remedy. Goldsmith might object to the judicial conclusion that the continued detention of the Uighurs was unlawful, but since the executive lacked adequate evidence to

The district court concluded that Qassim and Al-Hakim had a theoretical right to liberty, but that the right was ineffective in freeing them from the Guantanamo prison. As a result, Qassim and Al-Hakim appealed the district court's ruling to the circuit court. A hearing in the case was set for Monday, May 8, 2006. Three days before the hearing on May 5, the executive filed an emergency motion requesting that the appeal be dismissed as moot on the ground that the Uighurs were released to Albania.[58] The appeals court granted the motion.[59]

The transfer of five Uighurs to Albania left seventeen Uighurs at Guantanamo. The next Uighur challenge to their incarceration was decided by the Court of Appeals for the District of Columbia on June 20, 2008, two years after the *Qassim* case.[60] The petitioner in this case was Huzaifa Parhat. Parhat's factual claims were in accord with the general Uighur story. Parhat stated that he fled China in May of 2001 because of "oppression and torture" imposed by the Chinese government on the Uighur people;[61] that the oppression "'included harassment, forced abortions for more than two children, high taxes, the taking away of land, and the banishing of educated people to remote areas'"; that he arrived in a Uighur camp in Afghanistan in June 2001, which was destroyed in mid-October by "U.S. aerial strikes"; that he and others fled the camp, crossed into Pakistan and were cared for by local villagers who a few months later

establish that the Uighurs were in fact enemy combatants, Goldsmith's disposition is difficult to appreciate and seems blind to the important fact that the district judge concluded that he had no authority to remedy the injustice in the case presented.

[58] Qassim v. Bush, 466 F.3d 1073, 1074 (D.C. Cir. 2006). Five Uighurs were released to Albania on May 5, 2006. Their ISN numbers were 260, 276, 279, 283, and 293. It is unclear why the executive was willing to consider these five Uighurs not to be enemy combatants but not the remaining seventeen Uighurs.

[59] *Id.* at 1073. Harvard law professor and former Bush administration lawyer Jack Goldsmith conveniently overlooks the Bush administration's transfer of five Uighurs to Albania in May 2006, which was only a year and a half into George W. Bush's second term as president, and the Bush administration's decision to avoid contesting in the courts the factual question as to whether the Uighurs were enemy combatants, when he snidely states that it was only the "federal courts and the Obama administration" that decided that the Uighurs "were not part of al Qaida and thus not lawfully detained." Jack Goldsmith, Power and Constraint: The Accountable Presidency After 9/11, 44–45 (2012). As stated earlier in this chapter, the currently available public evidence indicates that the Bush administration decided as early as 2003 that the Uighurs were not "enemy combatants" as it defined the term. Furthermore, Goldsmith's verbal swipe at the Obama administration for failing to recognize the national security threat Goldsmith obviously thinks the Uighurs presented is not in accord with the Obama administration's fierce defense of its authority to detain and imprison two of the original twenty-two Uighurs until April of 2012, when they were transferred to El Salvador, and three other Uighurs until December of 2013, when they were transferred to Slovakia.

[60] Parhat v. Gates, 532 F.3d 834 (D.C. Cir. 2008).

[61] *Id.* at 837.

"handed them over to Pakistani officials who turned them over to the U.S. military";[62] and that in June of 2002, he was transferred to Guantanamo.

In 2003, a "military officer of the Criminal Investigation Force," part of the Department of Defense, concluded after investigating Parhat's case that Parhat be released "'under a conditional release agreement.'"[63] But Parhat was not conditionally released. Instead, on December 6, 2004, the CSRT held a hearing at Guantanamo to determine whether Parhat was an enemy combatant, defined as: "an individual who was part of or supporting Taliban or al Qaida forces, or associated forces that are engaged in hostilities against the United States or its coalition partners. This includes any person who has committed a belligerent act or has directly supported hostilities in aid of enemy armed forces."[64] The CSRT hearing consisted of an unclassified session at which Parhat was present and answered questions under oath, and a classified session at which "Parhat was not present and in which the Tribunal considered classified documents not made available to him."[65]

At the hearing, the "only evidence regarding the circumstances of Parhat's background and capture was his own interviews and testimony," that he "denied association with al Qaida or the Taliban," and that he "denied knowing anything about al Qaida or Taliban association with Uighur camps." Nonetheless, the Tribunal concluded that "Parhat was an enemy combatant." It found that Parhat was "'affiliated' with a Uighur independence group" that was "'associated' with al-Qaeda and the Taliban" and "engaged in hostilities against the United States and its coalition partners." The sole evidentiary basis for the charge that Parhat was affiliated with a Uighur independence group was that the "Uighur camp at which he lived and received training on a rifle and pistol was run" by a "leader" of the independence group. On that score, the Tribunal acknowledged that there was no other evidence establishing that Parhat had joined the independence group or had personally committed "any hostile acts against the United States or its coalition partners." The evidence pertaining to the second part of the charge that the independence group was "associated" with al Qaida and the Taliban and that it "was engaged in hostilities against the United States or its coalition partners, were statements in classified documents" that the court made clear "do not state (or, in most instances, even describe) the sources or rationales for those statements." Because it is likely that the Tribunal was concerned that the basis of its conclusion that Parhat was an enemy combatant was wafer thin, if not altogether

[62] Id.

[63] Parhat, 532 F.3d 834, 837.

[64] Id. at 838.

[65] Id.

dubious, it concluded that the "[d]etainee does present an attractive candidate for release," and urged favorable consideration for release. But the "Defense Department did not release him."[66]

At this point the procedural entanglement of Parhat's case is complex but sufficiently unrelated to the central issue so that it does not require description. What does matter is that while Parhat had a matter pending in the courts, "the government produced," on October 29, 2007, "to Parhat's counsel the record (both classified and unclassified) of what was actually presented to Parhat's CSRT."[67] A few days later, Parhat filed a motion in the D.C. Circuit Court "to review the CSRT's determination based solely upon that record." Parhat claimed that the "materials before the CSRT are sufficient to establish as a matter of law that he is not an enemy combatant," and that further delay in deciding this central issue was "unnecessary and unjust." The executive did not oppose Parhat's request for a judicial resolution of the enemy combatant issue.[68] In the end, the appeals court concluded "that the evidence that was before the CSRT is insufficient to categorize Parhat as an enemy combatant under" the Department of Defense's definition.[69] How the court got to that point is worthy of a short review.

The court asserted, without the executive objecting, that the conclusion that Parhat was an enemy combatant required evidence that supported three findings: (1) Parhat was "part of or supporting" the Uighur independence group, the East Turkistan Islamic Movement (ETIM); (2) the ETIM was associated with al-Qaeda or the Taliban; and (3) the ETIM "is engaged in hostilities against the United States or its coalition partners."[70] The court concluded that the last two factual findings lacked evidence. The court observed that the "principal evidence against Parhat" that supported a finding that Parhat was an enemy combatant consisted of "four government intelligence documents."[71] The four documents—one document was from the Department of State and "three from components of the Department of Defense"[72]—made assertions "about activities undertaken by ETIM, and about that organization's relationship to al Qaida and the Taliban."[73] But in doing so, the documents "repeatedly describe[d] those activities and relationships as having 'reportedly' occurred, as being 'said to' or 'reported to' have happened, and as things that 'may' be true or

[66] *Id.*

[67] *Id.* at 840.

[68] *Id.*

[69] *Id.* at 842.

[70] *Id.* at 843.

[71] *Id.* at 846.

[72] *Id.* at 844.

[73] *Id.* at 846.

are 'suspected of' having taken place." The court emphasized that "in virtually every instance, the documents do not say who 'reported' or 'said' or 'suspected' those things,"[74] nor do they provide any "underlying reporting upon which the documents' bottom-line assertions are founded, nor any assessment of the reliability of that reporting."[75] Because of those "omissions," the court concluded that neither the Tribunal nor the court was in a position to "assess the reliability of the assertions in the documents," and, as a result, the "assertions cannot sustain the determination that Parhat is an enemy combatant."[76] In reaching this result, the court emphasized that it was not taking the position that "hearsay evidence is never reliable," nor that the "government must always submit the underlying basis for its factual assertions in order to make such an assessment possible."[77] But it was insisting that the Tribunal and the court be in a position to assess the "reliability" of the hearsay evidence, and that the executive find "forms" of presentation of the evidence that "permit an appropriate assessment of the information's reliability while protecting the anonymity of a highly sensitive source."[78] The court remarked that insisting on "an opportunity to assess the reliability of the record evidence" was not "simply a theoretical exercise." In the end, the court concluded that Parhat offered "substantial support" for his claims that the "ultimate source of key assertions in the four intelligence documents is the government of the People's Republic of China."[79]

Concluding its analysis of the evidence, the court noted that it neither prescribed nor proscribed "ways in which the government may demonstrate the reliability of its evidence." However, what it did do was "reject the government's contention that it can prevail by submitting documents that read as if they were indictments or civil complaints," that asserted "as facts the elements required to prove that a detainee falls within the definition of enemy combatant."[80] To do otherwise, the court maintained, "would require the courts to rubber-stamp the government's charges, in contravention of our understanding that Congress intended the court 'to engage in *meaningful* review of the record.'"[81]

[74] *Id.*
[75] *Id.* at 846–847.
[76] *Id.* at 847.
[77] *Id.* at 849.
[78] *Id.*
[79] *Id.* at 848.
[80] *Id.* at 850.

[81] *Id.* In addition to this analysis, the court also had an alternative ground for finding that the submitted evidence was inadequate to support the second factual ground. To find Parhat to be an enemy combatant, the Tribunal had to find that "ETIM was 'associated' with al Qaida or the Taliban." *Id.* at 844. To support that finding, the executive relied "on the interview report of a single Uighur detainee, Akhdar Basit, which states that Basit told the interviewer that a leader at the camp told him that the camp 'had been provided to the Uigh[u]rs by the Taliban in order

The court's conclusion that Parhat could not be characterized as an enemy combatant on the evidentiary record developed at the CSRT hearing left open the question of a remedy. Parhat argued that a new CSRT hearing would be a useless endeavor, since the government had no additional evidence it could offer to support the charge that Parhat was an enemy combatant, and therefore urged the court to order his release or transfer to some country other than "China or any of its satellites." The court did not accept those alternatives as the only alternatives. Noting that it was possible that the "government has additional evidence that would cure the reliability issues we have identified,"[82] the court directed "the government to release Parhat, to transfer him, or to expeditiously convene a new CSRT to consider evidence submitted in a manner consistent with this opinion."[83] In allowing for a possible new CSRT, the court observed that it will not permit the executive "endless 'do-overs,'" but at the same time it did permit one do-over. That meant that Parhat, who had already been imprisoned at Guantanamo for six years, would continue to be a Guantanamo prisoner.

To put the matter in the language of judicial deference, although the court's decision was far from a rubber stamp in its analysis of the evidence the executive claimed warranted finding that Parhat was an enemy combatant, and although the court redefined and limited the conditions under which the executive could continue to imprison Parhat, it nonetheless granted the executive another opportunity to prove that Parhat was an enemy combatant.[84]

that the Uigh[u]rs could train to fight the Chinese oppression.'" *Id.* at 845. The court stated that reliance on "Basit's interview report is problematic because the CSRT was not provided with exculpatory evidence on the same point, which was required." *Id.* In another Uighur's CSRT hearing, which was conducted prior to Parhat's CSRT hearing, there was evidence that the "Uighur camp was actually in existence prior to the Taliban takeover of Afghanistan," but this "evidence was not presented to Parhat's CSRT." *Id.* Because the Tribunal "was not afforded an opportunity to consider contrary evidence" to what Basit reported, the court wrote that "we cannot conclude that reliance on the interview report 'was consistent with the standards and procedures specified by the Secretary of Defense.'" *Id.* at 846. And thus the finding—that "ETIM was 'associated' with al Qaida or the Taliban"—was not adequately established. *Id.* at 844.

[82] *Id.* at 850.

[83] *Id.* at 851.

[84] *Parhat* was an unusual case in that it was a direct appeal to the Court of Appeals for the District of Columbia from the CSRT decision finding Parhat an enemy combatant. The appeal was taken pursuant to a congressional statute, and the appeals court's authority in the matter was circumscribed by comparison to the authority of a court reviewing a petition for a writ of habeas corpus. In part because of the unusual character of the legal proceeding before the Court of Appeals, no party appealed the Court of Appeals decision. Parhat had prevailed with regard to having the CSRT finding of his status as an enemy combatant voided, and he was advised by the court, in the wake of the Supreme Court's decision in *Boumediene*, to pursue other relief by means

Although the available evidence does not disclose the details that led to the next development, the executive decided in the summer or early fall of 2008 that "it would no longer consider the 17 Uighurs detainees" who remained at Guantanamo as "enemy combatants."[85] Thus, with the wind of the *Boumediene* decision at their backs and a concession that they were not enemy combatants, the Uighur detainees "filed motions alleging that their continued detention is unlawful and requesting that the court order the government to release them into the United States."[86] All the Uighur proceedings were assigned to District Judge Ricardo M. Urbina.[87]

After setting forth the background of the case and asserting that the "government no longer treats the detainees as enemy combatants," Judge Urbina stated that "the only issues to be resolved are whether the government has authority to 'wind up' the petitioners' detention and whether the court has the authority to order the petitioners released into the United States."[88] After reviewing what he considered to be the relevant case law, Judge Urbina stated that the "constitutional authority to 'wind up' detentions during wartime ceases once (1) detention becomes effectively indefinite; (2) there is a reasonable certainty that the petitioner will not return to the battlefield to fight against the United States; and (3) an alternative legal justification has not been provided for continued detention. Once these elements are met, further detention is unconstitutional."[89] With those three elements in focus, Judge Urbina concluded that the detention of the Uighurs has become "effectively indefinite" in that the government has failed to resettle the Uighurs, even though it has "approached and re-approached almost 100 countries in its efforts to locate an appropriate resettlement location";[90] there is no evidence to support any concern "that the petitioners would return to the field of battle;"[91] there is no "alternative legal justification," other than the status of enemy

---

of a petition for a writ of habeas corpus. The government did not appeal because Parhat remained imprisoned and it had another opportunity to offer fresh evidence to support its claim that Parhat was an enemy combatant.

[85] *In re* Guantanamo Bay Detainee Litig., 581 F. Supp. 2d 33 (D.D.C. 2008) *rev'd and remanded sub nom.*, Kiyemba v. Obama, 555 F.3d 1022 (D.C. Cir. 2009) *vacated*, 559 U.S. 131 (2010) and *judgment reinstated as amended*, 605 F.3d 1046 (D.C. Cir. 2010). Judge Urbina offers the following details with regard to the status of the seventeen Uighurs. Sometime during the summer of 2003, "the government had already cleared 10" of the Uighurs for release. *Id.* The "government cleared an additional 5 for release or transfer in 2005, 1 for transfer in 2006 and 1 for transfer in May" of 2008. *Id.*

[86] *Id.* at 34.

[87] *Id.* at 35.

[88] *Id.*

[89] *Id.* at 38.

[90] *Id.* at 38 n.2.

[91] *Id.* at 38.

combatant for continued detention. At that point the judge simply stated: "the court concludes that the government's detention of the petitioners is unlawful."[92]

Under all of the circumstances, a judicial conclusion that the continued detention of the Uighurs was unlawful was not startling. They had been imprisoned for more than six years, the government admitted that they were not enemy combatants and not a threat in any way to the United States or its allies, and the government conceded that it had failed to resettle them and it had no concrete expectation that a resettlement plan was at hand, thus leaving open the possibility that these wrongfully imprisoned individuals might remain imprisoned for the indefinite future.

But the thorny issue was what to do about the fact that the Uighurs were unlawfully detained. They could not be transferred to China, and no other country had acceded to the request by the United States that they be accepted for resettlement. What that meant was that if the Uighurs were to be released, they would have to be released into the United States.

In addressing that central issue, the district judge conceded that the Supreme Court had "'repeatedly emphasized that over no conceivable subject is the legislative power of Congress more complete than it is over the admission of aliens.'"[93] Nonetheless, he insisted even this great power is "not absolute," and although a court would frequently reframe from insinuating "itself into a field normally dominated by the political branches," the court insisted that this case was "exceptional."[94] At that point, the district judge spelled out what he considered the exceptional circumstances:

> The government captured the petitioners and transported them to a detention facility where they will remain indefinitely. The government has not charged these petitioners with a crime and has presented no reliable evidence that they would pose a threat to U.S. interests. Moreover, the government has stymied its own efforts to resettle the petitioners by insisting (until recently) that they were enemy combatants, the same designation given to terrorists willing to detonate themselves amongst crowds of civilians.[95]

With regard to this last point, although Judge Urbina did not quote Supreme Court Justice Robert Jackson, he might well have quoted Jackson's dissent in a 1953 case.[96] In that case, an alien who had lived in the United States "for a

---

[92] *Id.*
[93] *Id.* at 40.
[94] *Id.*
[95] *Id.*
[96] Shaughnessy v. United States, 345 U.S. 206 (1953).

quarter of a century," "who seems to have lived a life of unrelieved insignifi-
cance," who "must have been astonished to find himself suddenly putting the
Government of the United States in such fear that it was afraid to tell him why it
was afraid of him," and who, after the United States attorney general refused to
honor his "visa for admission" and "turned him back as a menace to this Nation's
security," was refused admission by France, Great Britain, and "[t]welve countries of the American Hemisphere."[97] As Jackson wrote, the refusal of other
nations that were "less prosperous, less strongly established and less stable"
to accept this individual should not be surprising, since the United States had
"proclaimed him a Samson who might pull down the pillars of our temple."[98]
If Judge Urbina had borrowed from Justice Jackson's language, he might have
assessed the executive's characterization of the Uighurs as Samsons who were
ready to pull down the American pillars as unpersuasive, if not fanciful.

Against the analytical framework he set forth, Judge Urbina concluded that
it was not sufficient for the government to put forth its failed efforts to resettle
the Uighurs as a justification for their continued imprisonment. To endorse
such a view would be to accede to the "carte blanche authority the political
branches purportedly wield over the Uighurs" and that is not in keeping "with
our system of governance."[99] With that, the judge concluded that he was granting "the petitioners' motion for release into the United States," and to make
clear just how unjust it was to continue to imprison the Uighurs, he wrote that
an "Order consistent with this Memorandum Opinion is separately and con-
temporaneously issued this 8th day of October, 2008."[100]

Having decided to prohibit the seventeen Uighur petitioners from entering the
United States,[101] the executive appealed Judge Urbina's decision. The Court
of Appeals for the District of Columbia accelerated the appeal, hearing oral
arguments in the matter within six weeks of the district judge's opinion and
handing down a decision reversing and remanding the case three months later.

From the Uighurs' perspective, their case presented a fundamentally important question regarding their personal liberty. The Uighurs had left their historic home in western China because the Chinese government had oppressed

[97] *Id.* at 219.
[98] *Id.* at 219–220.
[99] *In re* Guantanamo Bay Detainee Litig., 581 F. Supp. 2d 33, 43 (D.D.C. 2008) *rev'd and remanded sub nom.*, Kiyemba v. Obama, 555 F.3d 1022 (D.C. Cir. 2009) *vacated*, 559 U.S. 131 (2010) and *judgment reinstated as amended*, 605 F.3d 1046 (D.C. Cir. 2010).
[100] *In re* Guantanamo Bay Detainee Litig., 581 F. Supp. 2d 33, 43 (D.D.C. 2008) *rev'd and remanded sub nom.*, Kiyemba v. Obama, 555 F.3d 1022 (D.C. Cir. 2009) *vacated*, 559 U.S. 131 (2010) and *judgment reinstated as amended*, 605 F.3d 1046 (D.C. Cir. 2010).
[101] Kiyemba v. Obama, 555 F.3d 1022, 1026 (D.C. Cir. 2009).

and tortured their people, and as a result of an unimaginable and unpredictable chain of events spurred by international developments unrelated to their struggle against the Chinese government, they spent years incarcerated on a Caribbean island halfway around the world from their homeland. When the D.C. Court of Appeals heard arguments in the appeal from Judge Urbina's decision, seventeen of the original twenty-two Uighurs remained at Guantanamo.

The circuit panel reversed Judge Urbina's decision. Judge Arthur Raymond Randolph, who had been appointed to the court by President George H. W. Bush in 1990 and was on senior status at the time, wrote the opinion. Given the complexity and importance of the issues raised by the appeal, Randolph's eight-and-one-half-page opinion was not exhaustive or convincing. Indeed, he devoted three of the pages to responding to particular points raised in the concurring opinion, so that his analysis of the central issues was only five and one-half pages.

Judge Randolph was able to decide the complex issues presented by the case in a short opinion because of how he characterized the petitioners and their legal claims. The petitioners asserted that because they were not and never had been enemies of the United States, nor enemy combatants, they were in effect civilians imprisoned in a military prison without pending charges against them. This was in violation of their right to liberty guaranteed by the United States Constitution, and that they were entitled to relief pursuant to the petition for the writ of habeas corpus. From this perspective, the petitioners maintained that their position was unusual if not unique, and that the executive had failed to reference any judicial decision that supported the executive's contention that a court lacked authority to grant relief under the circumstances.

In sharp contrast to the petitioners' characterization of their position, Judge Randolph converted the Uighurs' implausible circumstances into a conventional immigration matter in which an alien is taken into custody at the point of entry into the United States—for example, Ellis Island—by immigration officials and then requests that a federal court order the executive to release the alien into the United States over the executive's objection. By so doing, Judge Randolph was able to reference Cold War immigration cases in which federal courts refused to second-guess an executive judgment refusing to admit a particular alien into the United States on the ground that the alien in question presented a threat to the nation's security. Judge Randolph argued that federal courts took such a hands-off approach in these cases because it was, in his view, well established that immigration decisions were exclusively assigned to the politically accountable branches and that absent a specific grant of authority, federal courts had no authority to review the executive's decision.

Once he framed the dispute as an immigration matter, Judge Randolph was able to claim that the appeal raised one "critical question," and that was: "what law 'expressly authorized' the district court to set aside the decision of the Executive Branch and to order these aliens brought to the United States and released in Washington, D.C.?" In response, Judge Randolph was able to conclude that no statute or treaty specifically authorized Judge Urbina's order and that decisions of the Supreme Court and D.C. Circuit Court, which the district judge "must follow," had concluded that "the due process clause does not apply to aliens without property or presence in the sovereign territory of the United States."[102] Once that conclusion was placed next to Judge Randolph's operating premise, that the politically accountable branches of government—the executive and the Congress—had exclusive authority, there was nothing left for Judge Randolph to address other than to respond to points in the concurring opinion and to conclude, which is what he did in these words: "The government has represented that it is continuing diplomatic attempts to find an appropriate country willing to admit petitioners, and we have no reason to doubt that it is doing so. Nor do we have the power to require anything more."[103]

The Supreme Court granted the seventeen Uighurs' request for review on October 20, 2009. By then, four of the seventeen Uighurs had been resettled in Bermuda and within a few weeks of Supreme Court action, the executive transferred six Uighurs to Palau, leaving seven Uighurs in Guantanamo. Thus, although the executive had not yet been subject to a final judicial order to release any of the Uighurs, the judicial proceedings pressured the executive to quicken its efforts to resettle the Uighurs by persuading other nations to accept them.

After seven years of incarceration at Guantanamo, it would not be implausible for the remaining seven Uighurs to think that justice delayed was surely justice denied. At the same time, the very idea that the Supreme Court had agreed to decide "whether a federal court exercising habeas jurisdiction has the power to order the release of prisoners held at Guantanamo Bay 'where the Executive detention is indefinite and without authorization in law, and release into the continental United States is the only possible effective remedy,'" had to quicken the pulse of hope.[104] The hope was that as slow as the wheels of American justice might turn, the American aspiration that it was committed to the rule of law was not just table talk, but a bedrock principle of the governing scheme that imposed responsibilities on the Supreme Court that it was prepared to discharge.

But whatever hope had been kindled by the Supreme Court's grant of certiorari was squashed four months later when the high court, on March 1, 2010, announced that changed circumstances surrounding the incarceration of the

---

[102] *Id.*

[103] *Id.* at 129.

[104] Kiyemba v. Obama, 559 U.S. 131, 131 (2010).

Uighurs in Guantanamo had caused it to vacate the judgment of the District of Columbia Court of Appeals and to remand the matter to that court to "determine, in the first instance, what further proceedings in that court or in the District Court are necessary and appropriate for the full and prompt disposition of the case" in light of the new developments.[105] The Court characterized the changed circumstances as follows: "By now . . . each of the detainees at issue in this case has received at least one offer of resettlement in another country. Most of the detainees have accepted an offer of resettlement; five detainees, however, have rejected two such offers and are still being held at Guantanamo Bay." Against those circumstances—the transfer of six Uighurs to Palau on October 31, 2009, the transfer of two Uighurs to Switzerland on February 4, 2010, and the unaccepted offer of resettlement to the remaining five Uighurs—the Court stated that since no "court has yet ruled in this case in light of the new facts," it was declining "to be the first to do so" since it was a court of "review."[106] No member of the Court dissented from the decision.

Although vacating a grant of certiorari is not unusual and a change in circumstances that substantially alter the character of the dispute is an entirely plausible basis for vacating the granting of a certiorari petition, it is most unclear how the changed circumstances in this case redefined the nature of the legal question. It seems beyond doubt that the Uighurs preferred resettlement in the United States as opposed to Palau, Albania, or Bermuda, and because the United States was solely responsible for their being uprooted from Afghanistan and Pakistan, imprisoned for years, and subject to harsh treatment at Guantanamo, the Uighurs may have concluded that it was the United States, as opposed to another nation, that should accept the burden of their resettlement by allowing them to become a member of the Uighur community within the United States. If that was their position—and it is difficult to imagine why it would not have been—the nature of the legal question their case presented was not affected by the changed circumstances.

Moreover, it is doubtful that the members of the Supreme Court understood the matter any differently. If that is so, the question arises as to why the Court did vacate the grant of certiorari and remand the case, especially since the remand was to a panel of the District of Columbia Court of Appeals, which had already written a shallow and unpersuasive opinion on the issues. One explanation is that the Supreme Court was playing for time. It was hoping that a further delay in judicial proceedings would cause the five Uighur holdouts refusing a resettlement offer to accept the executive's offer, and that such a development would permit the Court to dismiss the case on the ground that it

---

[105] *Id.* at 132.
[106] *Id.*

was moot. Although agreeing to decide the legal questions the Uighurs presented would not necessarily mean that the high court would rule against the executive, it might have, and perhaps hoping to avoid such a confrontation, the Court took advantage of the changed circumstances the executive energetically engineered. In short, while in some situations there may be solid reasons prompting the Court to blink, the Court's blink in this case left five individuals imprisoned, even though the executive had concluded they were not a security threat and the fact that they had already been imprisoned eight years.[107]

The Court of Appeals heard oral argument in the Uighur case on April 22, 2010, and handed down a decision five weeks later. The opinion correctly noted that the "posture of the case now is not materially different than it was when the case was first before us."[108] The five Uighurs still imprisoned at Guantanamo had rejected three offers of resettlement, and though the Uighurs claimed that the offers were from countries that were not appropriate, the appeals panel stated that "an intervening opinion of this court precludes the sort of judicial inquiry petitioners seek,"[109] and made it clear that it is for the "political branches, not the courts, to determine whether a foreign country is appropriate for settlement."[110] The panel also noted that Congress had now passed legislation that "prohibited the expenditure of any funds to bring any Guantanamo detainee to the United States,"[111] and that the legislation did not trespass upon any detainee constitutional rights. As a result, the appeals panel reinstated its prior judgment, modified by the changes in a few facts.

Given the panel's first decision in the case, there was nothing surprising about its second decision. The only significant change was that the Uighurs had spent another year imprisoned at Guantanamo between the two opinions, and unless they accepted the offer of resettlement, their imprisonment would continue. But the five Uighurs did not accept the resettlement offers. Instead, they took the matter back to the Supreme Court.

One year later, on April 18, 2011, the Supreme Court refused by a unanimous vote to grant certiorari to the five Uighurs now imprisoned for ten years.

---

[107] In the *Boumediene* case, the Supreme Court decided—although it acknowledged the Court of Appeals did not reach the issue because it concluded it lacked jurisdiction—whether the Detainee Treatment Act provided "an adequate and effective substitute for habeas corpus." Boumediene v. Bush, 553 U.S. 723, 733, 772 (2008). Its failure to do the same in a case involving the Uighur request that they be released into the United States is just a further indication that the justices simply did not wish to decide this issue and risk a confrontation with both the Congress and the executive.

[108] Kiyemba v. Obama, 605 F.3d 1046, 1047 (D.C. Cir. 2010).

[109] The intervening decision was Kiyemba v. Obama, 561 F.3d 509 (D.C. Cir. 2009).

[110] Kiyemba v. Obama, 605 F.3d 1046, 1047 (D.C. Cir. 2010).

[111] *Id.* at 1048.

However, Justices Kennedy, Ginsburg, and Sotomayor joined Justice Breyer's short opinion concurring in the judgment. After a summary of the past developments, Justice Breyer wrote:

> In my view, these offers, the lack of any meaningful challenges as to their appropriateness, and the Government's uncontested commitment to continue to work to resettle petitioners transform petitioners' claim. Under present circumstances, I see no Government-imposed obstacle to petitioners' timely release and appropriate resettlement. Accordingly, I join in the Court's denial of certiorari. Should circumstances materially change, however, petitioners may of course raise their original issue (or related issues) again in the lower courts and in this Court.[112]

Whatever hope the Uighurs had that the Supreme Court would order the executive to resettle them in the United States vanished. As long as some other country was willing to resettle the Uighurs, the high court was not going to order their admission to the United States, and even if no other country offered to resettle the Uighurs, it was far from clear that five members of the Supreme Court would vote to order their admission to the United States. The Court was plainly hoping that the Uighurs would accept the resettlement offers and that the dispute would just go away.

One year after the Supreme Court decision, on April 18, 2012, two Uighurs were transferred to El Salvador, and two and one-half years after the Supreme Court decision, on December 30, 2013, three Uighurs were transferred to Slovakia.[113]

When the last of the Uighurs were transferred to Slovakia, the Pentagon spokesman called the development a "humanitarian gesture" and stated that the United States was grateful to Slovakia for the gesture and its "willingness to support U.S. efforts to close the Guantanamo Bay detention facility."[114]

In this public statement, irony runs deep. The United States could have made the same humanitarian gesture as did Slovakia years earlier, and if it had done so, it would have honored the rule of law and avoided the continued infliction of egregious harm on the Uighurs. But such a humanitarian gesture

---

[112] Kiyemba v. Obama, 563 U.S. 954, 1631–1632 (2011).

[113] Charlie Savage, *U.S. Frees Last of the Chinese Uighur Detainees From Guantanamo Bay*, N.Y. Times, Dec. 31, 2013; Charlie Savage, *Two Guantánamo Detainees Freed, the First in 15 Months*, N.Y. Times, Apr. 19, 2012.

[114] Charlie Savage, *U.S. Frees Last of the Chinese Uighur Detainees From Guantanamo Bay*, N.Y. Times, Dec. 31, 2013.

was beyond the reach of the United States, and though the executive's conduct in the shameful episode may be explained—not excused—by crippling politics that prevented the executive from treating the Uighurs justly, there is no comparable explanation for the Article III judges, who are intentionally insulated from political pressure so that they can enforce the law in the face of howling winds. The Supreme Court had an opportunity to uphold the rule of law in circumstances when such a ruling would have really mattered, and it walked away from the opportunity, betraying its own mission and mandate.

The Supreme Court's decisions in *Rasul, Hamdan,* and *Boumediene* contributed to creating a legal context that pressured the executive to depopulate Guantanamo. But it is not plausible to tease apart the importance of the legal dynamic from the political dynamic that resulted in a decline in the Guantanamo population, and thus the role of the judiciary in causing the number of incarcerated to decline cannot be concretely determined. But put aside the amorphous question of the general impact of the judiciary in that decline, and ask the following question instead: In how many cases was a Guantanamo prisoner released in direct response to a judicial order? That question can be answered.

On January 22, 2009, President Obama issued an Executive Order 13492, "calling for a prompt and comprehensive interagency review of the status of all individuals currently detained at the Guantanamo Bay Naval Base and requiring the closure of the detention facilities there."[115] One year later, the multiagency review was complete.[116] In surveying what it termed the "Transfer Decisions," the Final Report stated that "29 of the detainees subject to review were ordered released by a federal district court as the result of habeas litigation."[117] Of these twenty-nine detainees, eighteen were ordered released after the government "conceded the case," and Uighurs brought seventeen of those eighteen cases conceded by the executive.[118] The Final Report goes on to state that the "remaining 11 detainees were ordered released after a court reached

---

[115] Dep't of Justice, Dep't of Def., Dep't of State, Dep't of Homeland Security, Office of the Dir. of Nat'l Intelligence, Joint Chiefs of Staff, Guantanamo Review Task Force, Final Report I (Jan. 22, 2010). As of the writing of this book, President Obama has not closed the Guantanamo prison. The last footnote in this chapter contains references to recent news reports that discuss the issues central to the closing of the prison.

[116] The Task Force was composed of representatives from the Department of Justice, Department of Defense, Department of State, Department of Homeland Security, Office of the Director of National Intelligence, and Joint Chiefs of Staff. *Id.*

[117] *Id.* at 15. On the next page in a footnote, the Report states: "A total of 14 detainees have won their habeas cases on the merits in district court." *Id.* at 16 n.13. These statistics may be consistent with one another, but the consistency is not evident.

[118] *Id.* at 16 n.12.

the merits of the case and ruled, based on a preponderance of the evidence, that the detainee was not lawfully held because he was not part of, or did not substantially support, al-Qaida, the Taliban, or associated forces."[119] Thus, by the executive's own calculations in 2010, twenty-nine detainees were released as a response to a judicial order, and of those twenty-nine, seventeen were Uighurs.

Linda Greenhouse, the *New York Times* Supreme Court correspondent for three decades and a diligent student of all aspects of the Guantanamo litigation, asked the following question in 2014: "How many detainees actually got out due to the successful exercise of their right to habeas corpus?"[120] She answered her question as follows:

> The answer is not hundreds, not scores, but just a dozen or so. That number doesn't include the 17 Chinese Uighurs, hapless victims of global politics who even the Bush administration conceded were picked up by mistake . . . There is some imprecision in the number of habeas-driven releases, because some of these very low-value detainees might have been cleared by the various layers of review board and released anyway, as is happening bit by bit now . . . But whatever the precise number, it is tiny.[121]

Greenhouse then went on to summarize why the court-ordered releases have been "tiny." After studying the path of Guantanamo petitions, Greenhouse concluded that the district judges were not responsible for the "tiny" number of court-ordered releases. Indeed, Greenhouse's analysis persuaded her that the district judges "were granting habeas most of the time in the immediate post-*Boumediene* period."[122] The problem rested with the Obama administration, the D.C. Circuit Court of Appeals, and the Supreme Court. The Obama administration was responsible because it appealed the district court ruling and "stoutly defended its detention authority in court." The D.C. Circuit was responsible because in a "handful of major rulings," it instructed the district judges "to permit the government to draw every inference against the detainee and to evaluate the evidence according to a very relaxed standard of proof."[123] The Supreme Court was responsible because

---

[119] *Id.* at 16.

[120] Linda Greenhouse, *Guantanamo Dreams*, N.Y. Times, Dec. 24, 2014.

[121] *Id.*

[122] *Id.*

[123] The main cases were Al-Bihani v. Obama, 590 F.3d 866 (D.C. Cir. 2010), Ali Awad v. Obama, 608 F.3d 1 (D.C. Cir. 2010), and Al-Adahi v. Obama, 613 F.3d 1102 (D.C. Cir. 2010).

it "refused" to review the excessively deferential decisions of the District of Columbia Court of Appeals.[124]

It is often said—and properly so—that American tolerance for speech is not put to the test until the speech in question is speech that is hated. Only then is it possible to assess the nation's commitment to tolerating offensive, hateful, and despicable speech that stops short of "inciting or producing imminent lawless action."[125] A similar statement may be made with regard to the nation's, as well as the Supreme Court's, commitment to the rule of law. The strength of that commitment is only really tested when that commitment possibly conflicts with other important considerations. In the Guantanamo cases brought by the Uighurs, who were judged by the executive as not being a security threat, the rule of law principle conflicted with executive prerogatives, insisted upon because of general security considerations unrelated to the imprisoned individuals. In this context, a context that put the Supreme Court's commitment to the rule of law to the test, the high court had many opportunities after its *Boumediene* decision to uphold the rule of law, but it failed to do so.[126]

Over sixty years ago, Justice Robert Jackson wrote:

> Fortunately it still is startling, in this country, to find a person held indefinitely in executive custody without accusation of crime or judicial trial. Executive imprisonment has been considered oppressive and lawless since John, at Runnymede, pledged that no free man should be imprisoned, dispossessed, outlawed, or exiled save by the judgment of his peers or by the law of the land. The judges of England developed the writ of habeas corpus largely to preserve these immunities from executive restraint.[127]

However jarring it may be to national aspirations to "find a person held indefinitely in executive custody without accusation of crime or judicial

---

[124] Linda Greenhouse, *Guantanamo Dreams*, N.Y. Times, Dec. 24, 2014. The Supreme Court denied certiorari in each of the three cases cited in the previous footnote.

[125] Brandenburg v. Ohio, 395 U.S. 444 (1969).

[126] Jack Goldsmith, a Harvard law professor, takes a decidedly different view of these cases. He asserts in his book *Power and Constraint: The Accountable Presidency After 9/11* that federal judges "discarded their traditional reluctance to review presidential military decisions and threw themselves into questioning, invalidating, and supervising a variety of these decisions—decisions that in other wars had been the President's to make." Jack Goldsmith, Power and Constraint: The Accountable Presidency After 9/11, at xi (2012). Goldsmith's suggestion that the Supreme Court authorized substantial interference by federal judges with "presidential military decisions" is an unsupported claim that is contradicted by the Supreme Court with regard to Guantanamo prisoners.

[127] Shaughnessy v. United States, 345 U.S. 206, 218 (1953) (Jackson J., dissenting).

trial,"[128] the imprisonment of the Uighurs at Guantanamo establishes that the Supreme Court, as well as the nation as a whole, will, under some circumstances, accept indefinite confinement without the presentation of charges or judicial trial.[129]

[128] *Id.*

[129] In the fall of 2015, the Obama administration quickened the pace of transfers of Guantanamo prisoners to other countries. For example, see Charlie Savage, *Transfers Could Reduce Guantanamo Detainees to 90*, N.Y. Times, Dec. 16, 2015; Charlie Savage, *5 Yemeni Guantanamo Inmates are Sent to United Arab Emirates*, N.Y. Times, Nov. 15, 2015; Charlie Savage and Steven Erlanger, *Shaker Aamer is Released From Guantanamo Prison after 13 Years*, N.Y. Times, Oct. 30, 2015. Even after these efforts, many Guantanamo prisoners who have been approved for transfer to other countries remain incarcerated. In addition, there are several dozen Guantanamo prisoners not cleared for transfer who may remain imprisoned for an indefinite period of time. For recent commentary that discusses the major current issues concerning the closing of the Guantanamo prison, see Joseph Goldstein, *Once in Guantanamo, Alghan Now Leads War Against Taliban and ISIS*, N.Y. Times, Nov. 27, 2015; David M. Herszenhorn, *Senate Passes Military Bill that Bans Transfers of Guantanamo Detainees*, N.Y. Times, Nov. 10, 2015; Gregory B. Craig and Cliff Sloan, *The President Doesn't Need Congress's Permission to Close Guantanamo*, N.Y. Times, Nov. 6, 2015; Dianne Feinstein, *Let's Finally Close Guantanamo*, N.Y. Times, Nov. 4, 2015; Charlie Savage, *Guantanamo is Leaving Obama with Choices, Neither of them Simple*, N.Y. Times, Oct. 31, 2105; Charlie Savage, *Frustrated in Efforts to Close Guantanamo Prison, Officials Look to Reduce Population*, N.Y. Times, Dec. 2, 2015.

PART FOUR

BETWEEN ABDICATION
AND USURPATION

14

The Consequences of Deference

It is part of the national political and legal creed that the United States is committed to the rule of law.[1] And that general principle requires courts to provide a judicial remedy to an individual for a legal wrong. As John Marshall wrote long ago in his historic opinion in *Marbury v. Madison*:

> The very essence of civil liberty certainly consists in the right of every individual to claim the protection of the laws, whenever he receives an injury. One of the first duties of government is to afford that protection. . . . . [The] government of the United States has been emphatically termed a government of laws, and not of men. It will certainly cease to deserve this high appellation, if the laws furnish no remedy for the violation of a vested legal right.[2]

Providing a remedy for the violation of vested rights is central to an orderly society for, among other considerations, it strengthens societal norms, justifies

---

[1] Not unlike what many presidents have previously stated, President Barack Obama told the nation a little more than two centuries after Chief Justice Marshall penned his famous opinion in *Marbury v. Madison*, 5 U.S. 137 (1803): "In all that we do, we must remember that what sets America apart is not solely our power—it is the principles upon which our union was founded. We're a nation that brings our enemies to justice while adhering to the rule of law, and respecting the rights of all our citizens." President Barack H. Obama, Remarks by the President on the Way Forward in Afghanistan (June 22, 2011). Ten months after that, in a speech at Harvard Law School, the general counsel of the Central Intelligence Agency, Stephen W. Preston, stated that the "President has made clear that ours is a nation of laws, and that an abiding respect for the rule of law is one of our country's greatest strengths, even against an enemy with only contempt for the law." And to emphasize that the CIA was under that national mandate to be a nation committed to the rule of law, Preston stated that this "is so for the Central Intelligence Agency no less than any other instrument of national power engaged in the fight against al-Qaeda and its militant allies" and that the "CIA is an institution of laws and the rule of law is integral to Agency operations." Stephen W. Preston, *CIA and the Rule of Law*, 6 J. Nat'l Security L. & Pol'y 1, 1 (2012).

[2] Marbury v. Madison, 5 U.S. 137, 163 (1803).

the criminalization of self-help, vests legitimacy in judicial institutions charged with resolving disputes, and reaffirms the nation's commitment to the rule of law. As one judge stated, "for better or worse,"[3] courts are central to granting relief to individuals seeking redress, or as Woodrow Wilson set forth in his classic study, *Constitutional Government in the United States:* "So far as the individual is concerned, a constitutional government is as good as its courts; no better, no worse. Its laws are only its professions. It keeps its promises, or does not keep them, in its courts."[4] Thus, when John Marshall wrote over two centuries ago that the United States is a "government of laws, and not of men,"[5] he penned words that not only set forth a national aspiration at the time, but words that have echoed across the eras of American history as setting forth one of the nation's most fundamental commitments that has become part of America's identity among the nations of the world.

Over decades, the Supreme Court translated these ideals into law in action. Thus, the Court has ruled that illegally seized evidence must be suppressed in criminal cases, even if that results in the release of the criminal, on the ground that "[n]othing can destroy a government more quickly than its failure to observe its own laws."[6] Similarly, the Court ruled that a defendant must be given "Miranda rights" and that a confession that is not procured in compliance with those rules must be suppressed.[7] The Court also requires states to provide an indigent charged with a felony with a lawyer at the state's expense to give meaning to the ideal of the rule of law.[8] In civil cases, the Court provides a remedy against state and local officials, as well as private parties acting under color of law, for the deprivation of federal rights.[9] And the Court has fashioned a remedy against federal officials to deter future conduct that violates individual constitutional rights, because, as Justice John M. Harlan wrote: "it is important, in a civilized society, that the judicial branch of the nation's government stand ready to afford a remedy in these circumstances."[10]

---

[3] Arar v. Ashcroft, 585 F.3d 559, 630 (2d Cir. 2009) (Calabresi, J., dissenting).

[4] Woodrow Wilson, Constitutional Government in the United States 9 (Quid Pro Quo, LLC, 2011).

[5] *Marbury*, 5 U.S. at 163.

[6] Mapp v. Ohio, 367 U.S. 643, 659 (1961). In an earlier opinion, Justice Brandeis wrote: "our government is the potent, the omnipresent teacher. For good or for ill, it teaches the whole people by its example. . . . If the government becomes a lawbreaker, it breeds contempt for law; it invites every man to become a law unto himself; it invites anarchy." Olmstead v. United States, 277 U.S. 438, 485 (1928) (Brandeis, J., dissenting).

[7] Miranda v. Arizona, 384 U.S. 436 (1966).

[8] Gideon v. Wainwright, 372 U.S. 335 (1963).

[9] Monroe v. Pape, 365 U.S. 167 (1961).

[10] Bivens v. Six Unknown Agents of Federal Bureau of Narcotics, 403 U.S. 388, 411 (1971) (Harlan, J., concurring); Davis v. Passman, 442 U.S. 228 (1979); Carlson v. Green, 446 U.S. 14 (1980).

But as bedrock as this principle may be, it is not an absolute one.[11] The law does not provide a remedy for every injury caused by executive officers, and because of complex and competing values it may deny a remedy even when there is substantial evidence to believe that the executive branch has violated significant individual rights. But accepting that this important tenet is qualified does not by itself define the degree to which the principle should be qualified and the executive insulated from meaningful judicial review in national security cases. In other words, the idea that courts should provide a judicial remedy for the violation of a legal right, especially when government officers have allegedly acted unlawfully and the unlawful conduct has arguably violated constitutional limitations, is more than an aspiration; it is an important principle of a modern civilized society that should prevail except in the most limited of circumstances.

Nonetheless, during the last seven decades, courts—the very governing institution most responsible for assuring that Marshall's admonition is respected throughout the realm—have undermined this tenet by crafting and applying legal doctrines that shield executive conduct that is arguably unlawful. Indeed, against these widely accepted tenets, the idea of judges immunizing high-level executive officials from meaningful judicial accountability in circumstances in which there are compelling reasons to support the claim that these officials have acted unlawfully gives a strange cast to the national commitment to the rule of law.

Two cases, separated by three decades in which courts dismissed an action because of the state secrets privilege, illustrate this point. In 1978, the U.S. Court of Appeals for the District of Columbia Circuit utilized the privilege to dismiss an action in which individuals and organizations opposed to the United States military involvement in Vietnam claimed that former federal officials as well as private corporations acted in concert to conduct "warrantless interceptions of their international wire, cable and telephone communications."[12] The meaning of the dismissal meant—in the words of former Chief Judge of the U.S. Court of Appeals for the District of Columbia Circuit David L. Bazelon, who submitted a dissent—that the state secrets privilege "immunize[d] conduct that appears to be proscribed by the Fourth Amendment,"[13] and thus

---

[11] One important limitation on the principle courts should provide a remedy to vindicate a legal wrong is the doctrine of sovereign immunity. That doctrine, historically rooted and subject to congressional qualification, is discussed in Charles Alan Wright and May Kay Kane, Law of Federal Courts (6th ed. 2011), §22 "Civil Actions to which the United States is a Party" (pp. 127–133).

[12] Halkin v. Helms (*Halkin I*), 598 F.2d 1, 3 (D.C. Cir. 1978).

[13] Halkin v. Helms, 598 F.2d 1, 13 (D.C. Cir. 1979) (Bazelon, J., dissenting).

"becomes a shield behind which the government may insulate unlawful behavior from scrutiny and redress by citizens who are the target of the government's surveillance."[14]

In a post–September 11 case—*Mohamed v. Jeppesen Dataplan, Inc.*,[15] decided by the Ninth Circuit in 2010—five individuals claimed that the CIA, working in concert with other government agencies and officials of foreign governments, "operated an extraordinary rendition program to gather intelligence by apprehending foreign nationals suspected of involvement in terrorist activities and transferring them in secret to foreign countries for detention and interrogation by United States or foreign officials"[16] by "'methods that would [otherwise have been] prohibited under federal or international law.'"[17] The plaintiffs alleged that Jeppesen Dataplan, Inc., a U.S. corporation, had provided "flight planning and logistical support services to the aircraft and crew on all of the flights transporting each of the five plaintiffs among the various locations where they were detained and allegedly subjected to torture."[18] In relying upon the privilege to dismiss the complaint, Circuit Judge Raymond C. Fisher framed the issue as a collision in fundamental values between government under law and a secure government: "This case requires us to address the difficult balance the state secrets doctrine strikes between fundamental principles of our liberty, including justice, transparency, accountability and national security. Although as judges we strive to honor *all* of these principles, there are times when exceptional circumstances create an irreconcilable conflict between them."[19]

There are important differences between the executive and the judiciary on this matter. Federal judges, for example, who sustain the state secrets privilege to shield unlawful conduct are not themselves committing an unlawful act, nor are they responsible for directing such conduct. And there is an important difference between courts not requiring the executive branch to disclose certain information or documents that might be evidence of such unlawful conduct and courts actually approving of unlawful executive conduct. Nonetheless, these distinctions are not absolutions. Allegations of unlawful executive conduct are not new or even rare, and judges who dismiss cases on the ground that

---

[14] *Id.* at 13–14.

[15] Mohamed v. Jeppesen Dataplan, Inc., 614 F.3d 1070 (9th Cir. 2010) (en banc).

[16] *Id.* at 1073.

[17] *Id.*

[18] *Id.* at 1075.

[19] *Id.* at 1073. Judge Fisher's frank acknowledgment that the state secrets privilege shielded unlawful conduct is unusual. What is more common is the approach taken by Judge Edwards in the *Ellsberg* case and Judge Scalia in the *Molerio* case—that is, to just ignore the issue. See Chapter 6 for a discussion of these cases.

a doctrine of deference requires it do so knowing that they are shielding argu-ably unlawful conduct and creating a dynamic that encourages future unlaw-ful conduct. In other words, what the courts have knowingly done is to build into the functioning of the National Security State an insulating dynamic that permits, if not invites, public officials to violate the law with impunity.

When a court utilizes deferential doctrines to immunize the executive branch in an action in which a party asserts egregious claims as in an extraor-dinary rendition case, not only do the courts seem as if they are washing their hands[20] of the matter, but they may well be seen as if they are bowing to ex-ecutive authority,[21] if not complicit in the exertion of that authority. Although the degree to which such decisions undermine the public's trust in the courts and cut away at the courts' legitimacy is uncertain, it is worth recalling Justice John Paul Stevens's observation regarding the confrontation between the Supreme Court and President Nixon over whether the courts had the author-ity to require Nixon to "produce the tape recordings that eventually led to his resignation."[22] He wrote: "The decision not only had a historic effect on American politics and society but also powerfully illustrated the integrity and independence of the Court. It may well have done more to inspire the confidence in the work of judges that is the true backbone of the rule of law than any other decision in the history of the Court."[23] Justice Stevens's ob-servation is poignant. The Court gains public trust when it takes its indepen-dence seriously and holds the executive legally accountable.

No one claims that U.S. officials have a right to violate the law to protect the national security. There may well be a dispute as to whether specified con-duct does or does not violate the law, or whether a particular defendant has a defense such as qualified immunity.[24] But no one challenges the underlying premise that the law must be obeyed. Nor have recent presidential adminis-trations taken the widely criticized position insisted upon by President Nixon that an act that might otherwise be a violation of the law is not a violation when

---

[20] Judge Fisher's majority opinion in *Jeppesen*, dismissing a complaint alleging extraordinary rendition, wrote: "Our holding today is not intended to foreclose—or to preclude—possible non-judicial relief, should it be warranted for any of the plaintiffs." *Jeppesen*, 614 F.3d at 1091. Judge Fisher was surely as cognizant as any observer of the American governing structure as to how utterly unlikely it would be for the plaintiff in the case to secure relief from either the Congress or the executive. And yet he holds out this implausible possibility as an option.

[21] For two cases in which the judiciary is widely thought to have bowed to executive author-ity, see Ex parte Quirin, 317 U.S. 1 (1942), and Korematsu v. United States, 323 U.S. 214 (1944).

[22] John Paul Stevens, Five Chiefs: A Supreme Court Memoir 114 (2011).

[23] *Id.*

[24] The Supreme Court discussed qualified immunity in Clapper v. Amnesty Int'l USA, 133 S. Ct. 1138 (2013).

the president orders it to guard the national security,[25] nor have they espoused a utilitarian rationale that maintains that the protection of national security justifies breaking the law.[26] But yet the Court has, through its doctrines of deference, opened too wide a back door to the untenable doctrine that the executive may act unlawfully to protect national security. That doctrine eats away at the underpinnings of the entire governing structure.

Some insulation of the executive by means of technical doctrines of deference is required in some situations if the national security is to be protected. But accepting that what Learned Hand termed the "peril of war" may diminish substantive rights is a far cry from accepting that the incantation of the phrase "national security" should suffice as a basis for the dismissal of a case. And though case law does not insulate the executive with every incantation of the phrase "national security," the degree of insulation the Supreme Court now provides the executive substantially exceeds what is necessary to protect the nation.

The fact is that the judicial creation and application of technical doctrines of deference undermine the aspiration that a remedy be available for a violation of law and places a wedge between the national reality and principle. The most fundamental and driving theme underlying judicial deference in cases implicating national security is that the national interest in preserving and advancing national security is more important than providing a remedy to an individual who has arguably been wronged by the executive acting in service of national security. Or to put the matter in slightly different terms, as important as individual rights are under the Constitution, judges will, in cases implicating national security, allow speculative security considerations to trump protected individual rights.

Once the issue of granting or denying a remedy to an individual is understood from this perspective, the potential and damaging overreaching of a deferential disposition is laid bare. Because the concept of national security is extremely

---

[25] Richard M. Nixon, TV Interview with David Frost (May 20, 1977), http://youtube.com/watch?v=ejvyDn1TPr8 (last visited July 15, 2013). For two recent examples of presidential administrations not following in President's Nixon's footsteps, see Charlie Savage, *Obama Tests Limits of Power in Syria Conflict*, N.Y. Times, Sept. 8, 2013, http://www.nytimes.com/2013/09/09/world/middleeast/obama-tests-limits-of-power-in-syrian-conflict.html, and Secretary of State Colin Powell's speech to the United Nations Security Council seeking affirmation for the attack on Iraq because of the alleged threat presented by the regime's possession of weapons of mass destruction, http://www.theguardian.com/world/2003/feb/05/iraq.usa (last visited Sept. 9, 2013).

[26] Though no administration has formally made the claim that the ends justify the means, former Vice President Dick Cheney endorsed that position in December of 2014. *See* Anthony Zurcher, *Cheney: 'No problem' with Detaining Innocents*, BBC News (Dec. 15, 2014), http://www.bbc.com/news/blogs-echochambers-30485999.

broad and potentially covers a broad array of considerations, a broad deferential stance by the judiciary establishes a dynamic in which the judiciary generally fails to exercise the most minimal degree of review of executive national security claims. As a result, the judiciary fails to exert meaningful pressure on the executive to make distinctions among national security interests based on the scope or magnitude of a national security interest and that, in turn, results in individuals being denied a judicial remedy in far too many circumstances.

Almost eighty years ago, Supreme Court Justice Louis D. Brandeis warned of the consequences of the Supreme Court failing to fulfill its distinctive role in insisting that the conduct of the executive remain lawful. "In a government of laws," Brandeis wrote, "existence of the government will be imperilled if it fails to observe the law scrupulously. Our government . . . teaches the whole people by its example. Crime is contagious. If the government becomes a law-breaker, it breeds contempt for law; it invites every man to become a law unto himself; it invites anarchy." Brandeis went on to assert that to "declare that in the administration of the criminal law the end justifies the means—to declare that the government may commit crimes in order to secure the conviction of a private criminal—would bring terrible retribution. Against that pernicious doctrine this court should resolutely set its face."[27] Brandeis's observation was wise when he wrote it; it remains so today.[28]

The starting point for understanding how the Age of Deference undermines the constitutional order is James Madison's axiom put forth with unqualified certainty in *Federalist* No. 47. "No political truth," Madison contended, "is certainly of greater intrinsic value or is stamped with the authority of more enlightened patrons of liberty" than the claim that the "accumulation of all powers legislative, executive and judiciary in the same hands, whether of one, a few or many, and whether hereditary, self appointed, or elected, may justly be pronounced the very definition of tyranny."[29]

---

[27] Olmstead v. United States, 277 U.S. 438, 468 (1928) (Brandeis, J., dissenting).

[28] In a brief chapter entitled "Secrecy as Crime Concealer," Garry Wills brings into sharp focus the utility of secrecy during the post–World War II decades in hiding from the American public dozens upon dozens of instances in which the United States toppled other governments, usually in violation of international law. Wills concludes that the overthrowing of other governments usually led to "long-term results . . . damaging to the United States" and "created ill will from other nations and distrust or cynicism in our own." Garry Wills, Bomb Power: The Modern Presidency and the National Security State 183 (2010).

[29] The Federalist No. 47 (James Madison). In the same manner, Madison conceded that if the proposed Constitution could fairly be characterized as "having a dangerous tendency to such an accumulation, no further arguments would be necessary to inspire a universal reprobation of the system." But he argued that the charge that the proposed Constitution would lead to such a result

About 190 years after Madison wrote his newspaper articles aimed at convincing New Yorkers to approve the recommended new Constitution and which were eventually collected with those others written by Alexander Hamilton and John Jay in *The Federalist*, Arthur M. Schlesinger, Jr. wrote his seminal *The Imperial Presidency*, in which he affirmed the continued relevance of Madison's assertions. Schlesinger emphasized that the Founding Fathers based the American Constitution on the principle of separation of powers because they "saw conflict" over the exercise of government power "as the guarantee of freedom," and thus "institutionalized conflict in the very heart of the American polity."[30] They were surely aware that fractured power was inefficient and that such inefficiency could in its extreme threaten the ultimate goal of effective and fair government, but the founders were, in Schlesinger's words, "good Newtonians," intent on fashioning a well-balanced machine of government power that provided checks in order to diminish the concentration and abuse of power so as to "establish justice, insure domestic tranquility, promote the general welfare, and secure the blessings of liberty to ourselves and our posterity."[31]

But over time, developments betrayed the ideals of the founders. And this betrayal was in response to foreign policy and strategic national security considerations that pressed for the increased concentration of power in the executive branch. A prime example of the dynamic in which the executive argued on legal and policy grounds for enhanced presidential authority is set forth in the executive's legal brief filed before the Supreme Court in the famous *Steel Seizure* case of 1952. Although the executive's argument in this particular case did not win the day—the Supreme Court concluded that President Truman's seizure of the nation's steel mills during the Korean War, absent congressional authorization, was unconstitutional—the position set forth in the brief graphically illustrates the executive's claim for more authority. The executive framed its claim for executive power in historic terms: "One of the great problems of the age is whether the democracies can find sufficient vigor and energy to respond promptly and decisively to the crises of our time . . . There has been an enormous increase in the tempo at which events occur, and decisions must be made." That said, the brief went on to contend that the problems now challenging the viability of the democracy "can be met within the framework of our Constitution. But they can be met only by regarding the Constitution as a 'continuously operative charter of government' which is capable now as in

---

"cannot be supported" and that the "three great departments of power" would in fact be "separate and distinct," thus assuring "the preservation of liberty." *Id.*

[30] Arthur M. Schlesinger, Jr., The Imperial Presidency vii (1973).

[31] U.S. Const. preamble.

the past of adapting itself to the needs of new circumstances without sacrificing the basic principles of democracy and liberty." The brief then quoted the Court back to itself: "This Court has recently emphasized that 'it is of the highest importance that the fundamental purposes of the Constitution be kept in mind and given effect' and that 'in time of crisis nothing could be more tragic and less expressive of the intent of the people than so to construe their Constitution that by its terms it would substantially hinder rather than help them in defending their national safety.' "[32]

The position reflected many significant aspects of the American governing scheme. The Constitution gives the president authority to establish diplomatic relations, to negotiate executive agreements without congressional oversight, to negotiate treaties provided the Senate ratifies the treaty by a two-thirds majority, to be the commander-in-chief of the Army and Navy, and to direct the executive department and agencies such as the Departments of State and Defense as well as the FBI, CIA, and NSA. Not only is the president at the top of this ladder, but much of what happens within the executive branch happens in secret, which means that the Congress and the public often know little of what the executive does in the name of taking "care that the laws be faithfully executed."

The pragmatic argument for eroding constitutional checks and balances was forceful, and, as Schlesinger noted, the "assumption of that power by the Presidency was gradual and usually under the demand or pretext of emergency," and then accomplished as much by "congressional abdication as [by] presidential usurpation." As that pattern repeated itself, "there dwindled away checks, both written and unwritten, that had long held the Presidency under control. The written checks were in the Constitution. The unwritten checks were in the forces and institutions a President once had to take into practical account before he made decisions of war and peace—the cabinet and the executive branch itself, the Congress, the judiciary, the press, public opinion at home and the opinion of the world."[33]

Over time, as Schlesinger observed in the early 1970s, "a conception of presidential power" emerged that was so "spacious and peremptory as to imply a radical transformation of the traditional polity" so that "presidential primacy, so indispensable to the political order, has turned into presidential supremacy,"[34] and the "constitutional Presidency . . . has become the imperial Presidency and threatens to be the revolutionary Presidency."[35] As a result,

---

[32] Brief for Petitioner at 172–174, Youngstown Sheet & Tube Co. v. Sawyer, 343 U.S. 579 (1952) (No. 745) (internal citations omitted).

[33] Arthur M. Schlesinger, Jr., The Imperial Presidency ix (1973).

[34] *Id.* at viii.

[35] *Id.*

by Schlesinger's estimation, the American president by the early 1970s "had become on issues of war and peace the most absolute monarch (with the possible exception of Mao Tse-Tung of China) among the great powers of the world."[36]

In reaching this condemning conclusion, Schlesinger rejected the idea that America faced a stark choice between the president as a mere "messenger-boy"[37] and an Imperial Presidency. Instead, he insisted that "a middle ground between making the President a czar and making him a puppet" existed and urged Americans to find it and insist upon it.[38] Because, as Schlesinger himself conceded, he had contributed to "the rise of the presidential mystique,"[39] his claim that the nation had an Imperial Presidency was perhaps an unexpected judgment that sought to call the nation's attention to a trend that he contended threatened the constitutional order, as well as to a course of action that would avoid the perils of both an imperial and imprisoned presidency.

Today, over four decades later, there is broad agreement among scholars and commentators who assess the contemporary constitutional order with a focus on national security that the idea of an eighteenth-, nineteenth-, or early-twentieth-century Madisonian arrangement of checks and balances is not descriptive of American political reality. These observers may well disagree[40]—and in some cases they almost certainly do—as to the advantages and disadvantages of the

---

[36] *Id.* at ix.

[37] *Id.* at x

[38] *Id.*

[39] *Id.* at ix.

[40] *See, e.g.,* Bruce Ackerman, The Decline and Fall of the American Republic (2010); Eric K. Posner and Adrian Vermeule, The Executive Unbound: After the Madisonian Republic (2011); Peter M. Shane, Madison's Nightmare: How Executive Power Threatens American Democracy (2009). At the same time some of these commentators argue that there is no major need for change because new restraints on executive power have emerged, such as the restraints imposed by the press and what some call "lawfare." Although they are not critical of the increasing concentration of authority in the presidency, Posner and Vermeule agree that the Madisonian constitutional conception is either near death's door or already in the morgue. "We live in a regime of executive-centered government, in an age after separation of powers, and the legally constrained executive is now a historical curiosity . . . we argue that in the modern administrative state the executive governs, subject to legal constraints that are shaky in normal times and weak or nonexistent in times of crisis." Eric K. Posner and Adrian Vermeule, The Executive Unbound: After the Madisonian Republic 4 (2011). Harvard law professor Jack Goldsmith, who served in President George W. Bush's administration, echoes a similar view: "If Madison were alive today, he would be astonished and probably appalled to see the gargantuan presidency exercising so much power, much of it in secret, in an endless global war against nonstate actor terrorists. He would also be surprised by the reticulate presidential synopticon that has grown up to watch, check, and legitimate the presidency in war." Jack Goldsmith, Power and Constraint: The Accountable Presidency After 9/11, at 243 (2012).

increasing concentration of authority in the executive. But there is little disagreement about the fact that the president reigns supreme, and that the modern governing system is significantly different from what the framers experienced or envisioned, and that is certainly the case on national security matters.[41]

But can the Supreme Court perform an important role in making the executive accountable in meaningful ways in cases implicating national security and in restoring a system of checks and balances?

Generally, commentators do not think that the Supreme Court has the capacity—let alone the will—to make an important contribution to restoring more meaningful checks and balances in national security cases. Thus, Peter Shane, a strong advocate for the claim that the Madisonian governing scheme can be restored, wrote:

> Of the three branches, the judiciary has the least capacity to participate in an aggressive and systematic way in a recalibration of checks and balances and a taming of presidentialism. That is because courts cannot determine for themselves which questions and controversies will be brought before them for resolution, and uniformity of judicial response can be achieved only through decisions of the U.S. Supreme Court, which in recent years has decided fewer than one hundred cases per term.[42]

Shane's skepticism is not unfounded. Courts are passive governing institutions. They sit; they wait. Nothing happens until a party files a case. If no party

[41] For example, consider Peter Shane, who has written:

For the last quarter century, the checks and balances of American government have been increasingly battered by the merger of two powerful currents. One is the gathering concentration of power in the hands of the federal executive, a trend nurtured since the New Deal by Presidents both Democratic and Republican, although at different rates of acceleration. The second current has been the relentless campaign of the right wing of the Republican Party since 1981 to steer the capacities of our national government toward the fulfillment of a conservative social, economic, and foreign policy agenda. Together, the growing concentration of executive power and the campaign for partisan predominance have produced an era of aggressive presidentialism, a theory of government and a pattern of government practice that treat our Constitution as vesting in the President a fixed and expansive category of executive authority largely immune to legislative control or judicial review. This constitutional perfect storm has put the design of the democratic republic at risk, upending many of the norms and informal institutional practices that have helped to sustain the Madisonian check and balances in our national government, at least since the end of World War II. (Peter M. Shane, Madison's Nightmare: How Executive Power Threatens American Democracy 3 (2009))

[42] *Id.* at 193.

initiates a proceeding, there is no proceeding. Thus, courts have no authority to kick-start a legal proceeding or an investigation. They are entirely dependent upon others to commence legal proceedings and then they proceed one case at a time. Furthermore, the filing of a legal proceeding does not trigger a broad and open-ended judicial inquiry. Instead, the scope of the inquiry is shaped by the dispute between the parties, not the broader boundaries of the more general problem, and as a result, a court's focus is on how the parties define the issues in a case. In other words, courts are not roaming commissions, and that is true before and after an action is filed.

Courts mainly look backward, not forward. A legal action is a claim about what has been done, and it seeks appropriate relief. Thus, courts are at a disadvantage in limiting or controlling what the executive might do in the future, since the policies and actions that may be developed and implemented in the future will not be appropriate for legal action until actually implemented. Furthermore, courts act deliberately, if not slowly, so that the time lag between the challenged action—which generally is already a past event—and a judicial resolution may be many months if not two or three or four years. And by the time there is a judicial resolution of the matter that prompted the lawsuit, the executive and the Congress may well have changed policies and practices in light of changing circumstances, which in turn will minimize the impact of the judicial decision on current matters. Moreover, the remedial power of the judiciary is limited and courts tend to exercise that authority with restraint, especially on matters considered sensitive such as national security, prison order, and police conduct.

Thus, even if a party is successful in a lawsuit challenging one or another national security initiative, that legal victory may come some years well after the event that triggered the action and at a time when the significance of the issue has dissipated. Moreover, courts are inclined to be cautious because they are vulnerable institutions. For example, courts are dependent on the executive to enforce its orders directed against others and to comply voluntarily with its orders directed against the executive, and because of that, courts often seek to avoid what one chief justice once termed a "showdown" with the executive. Moreover, the scope of the court's jurisdiction and remedial power is subject to substantial congressional control.

And by comparison to the power possessed by Congress to rebalance the governing order, the judiciary has much less capacity. Congress has the power to make law that limits the executive. Congress has the power to pressure the executive into changing policy and practices by failing to confirm appointments, rejecting executive-sponsored legislative proposals, and utilizing the immense power of the purse. The court's authority is faint by comparison to these weapons of influence.

These considerations constitute a powerful lineup of reasons as to why courts cannot be expected to fulfill an important role in reversing the trend that makes the executive legally unaccountable on the many fronts implicating national security. And by and large, these reasons, and perhaps some others as well, along with courts' historic reluctance to intervene in national security matters, have persuaded most observers that courts will not in fact make an effort to alter their past practices and try to turn the tide in legal disputes that implicate national security.

Nonetheless, the Supreme Court has upended conventional wisdom over the history of the republic. Take, for example, the year 1937. In that year, the Court took a much more generous attitude toward the scope of national power to regulate social and economic affairs of the nation by means of its power under the commerce, spending, and taxing clauses of the Constitution. Simultaneously, the Court also put an end to an expansive interpretation of the Fourteenth Amendment to blunt state efforts at economic and social change and to a crabbed construction of Congress's authority to remedy economic and social problems. A combination of those decisions constituted a dramatic break with the past and ushered in a set of decisions that gave constitutional legitimacy to national and state regulation of social and economic matters.

In the aftermath of the defeat of Nazi racism and while the United States competed with the Soviet Union during the Cold War for the hearts and minds of peoples around the globe, the high court used its authority to salvage the reputation and standing of the United States from the depths of disrepute into which its history of slavery and Jim Crow laws had cast it by declaring that mandatory segregation in the public schools was unconstitutional.[43] Twenty years after the *Brown* decision, the Supreme Court altered its jurisprudence regarding the subjugation of women and began to take seriously its equal protection principles to dismantle deeply rooted discrimination that had placed women in significantly disadvantageous positions.[44] These decisions, as well as others, have reverberated well beyond even the outer boundaries of a law case and have had an impact on social policy, personal attitudes, and societal values.

The capacity of the court to help rebalance the governing structure should not be discounted. Judicial outcomes make a difference. They certainly do so within the boundaries of a case. Thus, forcing the executive to litigate a matter allegedly involving a state secret may yield important disclosures that do not in any way harm the nation's security and which change national policy in constructive ways. Allowing a claim to go forward against senior executive

---

[43] *See* Brown v. Board of Educ., 347 U.S. 483 (1954).

[44] For example, see United States v. Virginia, 518 U.S. 515 (1996); Mississippi Univ. for Women v. Hogan, 458 U.S. 718 (1982); Craig v. Boren, 429 U.S. 190 (1976).

officials involving torture, kidnapping, and extraordinary rendition may not only result in a damage award in favor of the injured individual, but may also force executive officials to change policies. Moreover, to the extent that past judicial outcomes have legitimated the rise of the Imperial Presidency and the National Security State, different outcomes going forward that constitute challenges to both trends may well have a salient impact on both. Lastly, there is little doubt that Supreme Court decisions are part of a national conversation that encompasses the executive, the Congress, state governments, and the people at large in a national conversation. Indeed, only a thin and porous wall separates legal discourse from political discourse, and thus legal opinions inevitably seep through the judicial membrane to the larger political culture and have an impact on changing attitudes and dispositions.

But the Supreme Court is more conservative today than at any time since the 1930s, and it may be more conservative today than that court was. So the possibility that a majority of the justices will suddenly or even gradually modify the intensity of their deferential stance in cases implicating national security is not great. But that does not mean that significant change is out of the question over some period of time. Concededly, the judiciary and the development of the law are generally cautious institutions, changing legal norms gradually over some extended period of time. But change does come, sometimes unexpectedly, and when it does come it is usually because the impulses for changes are powerful, and often because those impulses have generated severe criticism on the court.[45] And when the court inaugurates change, that change may well stimulate legislative change as well as galvanize public pressure in favor of both legislative and judicial change. In short, because of the complicated American governing structure, what commences as a judicial change of mind may infuse change throughout the American governing scheme. And although a majority of the current members of the Supreme Court may now seem as if they will resist change in cases implicating national security, the membership of the court will change in time.

---

[45] In each of these developments, the Supreme Court is more of a follower than a leader. The 1937 decisions followed many years of criticism by the president and the Congress of the Court. *Brown*'s trumpet of equality followed years of organized litigation intended to secure that result and a political context that supported a decision that was fiercely opposed across the South. The willingness of the Court to break ranks with prior decisions built on stereotypes that sentenced women to an inferior status only followed years of protest by women against discriminatory laws and practices. At the same time, it is apparent that while many forces created a context for these decisions, it is equally clear that the Court's decisions helped to shape the future. As Gordon Wood has observed: "Nowhere else in the modern world do courts wield as much power in shaping the contours of life as the Supreme Court does in the United States." Gordon Wood, Empire of Liberty: A History of the Early Republic, 1789–1815, at 442 (2009).

15

The Mind of Deference

Why is it that so many judges—but not all—over so many decades have favored and continue to favor a degree of deference and secrecy that denies relief to individuals arguably injured by the executive, undermines the scheme of checks and balances central to the constitutional order, and erodes the rule of law?

There is no definitive response to that important question. Moreover, attempting to penetrate the juristic mind of deference that has shaped an era of deference suggests that there is one mind, and that cannot be. There is no one juristic mind at any given point in time, and there certainly is no single juristic mind that encompasses hundreds of judges over seventy years. Furthermore, some judges may favor some reasons for deference and secrecy over others, and the different reasons underlying a deferential stance may in turn have an impact on a judge's willingness to employ certain doctrines of deference. Thus, the state secrets privilege is supported in large part by the claim that judges lack the competence to decide national security issues. The demise of the *Bivens* doctrine is mainly supported by the claim that courts should respect Congress's failure to pass a statute that authorizes a remedy and thus refrain from implying a remedy. The quasi-immunity doctrine is mainly upheld on the ground that the nation is better off when senior officials are immunized from liability and thus are more inclined to vigorously discharge their responsibilities. Some judges today argue that the law of standing that closes the courthouse door is warranted by separation of powers considerations. Plainly, the juristic mind that endorses deference and secrecy is complicated and versatile, and it is composed of entangled variables—precedent, values, pragmatic considerations, prejudices, aspirations, expectations—that may bleed into one another, reinforce one another, and vary in importance over time and with the context. As a result, any dissection of a juristic mind will not portray the thinking of all judges who embrace contemporary deference, and it certainly will not describe the thinking of judges who resist being unduly deferential. Nonetheless, to deny that there are main gravitational pulls in this mindset is untenable. And penetrating those gravitational pulls is important if post–World War II judicial deference is to be understood, and if judges who embrace undue deference are to be persuaded that values underlying individual liberty, the rule of law, and the democratic process require a different perspective.

At the core of the juristic mind of deference is the claim that judges are not competent to assess matters implicating national security.[1] As previously noted, Supreme Court Justice Robert Jackson wrote that these matters are "political, not judicial" in nature; they are "delicate, complex, and involve large elements of prophecy"; and they are decisions for which the "judiciary has neither aptitude, facilities nor responsibility and which has long been held to belong in the domain of political power not subject to judicial intrusion or inquiry."[2] From Jackson's perspective, no matter how much evidence is presented or how many experts testify, judges lack judgment seasoned by years of experience, and, as a result, judges, through no fault of trying or effort or intelligence, are not competent, as Jackson wrote, to "review and perhaps nullify" a decision made by members of the executive branch.[3]

---

[1] Most recently, Eric A. Posner's review of Rahul Sager's *Secrets and Leaks: The Dilemma of State Secrecy* (2013) is just one indication that the competency claim continues to be vital and current in the discussion of the Court's role in national security cases. Eric A. Posner, *The Paradox of Reforming the Secrecy-Industrial Complex*, The New Republic, Nov. 11, 2013, http://www.newrepublic. com/article/115291/rahul-sagars-secret-leaks-reviewed-eric-posner ("Judges have pled time and again that they lack the training and knowledge to second-guess soldiers and spies.").

[2] Chicago & S. Air Lines, Inc., v. Waterman S.S. Corp., 333 U.S. 103, 111 (1948). The views that Justice Jackson expressed in his opinion for the Court in *Chicago & South Air Lines, Inc.* were in accord with those in his dissent in *Korematsu v. United States*, 323 U.S. 214, 244–246 (1945) (Jackson, J., dissenting). But see United States v. Reynolds, 345 U.S. 1 (1953), in which Jackson dissented for the reasons expressed by the Third Circuit—that is, he supported an *in camera, ex parte* review by an Article III judge of the information that the executive asserted must be protected by the state secrets privilege. Jackson's broad experience in government, as well as being the chief American prosecutor at the Nuremberg trials, combined with his capacity to write an eloquent and elegant sentence, have given Jackson's views urging a hands-off attitude unusual authority and influence. But there is a modicum of evidence suggesting that Jackson revised his view on this crucial issue. For example, in *United States v. Reynolds*, Jackson dissented without opinion, but he did note that he endorsed the opinion of the Third Circuit Court of Appeals, which took the view that a district court should review the actual documents the executive sought to keep confidential under the state secrets privilege, and that the court had the authority to disagree with the executive over whether the privilege did or did not encompass the information in dispute and to make findings of fact against the government if the government refused to comply with a judicial order requiring the executive to disclose the information to the other side. *See* United States v. Reynolds, 345 U.S. 1, 12 (1953).

[3] For expressions of this perspective, see generally Hamdi v. Rumsfeld, 542 U.S. 507, 579–599 (2004) (Thomas, J., dissenting); New York Times v. United States, 403 U.S. 713, 752–759 (1971) (Harlan, J., dissenting); Youngstown Sheet & Tube Co. v. Sawyer, 343 U.S. 579, 667–710 (1952) (Vinson, C.J., dissenting). Jackson's statements in 1948 shed light on his 1944 opinion in *Korematsu*. In that historic opinion, Jackson concluded that the civilian courts should not

Initially it must be emphasized that the claim of judicial incompetence in national security cases is itself an unsupported surmise. There is no evidence that judges are incompetent to decide legal questions in cases involving national security. Given the intensity of judicial deference over the decades, it might be thought that no such evidence existed because, for example, the Supreme Court has not decided cases implicating national security and therefore their competence has not been tested. But that is not the case.[4] For example, the

"execute a military expedient that has no place in law under the Constitution." Jackson supported his claim with the assertion:

> In the very nature of things, military decisions are not susceptible of intelligent judicial appraisal. They do not pretend to rest on evidence, but are made on information that often would not be admissible and on assumptions that could not be proved. Information in support of an order could not be disclosed to courts without danger that it would reach the enemy. Neither can courts act on communications made in confidence. Hence courts can never have any real alternative to accepting the mere declaration of the authority that issued the order that it was reasonably necessary from a military viewpoint. (Korematsu v. United States, 323 U.S. 214, 245 (1944) (Jackson, J., dissenting))

See also Judge Richard A. Posner, Not a Suicide Pact 9 (2006) ("Judges, knowing little about the needs of national security, are unlikely to oppose their own judgments to that of the executive branch, which is responsible for the defense of the nation. They are especially unlikely to interpose *constitutional* objections because of the difficulty of amending the Constitution to correct judicial error.").

[4] In 1952, the president pressed the Supreme Court to uphold the seizure of the nation's steel mills so as to avoid a labor strike that would interrupt steel production and, that it asserted, would put American troops fighting a land war in Korea in danger. In trying to convince the Court to uphold the seizure, the executive's brief relied heavily on national security considerations. Thus, the brief recited some of the factual findings President Truman made in the Executive Order directing the seizure, which included the following:

> Whereas American fighting men and fighting men of other nations of the United Nations are now engaged in deadly combat with the forces of aggression in Korea, and forces of the United States are stationed elsewhere overseas for the purpose of participating in the defense of the Atlantic Community against aggression; and
>
> Whereas the weapons and other materials needed by our armed forces and by those joined with us in the defense of the free world are produced to a great extent in this country, and steel is an indispensable component of substantially all of such weapons and materials; and
>
> Whereas steel is likewise indispensable to the carrying out of programs of the Atomic Energy Commission of vital importance to our defense efforts; and
>
> Whereas a continuing and uninterrupted supply of steel is also indispensable to the maintenance of the economy of the United States, upon which our military strength depends; and
>
> Whereas a work stoppage would immediately jeopardize and imperil our national defense and the defense of those joined with us in resisting aggression, and would add to the continuing danger of our soldiers, sailors, and airmen engaged in combat in the

field (Brief for Petitioners at 29–30, Youngstown Sheet & Tube Co. v. Sawyer, 343 U.S. 579 (1952) (No. 745))

These findings linked steel production to, among other factors, providing armaments to "our soldiers, sailors, and airmen engaged in combat in the field," and they were supplemented with additional claims. The brief set the Korean War in a broader context so the war in Asia was part of a global pattern of Soviet Union aggression that had annexed Lithuania, Latvia, and Estonia; had established governing regimes in "Poland, Rumania, Hungary, Bulgaria, and Czechoslovakia," which "completely subordinated the interests of those countries to the interests of the Soviet Union"; had threatened the independence of Greece, Turkey, and Iran; and had attempted to "exploit the temporary weakness of the devastated nations of Western Europe." *Id.* at 31. Moreover, the brief pointed out that in 1949 "the Soviet Union produced an atomic explosion," thus doing away with the argument that the "United States' exclusive possession of atomic weapons constituted a powerful deterrent to Soviet aggression." *Id.* at 34.

Against those developments the brief set forth an argument linking "steel and defense," essentially claiming that steel is the "basic commodity involved in the manufacture of substantially all weapons, munitions, and equipment produced in the United States." *Id.* at 39. To make the point more powerful, the brief quoted Secretary of Defense Robert A. Lovett: "A work stoppage in the steel industry will result immediately in serious curtailment of production of essential weapons and munitions of all kinds; if permitted to continue, it would weaken the defense effort in all critical areas and would imperil the safety of our fighting men and that of the Nation." *Id.* at 41.

These were forceful claims made during wartime that tied the safety of combat troops to the seizure and prevention of a work stoppage. Nonetheless, the Court concluded that the president lacked the authority to seize the mills and ordered his secretary of commerce to return the running of the mills to its owners. Upon the return of the mills, a steel strike ensued for several weeks, but there was no steel shortage.

A second example is the Pentagon Papers case, *New York Times Co. v. United States,* 403 U.S. 713, 714 (1971). In 1971, the Nixon administration sued the *New York Times* and the *Washington Post,* claiming that further publication by the newspapers of a top-secret Pentagon history of America's involvement in Vietnam from 1945 to 1968—a history popularly known as the Pentagon Papers—would cause immediate and irreparable harm to the national security. The suit, commenced on Tuesday, June 15, was the first time the executive sought to restrain the press from publishing information in its control on the ground that the publication would seriously harm the nation's security. In each of the two cases—one in New York and one in Washington— the Nixon administration had the burden of proof, meaning that the executive had to submit evidence that warranted an injunction and its failure to submit such evidence would result in a denial of the requested relief, and that would be the case even if such evidence existed and the executive's lawyers—for whatever the reason—failed to offer it into evidence.

Eleven days after the commencement of the *New York Times's* lawsuit, the executive filed a sealed brief in the Supreme Court that set forth the main national security claims it argued warranted an injunction. In sum, the brief contended that future publication would "likely close up channels of communication which otherwise would have some opportunity of facilitating the closing of the Vietnam war"; would likely slow the "rate at which the United States could withdraw its troops from Vietnam"; could result in the disclosure of the "names and activities of CIA agents still active in Southeast Asia"; would disclose military plans of the South East Asia Treaty Organization"; could disclose United States intelligence estimate of the Soviet Union's "reaction to the Vietnam War," which in turn would provide the Soviets insights into United States intelligence activities; would disclose United States intelligence estimates of Soviet capacity to provide "various types of weapons to North Vietnam"; would likely endanger the United States if the newspapers reported on an internal memorandum of the Joint Chiefs of Staff "containing

Supreme Court ruled that President Truman's seizure of the nation's steel mills was unconstitutional, even though the Truman administration argued that the purpose of the seizure was to avoid a steel strike that would create a steel shortage and that such a shortage would put the safety of American armed forces fighting the Korean War in danger. A strike did result and there was no steel shortage. Also, the high court denied the Nixon administration an injunction barring *the New York Times* and *the Washington Post* from publishing excerpts from a secret Pentagon history of United States involvement in Vietnam from 1945 to 1968, even though the Nixon administration contended that further publication would irreparably harm the nation's security. The subsequent publications did no harm to the nation's security.

The competency claim highlights the fact the federal judges are generalists and may not have any special knowledge about or experience with security matters. But that might also be true for other matters of great importance to the nation, such as health care, antitrust matters, the financing of political campaigns, environmental issues, the economy,[5] health care,[6] and scientific study.[7] So if competence is the determinative factor in deciding whether judges should greatly defer to the executive in security cases, it is likely that judges would be disqualified in many other types of cases, and that is not the nation's practice.

If there is merit to Justice Jackson's suggestion that security matters are essentially political and not legal in nature, then it could be claimed that national security matters are indeed beyond the reach of judges. But Jackson never did explain why

---

a recommendation that a nuclear response might be required in the event of a Chinese attack on Thailand"; would disclose a 1968 telegram from the United States Ambassador to the Soviet Union; would disclose sensitive information pertaining to the activities of the National Security Agency that would be harmful to the national security; and would result in disclosures that might interfere with discussions aimed at securing the release of prisoners of war. David Rudenstine, The Day the Presses Stopped: A History of the Pentagon Papers Case 268–270 (1996).

Four days later, the Supreme Court ruled against the executive on the ground that it had failed to offer adequate evidence to support its most serious allegations. In reaching this conclusion, the Court ruled that "[a]ny system of prior restraints of expression comes to this Court bearing a heavy presumption against its constitutional validity," and for the executive to prevail, it "carries a heavy burden of showing justification for the imposition of such a restraint." New York Times Co. v. United States, 403 U.S. 713, 714 (1971). The Court concluded that the executive did not satisfy its burden of proof.

The *Times* and the *Washington Post* continued their publications, and some years later Erwin Griswold, the United States solicitor general who presented the executive's case to the Supreme Court, wrote: "In hindsight, it is clear to me that no harm was done by publication of the Pentagon Papers." David Rudenstine, The Day the Presses Stopped: A History of the Pentagon Papers Case 327 (1996).

[5] NLRB v. Jones & Laughlin Steel Corp., 301 U.S. 1 (1937).

[6] Nat'l Fed'n of Indep. Bus. v. Sebelius, 132 S. Ct. 2566 (2012).

[7] Ass'n for Molecular Pathology v. Myriad Genetics, Inc., 133 S. Ct. 2107 (2013).

national security issues could not be presented as legal issues, and before he died he twice indicated—by an opinion in one case[8] and by a vote in another[9]— that he had backed off from this very general point. More importantly, the suggestion that national security decisions are not amenable to the judicial process is inconsistent with past Supreme Court practice and lacks a coherent theoretical basis.

Closely allied to the idea that judges are not competent to decide security matters is the claim that the judicial process is totally inappropriate for making decisions that affect national security operations. Underlying this position is the fact that speed is often essential to ongoing operations that put the members of the armed forces in harm's way, and speed is not one of the virtues of the judicial process. Rather, the judicial process is slow and laden with procedural rules designed to enhance fairness and the search for the truth. As important as those considerations are, they may not be the most important considerations when the nation's security is imminently threatened.

Thus, there is no question that a lawsuit that challenged the legality of the D-Day invasion only days before the invasion on one ground or another would be completely inappropriate. Putting aside issues of subject matter and personal jurisdiction, the idea that an imminent military operation on which the fate of many nations depended could be upended by the initiation of a judicial proceeding is beyond conceivable. But an imagined D-Day hypothetical is fundamentally different from a lawsuit brought challenging the internment of the Japanese Americans during World War II, or the imprisonment of U.S. citizens identified as enemy combatants after 9/11, or the detention of those detained in Guantanamo. In these latter cases, as is true in so many other cases, the focus of a lawsuit is on past events that arguably resulted in the violation of important constitutional rights by executive officials. In such situations, the incomparable hazards presented by the D-Day hypothetical do not arise.

Quite apart from the issue of competence, judges may well shy away from the responsibility of making a decision that might affect national security for several other reasons. They might do this because they do not believe that the governing scheme has vested them with responsibility over such matters, or because they might resist having any responsibility for a decision affecting the nation's security. These are understandable inclinations. Making decisions that may have serious consequences for others—and in the case of judges making decisions that affect the national security, are grave decisions— should cause pause because the responsibility is great. And adopting a posture of deference in such cases may seem to be a responsible path that reflects Solomonic wisdom. But does it? Is it

---

[8] Youngstown Sheet & Tube Co. v. Sawyer, 343 U.S. 579 (1952).
[9] United States v. Reynolds, 345 U.S. 1 (1953).

Solomonic? Not deciding by employing doctrines of deference to avoid deciding the merits of a case is not a decision on the merits, but it is a decision, and it
does not leave matters untouched. Instead, the decision vests the executive with
judicially unreviewable discretion on the matter at hand, and that has serious,
harmful consequences. As a result, it is more illusion than reality that a judge
completely avoids responsibility in cases implicating national security by employing deferential doctrines to dismiss a case.

In some narrow circumstances, judges may fear that if they exercise a more
meaningful judicial review, the Congress might seek to exercise its substantial
powers over the courts or that the executive may not enforce judicial judgments or comply with them. That, too, is an understandable perspective. The
constitutional design provided checks for the exercise of judicial power by
granting the Congress control over the Supreme Court's appellate jurisdiction
and by making the courts dependent on the executive to enforce its judgments.
As a result, Congress has, on many occasions, sought to curtail the high court's
appellate jurisdiction, and there were celebrated historical moments when the
Court's dependency on the executive to enforce its judgments was highlighted.

A judicial recognition of the Court's own vulnerabilities and allowing such
recognition to influence the exercise of judicial authority receives some support in the scholarly literature on the ground that a court that adopts this posture in the appropriate circumstances is wise to avoid a "showdown" it could
not win in order to survive as a meaningful governing institution.[10] That is a
very appealing position and it favors judicial caution, if not retreat, in the face
of possible very serious conflict with the two coequal branches of government.
But it is a position that is not beyond question. No one would claim that the
potential power of the Congress or of the executive to blunt the courts should
always cause the court to be deferential. More to the point, no one puts forth
a set of guidelines that indicate when the Court should avoid a confrontation.
And the idea that courts should always defer to avoid a confrontation with the
executive is untenable and inconsistent with the Court's own history.

The Supreme Court is the least dangerous of the three coequal branches,
but it does itself and the nation a profound disservice when it allows its weakness to be a reason for it to be weak.

In one opinion, Chief Justice Rehnquist stated that it would be "unacceptable"
if judges in presiding over a matter made an error that injured the nation's security.[11] That may be the only time that a member of the Supreme Court set
forth a standard that would, if observed, more or less completely immobilize

---

[10] United States v. Reynolds, 345 U.S. 1, 11 (1953).

[11] Tenet v. Doe, 544 U.S. 1, 11 (2005).

the judiciary. Nonetheless, even though not expressed, it may be a disposition that influences the approach of many other judges.

The nub of this attitude would seem to be a view that the protection of the nation's security by far and away trumps any other countervailing value or consideration a case may put forward. At first blush, such a position may seem defensible. But that is only at first blush. The idea that it would be unacceptable for courts to participate in a process that injured national security might be plausible if the concept of national security was very narrowly and carefully defined, and if there was broad agreement on the concept. But these conditions do not exist.

In cases implicating national security, the executive, oddly enough, generally defines the concept of national security both too broadly and too narrowly. On the one hand, the executive would include within the term *national security* not only military plans, intelligence operations, ongoing CIA covert operations, and effective NSA surveillance programs but also just about every CIA and NSA operation, every nuance involving diplomatic relations, reasons for terminating government employees, files concerning events that occurred thirty or forty or even fifty years ago, and information that might be embarrassing and place a particular group and agency in an unfavorable light. On the other hand, the executive excludes from the concept of national security a range of other important considerations such as the preservation of separations of powers, upholding the rule of law, providing individuals allegedly wronged by the executive with a judicial remedy, and assuring that the electorate is adequately informed about national security matters so that it may responsibly exercise its right to vote.[12]

Furthermore, our national policy, which is dedicated to democratic values, individual liberty, and an open society, is premised on a more complex configuration of considerations than simply reducing to the greatest extent possible risks to the national security. For example, the nation runs the risk of the press reporting information that is classified and may injure national security so as to assure that the press is free of government censorship. It does that because of the assumption that an uncensored press is essential to a vital democracy.

---

[12] Furthermore, this outlook overlooks the importance of what is often termed "soft power," which emphasizes such factors as the freedom of American private and public institutions, the scope of individual liberties, and the preservation of American ideals such as the rule of law that greatly contribute to America's standing in the world. *See generally* Joseph S. Nye, Jr., Soft Power: The Means to Success in World Politics (2004). President Barack Obama recently acknowledged this basic political tenet in a speech at the National Defense University: "So America is at a crossroads. We must define the nature and scope of this struggle, or else it will define us. We have to be mindful of James Madison's warning that 'No nation could preserve its freedom in the midst of continual warfare.'" President Barack Obama, Remarks at the National Defense University (May 23, 2013), https://www.whitehouse.gov/the-press-office/2013/05/23/remarks-president-national-defense-university.

Or, in other words, protecting the nation's security is of vital importance, but it is not an absolute consideration—that means that it is a prominent consideration but is balanced by countervailing considerations in the distribution of rights, responsibilities, and authority in the constitutional arrangement.

A similar analysis is appropriate in thinking about the shared responsibilities between the executive and the Congress over national security matters. For example, under various federal statutes, the executive must give notice to Congress of classified national security policies and initiatives, even though the dissemination of that information to members of Congress and thus their staffs runs the risk of an unauthorized disclosure to the press. If the nation wanted to diminish the risk of unauthorized disclosure, it almost certainly would not prize a separation-of-powers rationale that favors checking and balancing the executive by means of congressional involvement. Yet that is what the nation does, and it does that because it is concerned about the concentration of unchecked power in the executive, even if that enhances the risk of an improper disclosure that might dilute the national security.

Against these important examples that illustrate that national security is a pivotal but not the only important consideration that guides the structure of the constitutional order, it is fair to ask why courts should drastically limit their authority so as to avoid making what Rehnquist considered an unacceptable error, when to do so requires courts to betray a fundamental role in the constitutional order. There is no persuasive response to this query, at least within the paradigm of trying to define the concept of security.

The stool of deference rests on still another leg. There are hints in opinions to the effect that the paramount importance of national security matters requires that the politically accountable branches, not the politically insulated judiciary, have primary if not exclusive responsibility in deciding such matters. As Robert Jackson claimed in 1948, decisions involving foreign affairs are by their "very nature" "political, not judicial" and are "wholly confided by our Constitution to the political departments of the government, Executive and Legislative."[13]

Initially, it should be emphasized that, just as with the claim of judicial competence, this claim that courts should be disabled because they are politically

---

[13] Chicago & S. Air Lines, Inc., v. Waterman S.S. Corp., 333 U.S. 103, 111 (1948). Chief Justice Earl Warren expressed a similar viewpoint in a 1962 speech. In referring to *Hirabayashi v. United States*, 320 U.S. 81 (1943), and *Korematsu v. United States*, 323 U.S. 214 (1944), Warren stated that these "decisions demonstrate dramatically that there are some circumstances in which the Court will, in effect, conclude that it is simply not in a position to reject descriptions by the Executive of the degree of military necessity. Thus, in a case like *Hirabayashi*, only the Executive is qualified to determine whether, for example, an invasion is imminent." Earl Warren, The Bill of Rights and the Military, 37 N.Y.U. L. Rev. 181, 192 (1962).

insulated is so sweeping in character that the scope of its sweep undermines its own plausibility. Because courts routinely decide many matters of high significance to the nation—such as same-sex marriage, abortion, affirmative action, the right to die, health care, voting rights, and campaign financing— it is hardly obvious why courts should be disabled because of the political accountability argument only in national security matters.[14] Moreover, because national security matters vary greatly in importance, it is unconvincing to claim that the political insulation of judges should prompt judges to defer to the executive to the same exceptional degree in all national security matters.

More important, the charge against courts that they are politically unaccountable is overly simplistic. Courts are hardly immune from political and popular influences. Congress has substantial control over the jurisdiction of the courts,[15] and the executive influences the direction of the courts through the appointment of judges.[16] Even more, there is substantial evidence indicating, as Professor Barry Friedman has observed, that, over time, public opinion has a shaping influence on judicial outcomes: history teaches that "through a dialogue with the justices, the Constitution comes to reflect the

---

[14] Indeed, there are some who take the position that courts should defer because of the anti-majoritarian nature of judicial review in all such cases, and they argue that judges should defer to the politically accountable branches except when a constitutional limitation is plain, concrete, and specific. That is, in fact, the argument that J. Harvie Wilkinson III sets forth in *Cosmic Constitutional Theory: Why Americans are Losing Their Inalienable Right to Self-Governance* (Oxford University Press, 2012). He urges a broad and radical form of judicial deference in almost all cases. For a critical review of the Wilkinson book, see David Rudenstine, *Self-Government and the Judicial Function*, 92 Tex. L. Rev. 161 (2013) (reviewing J. Harvie Wilkinson III, Cosmic Constitutional Theory: Why Americans Are Losing Their Inalienable Right to Self-Governance (2012)).

[15] Hamdan v. Rumsfeld, 548 U.S. 557 (2006); *see also* Ex parte McCardle, 74 U.S. 506 (1868). Chief Justice Earl Warren remarked on the chilling effect of congressional control over judicial power:

> In times of stress, the Court is not only vulnerable, to some extent, to the emotions of our people, but also to action by Congress in restricting what that body may consider judicial interference with the needs of security and defense. Following the Civil War, Congress actually exercised its constitutional powers to provide for the rules governing the appellate jurisdiction of the Supreme Court, for this very purpose. See Ex parte McCardle, 73 U.S. (6 Wall.) 318 (1867); 74 U.S. (7 Wall.) 506 (1868). (Earl Warren, The Bill of Rights and the Military, 37 N.Y.U. L. Rev. 181, 192 n.29 (1962))

[16] Charles M. Blow of the *New York Times* has highlighted the composition of the United States Supreme Court by the political party of the president who nominated each member of the Court. His statistics indicated that from 1976 to 2008, the Court membership consisted at any one time of no less than seven members appointed by a Republican Party president. In his editorial, Blow wrote that "Supreme Court justices . . . [are] where a president can exert power long after he has officially faded from power." Charles M. Blow, *Court Fight*, N.Y. Times, Nov. 1, 2013, http://www.nytimes.com/2013/11/02/opinion/blow-court-fight.html?_r=0.

considered judgment of the American people regarding their most fundamental values."[17]

More directly, instead of the federal judiciary being characterized as antidemocratic, the judiciary may be viewed as an effective "vehicle for self-government."[18] Almost a half century ago, Professor Louis Jaffe pointed out that it was, even at that time, "a commonplace that the individual citizen in our vast, multitudinous complexes feels excluded from government," and that as "governmental power expands, individual participation in the exercise of power contracts."[19] In light of that observation, the judicial process offered an injured individual an important forum for relief. And that is so not only for those seeking to vindicate minority rights against majority discrimination, but for others who seek to participate in the governing process but who are mainly outside the political process. From this vantage point, the judicial process enhances citizens' participation, which, Jaffe noted, is as much a part of American democracy as majority rule,[20] and as such is "thoroughly consistent with the primacy of majority rule."[21]

Furthermore, the implication of the antidemocratic charge against courts is that the office of the presidency, the executive administrative agencies, and the executive departments that comprise the National Security State are at the opposite end of the accountability spectrum and are highly politically accountable. But that is surely an exaggerated position that requires qualification. A second-term president holds office for four years on the legitimacy of the past presidential election but is no longer politically accountable.[22] More strikingly, the numerous departments and agencies directly responsible for national security function mainly in secret. Thus, the National Security Council, CIA, National Security Agency, and intelligence agencies within the Pentagon function in secret[23] and have only limited accountability to Congress, and

---

[17] Barry Friedman, *The Will of the People: How Public Opinion Has Influenced the Supreme Court and Shaped the Meaning of the Constitution* 367–368 (2009).

[18] Louis L. Jaffe, *The Citizen as Litigant in Public Actions: The Non-Hohfeldian or Ideological Plaintiff*, 116 U. Pa. L. Rev. 1033, 1045 (1968).

[19] *Id.* at 1044.

[20] *Id.* at 1045.

[21] *Id.* Supreme Court Justice William O. Douglas made a similar point in his concurrence in *Flast v. Cohen*, 392 U.S. 83, 111 (1968) ("The judiciary is an indispensable part of the operation of our federal system. With the growing complexities of government it is often the one and only place where effective relief can be obtained . . . . The individual is almost certain to be plowed under, unless he has a well-organized active political group to speak for him. The church is one. The press is another. The union is a third. But if a powerful sponsor is lacking, individual liberty withers—in spite of glowing opinions and resounding constitutional phrases.").

[22] U.S. Const. amend. XXII.

[23] Although the Constitution states that "a regular Statement and Account of the Receipts and Expenditures of all public Money shall be published from time to time," U.S. Const. art. I, §9, cl. 7,

then only to few members on select committees, and almost no accountability to the public.[24] Once the political accountability claim is placed in this light, the merits of the claim can be turned inside out for the very public nature of judicial proceedings, instead of being antidemocratic in nature, contribute to the transparency of national security policies and operations.[25]

the CIA's budget is secret. *See* United States v. Richardson, 418 U.S. 166 (1974). Thus, the voting public learns about CIA expenditures only when the executive makes such expenditures public or when a government official makes an unauthorized disclosure, as was very recently done regarding the "bags" of cash the CIA leaves in the office of Afghan President Hamid Karzai. *See* Matthew Rosenberg, *Karzai's Office Gets Bags Full of C.I.A. Cash*, N.Y. Times, Apr. 29, 2013, at A1, http://www.nytimes.com/2013/04/29/world/asia/cia-delivers-cash-to-afghan-leaders-office.html;   *see also* Robert M. Chesney, *National Security Fact Deference*, 95 Va. L. Rev. 1361, 1430–1431 (2009), for a reference to the undemocratic nature of "the decision making role for the Administrative Review Board (ARB) mechanism for Guantanamo detainees. . . .. [T]he nature of the ARB's composition . . . and the non-transparent nature of its work . . . call into question whether there is a meaningful nexus between ARB decisions and democratic accountability." *Id.*

[24] Unauthorized disclosures by government employees—so-called leaks—are a staple of national security reporting. Indeed, some even maintain that because of the enormous net cast by the United States classification system, there would be no meaningful national security reporting absent unauthorized disclosures. Max Frankel, Opinion, *Where Did Our 'Inalienable Rights' Go?*, N.Y. Times, June 23, 2013, at SR1, http://www.nytimes.com/2013/06/23/opinion/sunday/where-did-our-inalienable-rights-go.html; Andrew Beaujon, *Jill Abramson: Leak Prosecutions Threaten to "Rob the Public of Vital Information*,*"* Poynter, June 18, 2012, http://www.poynter.org/latest-news/mediawire/177554/jill-abramson-leak-prosecutions-threaten-to-rob-the-public-of-vital-information/ ; Arthur S. Brisbane, Opinion, *National Secrets and National Security*, N.Y. Times, June 17, 2012, at SR12, http://www.nytimes.com/2012/06/17/opinion/sunday/national-secrets-and-national-security.html. For an historic statement of the importance of unauthorized disclosures in informing the American public about national security matters, see the affidavit of Max Frankel, dated June 17, 1971, filed in the Pentagon Papers case, in which he stated: "Without the use of 'secrets' that I shall attempt to explain in this affidavit, there could be no adequate diplomatic, military and political reporting of the kind our people take for granted, either abroad or in Washington and there could be no mature system of communication between the Government and the people." Affidavit of Max Frankel, United States v. N.Y. Times, 328 F. Supp. 324 (S.D.N.Y. 1971) (No. 71 Civ. 2662). In that regard, the Obama administration has initiated aggressive investigation of leaks that "has led to more than twice as many prosecutions as there were in all previous administrations combined." Sharon LaFraniere, *Math Behind Leak Crackdown: 153 Cases, 4 Years, 0 Indictments*, N.Y. Times, July 21, 2013, at A1, http://www.nytimes.com/2013/07/21/us/politics/math-behind-leak-crackdown-153-cases-4-years-0-indictments.html.

[25] Much less significantly but worthy of comment, the claim that courts should defer to the politically accountable branches of government in national security cases exists within a broader perspective premised on the claim that an overreaching judiciary would sap vital energy from the political process and ultimately undermine the capacity of the people to self-govern. Over the decades, a chorus of legal giants advocated judicial restraint. Among others, they are James B. Thayer, Oliver Wendell Holmes, Learned Hand, Felix Frankfurter, Alexander M. Bickel, and John Marshall Harlan. Holmes captured that disposition in one of his elegant epigrams: "[t]he first duty of a judge is to remember that he is not God." David Rudenstine, *Self-Government and the Judicial Function*, 92 Tex. L. Rev. 161, 163 (2013) (quoting Felix Frankfurter, Calvert Magruder, 72 Harv. L. Rev.

The undemocratic nature of judicial review has been a central theme in assessing the proper role of courts for more than two centuries. But as important as the theme is, it has no special bearing on the scope of judicial review in national security cases as opposed to other important issues that are presented to the Supreme Court.[26]

There is still yet another twist to the arguments favoring judicial deference. This contention maintains that meaningful judicial review aimed at checking executive abuse is unnecessary because courts are not the only potential governing body capable of checking possible executive abuse. Congress has important oversight responsibilities, and former Chief Justice, William Rehnquist, on one important occasion, argued that senior executive officials

1201, 1202 (1959)). Those who urge judicial deference are as aware as any of the many ways that the Constitution is undemocratic. Thus, for example, they are cognizant that the Electoral College, not the popular vote, selects the president, and that the constitution of the Senate is undemocratic. Nonetheless, they insist that the undemocratic nature of judicial power presents a special threat to democratic values and for this reason judicial deference is required.

The general idea of deference should not be confused with complete abdication. Thus, proponents of deference would surely want courts to enforce the constitutional requirement that no one be "eligible" for the office of president "who shall not have attained to the age of thirty-five," or that the House or the Senate shall only punish a member for disorderly behavior with the "concurrence of two thirds" of the voting members. U.S. Const. art. II, §1. While each of these clauses leaves room for disagreement over the precise meaning of each clause, the scope of judicial discretion available is much narrower than it is in construing the grant of authority to Congress "to regulate commerce . . . among the several states," or the rule that the federal government shall not inflict "cruel and unusual punishments," or the prohibition that states may not "deprive any person of life, liberty, or property, without due process of law," or deny a person "equal protection of the laws." U.S. Const. With regard to these clauses, as well as others, proponents of deference want judges to construe such spacious words narrowly so that they do not severely limit the discretion of the politically accountable branches. Because advocates of deference favor a narrow construction of the open-ended clauses of the Constitution, they certainly oppose any construction of such clauses to protect, for example, the right of privacy, which today is a shorthand for such rights as the right to an abortion, to same-sex sex, or to same-sex marriage.

As is apparent, an aggressive posture of deference potentially cuts a broad swath through judicial authority. Indeed, as noted, a really aggressive expression of deference would run the risk of turning judges into rubber stamps for congressional and executive policies and conduct.

As may be evident, the core problem confronting anyone promoting deference is to define what role courts should have in the governing scheme. To simply assert that courts need to exhibit proper respect for the coordinate branches of government in deciding cases provides no guidance to a judge confronting a case in which an individual asserts a claim based on the Constitution against the state. And to claim that proper deference means that courts should always uphold legislation or executive action absent an unmistakable violation of a specific clause of the Constitution would more or less turn courts into a rubber stamp and eliminate them from fulfilling a meaningful role, even as the least dangerous branch, in governing.

[26] The role of courts in rendering decisions based on the Constitution that nullify actions of the politically accountable branches in a democratic society is complicated and well beyond the

could be relied upon to check the assertion of questionable executive authority.[27] In addition to these potential avenues of checking the executive, the press, watchdog groups, and what is termed "lawfare" also all contribute to checking the executive.

There is merit to the claim that the courts are not the only institution that can check executive power, and there is special merit to the claim that Congress has far more potential authority to check the executive than do the courts.[28] But conceding those important points is not the end of the analysis. In the constitutional scheme, courts have primary responsibility that neither of the other branches of government can perform effectively to provide wronged individuals with a remedy. In addition, to assure that the president and senior executive officials are not acting above the law in the national security context, courts must state what the law is, and courts cannot perform that function by dismissing cases on technical grounds. Lastly, there is no doubt that the Supreme

scope of this book. Nonetheless, it is important to note that the discussion often is framed in a paradigm that makes assumptions about the accountability of the political branches that is simplistic to a fault. Thus, a recent report by the *New York Times* on a 2,000-page tax and spending bill points out that "54 words that temporarily preserved a loophole sought by the hotel, restaurant and gambling industries, along with billionaire Wall Street investors, that allowed them to put real estate in trusts and avoid taxes" were added to the bill with "little time for lawmakers to consider" the merits of the proposal. The report also mentioned that a Mississippi senator obtained a provision to build a "$640 million National Security Cutter in Mississippi that the Coast Guard says it does not need," that a Maine senator secured "an extra $1 billion for a Navy destroyer" that is likely to be built in Maine, and that the Defense Department had "not requested money for the additional ship in this year's budget." Eric Lipton and Liz Moyer, *Hospitality and Gambling Interests Delay Closing of Billion-Dollar Tax Loophole*, N.Y. Times, Dec. 20, 2015.

[27] Federal Data Banks, Computers, and the Bill of Rights: Hearings Before the Subcommittee on Constitutional Rights on Federal Data Bank, Computers, and the Bill of Rights of the Committee on the Judiciary United States Senate, 92nd Cong. 1 (1971) (statement of William H. Rehnquist, Assistant Attorney General, Office of Legal Counsel, Department of Justice, Privacy, Surveillance, and the Law).

[28] As previously suggested, the claim that judicial oversight is unnecessary because, as then Assistant Attorney General William H. Rehnquist urged, the executive will discipline itself, was properly dismissed at the time by Senator Sam J. Ervin, Jr. as an "amazing theory" that was contradicted by indisputable facts known at the time Rehnquist made the claim. *See* Senator Sam J. Ervin, Jr., *Privacy and Government Investigations*, 1971 L.F. 137, 147–148 (1971). The following year, law professor George C. Christie noted that Rehnquist's suggestion that the American public should trust the executive "to insure that the Government's right of surveillance is not abused," was effectively undermined by the fact that the executive has not "informed the American people of the exact nature of its surveillance policies," and that it had not "told the American people how it determines who is a legitimate subject of surveillance," or "what criteria, if any, it uses in deciding when to terminate the surveillance of a particular individual or group once the surveillance has begun." George C. Christie, *Government Surveillance and Individual Freedom: A Proposed Statutory response to Laird v. Tatum and the Broader Problem of Government Surveillance of the Individual*, 47 N.Y.U. L. Rev., 871, 873 (1972).

Court has a special status in the republic and that the impact of its judgments goes well beyond the boundaries of the law and seeps into the nation's political discourse, affecting the making of policy at every level of government.

Judicial deference in national security cases rests on a dominating juristic mind driven by an unbending way of thinking that resists serious engagement over the merits of its premises. As a result, the legal doctrines that insulate the executive in cases implicating national security have expanded incrementally over many decades, gathering precedent after precedent in support of the mindset that in turn further insulates the mindset from a reexamination of its premises. This unfortunate dynamic makes it unlikely that the mindset will in fact be reconsidered before many of today's judges leave the bench and are replaced by judges not afraid to reassess accepted premises.

16

Be Last, Not First

No one quarrels with the claim that the Constitution allocates primary responsibility for the nation's security to the executive and Congress. But primary responsibility is not exclusive responsibility. And yet, all too frequently, the Supreme Court defers to the point of abdicating its responsibilities in national security cases out of respect for the executive's judgment. Because judicial abdication has resulted in profoundly harmful consequences to the nation, without necessarily protecting the nation's security, the members of the Supreme Court need to free themselves from the juristic mind that embraces undue deference and reshape the entire range of doctrines the Court has crafted over decades that combine to insulate the executive from meaningful judicial accountability.[1]

The Court can accomplish this reshaping by defining a disposition between abdication and usurpation.[2] That is so because the concept of judicial deference is elastic and fluid, and the various constructs of responsible deference fall out along a spectrum that, at one end, runs from abdication to, at the other end, usurpation.[3] In other words, just as there is a noteworthy gap between

---

[1] Although the degree of judicial abdication is striking and unsettling, for some it would seem that the federal courts can never be deferential enough. Thus, following the terrorist explosion of a Russian passenger plane, bombings in Lebanon, and the attacks in Paris—all in November of 2015—former U.S. Attorney General Michael B. Mukasey and former Assistant Attorney General Jamil N. Jaffer wrote a column in the *Wall Street Journal* complaining about the judiciary joining the Congress and President Obama in restricting "America's intelligence-gathering capabilities." Michael B. Mukasey and Jamil N. Jaffer, *Time to Remove the Surveillance Blinders*, Wall St. J., Nov. 24, 2015.

[2] Robert M. Chesney, *National Security Fact Deference*, 95 Va. L. Rev. 1361, 1377 (2009) (quoting Judge Harry Pregerson, who, in an argument before the Ninth Circuit in *Hepting v. AT&T Corp.*, charged that the government wanted the Court to be a "rubber stamp."). Hepting v. AT&T Corp., 539 F.3d 1157 (9th Cir. 2008).

[3] Although this approach to the idea of deference may be obvious, it is not always acknowledged. Thus, even a highly respected scholar is capable of turning the elastic concept of deference into an either/or dichotomy—that is, a court is either deferential or it is not deferential. *See* Robert M. Chesney, *National Security Fact Deference*, 95 Va. L. Rev. 1361, 1363 (2009)

the concept of president as messenger boy and the Imperial Presidency, or the concept of war as represented by World War II and the war on terror, there is a comparable gap between the concept of judicial abdication and usurpation.[4]

There is no need to set out here the doctrinal signposts for redesigning all of the relevant doctrines, since many of these guidelines are already set out in the law reports in dissenting opinions. For example, and as set forth in earlier chapters, the dissenting opinions in recent cases discussing standing,[5] quasi-immunity,[6] and pleading rules[7] point the direction for responsible judicial decision making that would help hold the executive meaningfully accountable. Nonetheless, the one doctrinal development that lacks such contemporary dissents concerns the state secrets privilege. That privilege, which is in many ways the most radical of the deference doctrines, is at the heart of the post–World War II era judicial deference. It is the executive's ultimate fallback legal claim, and it constitutes the executive's ace in the hole in persuading judges to dismiss cases without deciding the merits.[8]

The current rules regarding the state secrets privilege have vested the executive with de facto absolute authority to decide what information should be covered by the privilege. If the current de facto absolute privilege is to be brought under responsible judicial authority, the Supreme Court, which is solely responsible for the privilege's current definition, must use its authority to change the privilege in several respects.

Judges must redefine the phrase "state secrets," and that new definition should include three elements. First, the definition must address what kind of information constitutes a state secret. A state secret should protect information such as the development and location of weapons; the location of troops,

("Ultimately, I conclude that many arguments in favor of deference are unpersuasive, but that deference nonetheless may be justified in limited circumstances.").

[4] For an unusually thoughtful inquiry into what constitutes a "war," see Deborah N. Pearlstein, *Law at the End of War*, 99 Minn. L. Rev. 143 (2014). For two recent scholarly studies of the constitutional allocation of the power to make war, see Stephen M. Griffin, Long Wars and the Constitution (2013), and Mariah Zeisberg, War Powers: The Politics of Constitutional Authority (2013).

[5] *See, e.g.,* Clapper v. Amnesty Int'l USA, 133 S. Ct. 1138, 1155 (2013) (Breyer, J., dissenting).

[6] Nixon v. Fitzgerald, 457 U.S. 731 (1982).

[7] Ashcroft v. Iqbal, 556 U.S. 662 (2008) (Souter, J., dissenting).

[8] On September 23, 2009, the Obama administration announced new "Policies and Procedures Governing Invocation of the State Secrets Privilege" that would be administered by the Department of Justice. *See* Memorandum from Attorney Gen. addressed to Heads of Exec. Departments and Agencies and Heads of Department Components (Sept. 23, 2009). The initiative effectively acknowledges the abuse of the privilege and the need for the executive to impose some control over its invocation in the courts. As constructive as that step is, the new policies do not change the rules and procedures courts follow in adjudicating conflicting claims over the executive's assertion of the privilege in a particular case.

bases, and military equipment; current military contingency plans; important ongoing intelligence operations and methods of securing intelligence; and current diplomatic relations pertaining to significant national security matters. In contrast, the term "state secret" should not privilege information merely because it is classified;[9] discloses information that would be embarrassing to a department, agency, or one or more officials;[10] discloses conduct by executive branch officials that violated federal criminal law; or alleges an injury to the nation's security that is insignificant, improbable, and unlikely to occur in the foreseeable future. Second, the privilege should be sustained only when evidence establishes that there is at least a reasonable possibility, given all of the relevant considerations, that the threatened disclosure will, in fact, result in the predicted injury. Such a linkage may seem obvious, but current case law permits sustaining the privilege without any finding regarding the probability that the alleged injury will, in fact, result from the threatened disclosure.[11] Third, the privilege should be sustained only when evidence establishes that the disclosure of the information will cause the predicted injury within the foreseeable future, as opposed to some undetermined, remote, and indefinite time in the distant future. Presently, there is no such requirement.[12]

In cases in which documents are alleged to contain state secrets, courts must review the actual documents in dispute—as opposed to a summary of them—to guard against what Chief Justice Vinson termed executive "caprice"—a caprice dramatically illustrated in the *Reynolds* case itself.[13] Such a change requires discarding the rule set forth in the *Reynolds* case[14] because

---

[9] Many reports have criticized the practice of overclassification by the federal government. *See* Garry Wills, Bomb Power: The Modern Presidency and the National Security State (2010); Daniel Patrick Moynihan, Secrecy (1998); Morton H. Halperin and Daniel N. Hoffman, National Security and the Right to Know (1977). The result of this practice is that many documents are classified as confidential, secret, or top-secret, even though they contain no information that bears on national security. Moreover, the classification system has been criticized because of the enormous delay in declassifying documents that perhaps should never have been classified in the first place. Consequently, tying the state secrets privilege to the classification system would lead to a wholesale application of the privilege, which would not be justified.

[10] The prime example of using the state secrets privilege to keep confidential documents that would otherwise embarrass the executive is *Reynolds*. *See generally* David Rudenstine, *The Irony of a Faustian Bargain: A Reconsideration of the Supreme Court's 1953* United States v. Reynolds *Decision*, 34 Cardozo L. Rev. 1283 (2013).

[11] Mohamed v. Jeppesen Dataplan, Inc., 614 F.3d 1070 (9th Cir. 2010); El-Masri v. United States, 479 F.3d 296 (4th Cir. 2007).

[12] *See* David Rudenstine, *The Courts and National Security: The Ordeal of the State Secrets Privilege*, U. of Balt. L. Rev. 37, Part I (2014).

[13] United States v. Reynolds, 345 U.S. 1, 10 (1953).

[14] That rule provides that a court should sustain the executive branch's claim of privilege without forcing the actual disclosure of the disputed information to a judge, when that judge is able

that rule means that, as a practical matter, a judge will rarely, if ever, review a disputed document to determine whether the executive branch's claim that it falls within the privilege is justified.

Many unpersuasive arguments are offered in support of the idea that judges should not actually review the documents in dispute, as opposed to reading an affidavit summarizing the documents. First, it is feared that a judge or someone in the judge's chambers or the courthouse will intentionally or inadvertently disclose a sensitive document. While such a security breach is conceivable, diligent research has disclosed no instance of such an improper disclosure.[15] Second, there was once a concern that courthouses lacked the facilities to retain top-secret documents.[16] But that consideration seems no longer valid since federal judges routinely review sensitive documents in criminal cases[17] and in Freedom of Information Act cases.[18] Third, it is claimed that in camera, ex parte disclosure of disputed documents to a judge will prompt the opposing party to insist on also having access to the documents.[19] Putting aside for a moment whether opposing counsel should have access to a disputed document, the argument is unconvincing because a judge may simply deny the

to conclude from the overall context of the case that there is a reasonable probability that the disputed information contains a state secret that would, if publicly disclosed, injure the national security.

[15] In contrast, improper disclosures by members of the executive branch are frequent.

[16] A dramatic example of the lack of security in a courthouse occurred during the frenetic litigation between the United States and the *New York Times* over the newspaper's publication of what became popularly known as the Pentagon Papers. *See* David Rudenstine, The Day the Presses Stopped: A History of the Pentagon Papers Case 112 (1998).

[17] *See, e.g.,* Classified Information Procedures Act, 18 U.S.C.A. §App. 3, Refs & Annos (West 2013).

[18] *See, e.g.,* Freedom of Information Act (FOIA), 5 U.S.C.A. §552 (West 2013); *see generally* Christina E. Wells, *"National Security" Information and the Freedom of Information Act*, 56 Admin. L. Rev. 1195, 1205–1208 (especially cases cited in n.61 and the accompanying text); Operational Files of the National Security Agency, 50 U.S.C.A. §432b(f)(1) ("[W]henever any person who has requested agency records under section 552 of Title 5 alleges that the National Security Agency has withheld records improperly because of failure to comply with any provision of this section, judicial review shall be available under the terms set forth in section 552(a)(4)(B) of Title 5.").

[19] The House of Lords cited this contention in its World War II *Duncan* opinion in support of its conclusion that a British judge should not review disputed documents in camera and ex parte. Duncan v. Cammell, Laird & Co., [1942] A.C. 624, 640–641 (H.L.) (appeal taken from Eng.). This is an unpersuasive argument for the opposing party to make, given that one alternative to judges exercising ex parte review is that judges will exercise no review at all of the disputed information. Such a stance would grant to the executive sole authority for deciding what information is or is not privileged, and such an outcome would put the opposing party at a considerable disadvantage by comparison to a procedure that included ex parte judicial review of the disputed material.

claim of access, and there is no reason to think that merely raising a claim of access will compel it. Indeed, it is clear that in some current situations judges have access to information not shared with all parties.[20]

As just noted, when the executive currently submits documents to a judge in support of its claim for a state secrets privilege, opposing counsel is denied access to them. As a result, only a judge and the executive's representatives are present at in camera proceedings. This procedure should be changed. The available evidence suggests that judges are extremely deferential to the executive's judgment on national security matters, and when that inclination is combined with a process in which the executive's judgment is unchallenged by an opposing side, there is a basis to suspect that judges are at a serious disadvantage in deciding the issue of privilege, and that they defer to the executive's judgment without exercising reasonable oversight. The presence of opposing counsel who had the requisite security clearances would assist judges in assessing the merits of the executive's claims. The procedures used in other settings in which opposing counsel has access to sensitive information to assure against an improper disclosure can be utilized to safeguard confidentiality and security.[21]

Under current law, when a trial judge is unable to determine if there is a reasonable danger that disclosure of the information in dispute would injure national security, that judge has the authority to conduct an ex parte evidentiary hearing in which a government officer testifies as to why a judge should sustain the asserted claim of privilege. Nonetheless, research has identified not one case in which a judge has exercised that authority. If judges are to retain meaningful control of the evidence in a case, they must, in appropriate circumstances, be willing to conduct an evidentiary hearing on the application of the privilege to the information in dispute.[22]

The contemporary state secrets privilege is an absolute privilege. Accordingly, once a judge decides from the overall context that there is a reasonable probability that the disputed information or document would endanger the national security if disclosed, the judge must sustain the privilege no

---

[20] See David Rudenstine, *The Courts and National Security: The Ordeal of the State Secrets Privilege*, U. of Balt. L. Rev. 37, 84 n.294–295 (2014).

[21] S. 417, 111th Cong. (2009), introduced by Senator Patrick Leahy, would have permitted opposing counsel access to the disputed documents. Moreover, in the wake of disclosures by Edward Snowden in 2013 regarding National Security Agency surveillance activities and the consequential spotlight on the secret Foreign Intelligence Surveillance Court, many have recommended that the nonadversarial nature of the FISC be changed to permit lawyers with the requisite security clearances to oppose executive request for surveillance warrants.

[22] Even the remarkably deferential position adopted by Chief Justice Vinson in the *Reynolds* decision left open the possibility of such a hearing. See David Rudenstine, *The Courts and National Security: The Ordeal of the State Secrets Privilege*, U. of Balt. L. Rev. 37, Part I (2014).

matter how insignificant or remote the danger, or how important the information may be to a party claiming injury. Thus, the current definition of the contemporary state secrets privilege permits no balancing or weighing of the comparative importance of the information to the nation's security, to the vindication of an individual's legal claims, or even to the public's interest in knowing of the executive's conduct.

The absolute character of the privilege is supported by two claims. First, the judiciary has made a policy decision that any threatened injury to national security warrants sustaining the privilege, no matter how important the disputed information may be to an allegedly seriously injured party. Second, the absolute character of the privilege seems to rest on a distrust of the judiciary's competence to resolve questions implicating national security without seriously harming the nation's security.

Contrary to the premises underlying the absolute character of the privilege, the privilege can be qualified without harming the national security. Thus, a party seeking access to the disputed documents or information could be required to establish that the disputed documents or information may contain information central to establishing liability, that the information could not be obtained in any other way, and that the party seeks the vindication of important rights. For its part, the government would have an opportunity to establish the significance of the alleged national security injury, the likelihood that the injury would in fact follow from the disclosure, and that the injury would occur within some foreseeable time frame, as opposed to some undefined moment in the future. In considering these competing claims, a court would uphold the privilege, regardless of its significance to the injured party, if the government established with concrete evidence that the threatened injury was significant, that it would likely follow upon disclosure, and that it would occur within some reasonable time frame following disclosure. Such an approach would qualify the privilege while still protecting legitimate national security considerations.

Going forward, courts should curtail the use of the "unacceptable risk" rationale that requires a case to be dismissed before discovery is commenced or a responsive pleading is filed. As already noted, that remedial approach is based on a set of predictive decisions embodied in the unacceptable risk doctrine that are made long before issues may be sharply defined and the relevant evidence is inventoried. This is an excessively harsh outcome for an allegedly injured party. In privilege cases, courts should not abandon their traditional and strong preference of deciding issues in a concrete and a specific factual context, which, in privilege cases, would mean that courts should delay considering the dismissal of an action until the parties have concretely defined issues in dispute and identified, with some specificity, the evidence arguably covered by the privilege.

The extension of the privilege from information sought by the plaintiff to information sought by the defendant was consistent with *Reynolds*. But the disadvantages of the extension fall entirely on the plaintiff. Surely a defendant deserves a fair day in court; but then, so does a plaintiff. While it would be a "mockery"[23] of justice to impose a judgment on a defendant in a case in which the plaintiff's essential allegations were false, it is also a "mockery" of justice to dismiss a plaintiff's complaint merely because a defendant's cross-examination of a witness may be "hamper[ed]."[24]

As a result, judges should reshape the law so as to reallocate the burdens of the privilege. In addition to reforming the privilege in accord with the considerations noted earlier, in cases in which the privilege denies arguably helpful information to a defendant, judges should presumptively limit the dismissal of cases to situations in which it is evident that the plaintiff's essential allegations are false. In other cases, in which the privilege denies the defendant arguably helpful information, judges should presumptively treat the privileged information as if a witness had died, which would impose the burden on a defendant of offering a defense based on other available information. That presumption could be set aside if a judge set forth convincing reasons for doing so and for imposing the burdens triggered by the application of the privilege solely on the plaintiff.

The shape of the current state secrets privilege grants the executive a de facto absolute privilege, which in turn represents judicial abdication in assuring the integrity of the privilege's application. The Supreme Court should alter the state secrets privilege, and it can do that without usurping the executive's primary and dominating role in national security matters because there exists a broad spectrum of doctrinal choices with regard to the privilege between abdication and usurpation.

The constitutional order is seriously askew. It denies relief to individuals arguably wronged by members of the executive branch; it shields unlawful executive conduct; it undermines the scheme of checks and balances central to the governing scheme; it concentrates power in the executive; it diminishes transparency in government; it undermines the rule of law and weakens the constitutional order; and it undermines the respect the world may have for the United States as a nation dedicated to important governing principles.[25]

---

[23] Molerio v. FBI, 749 F.2d 815, 825 (D.C. Cir. 1984).

[24] Zuckerbraun v. General Dynamics Corp., 935 F.2d 544, 547 (2d Cir. 1991).

[25] Professor Owen Fiss of the Yale Law School recently offered a similar observation regarding the "unconstitutional policies" initiated by President George W. Bush (policies such as extraordinary rendition, imprisonment without trial, the denial of habeas corpus to individuals not charged with criminal conduct, the use of military commissions, and federal surveillance practices) that "have taken on a life of their own and have become durable features of our legal order. As such, they betray the proudest ideals of the nation, undermine one of the pillars of our

And all of this is done without there being any evidence that the legal doctrines of deference protect national security interests.

As dispiriting as these developments are, there is nothing surprising about the executive's assertion and accumulation of power with regard to national security matters. Indeed, given the constitutional structure of the national government and what might be thought of as the constitutional invitation for the three branches to compete for authority and power, it should be expected that the president, who is commander-in-chief and dominates in national security matters, will continually assert authority and press the other two coequal branches to cede to its requests and demands for enhanced authority.

At the same time, it is gravely disappointing that Congress so frequently fails to assert its own responsibilities over specific military and foreign affairs as well as more general national security matters. But no matter what Congress may do in the future to rebalance authority and responsibility with the executive over military and foreign affairs matters, it cannot fulfill the special role in the governing scheme the Supreme Court is assigned. Thus, it is the Supreme Court that is ultimately responsible for stating what the law is, and because of that responsibility the Court has ultimate responsibility for assuring that the United States is a "government of laws, not of men." No matter how much oversight the legislature exercised over the executive and the functioning of the National Security State, the legislature cannot fulfill this exceptionally important function within the governing scheme.

Against those constitutional obligations, it is a sharp disappointment that the Supreme Court has failed so regularly and for so long a time to wend its way through the thicket so as to respect simultaneously executive and congressional responsibilities to protect the national security, and to avoid surrendering its own independence and its responsibility to provide a meaningful check on executive power. But that is what the Supreme Court has done. For decades, it has crafted and shaped legal doctrines that effectively insulate the executive from meaningful judicial review.

There is no doubt that upending judicial abdication requires the redesigning of all of the doctrines that insulate the executive and enhance executive secrecy. That is so because these doctrines work in tandem with one another, and changing the architecture of only one or two of the doctrines would invite continued insulation of the executive from judicial accountability by permitting the remaining unmodified doctrines to continue to provide

self-understanding, and deny us—all of us, including [President Barack] Obama—the right to speak of the example of America as we once did—as a beacon for all the world." Owen Fiss, *A War Like No Other: The Constitution in a Time of Terror* 124 (2015).

robust insulation. Moreover, because the law of acquiescence is over seventy years old and legal norms tend to change slowly, the required changes will likely be evolutionary.

This is a deeply regrettable state of affairs. And although it is not here claimed that expanded executive authority will "plunge us straightaway into dictatorship," as Justice Jackson wrote in another context, it "is at least a step in that wrong direction."[26] And because, as Jackson also wrote, "men have discovered no technique for long preserving free government except that the Executive be under the law," although it may well be that free government "may be destined to pass away . . . it is the duty of the Court to be last, not first, to give [it] up."[27]

By charting the course it has for so long, the Supreme Court has diminished its own legitimacy and the quality and character of the constitutional order by denying a remedy to injured individuals, insulating unlawful conduct, needlessly reinforcing a secrecy system that is already grossly exaggerated, undermining the possibility of transparency, and eroding democratic value. In short, the failure of the Supreme Court to uphold its end of the constitutional bargain in legal matters affecting national security and its primary responsibility to assure the national commitment to the rule of law has done itself and the nation significant harm that only it can repair.

However, the prospect that a majority of the current members of the Supreme Court will abandon the posture of acquiescence is remote. And that is so even though the arguments in favor of change are powerful, and the change required is within the mainstream of acceptable doctrinal choices. That is regrettable, but it is no reason not to take the long view, which assumes that the unnecessary harmful consequences of the Age of Deference will one day be so apparent to so many that a mandate for change will be formidable.

If that development should come to pass, a majority of Supreme Court justices will chart a legal course in which the high court functions as a third coequal and independent branch of government that provides meaningful judicial review of executive policies and conduct in cases implicating national security. Although it is uncertain whether that will occur, the federal judiciary has surprised the nation before as it has confronted legal questions that reflect matters of the deepest importance to the nation, and if it does again, the nation's commitments to liberty and democracy will be strengthened.

---

[26] Youngstown Sheet & Tube Co. v. Sawyer, 343 U.S. 579, 653 (1952) (Jackson, J., concurring).
[27] Id. at 655.

INDEX